The Venture Capital Cycle

The Venture Capital Cycle

Paul A. Gompers and Josh Lerner

The MIT Press
Cambridge, Massachusetts
London, England

First MIT Press paperback edition, 2002

© 1999 Massachusetts Institute of Technology

This book was set in Palatino by Asco Typesetters, Hong Kong.

Printed and bound in the United States of America.

Library of Congress Cataloging-in-Publication Data

Gompers, Paul A. (Paul Alan)
  The venture capital cycle / Paul A. Gompers and Josh Lerner.
     p.   cm.
  Includes bibliographical references and index.
   ISBN 0-262-07194-0 (hc : alk. paper), 0-262-57158-7 (pb)
   1. Venture capital—United States. I. Lerner, Josh. II. Title.
HG4963.G66   1999
332'.0415'0973—dc21   99-13957
                                                  CIP

Contents

Acknowledgments

The research that forms the basis for this book has been drawn from many sources. First, we have relied on a number of investors in and consultants to venture capital funds and organizations. Without their cooperation, we would not have been able to access the information that forms the basis of these analyses. We thank in particular Tim Bliamptis, Mark Dibner, Mark Edwards, Michael Eisenson, T. Bondurant French, David Gleba, Kelly McGough, Robert Moreland, Tom Philips, Jesse Reyes, Rolf Selvig, Scott Sperling, David Witherow, and several organizations—the Harvard Management Company, Brinson Partners and its various affiliate limited partnerships, Kemper Financial Services, North Carolina Biotechnology Center, Recombinant Capital, RogersCasey Alternative Investments, the US West Investment Trust, Venture Economics, and a major corporate pension fund—for generous access to their files. The role of several of our current and former colleagues—in particular, Jay Light, William Sahlman, Jeffry Timmons, and Robert Vishny—in providing introductions should also be acknowledged.

Second, we relied on the many hours of patient work by our research assistants. The careful and painstaking work of Rob Bhargava, Alon Brav, Amy Burroughs, Tim Dodson, Meredith Fitzgerald, Victor Hollender, Leo Huang, Brian Hunt, Taras Klymchuk, Laura Miller, Bac Nguyen, Sanjeev Verma, and Jay Yang was essential to the completion of the analyses in this volume. Chris Allen and Phil Hamilton of Harvard Business School and Neil Bania and Michael Fogarty of Case Western Reserve University provided computational support. The financial support provided by the Center for Research in Security Prices, University of Chicago, the Center for Science and International Affairs, John F. Kennedy School of Government, Harvard University, the Consortium on Competitiveness and Cooperation, and the Division of Research, Harvard Business School, was also critical in this process. Our two administrative assistants, Marianne

D'Amico and Peggy Moreland, provided patient and indispensable support throughout all phases of this project.

Third, we would like to acknowledge the support of our fellow academic professionals. Rick Carter, Charles Lee, Harold Mulherin, Jay Ritter, and Michael Vetsuypens generously shared data from earlier research projects. Alon Brav, who was the coauthor of chapter 14, generously gave permission for the work to be included here. Our analyses were greatly improved by the helpful comments of our peers. We would also like to thank George Baker, Chris Barry, Eli Berman, Dennis Carlton, Gary Chamberlain, Susan Chaplinsky, Judy Chevalier, Jeff Coles, Robert Dammon, Joanne Dushay, Joetta Forsyth, Ken Froot, Chris Geczy, Michael Gibbs, Stuart Gilson, Kathleen Hanley, Oliver Hart, J. B. Heaton, Michael Jensen, Shmuel Kandel, Steven Kaplan, Tarun Khanna, Stacey Kole, Ralph Lerner, Marc Lipson, Andrew Metrick, Lisa Meulbroek, Wayne Mikkelson, Mark Mitchell, Kevin J. Murphy, Steve Orpurt, Peter Pashigian, Sam Peltzman, Mitchell Petersen, Canice Prendergast, James Poterba, Raghuram Rajan, Edward Rice, Jay Ritter, F. M. Scherer, Stephen Schurman, Erik Sirri, Howard Stevenson, René Stulz, Eli Talmor, Richard Thaler, Manuel Trajtenberg, Peter Tufano, Michael Vetsuypens, Rob Vishny, Jerry Warner, Michael Weisbach, Karen Wruck, Luigi Zingales, a number of anonymous referees, and seminar participants at many universities and conferences for their helpful comments and suggestions. A number of practitioners—especially Jonathan Axelrad, Tom Judge, Robin Painter, David Swensen, and Katherine Todd—also provided helpful comments. Particular thanks goes to the members of our dissertation committees, who read and commented on early versions of a number of these essays: Carliss Baldwin, Richard Caves, Zvi Griliches, Richard Ruback, William Sahlman, Andrei Shleifer, and Jeremy Stein. All errors and omissions, of course, are our own.

Finally, we would like to dedicate this work to Wendy and Jody, without whom this book would not have been possible.

Several chapters in this book are based on previously published material:

Chapter 3: Paul A. Gompers and Josh Lerner, "The Use of Covenants: An Analysis of Venture Partnership Agreements," *Journal of Law and Economics* 39 (October 1996): 463–498.

Chapter 4: Paul A. Gompers and Josh Lerner, "An Analysis of Compensation in the U.S. Venture Capital Partnership," *Journal of Financial Economics* 51 (January 1999): 3–44.

Chapter 5: Paul A. Gompers and Josh Lerner, "The Determinants of Corporate Venture Capital Success: Organizational Structure, Incentives, and Complementarities," in Randall Morck, editor, *Concentrated Corporate Ownership* (Chicago: University of Chicago Press for the National Bureau of Economic Research, 1999), forthcoming.

Chapter 7: Paul A. Gompers, "Optimal Investment, Monitoring, and the Staging of Venture Capital," *Journal of Finance* 50 (December 1995): 1461–1490.

Chapter 8: Josh Lerner, "Venture Capitalists and the Oversight of Private Firms," *Journal of Finance* 50 (March 1995): 301–318.

Chapter 9: Josh Lerner, "The Syndication of Venture Capital Investments," *Financial Management* 23 (Autumn 1994): 16–27.

Chapter 11: Josh Lerner, "Venture Capitalists and the Decision to Go Public," *Journal of Financial Economics* 35 (June 1994): 293–316.

Chapter 12: Paul A. Gompers, "Grandstanding in the Venture Capital Industry," *Journal of Financial Economics* 43 (September 1996): 133–156.

Chapter 13: Paul A. Gompers and Josh Lerner, "Venture Capital Distributions: Short-Run and Long-Run Reactions," *Journal of Finance* 53 (December 1998): 2161–2183.

Chapter 14: Alon Brav and Paul A. Gompers, "Myth or Reality? The Long-Run Underperformance of Initial Public Offerings: Evidence from Venture Capital and Nonventure Capital-Backed Companies," *Journal of Finance* 52 (December 1997): 1791–1822.

1   Introduction

Why This Volume?

Over the past two decades, the venture capital industry in the United States has experienced dramatic growth. Annual inflows into venture funds have expanded from virtually zero in the mid-1970s to $17.2 billion in 1998. Disbursements by these funds into portfolio companies have displayed almost as great a growth. Many of the most visible new firms over the past decades—including Apple Computer, Genentech, Intel, Lotus, and Microsoft—have been backed by venture capital funds. This growth has led to increasing attention to the venture capital industry from the popular press, executives of major corporations, and policymakers worldwide.

Yet despite this recent attention, misconceptions persist about the nature and role of venture capitalists. One claim, frequently encountered in guides for entrepreneurs, is that venture capitalists are purely passive financiers of entrepreneurial firms who are unlikely to add much value. An extreme, though not unrepresentative, example is Manweller's (1997) *Funding High-Tech Ventures*. In a chapter entitled "Venture Capitalists: The Companynappers," the author observes:

> The term Venture Capitalists (V/C) is an oxymoron. It should be U/Bs (Unadventurous Brokers), especially in hard times. V/Cs today prefer to invest in products which are being developed by sedate, well entrenched companies. If that's your company, V/Cs are a good source to approach for additional equity funding.... [The V/Cs] have developed personality traits more akin to professional wrestlers than professional investors. If you've got the time, try it. You'll get a real education in how to string along future vendors.

Another common misperception relates to how venture capitalists unwind their holdings in young firms. As discussed later in the volume, the exiting of venture capital investments is a controversial area, and venture funds have been known to behave in opportunistic ways. But the discussion of this process is often extremely one-sided and not representative of the broader historical record. A recent discussion in the *Washington Post* (Sloan 1997) is representative:

Venture capitalists … take a company public while the ink is still drying on its incorporation papers. Venture capitalists would rather have you risk your money than risk their own. Besides, going public lets them profit now, rather than waiting.

Distorted perceptions about the venture capital industry are commonplace among policymakers. One of many examples is Dr. Mary Good, Undersecretary of Commerce for Technology, commenting before the U.S. Senate Governmental Affairs Committee (1997):

As the competitive pressures of the global marketplace have forced American firms to move more of their R&D into shorter term product and process improvements, an "innovation gap" has developed…. Sit down with a group of venture capitalists. The funding for higher-risk ventures … is extraordinarily difficult to come by.

More disturbing than these accounts, however, have been the actions taken by entrepreneurs, corporations, and academic institutions based on misconceptions about the venture capital industry. Particularly misguided is the belief that venture capitalists can add little value to young firms aside from money or can be easily duplicated by an institution whose core strengths are very different. These misconceptions have often led to a failure to capitalize on attractive opportunities and to the substantial destruction of value.

One example that illustrates this point is an instance where a university sought to duplicate the role of venture capitalists, with few of the venture funds' checks and balances and little understanding of the potential pitfalls. In 1987, Boston University invested in a privately held biotechnology company founded in 1979 by a number of scientists affiliated with the institution. As part of its initial investment, the school bought out the stakes of a number of independent venture capital investors, who had apparently concluded after a number of financing rounds that the firm's prospects were unattractive. Between 1987 and 1992, the school, investing alongside university officials and trustees, provided at least $90 million to the private firm. (By way of comparison, the school's entire endowment in the fiscal year in which it initiated this investment was $142 million.) Although the company succeeded in completing an initial public offering, it encountered a series of disappointments with its products. At the end of 1997, the university's equity stake was worth only $4 million.[1]

These misconceptions have motivated us to undertake this volume, which draws together our recent research into the form and function of venture capital funds.[2] We have two goals. First, we seek to gather our research efforts into a more accessible volume than the various finance and economics journals in which they originally appeared. Second, we want to draw out some of the common themes in these studies with a series of interpretative essays about venture capital fundraising, investing, and exiting.

Three key themes run throughout this volume. The first is the tremendous incentive and information problems that venture capitalists must overcome. Venture investors typically concentrate in industries with a great deal of uncertainty, where the information gaps among entrepreneurs and investors are commonplace. These firms typically have substantial intangible assets, which are difficult to value and may be impossible to resell if the firm fails. Similarly, market conditions in many of these industries are highly variable. The nature and magnitude of the information gaps and uncertainty at each stage of the cycle leave many opportunities for self-interested behavior by the various parties. At each stage of the cycle, the venture capital industry has developed novel checks and balances, ensuring that incentives are properly aligned and increasing the probability of success.

The second theme is the interrelatedness of each aspect of the venture capital process. Venture capital can be viewed as a cycle that starts with the raising of a venture fund; proceeds through the investing in, monitoring of, and adding value to firms; continues as the venture capitalist exits successful deals and returns capital to their investors; and renews itself

1. This account is based on Seragen's filings with the U.S. Securities and Exchange Commission. In a 1992 agreement with the State of Massachusetts' Attorney General's Office, the university agreed not to make any further equity investments. The school, however, made a $12 million loan guarantee in 1995 (subsequently converted into equity) and a $5 million payment as part of an asset purchase in 1997. The firm was merged in 1998 into a subsidiary of another biotechnology company. Even if all the contingent payments associated with the transaction are made, the university will have received far less than the amount it invested.
2. The distinction between venture capital and private equity funds is not precise. Private equity funds include funds devoted to venture capital, leveraged buyouts, consolidations, mezzanine and distressed debt investments, and a variety of hybrids such as venture leasing and venture factoring. Venture capital funds are those primarily devoted to equity or equity-linked investments in young growth-oriented firms. Many venture capital funds, however, occasionally make other types of private equity investments.

with the venture capitalist raising additional funds. To understand the venture capital industry, one must understand the whole "venture cycle." The organization of this volume mirrors this cycle. Each part will highlight the interrelated nature of the various aspects of the cycle.

A final theme is how slowly the venture capital industry adjusts to shifts in the supply of capital or the demand for financing. Academics are used to thinking that financial markets instantaneously adjust to the arrival of new information. This does not appear to be true in the venture capital market, where regulatory and policy shifts generate disruptions that take years to resolve. Put another way, long-run adjustments in supply and demand curves can be very slow to respond to short-run shocks.

The nature of venture-backed companies contributes to this slow adjustment. Because venture funds must make long-run illiquid investments in firms, they need to secure funds from their investors for periods of a decade or more. The supply of venture capital consequently can not adjust quickly to changes in investment opportunities, as is the case in mutual or hedge funds. More generally, even identifying which sectors or groups are likely to be receiving too much or too little investment is often difficult. The supply of venture capitalists is also difficult to adjust in the short run. Not only is it difficult to raise a new venture capital fund without a track record, but the skills needed for successful venture capital investing are difficult and time-consuming to acquire.[3] During periods when the supply of or demand for venture capital has shifted, adjustments in the number of venture capitalists and venture capital organizations appear to take place very slowly.

The Nature and History of Venture Capital

Before turning to a discussion of venture capital fundraising, it is helpful to review the nature and history of the venture capital industry. Venture capitalists' role is an old one. Entrepreneurs have long had ideas that require substantial capital to implement but lacked the funds to finance these projects themselves. While many entrepreneurs have used bank

3. Practitioner accounts emphasize that venture capitalists have highly specialized skills, which are difficult to develop or even identify. For instance, Robert Kunze (1990) of Hambrecht and Quist notes: "The life of the associate [in a venture capital organization] is akin to playing house. Since associates never make the actual investment decision ... it's impossible to tell whether or not they'll be successful venture capitalists if and when they get the chance."

loans or other sources of debt financing, start up companies that lacked substantial tangible assets, expected several years of negative earnings, and had uncertain prospects have often been forced to struggle to find alternatives. Solutions to this problem date back at least as far as Babylonian partnerships at the time of Hammurabi (Lutz 1932). Venture capitalists represent one solution to financing these high-risk, potentially high-reward projects.

The venture capital industry today is a well established, if modestly sized, industry. The industry consists of several thousand professionals, working at about 500 funds concentrated in California, Massachusetts, and a handful of other states. These individuals undertake a variety of roles. The first is maintaining relationships with investors—primarily institutions such as pension funds and university endowments, but also wealthy individuals—who provide them with capital. Venture capitalists typically raise their capital not on a continual basis, but rather through periodic funds. These funds, which are often in the form of limited partnerships, typically have a ten-year life, though extensions of several years are often possible. Eventually, however, the funds must be returned to the investors, and a new fund raised. A venture organization usually will raise a fund every two-to-five years. Taken collectively, the venture industry today is managing funds with a total capital, including capital that the investors have promised to provide, even if it is not all drawn down, of about $50 billion.

Venture capitalists play a second role in the review of proposed investments, and the oversight of those that are selected for investment. The typical venture organization receives many dozens of business plans for each one it funds. Although most proposals are swiftly discarded, serious candidates are extensively scrutinized through both formal studies of the technology and market strategy and informal assessment of the management team. (It is not unusual for a venture team to complete 100 or more reference checks before deciding to invest in a firm.) The decision to invest is frequently made conditional on the identification of a syndication partner who agrees that this is an attractive investment.

Once the decision to invest is made, venture capitalists frequently disburse funds in stages. Managers of these venture-backed firms are forced to return repeatedly to their financiers for additional capital to ensure that the money is not squandered on unprofitable projects. In addition, venture capitalists intensively monitor managers. These investors demand preferred stock with numerous restrictive covenants and representation on the board of directors.

The final role of venture investors is managing the exiting of these investments. Typically, venture capitalists seek to take public the most successful firms in their portfolios. While a relatively modest fraction—historically, between 20 and 35 percent—of portfolio firms are taken public, they account for the bulk of the venture returns. Even among these offerings, often a small number of firms account for the bulk of the returns; the distribution is highly skewed. Other, less successful firms are liquidated, sold to corporate acquirers, or else remain operational at a modest level of activity.

Given the intensity of interest in replicating the U.S. venture model, it is easy to forget how young the formal venture industry is in this country. The first modern venture capital firm, American Research and Development (ARD), did not appear until after World War II. It was formed in 1946 by MIT President Karl Compton, Harvard Business School Professor Georges F. Doriot, and local business leaders who sought to commercialize the technologies developed for World War II, particularly innovations undertaken at MIT. The success of the investments ranged widely. Almost half of ARD's profits during its twenty-six years as an independent entity came from its $70,000 investment in Digital Equipment Company in 1957, which grew in value to $355 million. Because institutional investors were reluctant to invest, ARD was structured as a publicly traded closed-end fund and marketed mostly to individuals (Liles 1977).

A handful of other venture funds were established in the decade after ARD's formation. Most, like ARD, were structured as publicly traded closed-end funds (mutual funds whose shares must be sold to other investors, rather than redeemed from the issuing firm). The first venture capital limited partnership, Draper, Gaither, and Anderson, was formed in 1958. Imitators soon followed, but limited partnerships accounted for a minority of the venture pool during the 1960s and 1970s. The remainder of venture capital industry was either closed-end funds or small business investment companies (SBICs), federally guaranteed risk-capital pools that proliferated during the 1960s. The annual flow of money into new venture funds during these years never exceeded a few hundred million dollars and usually was much less.

As figure 1.1 shows, funds flowing into the venture capital industry increased dramatically during the late 1970s and early 1980s. The increase in new capital contributions outpaced growth in the number of active organizations, due to the rigidities that limit adjustments in the short-run supply of venture organizations and venture capitalists discussed above.

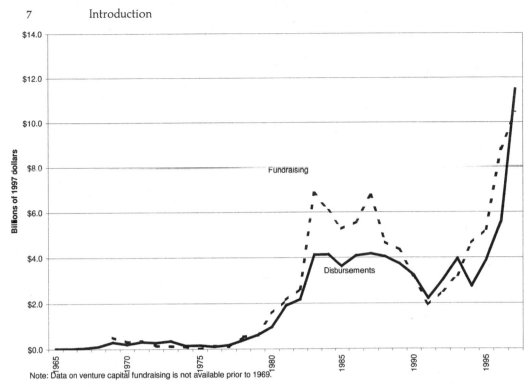

Figure 1.1
Venture capital fundraising and disbursements, 1965–1997.

An important contributing factor to the increase in money flowing into the venture capital sector was the 1979 amendment to the "prudent man" rule governing pension fund investments. Prior to that date, the Employee Retirement Income Security Act (ERISA) prohibited pension funds from investing substantial amounts of money in venture capital or other high-risk asset classes. The Department of Labor's clarification of the rule explicitly allowed pension managers to invest in high-risk assets, including venture capital. This rule change opened the door to pension funds' tremendous capital resources. Table 1.1 shows that in 1978, when $481 million was invested in new venture capital funds,[4] individuals accounted for the largest share (32 percent). Pension funds supplied just 15 percent. Eight years later, when more than $4.8 billion was invested, pension funds accounted for more than half of all contributions.

An associated change during the 1980s was the increasing role of investment advisors. During the late 1970s and early 1980s, almost all pension funds invested directly in venture funds. Because venture capital

4. The annual commitments represent pledges of capital to venture funds raised in a given year. This money is typically invested over three to five years starting in the year the fund is formed.

Table 1.1
Summary statistics for venture capital fundraising by independent venture partnerships. All dollar figures are in millions of 1997 dollars.

	1978	1979	1980	1981	1982	1983	1984	1985
First closing of funds								
Number of funds	23	27	57	81	98	147	150	99
Size (millions of 1997 $)	457	517	1,333	1,831	2,234	5,832	5,176	4,482
Sources of funds								
Private pension funds	15%	31%	30%	23%	33%	26%	25%	23%
Public pension funds	a	a	a	a	a	5%	9%	10%
Corporations	10%	17%	19%	17%	12%	12%	14%	12%
Individuals	32%	23%	16%	23%	21%	21%	15%	13%
Endowments	9%	10%	14%	12%	7%	8%	6%	8%
Insurance companies and banks	16%	4%	13%	15%	14%	12%	13%	11%
Foreign investors and other	18%	15%	8%	10%	13%	16%	18%	23%
Independent venture partnerships as a share of the total venture pool[b]			40%	44%	58%	68%	72%	73%

a. Public pension funds are included with private pension funds in these years.
b. This series is defined differently in different years. In some years, the *Venture Capital Journal* states that nonbank SBICs and publicly traded venture funds are included with independent venture partnerships. In other years, these funds are counted in other categories. It is not available after 1994.
Source: Compiled from the Venture Economics funds database and various issues of the *Venture Capital Journal*.

was a small portion of their portfolios, few resources were devoted to monitoring and evaluating these investments. During the mid-1980s, investment advisors (often referred to as "gatekeepers") entered the market to advise institutional investors about venture investments. The gatekeepers pooled resources from their clients, monitored the progress of existing investments, and evaluated potential new venture funds. By the 1990s, one-third of all pension fund commitments was made through an investment advisor, and one-fifth of all money raised by new funds came through an investment advisor.

A final change in the venture capital industry during this period was the rise of the limited partnership as the dominant organizational form, depicted schematically in figure 1.2. In a venture capital limited partnership, the venture capitalists are general partners and control the fund's activities. The investors serve as limited partners. Investors monitor the fund's progress and attend annual meetings, but they cannot become involved in the fund's day-to-day management if they are to retain limited liability. Venture partnerships have pre-determined, finite life spans. The limited partnership agreement explicitly specifies the terms that govern

1986	1987	1988	1989	1990	1991	1992	1993	1994	1995	1996	1997
86	112	78	88	50	34	31	54	105	72	97	136
4,735	5,752	3,977	3,698	2,681	1,635	2,151	2,722	5,098	4,876	8,477	11,699
39%	27%	27%	22%	31%	25%	22%	59%	47%	38%	43%	40%
12%	12%	20%	14%	22%	17%	20%	a	a	a	a	a
11%	10%	12%	20%	7%	4%	3%	8%	9%	2%	13%	30%
12%	12%	8%	6%	11%	12%	11%	7%	12%	17%	9%	13%
6%	10%	11%	12%	13%	24%	18%	11%	21%	22%	21%	9%
10%	15%	9%	13%	9%	6%	14%	11%	9%	18%	5%	1%
11%	14%	13%	13%	7%	12%	11%	4%	2%	3%	8%	7%
75%	78%	80%	79%	80%	80%	81%	78%	78%			

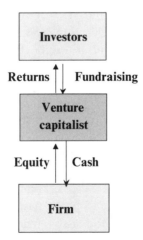

Figure 1.2
An overview of the venture capital process.

the venture capitalists' compensation over the entire ten-to-thirteen year life of the fund. It is extremely rare that these terms are renegotiated. The specified compensation has a simple form. The venture capitalist typically receives an annual fixed fee, plus variable compensation that is a specified fraction of the fund's profits. The fixed portion of the specified compensation is usually between 1.5 and 3 percent of the committed capital or net asset value, and the variable portion is usually about 20 percent of fund profits. Table 1.1 shows that partnerships have grown from 40 percent of the venture pool in 1980 to 81 percent in 1992.

As a result of this growth, venture capitalists have increased their rate of investment, as figure 1.1 demonstrates. As the rate of investment has increased, venture capitalists continued to focus their investments on information technology and health care, as well as on California and Massachusetts firms. Table 1.2 presents an aggregated summary of investments by industry (in manufacturing firms only) over the past three decades; and table 1.3 provides a summary of investments in the ten states with the most venture capital activity over the past three decades. The result of this growth was intense competition for transactions among venture groups.

The steady growth of commitments to the venture capital industry was reversed in the late 1980s. Returns on venture capital funds declined because of overinvestment in various industries and the entry of inexperienced venture capitalists. As investors became disappointed with returns, they committed less capital to the industry.

The departure of many inexperienced venture capitalists from the industry—along with the robust market for initial public offerings (IPOs)—has led to an increase in returns in recent years. (Table 1.4 summarizes the exiting of venture capital investments through IPOs as well as comparable data on nonventure capital offerings.) New capital commitments have risen accordingly. The surge in fundraising during the past several years has put upward pressure on prices and led to massive increases in stock distributions to venture capital investors. Additionally, venture capitalists have responded to greater capital in a variety of ways. First, the amount of money invested in the typical venture-backed company has increased. Venture capitalists have also been able to increase their compensation and reduce the restrictiveness of the limited partnership agreements that govern their investment behavior.

The recent growth of the U.S. venture industry has raised concerns among many venture capitalists and institutional investors about the future prospects of the industry. In response to these changes, investors—

and venture capital organizations themselves—are increasingly looking abroad for investment opportunities. Table 1.5 provides an international comparison of venture capital activity. In Chapter 15, we will discuss some of the future developments that we believe are likely in the venture capital industry.

Limitations of this Volume

Before ending this introduction, three limitations of this book should be acknowledged. First, there are many fascinating topics relating to venture capital that are not considered in this volume. These include the relative performance of venture capital and other financial assets, the degree to which public policies affect the formation of venture capital funds, and the extent to which the U.S. model of venture capital investment will be transferred into foreign markets. Throughout *The Venture Capital Cycle* we will highlight some of these research opportunities.

Second, we do not attempt to duplicate the guides that explain the intricacies of the venture financing process to practitioners. Numerous excellent volumes exist (especially Bartlett 1995, Halloran, et al. 1995, and Levin 1995) that document the legal and institutional considerations associated with raising venture financing at much greater depth than could be done in this volume.

Finally, we do not consider many interesting and related forms of financing that also deserve scrutiny. In particular, we define venture capital as independently managed, dedicated pools of capital that focus on equity or equity-linked investments in privately held, high-growth companies. A more ambitious volume might examine the entrepreneurial finance function more generally,[5] while our focus is exclusively on venture capital. This is partially because of the size of the venture capital market. Although evidence on the financing of these firms is imprecise, Freear and Wetzel's (1990) survey suggests that venture capital accounts for about two-thirds of the external equity financing raised by privately held technology-intensive businesses from private-sector sources.[6]

---

5. Merton (1995) has argued that the actual institution is not the important element of the financial system, it is the function. The same economic function can be performed by different institutions in different markets.

6. While many more firms receive funding from individual investors than venture capitalists, Freear and Wetzel (1990) report that median financing round raised by private high-technology firms from individual investors was about $200,000. 82% of the rounds from individuals were under $500,000. A more recent study of high-technology initial public offerings by Fenn, Liang, and Prowse (1997) largely corroborates this survey evidence.

Table 1.2
Number and dollar amount of venture capital disbursements for U.S. manufacturing industries, by industry and five-year period. The count of venture capital investments in each five-year period is the sum of the number of firms receiving investments in each year. All dollar figures are in millions of 1997 dollars.

Panel A: Venture capital investments (# s)

#	Industry	1965–69	1970–74	1975–79	1980–84	1985–89	1990–96
1	Food and kindred	1	9	6	23	80	93
2	Textile and apparel	4	12	9	19	27	70
3	Lumber and furniture	2	8	6	24	62	37
4	Paper	2	2	2	2	12	14
5	Industrial chemicals	1	1	1	6	18	23
6	Drugs	1	12	34	245	554	746
7	Other chemicals	1	7	8	10	52	46
8	Petroleum refining and extraction	3	3	26	92	27	14
9	Rubber products	1	5	6	19	11	7
10	Stone, clay, and glass products	0	1	3	14	48	31
11	Primary metals	0	3	5	20	44	33
12	Fabricated metal products	0	0	0	2	1	2
13	Office and computing machines	39	84	108	744	641	442
14	Other nonelectrical machinery	12	12	32	254	280	162
15	Communication and electronic	23	65	60	497	736	709
16	Other electrical equipment	0	6	16	36	52	50
17	Transportation equipment	1	7	5	6	24	25
18	Aircraft and missiles	0	0	0	12	20	4
19	Professional and scientific instruments	13	37	70	383	549	544
20	Other machinery	7	14	16	62	89	98
	Total	111	288	413	2,470	3,327	3,150

Panel B: Venture capital disbursements (millions of 1997 $s)

#	Industry	1965–69	1970–74	1975–79	1980–84	1985–89	1990–96
1	Food and kindred	5	22	8	28	241	2?3
2	Textile and apparel	7	17	16	31	51	2?1
3	Lumber and furniture	5	19	10	30	227	4?2
4	Paper	1	9	3	3	25	?2
5	Industrial chemicals	0	1	1	47	39	?7
6	Drugs	0	17	154	707	2,121	3,4?3
7	Other chemicals	1	45	5	10	176	?9
8	Petroleum refining and extraction	14	7	104	407	125	?3
9	Rubber products	1	3	17	32	9	20
10	Stone, clay, and glass products	0	1	6	39	112	?1
11	Primary metals	0	9	12	28	76	1?8
12	Fabricated metal products	0	0	0	1	0	1
13	Office and computing machines	76	458	327	3,691	2,827	1,6?8
14	Other nonelectrical machinery	73	19	42	768	759	3?7
15	Communication and electronic	50	214	93	1,981	3,002	2,9?1
16	Other electrical equipment	0	9	60	89	121	11?
17	Transportation equipment	0	11	5	10	53	10?
18	Aircraft and missiles	0	0	0	22	22	?
19	Professional and scientific instruments	15	98	129	920	1,644	1,71?
20	Other machinery	8	32	25	128	200	39?
	Total	$255	$992	$1,016	$8,972	$11,827	$12,12?

Source: Based on Kortum and Lerner (1998) and supplemented with tabulations of unpublished Venture Economics databases.

Table 1.3
Number and dollar amount of venture capital disbursements for all industries in the ten states with the most venture capital activity, by state and five-year period. The count of venture capital investments in each five-year period is the sum of the number of firms receiving investments in each year. All dollar figures are in millions of 1997 dollars.

Panel A: Venture capital investments (#s)

State	1965–69	1970–74	1975–79	1980–84	1985–89	1990–96
California	65	179	310	1,863	2,645	3,380
Massachusetts	45	93	155	708	1,014	1,028
Texas	18	71	84	373	584	489
New York	28	90	73	311	324	276
New Jersey	15	35	47	171	291	336
Colorado	5	22	31	194	258	298
Pennsylvania	8	21	32	120	290	311
Illinois	16	29	31	133	214	312
Minnesota	12	34	42	170	186	194
Connecticut	3	20	37	136	217	210
Total, all states	302	847	1,253	5,365	8,154	9,406

Panel B: Venture capital disbursements (millions of 1997 $s)

State	1965–69	1970–74	1975–79	1980–84	1985–89	1990–96
California	247	620	784	7,615	10,973	15,436
Massachusetts	69	176	224	2,205	3,210	3,842
Texas	42	159	168	1,317	2,463	2,281
New York	36	175	184	781	1,593	1,582
New Jersey	37	93	87	420	1,378	1,942
Colorado	14	57	52	559	913	1,079
Pennsylvania	20	47	132	420	1,736	1,258
Illinois	67	152	133	326	1,371	1,603
Minnesota	7	102	50	306	461	592
Connecticut	1	36	96	362	1,660	822
Total, all states	$780	$2,196	$2,563	$17,317	$34,884	$42,169

Source: Based on tabulations of unpublished Venture Economics databases.

Table 1.4
The distribution of venture-backed and nonventure IPOs for the period 1978–1997. This table compares the distribution of IPOs in this sample versus all IPOs recorded over this period of time. All dollar figures are in millions of 1997 dollars.

Year	Number of venture-backed IPOs	Amount raised in venture-backed IPOs	Total number of IPOs	Total amount raised in all IPOs	Venture-backed IPOs as percent of all IPOs (number)	Venture-backed IPOs as percent of all IPOs (amount)
1978	6	$152	42	$550	12.50	21.59
1979	4	$70	103	$882	3.74	7.34
1980	24	$760	259	$2,641	8.48	22.35
1981	50	$888	438	$5,501	10.25	13.91
1982	21	$837	198	$2,157	9.59	27.97
1983	101	$3,916	848	$20,424	10.64	16.09
1984	44	$829	516	$5,877	7.86	12.37
1985	35	$929	507	$15,100	6.46	5.80
1986	79	$2,273	953	$27,122	7.66	7.73
1987	69	$1,818	630	$22,378	9.87	7.52
1988	36	$1,038	435	$7,579	8.28	13.70
1989	39	$1,260	371	$7,674	10.51	16.41
1990	43	$1,440	276	$5,478	15.58	16.29
1991	119	$4,352	367	$19,145	32.43	22.73
1992	157	$4,899	509	$27,222	30.84	17.99
1993	193	$5,566	707	$45,906	27.30	12.12
1994	159	$3,867	564	$31,529	28.19	12.26
1995	205	$7,093	566	$41,099	36.22	17.26
1996	284	$12,455	845	$43,398	33.61	28.70
1997	134	$4,845	628	$45,704	21.34	10.60

Sources: Barry, et al. (1992), Ritter (1997), and various issues of the *Going Public: The IPO Reporter* and the *Venture Capital Journal.*

Table 1.5
The size of the venture capital investments in 21 nations in 1995. We use Jeng and Wells's figures for early stage funds in each country outside the United States because we believe it to be most comparable to venture capital funds as defined in the United States. Figures for Australia and New Zealand are 1994 estimated levels; figures for Israel are a 1995 estimate; and figures for Portugal are the actual level in 1994. All dollar figures are in millions of 1997 U.S. dollars.

Country	Total venture capital invested
Australia	54
Austria	0.4
Belgium	8
Canada	182
Denmark	4
Finland	1
France	35
Germany	116
Ireland	1
Israel	550
Italy	60
Japan	11
Netherlands	100
New Zealand	1
Norway	7
Portugal	9
Spain	24
Sweden	9
Switzerland	1
United Kingdom	36
United States	3,374

Source: Compiled from Jeng and Wells (1998), as slightly amended by the authors.

More generally, the venture capital market represents a particularly refined, if still evolving, solution to the difficult problems associated with financing young firms. Understanding the approaches developed by these investors should be more generally applicable, whether to corporations seeking to encourage internal entrepreneurship or to policymakers seeking to promote greater innovation and economic development through start-up companies.

1 Venture Capital Fundraising

2 An Overview of Venture Capital Fundraising

This exploration of the venture capital cycle begins by examining the issues associated with raising venture capital funds. The process of raising capital and structuring funds is complex and little understood outside the industry. Private equity partnership agreements are daunting documents, often extending for hundreds of pages and addressing almost any possible eventuality. Practitioner discussions of the structure of these firms are rife with obscure terms such as "reverse claw-backs."

But understanding the process of raising a fund and structuring a partnership is central to an understanding of the venture capital cycle. The features of private equity funds—whether management fees, profit-sharing rules, or contractual terms—have long-lasting effects on the behavior of venture capitalists. The choices made in structuring these funds have profound implications for the entrepreneur financing a company through these investors, the investment banker underwriting a firm backed by private equity funds, the corporate development officer investing alongside venture capitalists in a young company, and the pension fund manager placing an institution's capital into a fund.

An example—discussed at length in chapter 12—may help to illustrate how form influences behavior. Almost all venture and buyout funds are designed to be "self-liquidating," that is, to dissolve after ten or twelve years. The need to terminate each fund imposes a healthy discipline, forcing private equity investors to take the necessary, but painful, step of terminating underperforming firms in their portfolios. (These firms are sometimes referred to as the "living dead" or "zombies.") But the pressure to raise an additional fund can sometimes have less pleasant consequences. Young private equity organizations frequently rush young firms to the public marketplace to demonstrate a successful track record, even if the companies are not ready to go public. This behavior, known as "grandstanding," can have a harmful effect on the long-run prospects of firms dragged prematurely into the public markets.

Many features of private equity funds can be understood as responses to an uncertain environment, rife with many information gaps. Investing in a private equity fund is, in some respects, a "leap of faith" for institutional investors. Most pension funds and endowments typically have very small staffs. At the largest organizations, a dozen professionals may be responsible for investing several billion dollars each year. Meanwhile, private equity funds frequently undertake investments in risky new firms pursuing complex new technologies or in troubled mature companies with numerous organizational pathologies and potential legal liabilities.

Limited and general partners have gradually developed a variety of mechanisms to ensure that value is maximized in spite of these uncertainties. For instance, the "carried interest"—the substantial share of profits that are allocated to the private equity investors—helps address these information asymmetries by ensuring that all parties gain if the investment does well. Pension funds frequently hire gatekeepers who play a consultative role, recommending sophisticated private equity funds with well-defined objectives to their clients. In other cases, these intermediaries organize "funds-of-funds." In addition, venture organizations are increasingly hiring placement agents who facilitate the fundraising process. Specialized investors concentrate on particular niches of the private equity industry, such as buying and selling interests in limited partnerships from institutional investors.

At the same time, other features of private equity funds can be seen as attempts to transfer wealth between parties rather than efforts to increase the size of the overall amount of profits generated by private equity investments. An example was the drive by many venture capital funds in the mid-1980s—a period when the demand for their services was very strong—to change the timing of their compensation. Prior to this point, venture capital funds had typically disbursed all the proceeds from their first few successful investments to their investors, until the investors had received their original invested capital back. The venture capitalists would then begin receiving a share of the subsequent investments that they exited. Consider a fund that had raised capital of $50 million, whose first three successful investments yielded $25 million each. Under the traditional arrangement, the proceeds from the first two offerings would have gone entirely to the limited partners in their fund. The venture capitalists would have begun receiving a share of the proceeds only at the time that they exited the third investment.

In the mid-1980s, venture capitalists began demanding and receiving the right to start sharing in even the first successfully exited investments. The primary effect of this change was that the venture capitalists began receiving more compensation early in their funds' lives. Put another way, the net present value of their compensation package increased considerably. It is not surprising, then, that as the inflow into venture capital weakened in the late 1980s, limited partners began demanding that venture capitalists return to the previous approach of deferring compensation.

This tension between behavior that increases the size of the "pie" and actions that simply change the relative sizes of the slices runs throughout part I of this book. We attempt to both understand the reasons for and the workings of the key features of these funds using this framework.

Related Research

While theoretically and empirically oriented economists have extensively scrutinized the interactions among venture capitalists and portfolio firms, the formation of venture funds has received relatively little attention. The rationales for the limited partnership structure and the drivers of variability of capital inflows have attracted little formal attention.

Limited earlier work has focused on the highly variable commitments to the venture capital industry. Understanding the determinants of this variability has been a topic of some interest. Much of this work has been policy oriented, attempting to derive implications for programs to promote venture capital.

Various factors may affect the level of commitments to venture capital organizations. Poterba (1987, 1989) argues that many of the changes observed in venture capital fundraising could arise from changes in either the supply of or the demand for venture capital. By supply of venture capital, we mean the relative desire of institutional investors to commit capital to the sector. The number of entrepreneurs with good ideas who want venture capital determines the demand for venture capital. It is very likely, Poterba argues, that decreases in capital gains tax rates might increase commitments to venture capital funds, even though the bulk of the funds would come from tax-exempt investors. Through a formal model, he shows that a drop in the tax rate may have a substantial effect on the willingness of corporate employees to become entrepreneurs, thereby increasing the need for venture capital. This increase in demand due to greater entrepreneurial activity may lead to more venture capital fundraising.

Other work has approached these issues on a more qualitative basis. Black and Gilson (1998) argue that there should be a strong tie between the health of the public equity markets and venture capital fundraising, both in the United States and abroad. They believe that the health of the venture capital market depends on the existence of a vibrant public market that allows new firms to issue shares. Only with such a public market can venture capitalists make a credible commitment to entrepreneurs that they will ultimately relinquish control of the firms in which they invest.

Jensen (1991) and Sahlman and Stevenson (1986) have discussed the apparent cyclicality in the amount of venture funds raised. They have argued that institutional investors are prone to either over- or underinvest in speculative markets such as venture capital. They suggest that this apparently irrational pattern of investing can explain the extreme swings in fundraising. Furthermore, these works argue that such dramatic swings may hinder entrepreneurship and innovation in the American economy.

Our work elsewhere (Gompers and Lerner 1998) explores the suggestions of Poterba and Black and Gilson empirically. We find support for the claims on capital gains tax rates: lower capital gains taxes appear to have a particularly strong effect on the amount of venture capital supplied by tax-exempt investors. This suggests that the primary mechanism by which capital gains tax cuts affect venture fundraising is by increasing the demand of entrepreneurs for capital. If the effect were on the supply of funds, changes in tax rates should have affected the contribution by taxable entities more dramatically.

A number of other factors also influence venture fundraising. Not surprisingly, regulatory changes such as the Department of Labor's shift in ERISA policies have had an important impact on commitments to venture capital funds. We also show that performance influences fundraising. Higher returns lead to greater capital commitments to new funds. The returns to venture capital have been quite variable.[1] In the early 1980s, returns on venture investments were quite high. From the mid-1980s through early 1990s, however, returns were extremely low. Average returns on venture investments were largely in the single digits. Starting in 1993, returns increased substantially.

---

1. As discussed in chapter 4, the actual calculation of returns for venture investments and their correlation with other asset returns is problematic. New research is needed to improve these measures. See also the discussion in Gompers and Lerner (1997b).

These returns were largely driven by the strength of the IPO market. A venture capitalist must liquidate a return in private firms to make money. By far the most profitable exit is an IPO. A Venture Economics study (1988a) finds that a $1 investment in a firm that goes public provides an average cash return of $1.95 in excess of the initial investment, with an average holding period of 4.2 years. The next best alternative as estimated by Venture Economics, an investment in an acquired firm, yields a cash return of only 40 cents over a 3.7 year average holding period.

A comparison of annual fundraising by venture capitalists in figure 1.1 with the annual volume of venture-backed IPOs in table 1.4 makes this link explicit. Few firms went public in the 1970s and very little venture capital was raised. The growth of the venture capital industry in the early 1980s was mirrored by a similar growth in venture-backed firms going public. The decline in fundraising in the late 1980s was preceded by a decline in the IPO market. Finally, the growth in venture capital fundraising in the 1990s was also preceded by increases in IPO market activity.

In a related study, Jeng and Wells (1997) examine the factors that influence venture capital fundraising in twenty-one countries. They find that the strength of the IPO market is an important factor in determining venture capital commitments, echoing the conclusions of Black and Gilson. Jeng and Wells find, however, that the IPO market does not appear to influence commitments to early stage funds as much as later stage ones. While this work represents an important initial step, much more remains to be explored.[2]

One provocative finding from the Jeng and Wells analysis is that government policy can have a dramatic impact on the current and long-term viability of the venture capital sector. In many countries, especially those in continental Europe, policymakers face a dilemma. The relatively few entrepreneurs active in these markets face numerous daunting regulatory restrictions, a paucity of venture funds focusing on investing in high-growth firms, and illiquid markets where investors do not welcome IPOs by young firms without long histories of positive earnings. It is often unclear where to begin the process of duplicating the success of the United States. Only very recently have researchers begun to examine the ways in which policymakers can catalyze the growth of venture capital and the companies in which they invest. (Three recent exceptions are Irwin and

---

2. One potential source of confusion is that the term venture capital is used differently different in Europe and Asia. Abroad, venture capital often refers to all private equity, including buyout, late stage, and mezzanine financing (which represent the vast majority of the private-equity pool in most overseas markets). In the United States, these are all separate classes.

Klenow 1996, Lerner 1999, and Wallsten 1996.) Clearly, much more work needs to be done in this arena.

A topic that has attracted even less attention than determining fundraising patterns is the rationale for the structure of venture capital organizations. The independent private-equity firm is an organizational form that has often been hailed as a dramatic improvement over the typical American corporation with dispersed shareholders (Jensen 1993, Shleifer and Vishny 1997b). As noted in chapter 1, the organizational form that dominates the venture industry is the limited partnership. The contracts spell out the compensation and conditions that govern the relationship between investors (limited partners) and the venture capitalist (general partner) during the fund's life. These claims, however, have attracted little prior scrutiny. This absence of attention is surprising given the longevity of the limited partnership as an organizational structure and the unvarying nature of its central features since the Italian *commenda* of the tenth century (De Roover 1963, Lopez and Raymond 1955).

An Overview of Part I

In the three chapters that follow, we present three analyses of these issues. In chapters 3 and 4, we examine the structure of venture partnerships. We show that the need to provide adequate incentives and shifts in relative negotiating power have important impacts on the terms of venture capital limited partnerships. In the final chapter of part I, we consider the more general question of the importance of the limited partnership structure employed by most venture capital funds. Our findings—while tentative—raise provocative questions about the assumptions on this organizational form.

Covenants and compensation are critical for aligning the incentives of venture capitalists with those of investors. The limited partnership places restrictions on the ability of investors to intervene in the day-to-day activities of the venture fund. Few of the common corporate control mechanisms—for example, active boards of directors or a market for corporate control—are utilized in venture limited partnerships. Consequently, the terms of the partnership agreement are extremely important for controlling activities of the venture capitalists that might ultimately be harmful to investors.

Covenants and restrictions often play an important role in limiting conflicts among investors and venture capitalists. In chapter 3, we explore two complementary hypotheses that may help explain the use of covenants and restrictions in venture capital limited partnerships. The hypotheses have implications for both cross-sectional and time-series variation in contractual form.

First, because negotiating and monitoring specific covenants are costly, contracting parties should weigh the potential costs and benefits of covenant inclusion. The ease of monitoring and the potential to engage in opportunistic behavior may vary among funds, leading to different sets of optimal covenants in different contracts. Costly contracting implies that more restrictive contracts will be employed when monitoring is easier and the potential for opportunistic behavior is greater.

A second hypothesis relates covenant composition to supply and demand conditions. In the short run, the supply of venture capital services may be fixed, with a modest number of venture partnerships raising funds of carefully limited size each year. Demand for venture investing services has shifted sharply over the past decades. Increases in demand may lead to higher prices when contracts are written. Higher prices may include not only increases in monetary compensation, but also greater consumption of private benefits through fewer covenants and restrictions.

Chapter 3 examines a sample of 140 executed partnership agreements from a major endowment and two investment managers that select venture capital investments for pension funds and other institutional investors. Because investors in a limited partnership avoid direct involvement in the activities of the fund, the covenants and restrictions in the partnership contract are critical in determining the general partners' behavior. Considerable time and expense are devoted to negotiating the final form of the document. A single limited partnership agreement governs the relationship between the limited and general partners over the fund's life of a decade or more. Unlike other agreements (for example, employment contracts or strategic alliances), these contracts are rarely renegotiated. The heterogeneity of venture organizations helps us to analyze the importance of demand shifts and costly contracting in determining the extent of covenant inclusion in partnership agreements.

The evidence indicates that both supply and demand conditions and costly contracting are important in determining contractual provisions. In univariate comparisons and regression analyses, fewer restrictions are found in funds established during years with greater inflows of new capital, funds in which limited partners do not employ investment managers, and funds where general partners enjoy higher levels of compensation. The evidence illustrates the importance of general market conditions on the restrictiveness of venture capital limited partnerships. In periods when venture capitalists have relatively more bargaining power they are able to raise money with fewer strings attached.

In chapter 4, we examine compensation terms in 419 venture partnership agreements and offering memoranda for funds formed between 1978 and 1992. We explore the cross-sectional differences in compensation (comparing one venture capital organization to another), as well as the time-series variation (how contracts change as organizations become more seasoned). We find that compensation for older and larger venture capital organizations is more sensitive to performance than the compensation of other venture groups. For example, the oldest and largest venture groups command about a 1 percent greater share of the capital gains than their less established counterparts. This greater profit share matters little if the fund is not successful, but can represent a 4 percent or greater increase in the net present value of total compensation if the fund is successful. These differences are statistically significant whether we examine the percentage of profits accruing to the venture capitalists (though these analyses are very noisy) or the elasticity of compensation with respect to performance. The cross-sectional variation in compensation terms for younger, smaller venture organizations is considerably less than for older, larger organizations. The fixed component of compensation is higher for smaller, younger funds and funds focusing on high-technology or early stage investments. Finally, we do not find any relationship between the incentive compensation and performance.

Chapter 4 also discusses two models that might explain the cross-sectional and time-series variation in compensation, a learning and a signaling model. The empirical results are consistent with the primary predictions of the learning model. In this model, neither the venture capitalists nor the investor knows the venture capitalist's ability. In early funds, venture capitalists will work hard even without explicit pay-for-performance incentives because, if they can establish a good reputation for either selecting attractive investments or adding value to firms in their portfolios, they will gain additional compensation in later funds. These reputation concerns lead to lower pay-for-performance for smaller and younger venture organizations. Once a reputation has been established, explicit incentive compensation is needed to induce the proper effort levels. The signaling model, in which venture capitalists know their ability but investors do not, predicts that new funds should have higher pay-for-performance sensitivities and lower base compensation because high-ability venture capitalists try to reveal their type by accepting riskier pay.

Finally, chapter 5 contrasts the structure and success of investments by venture capital limited partnerships with those of corporate venture programs. The corporate funds have very different organizational forms, typically structured as subsidiaries of the parent firm with little incentive compensation. Nonetheless, they undertake similar investments with similar personnel, suggesting that a comparison with traditional venture funds may be fruitful. In particular, we seek to determine whether—as arguments about the importance of the structure of independent venture capital organizations might suggest—the corporate funds are less successful than their independent counterparts. We also examine whether the corporate programs enjoy some benefits that may offset some of these costs. In particular, a substantial body of work on complementarities in the strategy literature suggests that corporate funds select better investments related to their existing business areas or add greater value to the firms in which they invest.

To test these concepts, we examine over 30,000 investments by corporate and independent venture funds into entrepreneurial firms. We examine the ultimate outcome of the firms receiving the capital, the valuations assigned to the firms at the time of the investments, and the duration of the venture organizations or subsidiaries themselves.

The evidence supports the importance of complementarities. Portfolio companies receiving funds from corporate investors with a well-defined strategic focus enjoy greater success. Investments are made at a premium, but this may reflect the indirect benefits that the corporation receives. Corporate programs with a well-defined strategic focus are as stable as traditional independent venture organizations. Among the corporate funds without a strong strategic focus, we see significantly less success in the investments and less stability than among the focused funds. Thus, it may be that earlier work suggesting the critical nature of the venture capital limited partnership was somewhat misguided. Instead, the evidence argues that strategy and incentives are critical to successful venture capital investing.

Final Thoughts

In short, these three essays underscore the complexity and multifaceted nature of venture capital organizations. Certainly, this is an organizational form that defies facile generalizations. It is clear that this is an organizational structure that has evolved—and continues to adjust—to address the challenging problems posed by investments in entrepreneurial firms.

Yet many recent shifts in the structure of these funds, such as the relaxation of covenants during periods of substantial growth, appear to reflect the changing supply-and-demand conditions for venture capital itself rather than any concerns about the optimal structure for investing. Nor is it clear that the venture capital limited partnership is the only structure in which successful investments into entrepreneurial firms can take place.

Part I ends with more questions than it answers. Will the structures of funds converge over time to a few templates that have been shown to be most effective in generating high returns? Or will the tension among adding features that maximize overall value and those that merely transfer wealth continue to characterize the industry? To what extent will the venture capital limited partnership emerge as the dominant organizational form outside the United States, or will alternative structures predominate? Thus, the structure of venture capital organizations is likely to be a topic of continuing interest to academic professionals and practitioners alike.

3   How Are Venture Partnerships Structured?

Here we explore the use of covenants and restrictions in long-term contracts governing venture funds. As discussed in chapter 2, the initial partnership agreement governs the partnership over its life. This agreement is important because it is the crucial mechanism for limiting the behavior of venture capitalists. Many of the oversight mechanisms found in corporations—for example, powerful boards of directors and the market for corporate control—are not available here. While limited partners can serve on advisory boards that review certain policy issues, if they become involved in the day-to-day management of a venture fund, they risk losing their limited liability (Levin 1995). No liquid market for partnership interests exists, and limited partners are frequently restricted from selling their partnership interests. Consequently, the primary remedy for the limited partners is legal action triggered by a violation of the covenants.[1]

We analyze 140 U.S.-based independent private partnerships primarily engaged in venture capital investments in equity or equity-linked securities of private firms with active participation by the fund managers in the management or oversight of the firms. We characterize each venture partnership using a series of proxies that measure the probability of opportunistic behavior and supply and demand conditions for venture capital services. We examine whether fourteen major classes of covenants are included in each agreement, and how the inclusion of covenants varies with these proxies.

---

1. For accounts of recent litigation, see Asset Alternatives (1994a) and Ely (1987). For a more detailed discussion of the latter case, see Lincoln Nt'l Life Ins. Co. v. Silver, 1987 U.S. Dist. LEXIS 240 (N.D. Ill., Jan. 13, 1987), count dismissed, 1990 U.S. Dist. LEXIS 13667 (N.D. Ill., Oct. 4, 1990), 1991 U.S. Dist. LEXIS 13584 (N.D. Ill., Sep. 24, 1991), 1991 U.S. Dist. LEXIS 13857 (N.D. Ill., Sep. 30, 1991), adopted, summary judgement granted, 1991 U.S. Dist. LEXIS 15758 (N.D. Ill., Oct. 30, 1991), 1991 U.S. Dist. LEXIS 15804 (N.D. Ill., Oct. 30, 1991), summary judgement granted, 1992 U.S. Dist. LEXIS 8968 (N.D. Ill., Jun. 23, 1992), motion granted, motion denied, 1993 U.S. Dist. LEXIS 11325 (N.D. Ill., Aug. 12, 1993).

The results indicate that both sets of proxies are important in explaining the number of covenants. In univariate comparisons, the most significant differences are associated with measures of relative supply and demand conditions, especially the inflow of venture capital in that year. In regressions—whether cross-sectional analyses of the entire sample or first-difference analyses of those organizations that raised multiple funds—both sets of proxies have significant explanatory power.

This chapter is organized as follows. The next section presents the theoretical literature on contractual completeness and its empirical implications. In the third section, the types of terms found in the contracts are introduced. The empirical analysis is presented in the fourth section. The fifth section concludes the chapter.

Determinants of Covenants

Theoretical Suggestions

Economists have argued that transactions subject to repeated bargaining problems should be governed by long-term contracts (Klein, Crawford, and Alchian 1978; Williamson 1979). For example, a coal mine operator may seek to expropriate rents by raising prices once a utility has built a plant near the mine shaft. The terms and conditions that govern the contractual relationship between the two parties are critical to limiting opportunistic behavior and ensuring allocational efficiency. A venture partnership presents many of the same problems: once the funds have been raised, the limited partners have very limited recourse to these funds. One of the few remedies is to insist on terms and conditions that will limit the general partner's ability to behave opportunistically.

Two approaches to understanding the determinants of contractual provisions have emerged in the financial and organizational literatures. Both approaches assume that observed contracts are optimal given the contractual environment. The two hypotheses should be viewed as complements. Both effects may be at work simultaneously. Our tests examine the relative importance of each hypothesis in determining contractual outcomes.[2]

---

2. Grossman and Hart (1986) suggest an alternative approach to the question of covenant inclusion. These authors argue that ownership is the ability to exclude someone from access to a particular asset. Ownership should be assigned to the party who will be least likely to engage in wasteful ex post renegotiating. Contractual covenants can be loosely interpreted as a mechanism that reserves ownership of particular activities for the limited partners. (Under partnership law, the general partner is assumed to have those rights not explicitly reserved by the limited partners.)

The costly contracting theory predicts that because negotiation and enforcement of explicit provisions are costly, covenants are included only when the benefits of restricting activity are greater than the costs. Williamson (1985) advances similar arguments about factors that influence contractual completeness. Because the ease of monitoring and incentives to pursue opportunistic behavior vary, the optimal set of restrictions differs across contracts.

Various investigations provide support for the costly contracting hypothesis. Smith and Warner (1979) argue that the complexity of debt contracts reflects the cost of contracting. Crocker and Reynolds (1993) argue that the degree of specificity in payment terms found in U.S. government jet engine procurement contracts is related to the level of technological and production uncertainties. Malitz (1986) shows that three specific classes of bond covenants are more common for issuers with characteristics that may proxy for a greater need for monitoring.

A second hypothesis contends that relative supply and demand conditions in the venture capital market affect the covenants and restrictions in long-term contracts. If the demand for the services of experienced venture capitalists changes rapidly while the supply of those venture capitalists is fixed in the short run, the price of venture capital services should rise. Venture capitalists' expected total compensation should increase.

The price of venture capital services is the compensation that general partners of the fund receive. This compensation has two components. The first component is monetary compensation paid to fund managers. The venture capitalist may also receive private benefits from certain activities. For ease of explication, we focus on private benefits that enhance the venture capitalist's reputation in a certain area. For example, venture capitalists may seek to invest in leveraged buyouts because if they succeed, they can raise a specialized LBO fund. The benefits of these reputation-building activities accrue exclusively to the venture capitalist. Because the expected return to the limited partners is likely to be diminished by these activities, they should seek to prohibit them.

The numbers of venture capitalists and investors are small, so the allocation of private benefits will be affected by relative supply and demand conditions. A sudden increase in demand for venture capital investing services—that is, if institutional investors suddenly increase their allocation to venture capital funds—should increase their price. Competition among venture capitalists does not lead to allocating all the gains to the investor because venture capital funds are imperfect substitutes for each other. Only a small number of venture capitalists may be raising a fund at any particular time, and these firms are likely to be differentiated by size, industry focus, location, and reputation. Many venture organizations will limit both how often they raise funds and the size of the funds that they raise, in the belief that excessive growth reduces returns. Meanwhile, managers who allocate alternative investments for institutions often operate under limitations about the types of funds in which they can invest (for instance, rules that prohibits investments into first funds raised by venture organizations), and they are pressured to meet allocation targets by the end of the fiscal year. Institutional investors have few alternatives to investing in new partnerships: the market for secondary interests in existing venture partnerships is illiquid and very thin.

It might appear puzzling that much of the adjustment takes place through *both* the insertion and deletion of covenants and explicit monetary compensation. Why should the entire adjustment not take place through the adjustment of compensation? One possibility is that these adjustments in the consumption of private benefits are an optimal response. The combination of expected fund returns and reputation-building activity by the venture capitalist define a Pareto frontier of possible contracts. The level of expected returns cannot be increased without curtailing reputation-building activity and vice versa. If venture capitalists optimize the mixture of compensation, then increases in demand are likely to lead to both increased monetary compensation and reduced restrictiveness. In many cases, it may be easier and cheaper to adjust contractual restrictiveness.

A related explanation is suggested by the literature on agency issues among institutional investors (Lakonishok, Shleifer, and Vishny 1992). These covenants represent a less visible way to make price adjustments than explicit modifications of the split in capital gains. Deviations from the standard 80 to 20 percent division of profits are likely to attract widespread attention in the institutional investor community (for a recent example, see Asset Alternatives 1994b). The inclusion or deletion of covenants, however, is much less likely to attract notice. Investment officers responsible for choosing venture capital investments may find that concessions made in this manner attract less scrutiny from regulators or superiors.

Although they are featured prominently in practitioners' accounts of contracting, supply and demand theories of contractual design have received little attention in academic circles. Hubbard and Weiner (1991) present a model that derives predictions about the relative importance of transaction costs and market power in determining contractual provisions. They test those predictions in a sample of natural gas contracts. While they find some monopsonistic effects on the initial contract prices (by using absolute and relative size of the transacting parties as a proxy for market power), they find little support for market power in other contractual provisions.[3]

Empirical Implications of Costly Contracting

The costly contracting theory predicts that contracting parties should balance the benefits of restricting activities with the cost of negotiating the provisions, writing the contractual clauses, and monitoring compliance. Fund- and firm-specific factors that increase the benefits of restrictions or decrease monitoring costs should lead to a greater number of restrictions.

Monitoring costs may be related to fund size. A large fund should be easier to monitor because it makes more investments and provides more opportunities to evaluate the policies of the venture capitalists. If that were the case, we would expect that larger funds would have more covenants and restrictions. The benefits of restricting certain activities may also be greater in larger funds. Because larger funds may have greater scope to make investments that do not necessarily benefit the limited partners (for example, substantial investments in leveraged buyouts or other venture funds), restrictions on these types of investments may be important.

Investors may not need to restrict the activities of venture organizations that have reputations as fair and reasonable players. Reputational concerns make opportunistic behavior less attractive and reduce the need for covenants. The likelihood of including covenants that restrict activities of the general partner should be significantly reduced for reputable venture capital organizations.

The sensitivity of compensation to performance may also reduce restrictions. Jensen and Meckling argue that agency costs decline as the

---

3. The costly contracting and supply-and-demand hypotheses are not mutually exclusive. In fact, the supply-and-demand hypothesis assumes that certain activities of the general partner impose costs on limited partners and need to be controlled by restricting those activities. A third possibility is that contractual provisions are benign and persist because there are no costs or benefits to their inclusion. This suggestion appears to run counter to the protracted and costly bargaining over covenants that precedes the signing of venture partnership agreements and many other types of contracts.

financial rewards of managers become more closely tied to the firm's future prospects.[4] Increasing the sensitivity of the venture capitalists' compensation to performance should reduce incentives to make investments that do not maximize limited partners' returns. The perceived need for covenants should thus fall.

The relative benefits of covenants may also increase as the scope for opportunistic behavior rises. Investments in early-stage and high-technology companies may increase the venture capitalist's ability to engage in opportunistic activities. These investment classes potentially involve the greatest asymmetric information and allow venture capitalists more opportunity to exploit their knowledge. Accounting performance may shed little light on the performance of a young firm; assessing the health of a high-technology firm is likely to require a detailed understanding of the technical position of the company and its competitors. Restrictions on activities of the general partners may thus be more likely. Monitoring compliance with the covenants in these types of funds, however, may be more difficult. Consequently, we have an ambiguous prediction about the relationship between the type of fund and the number of covenants.

A final empirical implication of the costly contracting view is that the number of covenants may change over time if investors learn about the venture capital industry. Because venture limited partnerships have become widespread only during the past fifteen years, and the market has only gradually learned about the incentives and activities of venture capitalists, early contracts may be significantly different from more recent agreements. In particular, early contracts may have far fewer covenants and restrictions than later contracts. If all potential future outcomes cannot be foreseen, the cost of writing and monitoring specific contracts may be very high. As the process and incentives become better understood, contracts could include more specific restrictions.[5]

---

4. Jensen and Meckling (1976). While the more visible portion of venture capitalists' return, their share of profits, is bunched between 20 and 21 percent, other aspects of compensation vary. Consequently, the sensitivity of pay to performance varies considerably, as discussed in chapter 4.

5. The structure of railroad sidetrack agreements in the late nineteenth and early twentieth centuries is examined in Pittman (1991). The author argues that the provisions in these contracts evolved in response to specific opportunistic behavior that took place. Similarly, evidence that few debt contracts prior to the leveraged buyout boom of the mid-1980s included event covenants related to buyouts or recapitalizations is presented in Lehn and Poulsen (1991). After the risk of expropriation became known, these types of risks were addressed with new types of covenants.

Empirical Implications of Supply and Demand Hypothesis

The supply and demand hypothesis suggests that when the demand for venture capital services is high, relative to a fixed supply of venture capital providers, the number of restrictions should decline. The bulk of the covenants prevent behavior that enriches venture capitalists at the investors' expense. Thus, the general partner's "compensation" increases with reductions in the number of restrictions. Several factors proxy for shifts in relative demand.

While it is impossible to directly measure the supply of and demand for venture capital services, we can measure capital inflows relative to the existing venture pool. If the short-run supply of venture services is fixed, changes in inflows may primarily reflect changes in demand. When the annual influx of funds is a large fraction of the existing venture pool (demand is high), the average number of covenants should fall.

The presence of an investment manager may affect the likelihood of including restrictive covenants in venture agreements. Investment managers not only select the funds in which pension funds invest, but also negotiate the terms and conditions of the partnership agreement. Investment managers typically place the funds of several pensions into a single venture fund. Investment managers believe that this bundling allows them to insert restrictions that otherwise would not be included in the partnership agreement (see, for instance, Huemer 1992). Raising a fund without the participation of these investment managers should indicate that the demand for the experienced venture capitalists' services is high. Therefore, funds without gatekeepers should have fewer covenants.[6] Anecdotal evidence supporting this hypothesis is found in discussions of the fund-raising strategies of venture capital firms. Some established venture organizations, such as Greylock, explicitly refuse to take money from investment managers.

---

6. An alternative interpretation is that funds selected by investment managers have a greater potential for agency problems. A particular concern is that the investment manager and general partners may engage in collusive behavior. To address these potential problems, limited partners may demand more covenants. It is very difficult to design a test that can distinguish between these two interpretations, but there are at least two reasons why the agency hypothesis is problematic. First, it is unclear why the investment manager would want to engage in collusive behavior with the venture capitalists. Investment managers receive all their compensation from the limited partners. These fees are typically independent of the returns generated by the venture funds that they have selected and of the value of the funds' assets. Second, investment managers are very sensitive to reputational concerns. Most of their clients are pension funds and endowments whose trustees are under a considerable of amount of regulatory and public scrutiny. If an investment manager is revealed to have behaved in a questionable manner, the repercussions are likely to be severe.

The demand for top-performing venture capital organizations should also be high relative to the supply of their services. While older, better performing venture organizations do add general partners to their funds, they tend to limit growth in the belief that large organizations lose their ability to operate effectively. Although direct measures of past performance are difficult to find, several proxies for performance can be tested. First, older venture organizations are likely to be better on average than new firms, because poorly performing organizations will be unable to raise new funds. Older firms therefore should have fewer covenants. Second, funds with higher compensation should have fewer covenants. The level of compensation also proxies for high demand for the venture organization's services.

The supply and demand hypothesis also predicts that pay sensitivity should be negatively related to the number of covenants. If the venture capitalist is taking more compensation in the form of private benefits at the expense of potential returns, limited partners want to tie the venture capitalist's monetary compensation more closely to fund returns.

Two difficulties with these predictions must be discussed. First, age and total compensation may be related to reputation. The greater the venture capitalists' reputational capital, the less likely they are to engage in opportunistic behavior that might destroy future returns to their reputation. Larger and more highly compensated venture capital firms may have fewer restrictions because they have less incentive to exploit investors, not because their funds are in greater demand.

Second, the costly contracting hypothesis may generate a similar time-series pattern. In particular, it may be that the costs of opportunism for the venture capitalists vary over time. During periods when there is a particularly heavy inflow of funds, fewer covenants are needed, because the cost of opportunistic behavior (for instance, foregone future fundraising) is greater.

This interpretation, while seemingly plausible, is problematic for two reasons. First, venture partnerships typically raise funds only every several years. A year of rapid growth in the venture pool tends to be followed by another year of rapid growth, but there is no correlation across several years.[7] Thus, it is unclear why worries about future fundraising

---

7. The average venture organization that raised a fund between 1968 and 1987 and raised a follow-on fund did so 2.9 years later. Using data from 1968 to 1994, the flow into venture capital funds (expressed as a percentage of the venture pool in the previous year) has a correlation coefficient with its one-year lag of 0.873 (with a p-value of .000). The correlation coefficient with its three-year lag is -0.105 (with a p-value of .634).

should be particularly intense in high-growth years. Second, this hypo thesis assumes that limited partners can rapidly identify opportunistic behavior by venture capitalists. In fact, venture capital investments are long-term by nature, and it is often difficult for outsiders to assess the status of the private firms in a venture capitalist's portfolio. Consequently, it takes a long time for opportunistic behavior to be identified.[8]

A First Look at the Convenants

We construct a random sample of 140 partnership agreements. As described in chapter 16, we eliminated a variety of related funds. We use the 140 partnership agreements in the files of two gatekeepers and one limited partner. In chapter 16, we assess the completeness and representa- tiveness of this sample.

These partnership agreements are complex, often extending for 100 pages or longer. Our procedure for coding the documents was as follows. First, we reviewed the earlier literature and identified the broad areas in- volved in partnership agreements. (We employed Bartlett 1988, 1994; Dauchy and Harmon 1986; Halloran, et al. 1995; Sahlman 1990; and Venture Economics 1989b, 1992b.) A research assistant then culled the contractual provisions in these areas from a subsample of forty contracts. We then used these forty descriptions to design a coding form capturing the key features of the agreements. The coding of the 140 contracts was done by an MBA candidate who had previously received a law degree and spent several years practicing contract law.

Before presenting the analysis, we qualitatively discuss the fourteen classes of restrictions featured in our analysis. Each covenant is related to a particular type of opportunistic activity that the general partners might undertake for their own personal benefit but may impose costs on the limited partners. Our description of the covenants focuses on the poten- tial agency costs that might arise if the covenants were not included. The formal tests later in the chapter will examine how the number of cove- nants varies with potential agency problems in the fund and with the relative supply and demand for venture capital services.

---

8. To cite one example, Hambrecht and Quist raised a fund in 1981 that was plagued by a wide array of organizational problems and had exceedingly poor returns. The venture orga- nization was nonetheless able to raise one dozen funds with nearly half-a-billion dollars in capital over the remainder of the decade (see King 1990).

We focus on fourteen covenant classes in partnership agreements. These classes include all those restrictions that are found in at least 5 percent of the agreements in our sample and no more than 95 percent of agreements (in between 7 and 133 out of the 140 contracts). In this way, we enhance the tractability of the analyses by eliminating several classes that are either standardized "boilerplate" or else exceedingly rare.

Because the analysis is focused on the number of covenant classes employed, it does not do full justice to the restrictions' complexity. Many variants of each covenant are found in the partnership agreements. The qualitative descriptions of the fourteen classes of restrictions provide a sense of the complexity of these terms. In the descriptions and the analyses, we divide these covenants into three broad families: those relating to the overall management of the fund, the activities of the general partners, and the permissible types of investments.

Covenants Relating to Overall Fund Management

The first set of restrictions limits the amount invested in any one firm. These provisions are intended to ensure that the general partners do not attempt to salvage an investment in a poorly performing firm by investing significant resources in follow-on funding. The general partners typically do not receive a share of profits until the limited partners have received the return of their investment. The venture capitalists' share of profits can be thought of as a call option: the general partners may gain disproportionately from increasing risk of the portfolio at the expense of diversification. This limitation is frequently expressed as a maximum percentage of capital invested in the fund (typically called committed capital) that can be invested in any one firm. Alternatively, the limit may be expressed as a percent of the current value of the fund's assets. In a few cases, the aggregate size of the partnership's two or three largest investments is capped.

The second covenant class limits the use of debt. As option holders, general partners may be tempted to increase the variance of their portfolio's returns by leveraging the fund. Increasing the riskiness of the portfolio would increase the value of their call option at the investors' expense. Partnership agreements often limit the ability of venture capitalists to borrow funds themselves or to guarantee the debt of their portfolio companies (which might be seen as equivalent to direct borrowing). Partnership agreements may limit debt to a set percentage of committed capital or assets, and in some instances also restrict the maturity of the debt to ensure that all borrowing is short-term.[9]

The third restriction relates to coinvestments with the venture organization's earlier and/or later funds. Many venture organizations manage multiple funds formed several years apart. These can lead to opportunistic behavior.[10] Consequently, partnership agreements for second or later funds frequently require that the fund's advisory board review such investments or that a majority (or super-majority) of the limited partners approve these transactions. Contracts also address these problems by requiring that the earlier fund invest simultaneously at the same valuation. Alternatively, the investment may only be allowed if one or more unaffiliated venture organizations simultaneously invest at the same price.

A fourth class of covenant relates to reinvestment of profits. For several reasons, venture capitalists may reinvest capital gains rather than distributing the profits to the limited partners.[11] The reinvestment of profits may require approval of the advisory board or the limited partners. Alternatively, such reinvestment may be prohibited after a certain date, or after a certain percentage of the committed capital is invested.

---

9. A related provision—found in virtually all partnership agreements—is that the limited partners will avoid unrelated business taxable income. Tax-exempt institutions must pay taxes on UBTI, which is defined as the gross income from any unrelated business that the institution regularly carries out. If the venture partnership is generating significant income from debt-financed property, the limited partners may have tax liabilities (see Bartlett 1995). In the analysis below, we code funds as having a restriction on debt only if there are limitations beyond a clause concerning UBTI.

10. Consider, for instance, a venture organization whose first fund has made an investment in a troubled firm. The general partners may find it optimal for their second fund to invest in this firm in the hopes of salvaging the investment. Distortions may also be introduced by the need for the venture capitalists to report an attractive return for their first fund as they seek investors for a third fund. Many venture funds will write up the valuation of firms in their portfolios to the price paid in the last venture round. By having the second fund invest in one of the first fund's firms at an inflated valuation, they can (temporarily) inflate the reported performance of their first fund.

11. First, many partnerships receive fees on the basis of either the value of assets under management or adjusted committed capital (capital less any distributions). Distributing profits will reduce these fees. Second, reinvested capital gains may yield further profits for the general (as well as the limited) partners. A third reason why venture capitalists may wish to reinvest profits is that such investments are unlikely to be mature at the end of the fund's stated life. The presence of investments that are too immature to liquidate is a frequently invoked reason for extending the partnership's life beyond the typical contractual limit of ten years. In these cases, the venture capitalists will continue to generate fees from the limited partners (though often on a reduced basis).

Covenants Relating to Activities of the General Partners

Five frequently encountered classes of restrictions curb the activities of the general partners. The first of these limits the ability of the general partners to invest personal funds in firms. If general partners invest in selected firms, they may devote excessive time to these firms and may not terminate funding if the firms encounter difficulties. To address this problem, the size of the investment that the general partners can make in any of their fund's portfolio firms is often limited. This limit may be expressed as a percentage of the fund's total investment, or (less frequently) of the net worth of the venture capitalist. In addition, the venture capitalists may be required to seek permission from the advisory board or limited partners. An alternative approach employed in some agreements is to require the venture capitalists to invest a set dollar amount or percentage in every investment made by the fund.[12]

A second restriction addresses the reverse problem: the sale of partnership interests by general partners. Rather than seeking to increase their personal exposure to selected investments, general partners may sell their share of the fund's profits to other investors. While the general partnership interests are not totally comparable with the limited partners' stakes (for instance, the general partners will typically only receive distributions after the return of the limited partners' capital), these may still be attractive investments. Limited partners may worry that such a sale will reduce the general partners' incentives to monitor their investments. Partnership agreements may prohibit the sale of general partnership interests outright, or else require that these sales be approved by a majority (or super majority) of the limited partners.

A third area for restrictions on the general partners is fundraising. The raising of a new fund will raise the management fees that venture capitalists receive and may reduce the attention that they pay to existing funds. Partnership agreements may prohibit fundraising by general partners until a set percentage of the portfolio has been invested or until a given date.[13]

---

12. Another issue relating to coinvestment is the timing of the investments by the general partners. In some cases, venture capitalists involved in the establishment of a firm will purchase shares at the same time as the other founders at a very low valuation, then immediately invest their partnership's funds at a much higher valuation. Some partnership agreements address this problem by requiring venture capitalists to invest at the same time and price as their funds.

13. Alternatively, fundraising may be restricted to a fund of a certain size or focus. For instance, the venture organization may be allowed to raise a buyout fund, which would presumably be managed by other general partners.

Some partnership agreements restrict general partners' outside activities. Because outside activities are likely to reduce the attention paid to investments, venture capitalists may be required to spend "substantially all" (or some other fraction) of their time managing the investments of the partnership. Alternatively, the general partners' involvement in businesses not in the venture fund's portfolio may be restricted. These limitations are often confined to the first years of the partnership, or until a set percent of the fund's capital is invested, when the need for attention by the general partners is presumed to be the largest.

A fifth class of covenant relates to the addition of new general partners. By adding less experienced general partners, venture capitalists may reduce the burden on themselves. The quality of the oversight provided, however, is likely to be lower. As a result, many funds require that either the advisory board or a set percentage of the limited partners approve the addition of new general partners.

Although many issues involving the behavior of the general partners are addressed through partnership agreements, several others typically are not. One area that is almost never discussed in the sample is the vesting schedule of general partnership interests. If general partners leave a venture organization early in the life of the fund, they may forfeit all or some of their share of the profits. If venture capitalists do not receive their entire partnership interest immediately, they are less likely to leave soon after the fund is formed. A second issue is the division of profits among the general partners. In some funds, most profits accrue to the senior general partners, even if the younger partners provide the bulk of the day-to-day management. While these issues are addressed in agreements between the general partners, they are rarely discussed in the contract between the general and limited partners.

Covenants Restricting the Types of Investment

The third family of covenants limit the types of assets in which the fund can invest. These restrictions are typically structured in similar ways: the venture fund is allowed to invest no more than a set percent of capital or asset value in a given investment class. An exception may be made if the advisory board or a set percentage of the limited partners approve. Occasionally, more complex restrictions will be encountered, such as the requirement that the sum of two asset classes not exceed a certain percent of capital.

Two fears appear to motivate these restrictions on investments. First, compared to other investors in a particular asset class, the general partners may be receiving compensation that is inappropriately large. For instance, the average money manager who specializes in investing in public securities receives an annual fee of about 0.5 percent of assets (Lakonishok, Shleifer, and Vishny 1992), while venture capitalists receive 20 percent of profits in addition to an annual fee of about 2.5 percent of capital. Consequently, limited partners seek to limit the ability of venture capitalists to invest in public securities. Similarly, the typical investment manager receives a one-time fee of 1 percent of capital for investing an institution's money in a venture fund (Venture Economics 1989a). Partnership agreements often also include covenants that restrict the ability of the general partners to invest capital in other venture funds.

A second concern is that the general partners will opt for classes of investments in which they have little expertise in the hopes of gaining experience. For instance, during the 1980s, many venture funds began investing in leveraged buyouts (LBOs). Those that developed a successful track record proceeded to raise funds specializing in LBOs; many more, however, lost considerable sums on these investments.[14] Similarly, many firms invested in foreign countries during the 1980s. Only a relative handful proved sufficiently successful to raise funds specializing in these investments (for a practitioner discussion, see Kunze 1990).

Empirical Analysis

Univariate Comparisons

Table 3.1 summarizes representation of the fourteen primary covenant classes in the sample. Panel A indicates the percent of contracts that include each provision in three five-year periods (1978–82, 1983–87, and 1988–92). The initial impression is one of persistent heterogeneity in the distribution of these covenants. Differences are striking in view of the concentration of capital providers and advisors in this industry: relatively few limited partners provide the bulk of capital, and partnership documents are prepared by a modest number of law firms. Panel B demonstrates the marked increase in the number of covenant classes in agreements executed after 1987. This effect is driven by the pronounced

---

14. The poor performance of venture-backed LBOs, such as Prime Computer, has been much discussed in Gallese (1990); quantitative support of these claims is found in analyses of the returns of funds with different investment objectives by Venture Economics (e.g., 1998).

Table 3.1
The number of covenants in 140 venture partnership agreements by year. For the fourteen classes of covenants, the table indicates the percent of venture partnership agreements with such a restriction in each five-year period. The second panel indicates the number of partnership agreements in each period and the mean number of covenant classes (the simple average and the average weighted by fund size).

Panel A: Distribution of covenants

	Percent of contracts with covenant in		
	1978–82	1983–87	1988–92
Covenants relating to the management of the fund			
Restrictions on size of investment in any one firm	33.3	47.1	77.8
Restrictions on use of debt by partnership	66.7	72.1	95.6
Restrictions on coinvestment by organization's earlier or later funds	40.7	29.4	62.2
Restrictions on reinvestment of partnership's capital gains	3.7	17.6	35.6
Covenants relating to the activities of the general partners			
Restrictions on coinvestment by general partners	81.5	66.2	77.8
Restrictions on sale of partnership interests by general partners	74.1	54.4	51.1
Restrictions on fundraising by general partners	51.9	42.6	84.4
Restrictions on other actions by general partners	22.2	16.2	13.3
Restrictions on addition of general partners	29.6	35.3	26.7
Covenants relating to the types of investment			
Restrictions on investments in other venture funds	3.7	22.1	62.2
Restrictions on investments in public securities	22.2	17.6	66.7
Restrictions on investments in LBOs	0.0	8.8	60.0
Restrictions on investments in foreign securities	0.0	7.4	44.4
Restrictions on investments in other asset classes	11.1	16.2	31.1

Panel B: Summary of covenants

	1978–82	1983–87	1988–92
Total number of partnership agreements in sample	27	68	45
Average number of covenant classes	4.4	4.5	7.9
Average number of covenant classes (weighted by fund size)	4.4	4.6	8.4

increase in provisions about the management of the fund and types of investment. In fact, all nine covenant classes in these two families increase in frequency during the sample period. Weighting observations by fund size makes little difference in this analysis or in those reported below.

This increase contrasts with the decline in four of the five covenants about the activities of general partners. The overall pattern is consistent with the costly contracting hypothesis. During the early period when venture capital limited partnerships were a relatively recent phenomenon,

restricting the activities of general partners was important. Because
potential agency problems relating to the management of the fund or
investments were difficult to predict, restrictions were general in nature.
As investors learned about what agency costs were probable, specific
restrictions concerning fund management and investments were written.
General restrictions on venture capitalists' activities, which may have
limited their flexibility undesirably, were consequently dropped.

We analyze how the number of restrictions varies with eight variables,
four of which measure potential agency problems. The first two relate to
fund focus. General partners of early-stage and high-technology funds
may have more scope to engage in opportunistic behavior. The costly
contracting hypothesis predicts that limited partners in these funds
demand covenants that restrict potential agency problems. We determine
the fund's focus by examining the contracts and offering documents that
are used to promote the funds.[15]

A third proxy for potential agency costs is fund size.[16] All else being
equal, limited partners should add more restrictions to larger funds. There
should be increasing returns to scale in negotiating and monitoring compliance with covenants. Larger funds, however, are raised by more established venture firms that may not wish to risk their reputational capital by
engaging in opportunistic behavior. We determine fund size using the
Venture Economics funds database.

Our fourth measure is the elasticity of compensation to performance,
or pay sensitivity. Both the supply and demand hypothesis and costly

15. In many cases, the information will be in the offering document, but not in the partnership agreement. In the few cases where we do not have the offering document, we use the
information about the fund focus recorded in the Venture Economics funds database.
16. One concern is that fund size is a proxy for the reputational capital of the venture organization, not the individual venture capitalists. Ideally, we would have a measure of the
cumulative experience of the venture capitalists associated with the fund. Unfortunately,
constructing such a measure is problematic. Many venture capitalists have diverse backgrounds: for instance, as founders of entrepreneurial firms, corporate managers, or university
researchers. It is unclear how individual experience should be aggregated. Even if such a
measure could be designed, only about half of the private placement memoranda provide
detailed information on the general partners' backgrounds. Obtaining biographical information on venture capitalists elsewhere is often very difficult. To address this concern, we
examine whether the venture capitalists in older, larger venture organizations had more prior
experience. We look at 267 venture organizations established between 1978 and 1985 that
had a board seat on at least one firm that went public in the seven years after the fund closed.
To assess experience, we look at the boards on which the venture capitalists served prior to
the closing of the fund. (We total the inflation-adjusted market capitalization of all IPOs on
whose boards these venture capitalists served.) Older and larger venture organizations tend
to have more experienced venture capitalists. The correlation coefficients, 0.29 and 0.25
respectively, are significant at the 1 percent confidence level.

contracting hypothesis predict that fund managers who have compensation more closely tied to performance have fewer restrictive covenants.
As pay is more closely related to the fund's monetary returns, the need
for restrictive covenants is reduced. We compute compensation measures
using the detailed information on the management fees, division of profits, and timing of payments from the partnership agreements. For measures that cannot be computed in advance, we use historical averages. We
first calculate the elasticity of compensation to performance.[17] We then
compute the net present value of the base and variable compensation,
with the assumption that assets with the venture capitalists' management
grow by 20 percent annually.

The second set of variables controls for relative supply and demand
conditions in the venture capital market. The first measure is the inflow of
new capital into venture funds in the year the fund is established. Because
the supply of venture capital services is fixed in the short run, a large
growth in capital commitments suggests that demand for venture capital
services is high relative to supply, causing the number of covenants to
decline and total compensation to rise. While fundraising activity was
relatively sluggish before and after, the years 1982 through 1986 were
characterized by a dramatic growth in this capital pool. We measure the
growth of this pool by computing the ratio of total capital committed to
venture funds in the year the fund closed to the amount raised in the previous ten years.[18]

An alternative measure of the relative demand for the general partners'
services is the presence or absence of investment managers. The absence
of investment managers should be an indication of high demand. To determine whether an investment manager advised a client to invest in the
fund, we examine the lists of names and addresses of limited partners that

---

17. More specifically, we use the increase in the net present value of compensation associated with an increase in the asset growth rate from 20 to 21 percent. This is near the mean
of venture performance during the 1980s (Venture Economics 1998). The procedure is
described in detail in chapter 4.

18. The calculations are made using the Venture Economics funds database. We use
inflation-adjusted dollars throughout. Because we are concerned that the results may be sensitive to the definition of the venture growth rate, we also employ three alternative measures. These are (1) the ratio of total capital committed to venture funds in the year the fund
closed to the amount raised in the previous *five* years (to correct for the fact that much of the
capital of older funds already has been returned to the limited partners), (2) the ratio of new
capital to the number of active venture organizations (defined as those that had raised a fund
in the previous ten years), and (3) the absolute growth in venture capital pool in the year the
fund closed.

are typically appended to the partnership agreement. This is usually indicated when an investment manager advises the limited partner.[19] In addition, we obtain the names of the venture funds in which five major investment managers have allocated funds.

A third proxy for the venture capital supply and demand conditions is the total compensation they receive. Venture capitalists may increase both their monetary compensation and their consumption of private benefits in response to increased demand. As described above, we calculate total compensation, assuming a 20 percent growth rate and express it as a fraction of the fund's capital.

The final measure that we employ is the age of the venture organization. We anticipate that more experienced venture capitalists will have greater demand for their services. Older firms have been able to raise a series of funds and should have higher ability on average. Using the Venture Economics funds database, we compute the time from the closing of the venture organization's first fund to the closing of this fund.[20]

Table 3.2 summarizes the univariate comparisons of the number of restrictions. Fund focus and the presence of an investment manager are dummy variables that equal one for firms with each characteristic. In the other cases, funds are divided by whether they are above or below the median of each measure. We compare the mean and median number of restrictions.

We find significant differences in the number of restrictions when we divide the contracts by three measures suggested by the supply and demand hypothesis: the growth rate of the venture pool in the year of the fund's closing (measured in four different ways), the presence of an investment manager as an advisor to one or more limited partners, and total compensation of the general partners. Funds established at times when the venture pool grew rapidly, where an investment manager was not involved, or in which the venture capitalists were highly compensated have significantly fewer restrictions. The differences are significant whether we compare means or medians. When we divide the funds by indicators that we expect to be associated with a greater need for moni-

---

19. Because the investment manager will typically handle the continuing administrative work concerning the partnership (for example, liquidating stock distributions and responding to any proposed modifications of the partnership agreement), the address of the limited partner will be listed as care of the investment manager.

20. In a closing, an investor or group of investors sign a contract that binds them to supply a set amount of capital to a private equity fund, and they often provide a fraction of that capital immediately.

Table 3.2
The number of covenant classes in 140 venture partnership agreements for various subgroups.
The first two columns compare the mean and median (in brackets) number of covenant classes for funds in the sample that fall into various categories. In the first panel, firms are divided by their focus and the presence of an investment manager; in the second panel, by whether they are above or below the median on several measures. The third column presents the p-values of t-tests and Wilcoxon signed-rank tests (in brackets) of the null hypotheses that these distributions are identical.

Panel A: Binary variables

	Number of covenants for funds where this is		p-value, test of no difference
	True	False	
Focus on early-stage investments	5.0	5.3	0.567
	[5]	[5]	[0.524]
Focus on high-technology investments	5.3	5.2	0.790
	[5]	[5]	[0.877]
Presence of investment manager	5.8	3.8	0.001
	[6]	[3]	[0.001]

Panel B: Continuous variables

	Number of covenants for funds that are		p-value, test of no difference
	Above median	Below median	
Size of venture fund	5.2	5.2	0.691
	[5]	[5]	[0.752]
Sensitivity of general partner compensation to performance	4.7	5.9	0.717
	[5]	[6]	[0.534]
Rate of growth of venture pool in year of fund's closing[a]	4.0	7.2	0.000
	[4]	[8]	[0.000]
Total compensation of the general partners	4.2	6.4	0.017
	[4]	[6]	[0.033]
Age of venture organization in year of closing	5.5	5.0	0.414
	[5]	[5]	[0.464]

a. The rate of the growth of venture pool is significant at the 1 percent level using three alternative definitions.

toring—for instance, whether the fund focuses on early-stage and high-technology investments—we find no significant differences in the number of covenants.[21]

Regression Analyses

We examine these patterns using regression analyses in table 3.3. The dependent variable is the number of covenant classes included in the partnership agreement (out of a total of fourteen). We employ two econometric specifications, ordinary least squares (OLS) and Poisson. The latter may more accurately reflect the nonnegative, ordinal nature of the dependent variable.[22] Because the dummy variables for funds with an early-stage and high-technology focus are highly correlated, we use only one of these variables at a time. Since we are missing data in some cases, we employ only 124 out of the 140 observations.[23]

Panel A presents the OLS and Poisson regressions. In each, the coefficients of the variables measuring the growth rate of the venture pool and the presence of one or more investment managers are significant. Consistent with the supply and demand hypothesis, funds established at times when the venture capital pool is growing rapidly and in which investment managers do not advise the limited partners have fewer restrictions.

We test whether the independent variables that proxy for agency problems or supply and demand conditions jointly differ from zero. In Panel B, we present the p-values from tests of the null hypothesis of no difference. Using both specifications, the null hypothesis is rejected for

---

21. Our results are not driven by all-or-nothing covenant inclusion. Most covenant classes are positively correlated with other covenant classes, and many of the correlations are significant. The correlation coefficients are reasonably small, however. For example, the average correlation coefficient among restrictions on the fund's management is 0.169, and 33 percent are significant at the 1 percent confidence level. The highest correlation is among the restrictions on investments: 90 percent of the correlation coefficients are significant at the 1 percent level; the average correlation coefficient is 0.432. The largest correlation across covenant classes is between restrictions concerning fund management and investment activity. The average correlation coefficient is 0.258: 55 percent are significant at the 1 percent level, with 80 percent significant at the 5 percent level.

22. The standard errors in the OLS regression are heteroskedastic-consistent, while those in the Poisson regression are not adjusted in this manner. The usefulness of Poisson regressions in these settings is discussed in Maddala (1983).

23. In some cases, we do not know the size of the fund. In other cases, we cannot calculate the base compensation since it is set in a budget negotiated annually between the limited and general partners or else is based on the debt taken on by the firms in the venture capitalists' portfolio.

Table 3.3
Regression analysis of the number of covenant classes in venture partnership agreements. In the first panel, the dependent variable is the number of covenant classes (out of a total of fourteen) included in the partnership agreement. The first two rows present the coefficients of an ordinary least squares regression (with absolute heteroskedastic-consistent t-statistics in brackets); the second, a Poisson regression (with absolute t-statistics in brackets). The second panel presents the p-values of F- and χ^2-texts that the sets of variables which proxy for agency costs (early-stage focus, sensitivity of pay to performance, and size of the venture fund) and for the venture organization's market power (venture pool growth, presence of an investment manager, total compensation, and age of the venture organization) are equal to zero. The regressions use 124 partnership agreements for which complete data are available.

Panel A: Regression analyses

| | Independent variables | | | | | | | | | | | |
Specification	Early-stage focus?	Sensitivity of pay to profits	Size of venture fund	Venture pool growth	Investment manager?	Total compensation	Age of venture organ.	Constant	Adj. R²	Root MSE	χ^2-statistic	p-value
OLS	0.19	−51.67	0.005	−5.06	1.47	−13.19	−0.06	12.51	0.22	2.658		
	[0.34]	[1.63]	[1.45]	[5.83]	[2.23]	[1.33]	[1.11]	[2.85]				
Poisson	0.01	−8.30	0.001	−0.98	0.27	−2.23	−0.01	2.89			53.19	0.000
	[0.16]	[1.60]	[1.42]	[5.05]	[2.82]	[1.74]	[1.67]	[4.92]				

Panel B: Tests of significance

Specification	p-value, test of whether agency proxies are zero	p-value, test of whether market power proxies are zero
OLS	0.231	0.000
Poisson	0.214	0.000

supply-and-demand proxies at the 1 percent level. The variables seeking to measure the costly contracting hypothesis, however, cannot be shown to differ from zero. These regressions suggest that the relative demand for venture capital services is a critical determinant of the number of covenants.[24]

We examine the robustness of the analysis to the use of alternative dependent variables. We explore whether results could be driven by one covenant (or one set of restrictions) by considering each of the three covenant families separately. Table 3.4 presents three regressions that employ as dependent variables the number of restrictions relating to fund management, the activities of the general partners, and the investment type. We present only the regressions using an OLS specification; results using a Poisson specification are similar.

The results in table 3.4 support both the supply and demand and costly contracting hypotheses. The results show that fund size is important in determining the number of covenants on the management of the fund and the type of investment. The potential agency problems on fund management and investments are likely to increase with the size of the fund, while the potential for agency problems involving general partners may not. (The number of investments is likely to increase linearly with fund size, while the number of general partners typically only increases slowly with size.) In these two regressions, the costly contracting proxies are jointly different from zero. The coefficients of the venture pool growth and investment manager variables have the sign predicted by the supply and demand hypothesis in all three regressions (and are significant at the 5 percent confidence level in two). The measures of supply and demand

---

24. We undertake several modifications of these regressions to address concerns about their robustness. First, we add a variable that indicates the date that the fund closed to control for any trend in the number of covenants. While the primary results are robust to the addition of this variable, the trend term is positive and highly significant. This might indicate that the market has been learning about potential agency costs over time and continues to include more specific restrictions. Second, we address the concern that two of the independent variables—the amount and performance sensitivity of the compensation—are determined at the same time as the dependent variable. While a venture organization will typically announce a target fund size in advance, the compensation will be negotiated at the same time as the terms and conditions of the partnership. We rerun the regressions omitting these measures. Third, we reestimate the regressions using three alternative measures of the venture pool growth because we are concerned that the results may reflect the particular measure that we employ. Finally, we employ a dummy variable for a fund with a high-technology (rather than an early-stage) focus. In all cases, the independent variables associated with the supply and demand hypothesis remain jointly significant at the 1 percent confidence level. Those addressing the costly contracting hypothesis are in each case insignificant at conventional confidence levels.

Table 3.4
Regression analysis of the number of covenant classes in venture partnership agreements, divided into three families. The dependent variable is the number of covenant classes in each family included in the partnership agreement. The table presents the coefficients of an ordinary least squares regression (with absolute heteroskedastic-consistent t-statistics in brackets). The second panel presents the p-values of F-tests that the sets of variables which proxy for agency costs (early-stage focus, sensitivity of pay to performance, and size of the venture fund) and for the venture organization's market power (venture pool growth, presence of an investment manager, total compensation, and age of the venture organization) are equal to zero. The regressions use 124 partnership agreements for which complete data are available.

Panel A: Regression analyses

Dependent variable	Independent variables								Adj. R²	Root MSE
	Early-stage focus?	Sensitivity of pay to profits	Size of venture fund	Venture pool growth	Investment manager?	Total compensation	Age of venture organ.	Constant		
Number of covenants relating to the management of the fund	0.04 [0.17]	−17.78 [1.82]	0.003 [3.41]	−1.38 [3.06]	0.35 [1.48]	−3.74 [1.08]	−0.03 [1.11]	4.04 [2.76]	0.14	1.024
Number of covenants relating to the activities of the general partners	0.10 [0.40]	−1.34 [0.09]	0.001 [0.44]	−0.56 [1.38]	0.59 [2.02]	−3.16 [0.93]	−0.06 [2.27]	3.60 [2.12]	0.10	1.205
Number of covenants relating to the types of investment	0.05 [0.18]	−32.56 [2.02]	0.003 [2.42]	−3.12 [6.92]	0.53 [1.99]	−6.28 [1.16]	0.02 [0.84]	4.87 [2.11]	0.32	1.345

Panel B: Tests of significance

Dependent variable	p-value, test if agency proxies are zero	p-value, test of whether market power proxies are zero
Number of covenants relating to the management of the fund	0.005	0.011
Number of covenants relating to the activities of the general partners	0.954	0.000
Number of covenants relating to the types of investment	0.042	0.000

Table 3.5
The change in the number of covenant classes included in the current and previous venture partnership agreements. The observations are divided by a change in whether the fund has a gatekeeper among its investors, a change in fund focus (either to or from a focus on early-stage or high-technology investments), and a change in the growth rate of the venture capital pool in the year of the fund's closing. There are a total of 14 covenant classes. The second panel presents the results of t-tests and an F-test of the significance of these differences. The sample consists of 75 second and later venture funds where information is available on an earlier fund of the venture organization.

Panel A: Impact of change in fund characteristics on number of restrictions

	Change in number of restrictions		
	Mean	Standard error	Observations
Gatekeeper status			
When a gatekeeper invested in this fund but not in previous fund	+2.4	1.1	14
When a gatekeeper invested in this and in previous fund	+1.4	0.5	45
When no gatekeeper invested in this fund	+1.5	0.9	16
Stage focus			
When this is an early-stage fund and previous fund is not early stage	+4.3	2.4	6
When this and previous fund specialize in early-stage investments	+1.4	1.0	10
When this and previous fund do not specialize in early-stage investments	+1.6	0.5	49
When previous fund specializes in early-stage investments and this one does not	+0.6	1.4	10
Technology focus			
When this is a high-tech fund and previous fund is not high-tech	+3.6	1.5	11
When this and previous fund specialize in high-tech investments	+2.3	0.9	16
When this and previous fund do not specialize in high-tech investments	+1.2	0.5	41
When previous fund specializes in high-tech investments and this one does not	−0.4	1.7	7
When the growth rate of the venture pool at time of this fund's closing is			
Greater than at time of last fund's closing	−0.9	0.7	15
Between 0 and 10 percent below last fund's closing	+1.8	0.9	21
Between 10 and 20 percent below last fund's closing	+2.4	0.8	20
More than 20 percent below last fund's closing	+2.7	0.8	19

Panel B: Tests of significance

	Test statistic	p-value
Do cases where a gatekeeper invested in this fund and not in previous fund differ from others?	0.87	0.389
Do cases with an early-stage focus in this fund and not in previous fund differ from others?	1.85	0.068
Do cases where a high-tech focus in this fund and not in previous fund differ from others?	1.94	0.057
Do cases with various venture pool growth rate changes differ?	3.46	0.021

Table 3.6
Regression analysis of the change in the number of covenant classes in venture partnership agreements. The dependent variable is the difference in the number of covenant classes (out of a total of fourteen) included in the current and previous partnership agreements. Independent variables are the change in fund focus (either to or from a focus on early-stage or high-technology investments), the change in whether the fund has a gatekeeper among its investors, and the change in the growth rate of the venture capital pool in the year of the fund's closing. The table presents the coefficients of ordinary least squares regressions (with absolute t-statistics in brackets). The sample consists of seventy-five second and later venture funds where information is available on an earlier fund of the venture organization.

| | Independent variables | | | | | | | |
| | Change in whether early-stage focus | Change in whether high-tech focus | Change in gatekeeper presence | Change in growth rate of venture pool | Constant | Adj. R² | F-statistic | p-value |
Dependent variable								
Change in number of restrictions	1.90		-0.10	-3.77	1.30	0.08	3.15	0.030
	[2.07]		[0.13]	[2.46]	[2.85]			
Change in number of restrictions		2.01	-0.39	-3.28	1.17	0.09	3.56	0.018
		[2.33]	[0.52]	[2.16]	[2.58]			

are jointly significant in all three regressions. Formal tests of the significance of these variables are presented in panel B of table 3.4.

An alternative empirical approach examines first differences to determine if changes in the explanatory variables are related to changes in the number of covenants. Such a first-differences analysis eliminates many unobserved organization-specific characteristics that may be correlated with the explanatory variables. Table 3.5 shows how the number of covenant classes changes in subsequent funds of the same venture organization. We divide the funds by whether there were changes in the presence of a gatekeeper, the focus of the fund, or the rate of growth of the venture industry in the year of the fund's closing. The effects are in the expected direction. For example, the number of covenants increases by 2.4 when a gatekeeper supplies capital to the current fund but not to the previous fund. Declining growth rates in the venture pool also lead to an increase in the number of covenants. Both results are consistent with the supply and demand hypothesis. In addition, early-stage and high-technology funds have more scope to engage in opportunistic activities, so restricting their activities is more valuable. The second panel tests the significance of these differences. The differences in the number of covenants are significant at the 5 percent confidence level in the growth-rate analysis; those relating to fund focus are of borderline significance.

The first-difference regressions are presented in table 3.6. Unlike the earlier regressions, a change in the focus of the fund to either early-stage or high-technology investments increases the number of covenants significantly, by approximately two. This is consistent with the costly contracting hypothesis. Changes in the gatekeeper status do not significantly affect the number of covenants, which may reflect the smaller sample size in these first-difference analyses. Finally, a decline in the growth rate of the venture pool increases the number of covenants in the contracts. These results are generally consistent with both the costly contracting and supply and demand hypotheses.

Conclusions

This chapter examines the use of contractual covenants in venture capital partnership agreements. Two complementary explanations for the presence of these restrictions are analyzed: differences in the need for oversight and in supply and demand conditions for venture capital services. The evidence from a sample of 140 contracts indicates that both factors are important determinants of contractual restrictiveness. The proxies for supply and demand conditions are consistently significant in univariate and regression analyses. When the covenants are broken down into families, proxies for potential agency problems are significantly related to covenants that restrict the management of the fund and investment activities, while the supply and demand proxies are related to all three groups. The results are robust to a variety of modifications.

This research differs from earlier empirical analyses of contract structure. Earlier analyses have either focused exclusively on the costly contracting hypothesis or found weak support for the claim that supply and demand conditions affect contractual form. Our results suggest that the relative neglect of the supply and demand hypothesis is unwarranted. The paucity of academic work on supply and demand effects contrasts with the weight placed on this factor in practitioner accounts. While our description of the supply and demand hypothesis is informal, we hope that further theoretical and empirical work will examine the role of shifts in supply and/or demand in determining contractual forms.

4 How Are Venture Capitalists Compensated?

In addition to the terms and conditions discussed in chapter 3, venture capital limited partnership agreements clearly define the compensation over the fund's life to be paid to the venture capitalists. Typically, these agreements designate a percentage of the fund's capital or assets as an annual management fee and a percent of the profits to be paid out as investment returns are realized. Compensation is based on actual returns from the venture fund's investments. While compensation in the different funds raised by a venture organization may differ, the individual partnership agreements are rarely renegotiated, unlike executive employment contracts.[1]

Contractually specified compensation is particularly important in the venture capital setting. As discussed in chapter 2, the limited partners in venture capital funds cannot utilize many of the methods of disciplining managers found in corporations and must avoid direct involvement in the fund's activities. Removing a venture capitalist is a difficult and costly procedure. Consequently, as Venture Economics (1989b) notes, compensation is "one of the most contentious issues between limited and general partners of venture funds."

At first glance, the compensation terms in these models resemble one another. This is illustrated in figure 4.1 which presents the distribution of the percentage of profits allocated to the general partners after any provision for the return of invested capital, or of invested capital plus a premium. The share in our sample varies from 0.7 to 45 percent, but 81 percent of the funds are between 20 and 21 percent, inclusive. While superficially quite homogenous, there are many subtle differences across the compensation provisions in these agreements. Many of these differences, we will show, reflect the diversity the venture organizations

---

1. Similar schemes are found in funds devoted to leveraged buyout, mezzanine, real estate, and oil-and-gas investments as well as hedge funds.

Number of observations

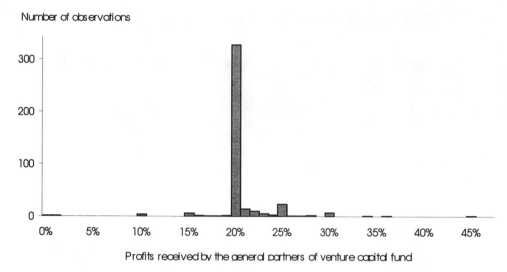

Figure 4.1
The share of profits received by venture capital organizations. The sample consists of 419 venture capital partnerships whose first closing was between January 1978 and December 1992. The profit figure indicates the average share of capital gains received by the venture capital organizations after any initial return of investment to the limited partners.

entering into the agreements. In this chapter we explore some of these differences and their causes.

Two models are given that might explain the variation in compensation in these contracts which have quite different empirical implications. We then analyze a sample of 419 U.S. venture capital partnerships. We find that compensation for older and larger venture capital organizations is more sensitive to performance and more variable than the compensation of other venture groups. The fixed component of compensation is higher for smaller, younger funds and funds focusing on high-technology or early-stage investments. No relationship is found between the incentive compensation and performance. The empirical results are consistent with the primary predictions of a model in which neither the venture capitalist nor the investor initially knows the venture capitalist's ability, but this information is gradually revealed over time.

The chapter is organized as follows. The next section discusses the theoretical models of the determinants of compensation. The third section analyzes the sample of partnership agreements. The fourth section examines the relationship between incentive compensation and performance. The fifth section concludes the chapter.

Determinants of Venture Capitalist Compensation

This section explores how information about the venture capitalist's ability should affect the time-series and cross-sectional variation of compensation for venture capitalists for both fixed and variable pay. We discuss two stylized models that generate predictions framing the empirical analyses. First, we adapt the compensation model from Gibbons and Murphy (1992) to the venture capital setting and derive the equilibrium compensation to explore the learning model. We assume that initially there is symmetric uncertainty about the ability of the venture capitalist. Then we assume the venture capitalist, but not the investor, is initially informed about the venture capitalist's ability in our discussion of the signaling model. Appendices A and B discuss the models in detail.

The Learning Model

An abstraction of the learning model is the assumption that venture capitalists raise two funds (partnerships) in two consecutive periods. The outcome of investments in the first fund, including any investment returns, is realized prior to the second fund being raised. No projects shift from the first fund to the second. The fund return is a function of the venture capitalists' ability to select high-quality projects and add value after the investment, their effort, and noise. While the venture capitalists' ability either to select attractive projects or to add value after the investment is uncertain, both venture capitalists and investors know the distribution of abilities in advance. Investors cannot observe the effort level chosen in either fund, because this information is private. The venture capitalists' compensation is assumed to be a linear function of fund returns.

Compensation contracts are written for each fund and are conditional on the information available from returns, if any exist. The compensation contract is set out before effort is chosen or investments are made. Investors in both funds can, but need not, be the same. Investors in the second fund, however, have verifiable information about the performance of the first fund. Appendix A of this chapter derives the equilibrium contract under the assumptions of the learning model.

The learning model has five implications for venture capitalist compensation:

• *Level of pay-for-performance sensitivity over time.* The sensitivity of compensation to performance is higher in the venture capitalists' second fund.

Venture capitalists have an incentive to work hard in their first fund because, if they increase effort, investors think they have higher ability. (This relation holds for fixed expectations about equilibrium effort choice.) Greater effort not only increases current income but also raises total compensation in the second period.[2]

• *Level of fixed fees over time.* The learning model is ambiguous about the relative fixed fees in new and old venture firms. While the level of variable compensation unambiguously increases in established venture firms, fixed fees could rise, fall, or remain unchanged.

• *Level of fixed fees and effort level.* Because we assume a Nash bargaining solution, fixed fees incorporate the cost of effort such that the higher cost of effort, the higher the fixed fees. All else being equal, higher investment and monitoring costs lead the venture capitalists to receive higher fixed fees.

• *Variance in pay-for-performance sensitivity over time.* This model also predicts that the cross-sectional variance should be lower for new and smaller venture organizations than for established organizations. Compensation schemes for small, young venture capital organizations should be clustered, because neither the venture capitalists nor the investors know the venture capitalists' abilities. As venture capitalists' abilities become known, compensation schemes can reflect the updated information about ability. If there is a distribution of abilities, then the cross-sectional variance of variable compensation should be higher for larger, older venture capital organizations.

• *Level of pay-for-performance sensitivity and performance.* Finally, the learning model predicts that pay-for-performance sensitivity across periods should be unrelated to the performance of the venture capital fund. In the

2. The comparison of first- and second-fund compensation can be viewed as indicative of patterns among venture capitalists with and without established reputations. If a venture capital firm has established a good reputation, it needs explicit incentives in the form of high pay-for-performance sensitivity to induce effort. To empirically assess this claim, we will use venture organization age and size as proxies for reputation. Older and larger venture capital organizations are likely to have established reputations and therefore need higher pay sensitivities to induce the desired effort level. New and smaller venture organizations work harder because they seek to establish a reputation that will allow them to command greater compensation in future funds. This implicit incentive means that less pay-for-performance sensitivity is necessary for small, young venture firms. An important issue that we do not model is whether reputation adheres to the venture organization or the individual venture capitalists. Although we show in the empirical analysis below that established venture capital organizations tend to be comprised of more experienced venture capitalists, exploring the ways in which reputation resides in and transfers among financial institutions is a fertile topic for future research.

first period, even though pay-for-performance is lower, the venture capitalist is driven to work hard by the desire to establish a reputation. In the second period, higher explicit incentives are required because the potential for higher compensation in the next period is not there. Put another way, incentive compensation is endogenous and elicits the optimal effort given the perceived ability of the venture capitalist. In a cross section of venture capital funds, pay sensitivity should have no predictive power for performance.

The Signaling Model

The principal-agent literature demonstrates that the nature of contracts changes dramatically once informational assumptions are altered. In the learning model, investors and venture capitalists both have the same initial information about venture capitalists' abilities. Symmetric uncertainty leads to the central result. If venture capitalists have better information before entering into a contract, however, the possible contracts signed in equilibrium states change. Under certain assumptions, high-ability venture capitalists will attempt to signal their type through the contracts they offer to investors in the first period.[3]

In this simple signaling model, the second fund's variable compensation is the same for high- and low-ability venture capitalists. This result follows from our assumption that marginal productivity after the first unit of effort and effort costs of both types of venture capitalists are identical. Because types are fully revealed in the first fund, second-period compensation differs only in the base compensation. High-ability venture capitalists receive higher fixed fees in subsequent funds. Once the ability type of the high-ability venture capitalists has been revealed, they desire more insurance, and hence receive higher fixed compensation and less variable compensation.

Deriving optimal first-period compensation schemes is more difficult. These classes of signaling models usually have a continuum of equilibrium points. Because low-ability venture capitalists set their compensation for their second fund under full information about ability, their optimal first-fund contract will be identical to the optimal second-fund contract. Low-ability venture capitalists act as if their type is completely known in their first fund.

---

3. Although we examine the Riley (1979) information equilibrium, it is likely that other separating, as well as pooling, equilibria exist.

High-ability venture capitalists offer a contract that maximizes their utility, subject to the constraint that low-ability venture capitalists are indifferent between accepting this contract and their own. As shown in appendix B of this chapter, the variable compensation for the high-ability venture capitalists in the first fund is more sensitive to performance than it is in the second fund. Likewise, the fixed component of compensation is smaller in the first fund. The fixed component in a first-fund contract might even be negative, in which case high-ability venture capitalists would pay for the opportunity to invest in start-up companies in their first fund. For high-ability venture capitalists to separate from low-ability types, they must be willing to accept more risk. Linking compensation more closely to uncertain future returns increases the risk that the high-ability venture capitalists bear. The higher expected level of pay compensates these venture capitalists for the greater risk. Pay-for-performance sensitivity in the first fund for high-ability venture capitalists increases as the difference in ability increases. The difference in second-period compensation is greater, and therefore low-ability venture capitalists have more to gain from imitating high-ability types.

The signal in this model is the level of risk that the venture capitalists bear. Variable compensation divides an uncertain payoff between venture capitalists and investors. Unlike signaling models in which the signal is explicitly nonproductive, such as education, the use of pay sensitivity as a signal has a second effect of inducing different effort choices in equilibrium.

Heinkel and Stoughton (1994) examine the case in which investors evaluate portfolio managers on both the contracts offered and past performance. Their optimal contracts are complex, but qualitatively resemble the learning model. This is because their model has both learning and signaling components. Adding a noisy signal of ability, like performance, creates incentives to work harder. Heinkel and Stoughton show that under their assumptions, the learning effect is stronger. In the model used here, however, investors do not have an opportunity to use past returns to update beliefs. Types are totally revealed to investors by the contracts offered in the first fund before the venture capitalists have any performance. In the learning model discussed earlier, both the venture capitalists and investors infer the venture capitalists' ability through realized returns. Our empirical analysis can be seen as a comparison of the power of these two effects, which are depicted in extreme form in our models. Our central empirical result—the greater pay-for-performance sensitivity of more established venture organizations—is consistent with the predictions presented in Heinkel and Stoughton (1994) and the learning model.

In our signaling model, where venture capitalists know their ability to select and oversee entrepreneurs before raising a fund, the predicted empirical patterns differ from those derived in the learning model, where venture capitalists and investors have equally poor initial information about ability:

• *Level of pay-for-performance sensitivity over time.* The signaling model predicts that new and smaller venture organizations, which are confident that they have high ability, will increase their pay-for-performance sensitivity in early funds. Once the venture capitalists' ability has been revealed through their contract choice, the desire for insurance on the part of the risk-averse venture capitalists causes incentive compensation in subsequent funds to decline. Older and larger venture capital organizations with established reputations should have less incentive compensation.

• *Level of fixed fees over time.* Fixed fees for older and larger venture capital firms should be higher because these organizations will demand insurance.

• *Level of fixed fees and effort level.* As in the learning model, higher investment and monitoring costs should lead the venture capitalists to receive higher fixed fees.

• *Variance in pay-for-performance sensitivity over time.* We also expect that the cross-sectional variance in pay-for-performance sensitivities will be smaller in older, larger organizations. In the model where each type's marginal product is equal, there is no variance in the variable compensation for the later fund. Thus, both the level and the cross-sectional variance of pay-for-performance sensitivities should be higher for younger venture capital firms. Both of these predictions are the reverse of the predictions of the learning model.

• *Level of pay-for-performance sensitivity and performance.* Finally, the signaling model predicts that pay sensitivity should be positively related to performance. High-ability venture capitalists increase their pay-for-performance sensitivity to signal their quality. Young, high-ability venture capitalists will work hard because of the higher variable compensation and have higher returns.

The Form of Compensation

We examine 419 venture partnership agreements and offering memoranda for funds formed between 1978 and 1992. The construction of the sample is described in chapter 16.

The form of venture capitalist compensation in these contracts is analyzed in three ways. First, we examine the most visible aspect of compensation, the percentage of profits received by the venture capitalists. Second, we examine the net present value (NPV) of the fixed management fees. Finally, we examine the elasticity of venture partnerships' compensation, defined as the percentage change that will occur in the NPV of total compensation in response to a 1 percent change in performance. The elasticity is a function of both the percentage of profits retained by general partners and the base compensation, and therefore it is the best measure of the sensitivity of compensation to performance.

The Percentage of Profits

As highlighted in figure 4.1, there is a great deal of bunching in the share of profits. This concentration is broadly consistent with a learning model in which information is revealed slowly. If investment ability is uncertain, venture capitalists negotiate very similar compensation terms.

But there are also substantial differences. Panel A of table 4.1 presents the mean level of variable compensation. We divide the observations in several ways. As discussed above, we use two measures of venture organization reputation. The first measure is the age of the venture organization, or the time from the closing of the first partnership that the venture organization raised to the closing of this fund. We use this measure for age because investors should know more about the ability of older venture organizations. These older venture organizations, however, may also be of higher quality. Low-quality venture capitalists should eventually be unable to raise new funds. The average level of compensation should rise because we do not observe the low compensation of poor venture capitalists in later funds.

Venture organization age will not, however, capture the fact that venture capitalists beginning a new organization may have had considerable experience at another venture group or elsewhere. We consequently employ a second proxy for the experience of the venture capitalists, which is the size of the venture organization's previous funds. Venture organization size is a potentially useful measure of uncertainty concerning ability. Investors may provide larger sums to venture capitalists with proven track records, even if they have not raised any earlier funds. We total the capital invested in the organization's funds, using 1997 dollars, whose first closing was in the ten calendar years prior to the year that this fund closed. Because the size of the venture pool increased dramatically over

Table 4.1
The share of profits received by venture capital organizations. The sample consists of 419 venture capital partnerships whose first closing was between January 1978 and December 1992. We present the mean share of capital gains received by the venture capital organizations (VCs) after any initial return of investment to the limited partners. We also present the number of observations. The size of the venture organization is the ratio of the capital invested in the organization's funds, in constant dollars, whose first closing was in the ten calendar years prior to the year that this fund closed, to the total amount raised by all venture organizations in these years, again in constant dollars. Panel B tests the significance of these patterns.

Panel A: Mean percentage of profits received by venture capitalists

	Percent of profits received by VCs	Number of observations
Age of venture organization		
No earlier funds	20.5	146
Four years or less	20.7	88
Between four and eight years	20.6	94
More than eight years	21.4	91
Size of venture organization		
No earlier funds[a]	20.4	170
Between 0.0 and 0.2 percent	20.9	84
Between 0.2 and 0.7 percent	20.5	88
Greater than 0.7 percent	21.6	77
Objective of fund		
Focus on high-technology firms	21.2	199
Other industry focus (or no focus)	20.3	220
Focus on early-stage investments	21.1	173
Other stage focus (or no focus)	20.5	246
Date of closing		
January 1978–December 1984	20.5	100
January 1985–June 1986	20.9	111
June 1986–December 1988	20.7	120
January 1989–December 1992	20.9	85

Panel B: Tests involving percentage of profits

Variables	Coefficient	p-value
Correlation, age of venture organization and percent of profits	0.104	0.032
Correlation, size of venture organization and percent of profits	0.109	0.026
Correlation, date of closing and percent of profits	0.027	0.577
t-Test, high-technology focus and percent of profits		0.004[b]
t-Test, early-stage focus and percent of profits		0.047[b]
Variance test, organizations below and above 0.7 percent of pool		0.000[c]
Variance test, organizations below and above ten years old		0.022[c]

Table 4.1 (continued)

a. This category also includes funds that raised a previous fund whose size cannot be determined.
b. p-value from a t-test comparing the percentage of profits received by funds with and without this investment focus.
c. p-value from an F-test comparing the variance of profits received by experienced and inexperienced venture organizations.

these years, we employ a measure of relative size. We divide this sum by the total amount raised by venture organizations in these years, again using 1997 dollars.

Neither measure of experience is perfect. Ideally, we would have a measure of the cumulative experience of the venture capitalists associated with the fund, but unfortunately, constructing such a measure is problematic. Many venture capitalists have diverse backgrounds, including experience as founders of entrepreneurial firms, corporate managers, or university researchers. It is unclear how individual experience should be aggregated. Even if such an experience measure could be designed, only about half of the private placement memoranda provide detailed information on the backgrounds of the general partners. Obtaining biographical information on venture capitalists elsewhere is often very difficult. To address this concern, we examine whether the venture capitalists in older and larger venture organizations had more prior experience. We look at 267 venture funds established between 1978 and 1985, including some not in the sample, that had a board seat on at least one firm that went public in the seven years after the fund closed. To assess experience, we look at the boards on which the venture capitalists served prior to the closing of this fund. We total the inflation-adjusted market capitalization of all IPOs on whose boards these venture capitalists served. Older and larger venture organizations tend to have more experienced venture capitalists. The correlation coefficients, 0.29 and 0.25 respectively, are significant at the 1 percent confidence level.

The oldest and largest funds command about a 1 percent greater share of profits than less established funds. As the correlation analysis in panel B of table 4.1 demonstrates, these effects are significant at least at the 5 percent confidence level. Similarly, firms with a focus on high-technology or early-stage investments receive a significantly higher percent of profits. No significant time effect appears. Again, consistent with the learning model, larger and older venture capital organizations also have significantly greater variance in the share of profits that they receive.

Even if the differences between more and less established funds are statistically significant, they may not be economically meaningful. To address this concern, we examine a representative fund, using the assumptions outlined in appendix C. A 1 percent difference in the share of profits matters very little if the venture fund does not perform well. For instance, if the fund's investments grow only at an annual rate of 10 percent, an increase in the venture capitalists' profit share from 20 to 21 percent boosts the NPV of total compensation by only 0.3 percent. The small magnitude of this change occurs because the compensation in this case is dominated by the fixed fee. If, however, the fund's investments perform well, a very different picture emerges. For example, if the fund's investments grow at an annual rate of 50 percent, an increase in the profit share for the venture capitalists from 20 to 21 percent raises the NPV of total compensation by 4.2 percent.

Table 4.2 reports the results from several regression analyses. The first is an ordinary least squares (OLS) analysis. The dependent variable is the venture capitalists' share of profits. We express this variable as a number between 0 and 100, where 21.2 represents a profit share of 21.2 percent. Independent variables are the date of the closing, venture organization size and age, and dummy variables denoting whether the fund focuses on high-technology or early-stage firms. We include the dummy variables for fund focus to control for other factors that may influence base compensation and that may also be associated with fund reputation to isolate the effect of the reputation measures. These dummy variables take on a value of 1 if the fund has such a focus.

We are unsure, however, whether OLS is the proper specification, so we also employ three alternatives. First, we classify funds into those where venture capitalists' percentage of profits is in five ranges and run an ordered logit regression. We code funds receiving below 20 percent as 0, those between 20 and 21 percent as 1, those between 21 and 25 percent as 2, those between 25 and 30 percent as 3, and those above 30 percent as 4. Second, we perform a Tobit regression, where we examine whether the venture organization received more than 21 percent of the profits, and if so, how much more. The use of this specification is motivated by the fact that the vast majority of contracts fall into the range between 20 and 21 percent, or else are greater than 21 percent. The final set of regressions employs a maximum likelihood approach. We estimate if the venture capitalists received between 20 and 21 percent of the profits, and if not, what percentage was received. We assume that the percentage received by the

Table 4.2
Regression analyses of the share of profits received by venture capital organizations. The sample consists of 419 venture capital partnerships whose first closing was between January 1978 and December 1992. The first three regressions are ordinary least squares (OLS) analyses, with the capital gains received by the venture capital organizations after any initial return of investment to the limited partners as the dependent variable. The next two regressions are ordered logit analyses, with funds receiving below 20 percent coded as 0, those between 20 and 21 percent as 1, those between 21 and 25 percent as 2, those between 25 and 30 percent as 3, and those above 30 percent as 4. The sixth is a Tobit analysis of whether the percentage of profits is above 21 percent, and if so, by how much. The final two regressions are a maximum likelihood analysis of whether the fund receives between 20 and 21 percent of profits, and if not, what the level is, assuming a normal distribution for those observations not between 20 and 21 percent. Independent variables include the date of the closing, with January 1, 1978, coded as 1978.0, and so forth, the size of the venture capital organization, measured as the ratio of capital raised in the ten calendar years prior to the year in which the fund closed to the total amount raised by venture capital organizations in that time, the age of the venture organization at the time of the fund closing, in years, and dummy variables indicating whether the fund focused on high-technology or early-stage investments, with 1 denoting such a fund. Absolute t-statistics in brackets.

	OLS	OLS	OLS	Ordered logit	Ordered logit	Tobit	Maximum likelihood	
Dependent variable: Percentage of profits received by venture capital organization							Profits in target range?	Actual profits
Date of closing	0.04 [0.80]	−0.002 [0.03]		0.01 [0.19]	−0.03 [0.73]	−0.21 [1.07]	0.05 [1.94]	0.12 [0.61]
Fund closed in 1978–1982?			−0.01 [0.02]					
Fund closed in 1983–1987?			−0.27 [0.80]					
Size of venture organization	50.67 [2.54]		48.19 [2.40]	42.57 [2.86]		189.78 [2.60]	−17.90 [2.05]	117.58 [1.86]
Age of venture organization		0.07 [2.47]			0.05 [2.11]			
Fund focuses on high technology?	0.93 [3.08]	0.94 [3.13]		0.61 [2.41]		1.57 [2.27]	0.10 [0.72]	4.18 [3.19]

Fund focuses on early stages?		0.75 [2.41]			0.35 [1.39]			−210.63 [0.55]
Constant	−58.52 [0.60]	23.53 [0.23]	20.26 [60.04]			433.26 [1.10]	−91.38 [1.93]	
Adjusted R²	0.03	0.02	0.03					
F-statistic	5.07	3.49	3.83					
Log likelihood				−306.07	−309.52	−328.16	−461.74	
χ^2-statistic				12.42	5.52	9.78	22.07	
p-value	0.002	0.016	0.005	0.006	0.137	0.020	0.001	
Number of observations	416	416	416	416	416	416	416	

venture capitalists, if not in the 20 to 21 percent range, has a normal distribution. This allows us to use funds receiving less than 20 percent as well as those getting more than 21 percent. It also allows us to estimate separate coefficients for the decision to deviate from the standard range and the extent of the deviation.

As reported in table 4.2, the venture organization's size and age are positive and significant in the first six regressions. While the regressions are noisy and the adjusted R^2s are quite low, the results are consistent with the learning model. In the final pair of maximum likelihood regressions, larger venture capitalists are more likely to deviate from the 20 to 21 percent range, and to receive a larger share of profits (at the 10 percent confidence level).

Base Compensation

We next examine fixed fees, also known as management fees. Because these fees are a significant fraction of venture capitalist's compensation, and are calculated in many different ways, omitting them may give a misleading impression. Fixed fees may be specified as a percent of the committed capital (that is, the amount of money investors have committed to provide over the life of the fund), the value of fund's assets, or some combination or modification of these two measures. Both the base used to compute the fees and the percentage paid as fees may vary over the life of the fund. To examine management fees, we compute the NPV at the time of the partnership's closing of the fixed fees that are specified in the contractual agreement. We express the value as a percent of the committed capital. We discount relatively certain compensation, such as fees based on committed capital, at 10 percent, while applying a 20 percent discount rate to more uncertain compensation, such as fees based on net asset value. The results do not change significantly when we use other discount rates. When necessary, for example, in cases where fees are based on net asset value, we make a series of assumptions about fund performance, which are summarized in appendix C of this chapter.

Table 4.3 reports the mean NPV of the base compensation as a percentage of committed capital. Older and larger venture capital organizations receive lower base compensation than younger, smaller ones. Funds focusing on early-stage and high-technology investments have higher base compensation. The NPV of base compensation appears to have increased over time, rising by nearly 2 percent since 1984.

Table 4.3

Base compensation and sensitivity of compensation to performance for venture capital organizations. The sample consists of 419 venture capital partnerships whose first closing was between January 1978 and December 1992. We present base compensation as the mean net present value of the fixed fees as a percentage of committed capital, and sensitivity of compensation to performance as the mean percentage increase in the net present value of total compensation associated with an increase in the asset growth rate from 20 to 21 percent. We discount relatively certain compensation, such as fees based on committed capital, at 10 percent, and uncertain compensation, such as the venture capitalists' share of the capital gains, at 20 percent. The size of the venture organization is the ratio of the capital, in constant dollars, invested in the organization's funds whose first closing was in the ten calendar years prior to the year that this fund closed to the total amount, again in constant dollars, raised by all venture organizations in these years. Panels B and C test the significance of these patterns.

Panel A: Mean base compensation and sensitivity of compensation to performance

	Mean base compensation	Mean sensitivity of compensation to performance
Age of venture organization		
No earlier funds	18.9	4.5
Four years or less	18.5	4.5
Between four and eight years	19.3	4.3
More than eight years	15.9	4.9
Size of venture organization		
No earlier funds[a]	18.8	4.5
Between 0.0 and 0.2 percent	19.9	4.4
Between 0.2 and 0.7 percent	18.2	4.5
Greater than 0.7 percent	15.1	5.1
Objective of fund		
Focus on high-technology firms	18.8	4.6
Other industry focus (or no focus)	17.8	4.6
Focus on early-stage investments	19.2	4.6
Other stage focus (or no focus)	17.6	4.6
Date of closing		
January 1978–December 1984	16.7	5.2
January 1985–June 1986	18.8	4.6
June 1986–December 1988	18.9	4.3
January 1989–December 1992	18.3	4.4

Table 4.3 (continued)

Panel B: Tests involving base compensation

Variables	Coefficient	p-value
Correlation, age of venture organization and base compensation	−0.238	0.000
Correlation, size of venture organization and base compensation	−0.330	0.000
Correlation, date of closing and base compensation	0.134	0.008
t-test, high-technology focus and base compensation		0.041[b]
t-test, early-stage focus and base compensation		0.001[b]
Variance test, organizations below and above 0.7 percent of pool		0.417[c]
Variance test, organizations below and above ten years old		0.227[c]

Panel C: Tests involving sensitivity of compensation to performance

Variables	Coefficient	p-value
Correlation, age of venture organization and performance sensitivity	0.109	0.031
Correlation, size of venture organization and performance sensitivity	0.242	0.000
Correlation, date of closing and performance sensitivity	−0.274	0.000
t-test, high-technology focus and performance sensitivity		0.950[b]
t-test, early-stage focus and performance sensitivity		0.459[b]
Variance test, organizations below and above 0.7 percent of pool		0.042[c]
Variance test, organizations below and above ten years old		0.043[c]

a. This category also includes funds that raised a previous fund whose size cannot be determined.
b. p-value from a t-test comparing the performance sensitivity in funds with and without this investment focus.
c. p-value from an F-test comparing the variance of performance sensitivity in funds of experienced and inexperienced venture organizations.

Regression results are presented in table 4.4. The dependent variable is the NPV of base compensation as a percent of committed capital. Fees totaling 20 percent of committed capital would again be expressed as 20. Independent variables include the date of the fund's closing, venture organization size and age, and dummy variables denoting whether the fund focuses on high-technology or early-stage investments, with 1 denoting such a fund. We find that larger and older venture organizations are associated with significantly lower fees, while funds specializing in early-stage or high-technology investments have significantly larger base compensation.

The results are consistent with the predictions of the learning model which suggests that established firms will receive a greater share of their compensation in the form of variable payments. The signaling model, however, predicts that base compensation should be higher for older and larger venture capital organizations. Once they have established reputa-

Table 4.4
Regression analyses of the net present value of base compensation of venture capital organizations. The sample consists of 419 venture capital partnerships whose first closing was between January 1978 and December 1992. The dependent variable is the net present value of the expected base compensation paid to venture capitalists as a percentage of committed capital. We assume an annual asset growth rate of 20 percent, and discount relatively certain compensation, such as fees based on committed capital, at 10 percent, and uncertain compensation, such as fees based on net asset value, at 20 percent. Independent variables include the date of closing, with January 1, 1978, coded as 1978.0, and so forth, the size of the venture capital organization, measured as the ratio of capital raised in the ten calendar years prior to the year in which the fund closed to the total amount raised by venture capital organizations in that period, the age of the venture organization at the time of the closing of the fund, in years, and dummy variables indicating whether the fund focused on high-technology or early-stage investments, with 1 denoting such a fund. Absolute t-statistics in brackets.

	Dependent variable: Net present value of base compensation as a percent of committed capital			
	With dummy for high-tech focus		With dummy for early-stage focus	
Date of closing	0.22	0.35	0.23	0.35
	[2.82]	[4.29]	[2.97]	[4.31]
Size of venture organization	−225.51		−214.99	
	[6.83]		[6.48]	
Age of venture organization		−0.25		−0.23
		[5.88]		[5.35]
Fund focuses on high technology?	0.86	1.02		
	[1.88]	[2.21]		
Fund focuses on early stages?			1.29	1.32
			[2.78]	[2.78]
Constant	−419.58	−680.11	−442.25	−681.20
	[2.70]	[4.17]	[2.85]	[4.19]
Adjusted R^2	0.13	0.10	0.14	0.11
F-statistic	19.96	15.82	21.56	16.88
p-value	0.000	0.000	0.000	0.000
Number of observations	393	393	393	393

tions, venture capitalists should demand insurance through higher base compensation. This prediction is not borne out in the data.

The Sensitivity of Compensation to Performance

An alternative measure of variable compensation is the elasticity of compensation to fund performance. This allows us to get a more complete picture of the sensitivity of compensation to performance, as we can assess the impact of both the base and variable compensation. To determine the elasticity, we calculate the NPV of the total compensation under reasonable assumptions.

We discount the payments back to the date of the partnership's formation. We undertake the calculation at two asset growth rates, 20 and 21 percent. By comparing these two values, we can examine the incremental value of a small amount of additional performance at a level of performance that is typical for this period. For example, Venture Economics (1998) estimates that funds established prior to 1982 that were still active in 1989 had a mean return of 17.6 percent, with a standard deviation of 14.2 percent. We once again discount relatively certain compensation, such as that based on committed capital, at 10 percent, while applying a 20 percent discount rate to more uncertain compensation, such as expected profits. Additional assumptions are described in appendix C. Figure 4.2 displays considerably greater dispersion in the sensitivity to performance than in the share of profits.

An alternative approach to measuring the elasticity of compensation to performance would be to view the venture capitalist's compensation as consisting of two securities: a bond—the base compensation—and an option on the percentage of the assets of the partnership, which would be the variable compensation. We could then compute the value of the bond and the option. While Sahlman (1990) computes the value of such an option in a simple case, undertaking such a calculation for several hundred funds with different payout structures would be prohibitively difficult.

Table 4.3 reports the mean elasticity of compensation to performance. Older and larger venture organizations have significantly greater performance sensitivity. Funds specializing in high-technology and early-stage investments, which command both higher base and variable compensation, display no difference in the sensitivity of compensation to performance. The variance of the performance sensitivity is significantly higher for larger and older venture organizations.

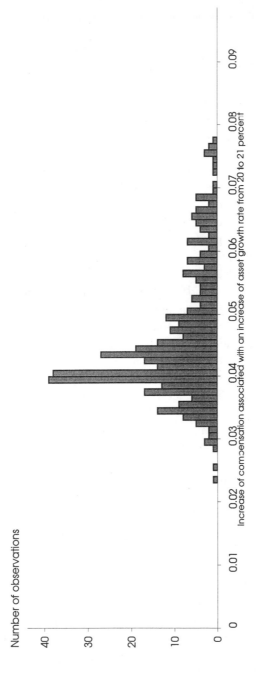

Figure 4.2
The sensitivity of venture capitalist compensation to performance. The sample consists of 419 venture capital partnerships whose first closing was between January 1978 and December 1992. The figure indicates the percentage increase in compensation associated with an increase in the asset growth rate from 20 to 21 percent. We discount relatively certain compensation, such as fees based on committed capital, at 10 percent, and uncertain compensation, such as the venture capitalists' share of the capital gains, at 20 percent.

Table 4.3 presents regression analyses of compensation sensitivity to performance. The dependent variable is the change in the NPV of total compensation associated with increasing the asset growth rate from 20 to 21 percent. Compensation for larger and older venture organizations displays greater performance sensitivity, while compensation for funds specializing in early-stage and high-technology firms does not.

Here are two observations about the level and pattern of elasticity measures. The first is the relatively large impact of an increase in performance on the pay of the venture capitalists. An increase in the asset growth rate from 20 to 21 percent leads to a 4 to 5 percent increase in compensation. This increase results from the highly leveraged position of the venture capitalists, who receive a share of the profits only after the return of the investors' committed capital. This sensitivity is magnified among the older and larger firms due to the greater sensitivity of their compensation to performance.

Second, our analyses have a significant bias against finding the patterns displayed in tables 4.3, 4.4, and 4.5. Several of the oldest and largest venture organizations do not charge a fixed annual fee based on committed capital or assets. Rather, they negotiate annual budgets with their limited partners. These organizations are reputed to have very low fee structures. This claim is corroborated through an examination of recent annual reports for eight such funds in the Harvard Management Company files. The funds charged an average fee of 1.6 percent of committed capital, considerably below the standard 2.5 percent. These funds are not included in our analyses of base compensation or performance sensitivity since their compensation is not fixed in advance. Were we able to include them, the level of base compensation would decline, and the level and variance of the performance sensitivity would increase for the oldest and largest funds.

The elasticity results are consistent with the predictions of the learning model but not the signaling one. As the abilities of venture capitalists become known with greater certainty, explicit incentives, typically in the form of variable performance compensation, replace implicit career concerns. The variance in compensation schemes rises over time as investors and venture capitalists learn about abilities. If early-stage and high-technology venture funds differ from other funds only in the level of effort necessary to monitor the portfolio, fixed fees should be higher, but performance sensitivity should not differ between the groups. This difference is what we find empirically.

Table 4.5

Regression analyses of the sensitivity of compensation to performance for venture capital organizations. The sample consists of 419 venture capital partnerships whose first closing was between January 1978 and December 1992. The dependent variable is the percentage increase in the net present value of total compensation associated with an increase in the asset growth rate from 20 to 21 percent. We discount relatively certain compensation, such as fees based on committed capital, at 10 percent, and uncertain compensation, such as the venture capitalists' share of the capital gains, at 20 percent. Independent variables include the date of closing, with January 1, 1978, coded as 1978.0, and so forth, the size of the venture capital organization, measured as the ratio of capital raised in the ten calendar years prior to the year in which the fund closed to the total amount raised by venture capital organizations in that time, the age of the venture organization at the time of the closing of the fund, in years, and dummy variables indicating whether the fund focused on high-technology or early-stage investments, with 1 denoting such a fund. Absolute t-statistics in brackets.

	Dependent variable: Sensitivity of compensation to performance			
	With dummy for high-tech focus		With dummy for early-stage focus	
Date of closing	−0.10	−0.12	−0.10	−0.12
	[5.73]	[6.53]	[5.76]	[6.54]
Size of venture organization	36.72		36.15	
	[5.05]		[4.93]	
Age of venture organization		0.04		0.04
		[3.87]		[3.73]
Fund focuses on high technology?	0.02	−0.01		
	[0.18]	[0.09]		
Fund focuses on early stages?			−0.05	−0.06
			[0.44]	[0.53]
Constant	200.74	238.79	202.06	239.18
	[5.86]	[6.66]	[5.89]	[6.67]
Adjusted R^2	0.13	0.10	0.13	0.10
F-statistic	19.74	15.94	19.80	16.05
p-value	0.000	0.000	0.000	0.000
Number of observations	393	393	393	393

Table 4.6

Regression analyses of the performance of venture capital funds. The sample consists of 234 venture capital partnerships whose first closing was between January 1978 and December 1986. The first regression is an ordinary least squares (OLS) analysis, with the ratio of the value of the fund's stakes in firms which had gone public in an initial public offering (IPO) by December 1992 to the total amount raised by the fund as the dependent variable. The value of the firm is determined eighteen months after the IPO. To control for the different maturities of the portfolios, the ratio of the mean fund begun in each year is normalized as 1.0. The second regression employs a Tobit specification, the third, a two-stage least squares approach, for which only the second-stage regression is reported. Independent variables include the date of closing, with January 1, 1978, coded as 1978.0, and so forth, the size of the venture capital organization, measured as the ratio of capital raised in the ten calendar years prior to the year in which the fund closed to the total amount raised by venture capital organizations in that time, and the percentage of profits received by the venture organization. Absolute t-statistics in brackets.

	Dependent variable: Dollar volume of IPOs relative to capital raised		
	OLS analysis	Tobit analysis	Two-stage least squares analysis
Date of closing	0.004	−0.05	−0.12
	[0.09]	[0.78]	[0.29]
Size of venture organization	11.79	23.77	0.01
	[1.07]	[1.70]	[0.11]
Venture capitalists' percentage of profits	0.004	0.001	17.92
	[0.15]	[0.04]	[0.76]
Constant	−6.92	91.27	−6.86
	[0.08]	[0.79]	[0.07]
Adjusted R^2	−0.008		
F-statistic	0.41		0.40
Log likelihood		−388.64	
χ^2-statistic		4.06	
Root MSE			1.454
p-value	0.744	0.255	0.757
Number of observations	234	234	234

Ex Ante Compensation and Ex Post Performance

Our two models also differ in their predicted relationship between ex ante sensitivity of compensation to performance and ex post performance. In other words, each model provides different predictions on whether performance-sensitive compensation negotiated at the time of the partnership agreement will be associated with higher returns. The learning model suggests that there will not necessarily be any relationship between pay sensitivity and performance. Reputational concerns lead young venture capitalists with little explicit incentive compensation to work hard and perform well. The signaling model, on the other hand, suggests a positive relationship between pay sensitivity and success. Higher ability venture capitalists signal their ability by taking more risk and then work harder. In this section we empirically examine this relationship. Consistent with the learning model, we do not find any evidence of a relationship between pay sensitivity and performance.

Several data constraints limit our analysis. First, we do not have access to the internal rate of return (IRR) information for the funds in our sample. While this information is compiled by several monitoring organizations, it is considered proprietary information. Second, our sample consists primarily of funds from the 1980s and 1990s. Few of these funds have yet been concluded. The ten-year contractual life for most venture funds is often extended by several years. Consequently, most of our funds have investments remaining in their portfolios. Because valuations of private firms are often very subjective, even if they were available, rates of return would be of limited value.

Thus, we employ an alternative measure of performance which is the ratio of the market value of the fund's stakes in firms that went public to the total amount raised by the fund. This measure is highly correlated with the fund's final IRR. As discussed in chapter 2, venture capitalists generate the bulk of their profits from firms that go public.

We identify potential venture-backed initial public offerings (IPOs) using three sources. The first is the listings of venture-backed IPOs published in Venture Economics' *Venture Capital Journal*. This is the same source used by Barry, et al. (1990), and Megginson and Weiss (1991). Venture Economics' listings, however, do not include approximately 15 percent of all venture-financed firms (see chapter 16). We consequently use listings of security distributions by venture funds. Venture capitalists typically divest their successful investments by distributing shares to their partners. We obtain lists of the distributions received by a major pension fund and three investment managers. Most of the successful investments by 135 venture funds can be identified from these lists. The final source is the private placement memoranda used to raise new venture funds. In these offering memoranda, venture organizations often list successful past investments. We examine over 200 memoranda in the files of Venture Economics. We then examine the firms' IPO prospectuses and note each venture capital fund holding an equity stake of at least 5 percent. We identify 835 IPOs between 1972 and 1992 where one or more venture capitalists held such an equity stake. We then determine which venture capital funds in our sample of 419 partnerships held an investment in one of the IPO companies.

Venture capitalists typically do not sell their holdings at the time of the IPO, but hold them for approximately one-and-a-half years thereafter (see chapter 13). We do not know the precise date at which they liquidated these investments in most cases. We consequently value the venture capitalists' stakes at the market price eighteen months after the IPO date, using the Securities Data Company Corporate New Issues and Center for Research in Security Prices databases.

These analyses, reported in table 4.6, employ all 234 funds begun before January 1987, which include those out of the sample of 419 with at least six years to take firms public. The dependent variable is the ratio of the dollar value of each fund's stake in IPOs, summing the amount in 1997 dollars, to the fund's total committed capital. Because older funds have had more time to harvest their portfolios, we normalize the ratio of the mean fund in each year to one. Independent variables include the date of the fund's closing, venture organization size, and the percent of profits accruing to the general partners. One concern in choosing the sample of firms to review is that different venture organizations may take companies public at different times. Chapter 12 shows that a new venture capital organization may take companies public earlier to impress potential investors in its second fund. Consequently, IPOs in the first years of a fund's life may not provide a clear indicator of ultimate performance. We address this concern in unreported regressions by examining only the subset of funds begun before January 1983. For these funds, we can observe all IPOs over the first ten years of the fund's life. Neither the magnitude nor the significance of the relationship between compensation and performance differs appreciably when this subset is used.

In the first regression, we use an OLS specification. Because the dependent variable is bounded by zero, this may produce biased coefficients. We thus employ a Tobit specification in the second regression. Finally, we employ a two-stage approach to control for factors that may explain the percentage of profits received by the venture capitalist. In each, the compensation measure has virtually no explanatory power. We explore several alternative approaches in unreported regressions. First, we use the measure of pay sensitivity defined above, then we add additional independent variables, such as venture organization age. In none of these regressions is there a significant relationship between compensation and performance. This result is consistent with the predictions of the learning model.

An interesting unanswered question is whether the variance of returns of high- and low-ability venture capitalists differs. The models presented constrain the variance of these two group's returns to be the same. It could be that experienced venture capitalists invest in less risky firms, or reduce these risks by engaging in active management of these firms. This question has not been empirically explored to date by financial economists, but is a topic that we are currently examining in a research project.

Conclusions

Because they have few alternatives, investors in limited partnerships must rely on incentive schemes to control managers. The small number of general partners, and the accuracy with which their success can be measured, ensure that compensation schemes can effectively motivate management actions. The terms of the compensation schemes are clearly defined in the initial partnership agreements and are rarely renegotiated.

Evidence from 419 U.S. venture partnerships formed between 1978 and 1992 is generally consistent with the view that reputation is an important motivation for young, unseasoned venture capitalists. Using two proxies for reputation—the age and size of the venture organization—we find that the compensation of established funds is significantly more sensitive to performance and more variable than that of other funds. Older and larger firms have lower base compensation as well. Performance and pay sensitivity do not appear to be related.

The results indicate that venture capital entrants may not have superior information about their investment abilities, and may be concerned about establishing a reputation. This interpretation seems plausible. The venture capital industry may require skills that were not used in venture capitalists' previous employment. As discussed in chapter 2, venture capitalists argue that it is difficult to predict success of new partners in advance. Meanwhile, investors are sophisticated institutions that closely track performance. It is reasonable to expect that neophyte venture capitalists do not know their own investment abilities any better than their investors do.

While we have only tested the learning model against the signaling model, other factors may help explain compensation patterns. A leading alternative is a human capital model. Leading venture capitalists may be able to extract higher pay than their less-seasoned counterparts because more investors want to invest in their next funds. This trend might lead to a similar pattern of older venture organizations, whose venture capitalists often have extensive investment experience, receiving higher compensation as a return on their superior human capital. It is difficult to build a human capital model, however, that has the higher pay occurring only in the variable compensation. If venture capitalists are risk averse, they should demand more insurance. Established venture capital firms should raise new funds with higher base and variable compensation, if the venture capitalists extract higher pay with both components, or with higher base and lower variable compensation, if the demand for insurance predominates. The above section demonstrates that older and larger venture capital organizations receive higher variable and lower base compensation. This pattern is not what a human capital model would suggest, but it is consistent with our learning model.

These empirical patterns raise several unanswered questions. One unresolved issue is why there is so much uniformity in the most visible aspect of compensation, the distribution of carried interest. Clustering of the visible portion of compensation is very common. For instance, many lawyers work for a 33 percent contingent fee and most real estate brokers in an area charge the same sales commission. An interesting theoretical model would attempt to explain this lack of variation within professions and the factors that lead to these focal equilibria. A second puzzle is how compensation arrangements in limited partnerships interact with the many restrictions in these arrangements. As chapter 3 discusses, there is considerably more variability in the use of covenants and restrictions in venture capital limited partnership agreements. These variations in covenants might be thought of as prices as well. Why the price of restrictions is more variable than explicit compensation terms is a fertile area for future research.

Appendix A: Derivation of the Learning Model

We assume that there is symmetric uncertainty about the ability of the venture capitalist, η. This can represent either the venture capitalist's skill in selecting portfolio companies (either through screening or through proactively identifying transactions), or an ability to add value after the investment. Venture capitalists and investors believe that η is distributed normally, with mean m_0 and variance σ_0^2. Neither side has private information about the venture capitalist's quality in advance of the project.

Venture capitalists raise two partnerships in two consecutive periods. The outcome of investments in the first fund and any investment returns are realized prior to the second fund being raised. No projects shift from the first fund to the second. The fund return in period t, π_t, is a function of ability, the venture capitalist's effort (e_t), and noise (ε_t):

$$\pi_t = \eta + e_t + \varepsilon_t. \tag{A1}$$

We use the simple additive production function to simplify the derivation of the optimal contract. We have also derived results for a multiplicative production function (i.e., ηe). Using this alternative production function, the feature of the learning model that distinguishes it from the signaling model presented below remains the same: early funds have lower pay-for-performance sensitivity. The multiplicative production function, however, leads to second-period compensation schemes in which high-ability venture capitalists have lower pay-for-performance sensitivity than the others. In reality, certain activities of the venture capitalist appear to be additive, such as providing contacts and advice, while others, like reputational spillovers, seem to be multiplicative.

In equation (A1), noise (ε_t) is distributed independently and identically normal with mean 0 and variance σ_ε^2. The number of projects in a venture fund is typically small enough that residual uncertainty about returns exists. At the time a venture capitalist raises the next fund, considerable uncertainty about abilities is likely to remain. While venture capitalists and investors have the same beliefs about ability before the funds are formed, investors cannot observe the effort level chosen in either fund. Effort choice is private information.

The venture capitalist's compensation, w_t, is a linear function of fund returns. Holmstrom and Milgrom (1987) show that when effort choice and output are continuous, but monitoring by the principal is periodic, linear sharing rules are optimal. An added motivation for using a linear scheme in the model is the prevalence of such agreements in venture partnership agreements. The venture capitalist receives some fixed payment, f_t, and variable compensation that represents a share, v_t, of the return on the fund:

$$w_t(\pi_t) = f_t + v_t \pi_t. \tag{A2}$$

$C(e_t)$ is the direct disutility, in monetary terms, of effort. Both the venture capitalist and the investor know $C(e_t)$. $C(e_t)$ is convex, and $C'(0) = 0$, $C'(\infty) = \infty$, and $C''' \geq 0$. $C''' \geq 0$ ensures uniqueness of the equilibrium contract. The investor is risk neutral, but the venture capitalist is risk averse, with a coefficient of risk aversion, r, and a constant per-period discount rate, δ. The venture capitalist's utility function is given by equation (A3):

$$U(w_1, w_2; e_1, e_2) = -\exp\left(-r\left[\sum_{t=1}^{2} \delta^{t-1}[w_t - C(e_t)]\right]\right). \tag{A3}$$

As in Gibbons and Murphy (1992), this utility function is not additively separable. The utility function displays constant absolute risk aversion and makes the derivation of two-period incentive schemes easier. Because investors in venture funds are primarily large institutions, such as pension funds and insurance companies, investor risk neutrality is reasonable. Venture capitalist risk aversion may result from wealth constraints or lack of investment portfolio diversification (for survey evidence, see Tyebjee and Bruno 1984).

Compensation contracts are written for each fund, conditional on the information available from returns, if any exist. The terms of the compensation contract are set out before effort is chosen or investments are made. Investors in both funds can, but need not be, the same investors as in the first fund. Investors in the second fund, however, have verifiable information about the performance of the first fund. We assume that one investor and one venture capitalist negotiate over the terms of the compensation and that a Nash (1950) bargaining solution is relevant, that is, the compensation package evenly splits the expected gains from investment:

$$f_1(v_1) + v_1 E(\pi_1|\hat{e}_1) - C(\hat{e}_1) = \tfrac{1}{2}[E(\pi_1|\hat{e}_1) - C(\hat{e}_1)]; \tag{A4}$$

$$f_2(v_2) + v_2 E(\pi_2|\pi_1, \hat{e}_1, \hat{e}_2) - C(\hat{e}_2) = \tfrac{1}{2}[E(\pi_2|\pi_1, \hat{e}_1, \hat{e}_2) - C(\hat{e}_2)] \tag{A5}$$

A Nash bargaining solution, which assumes equal bargaining power, seems appropriate for venture capital settings where only a small number of potential players are involved in the negotiations. The number of investors and venture capitalists is not large. The model's theoretical predictions are robust to other divisions of the surplus.

The venture capitalist maximizes expected utility in both funds:

$$\max - E[\exp(-r[f_1 + v_1(\eta + e_1 + \varepsilon_1) - C(e_1)]$$
$$- r\delta[f_2 + v_2(\eta + e_2 + \varepsilon_2) - C(e_2)])]. \qquad (A6)$$

The optimal schedule of incentives is derived by starting in the second period. Conditional on first fund returns of π_1, venture capitalists choose effort to maximize:

$$\max - E[\exp(-r[f_2 + v_2(\eta + e_2 + \varepsilon_2) - C(e_2)])|\pi_1] \qquad (A7)$$

If the investor observes a return of π_1 and believes that the venture capitalist exerted $\hat{e}_1$ in the first fund, the investor's posterior estimate of the venture capitalist's ability will be:

$$m_1(\pi_1, \hat{e}_1) = \frac{\sigma_\varepsilon^2 m_0 + \sigma_0^2(\pi_1 - \hat{e}_1)}{\sigma_\varepsilon^2 + \sigma_0^2}. \qquad (A8)$$

The intuition behind equation (A8) is that the higher first-period returns are, the larger the revision in beliefs about ability will be. The higher the variance of noise relative to the variance in abilities is, the smaller the revision in beliefs will be. If equation (A7) is maximized with respect to e_2, we get the first order condition for the optimal second-period effort:

$$C'(e_2) = v_2 \qquad (A9)$$

Equation (A9) says that venture capitalists work until their marginal share of the expected increase in return equals their marginal effort cost. We substitute equation (A5) into equation (A7), and take the expectation, to get:

$$\max - \exp\left[-\frac{r}{2}\left[m_1(r_1, \hat{e}) + e_2(v_2) - C(e_2(v_2)) - \frac{r}{2}v_2^2(\sigma_\varepsilon^2 + \sigma_1^2)\right]\right]. \qquad (A10)$$

Note that $E\{\exp(-kx)\} = \exp(-k\mu + \frac{1}{2}k^2\sigma^2)$. Maximizing equation (A10) gives the first-order condition for v_2^*. Equation (A11) gives the expression derived from that solution:

$$v_2 = \frac{1}{1 + 2r(\sigma_\varepsilon^2 + \sigma_1^2)C''(e_2^*(v_2))} \qquad (A11)$$

To get a value for v_1, equations (A5) and (A4) are substituted into equation (A6), to yield:

$$\max - E\left[\exp\left(-r\left[\frac{1}{2}[(1-2v_1)(m_0+\hat{e}_1(v_1))+C(\hat{e}_1(v_1))]\right.\right.\right.$$

$$+ v_1[\eta+e_1(v_1)+\varepsilon_1]-C(e_1^*(v_1))\bigg]$$

$$- r\delta\left[\frac{1}{2}\left[(1-2v_2)\left[\frac{\sigma_\varepsilon^2 m_0+\sigma_0^2(y_1-\hat{e}(v_1))}{\sigma_\varepsilon^2+\sigma_0^2}+\hat{e}_2(v_2)\right]+C(\hat{e}_2(v_2))\right]\right.$$

$$\left.\left.\left.+v_2[\eta+e_2(v_2)+\varepsilon_2]-C(e_2(v_2))\right]\right)\right]. \tag{A12}$$

Taking the expectation of equation (A12) yields:

$$\max - \exp\left\{-r\left[\frac{1}{2}((m_0+\hat{e}_1(v_1)-C(\hat{e}_1(v_1))\right]\right.$$

$$-\frac{1}{2}r\delta[m_0+e_2(v_2)-C(e_2(v_2))]$$

$$+\frac{1}{2}r^2v_1^2[\sigma_\varepsilon^2+\sigma_0^2]+\frac{1}{8}\frac{r^2\delta^2(1-2v_2)^2(\sigma_0^2)^2(\sigma_\varepsilon^2+\sigma_0^2)}{(\sigma_\varepsilon^2+\sigma_0^2)^2}$$

$$+\frac{1}{2}r^2\delta^2v_2^2(\sigma_\varepsilon^2+\sigma_0^2)+\frac{1}{2}\frac{r^2\delta v_1(1-2v_2)(\sigma_0^2)(\sigma_\varepsilon^2+\sigma_0^2)}{\sigma_\varepsilon^2+\sigma_0^2}$$

$$+\frac{1}{2}\frac{r^2\delta^2v_2(1-2v_2)\sigma_0^2}{\sigma_\varepsilon^2+\sigma_0^2}+r^2\delta v_1v_2\sigma_0^2\bigg\}. \tag{A13}$$

The v_1 that satisfies the first-order condition for equation (A13) will be the optimal variable compensation sensitivity. The first-order condition is:

$$-\frac{1}{2}+\frac{1}{2}C'(e_1^*(v_1))+rv_1(\sigma_\varepsilon^2+\sigma_0^2)C''(e_1^*(v_1))$$

$$+\frac{1}{2}r\delta(1-2v_2)\sigma_0^2C''(e_1^*(v_1))=0. \tag{A14}$$

From equation (A12), we know that the venture capitalist's optimal effort level in period 1, e_1, must be given by:

$$C'(e_1^*(v_1))=v_1+\delta(1-2v_2)\frac{\sigma_0^2}{\sigma_\varepsilon^2+\sigma_0^2}. \tag{A15}$$

We substitute equation (A15) into equation (A14) and solve for the optimal variable compensation in period 1:

$$v_1 = \frac{1}{1 + 2r(\sigma_\varepsilon^2 + \sigma_0^2)C''[e_1^*(v_1)])}$$

$$- \delta(1 - 2v_2^*) \frac{\sigma_0^2}{\sigma_\varepsilon^2 + \sigma_0^2} - \frac{2r\delta v_2^* \sigma_0^2 C''[e_1^*(v_1)]}{1 + 2r(\sigma_\varepsilon^2 + \sigma_0^2)C''[e_1^*(v_1)]}. \tag{A16}$$

The level of fixed fees is determined by substituting equations (A11) and (A16) into equations (A5) and (A4), respectively, taking expectations, and solving, to yield f_1 and f_2:

$$f_1(v_1^*) = \frac{1}{2}[(1 - 2v_1^*)[m_0 + e_1^*(v_1^*)] + C(e_1^*(v_1^*))]. \tag{A17}$$

$$f_2(v_2^*|\pi_1) = \frac{1}{2}\left[(1 - 2v_2^*)\left[\frac{\sigma_\varepsilon^2 m_0 + \sigma_0^2(\pi_1 - e_1^*(v_2^*))}{\sigma_\varepsilon^2 + \sigma_0^2} + e_2^*(v_2^*)\right] + C(e_2^*(v_2^*))\right]; \tag{A18}$$

Appendix B: Derivation of the Signaling Model

We continue to employ the basic framework and notation of appendix A, except that we assume venture capitalists initially know their ability type, η^H, but investors do not. For ease of exposition, we assume that venture capitalists can have two types, high-ability (H) or low-ability (L), with $\eta^H > \eta^L$. Effort after the first unit is equally productive for both types because we have assumed an additive return function. To determine the optimal contract that will be offered by high-ability venture capitalists, we first need to assume that we are constructing a separating equilibrium. Not only will other separating equilibria exist, but pooling equilibria are also likely to exist for various parameter values. Because we are interested in the case in which high-ability types are able to distinguish themselves, we will only focus on the Riley (1979) separating equilibrium.

We again assume that venture capitalists and investors split the expected surplus from investments:

$$f_2^H + v_2^H[\eta^H + \hat{e}(v_2^H)] - C(\hat{e}(v_2^H)) = \tfrac{1}{2}[E(\eta^H + \hat{e}(v_2^H) - C(\hat{e}(v_2^H)))]; \tag{B1}$$

$$f_2^1 + v_2^L[\eta^L + \hat{e}(v_2^L)] - C(\hat{e}(v_2^L)) = \tfrac{1}{2}[E(\eta^L + \hat{e}(v_2^L) - C(\hat{e}(v_2^L)))]. \tag{B2}$$

The single-period maximization problem then becomes a problem of maximizing expected utility in the second period, assuming full information.

Because we are constructing separating equilibria, information about abilities is totally revealed in the first period. Contracts signed in the second period reflect this information. For high-ability venture capitalists, we solve:

$$\max - E[\exp(-r[f_2^H + v_2^H(\eta^H + e_2 + \varepsilon_2) - C(e_2)])]. \tag{B3}$$

The second fund's variable compensation for both high- and low-ability venture capitalists is:

$$v_2^H = v_2^L = \frac{1}{1 + 2r\sigma_\varepsilon^2 C''[e_2^*(v_2)]} = v_2. \tag{B4}$$

The result in equation (B4) is not surprising, because we assume that marginal productivity and effort costs of high- and low-ability venture capitalists are the same. Because types are fully revealed in the first period, second-period compensation differs only in the base component of compensation. This is true because the utility function we choose does not display any wealth effects. The level of expected income does not affect risk aversion. Fixed compensation for the two types is given by equations (B5) and (B6):

$$f_2^H(v_2^*) = \tfrac{1}{2}[(1 - 2v_2^*)[\eta^H + e_2^*(v_2^*)] + C(e_2^*(v_2^*))]; \tag{B5}$$

$$f_2^L(v_2^*) = \tfrac{1}{2}[(1 - 2v_2^*)[\eta^L + e_2^*(v_2^*)] + C(e_2^*(v_2^*))]. \tag{B6}$$

The difference in second-period fixed compensation is directly proportional to the difference between high- and low-ability venture capitalists:

$$f_2^H - f_2^L = \tfrac{1}{2}(1 - 2v_2^*)[\eta^H - \eta^L]. \tag{B7}$$

The optimization program for the high-ability venture capitalist in period one is given by equation (B8):

$$\max - E[\exp\{-r[\tfrac{1}{2}[(1 - 2v_1^H)[\eta^H + e_1(v_1^H) + C(e_1(v_1^H))]$$

$$+ v_1^H[\eta^H + e_1(v_1^H) + \varepsilon_1] - C(e_1(v_1^H))]\}]$$

$$\text{s.t.} - E[\exp\{-r[\tfrac{1}{2}[(1 - 2v_1^L)[\eta^L + e_1^*(v_1^L) + C(e_1^*(v_1^L))]$$

$$+ v_1^L[\eta^L + e_1^*(v_1^L) + \varepsilon_1] - C(e_1^*(v_1^L))$$

$$+ \delta\{(1 - 2v_2^L)[\eta^L + e_2^*(v_2^L) + C(e_2^*(v_2^L))]$$

$$+ v_2^L[\eta^L + e_2^*(v_2^L) + \varepsilon_2] - C(e_2^*(v_2^L))\}]\}]$$

$$= -E[\exp\{-r[\tfrac{1}{2}[(1 - 2v_1^H)[\eta^H + e_1^*(v_1^H) + C(e_1^*(v_1^H))]$$

$$+ v_1^H[\eta^L + e_1^*(v_1^H) + \varepsilon_1] - C(e_1^*(v_1^H))]$$

$$+ \delta\{(1 - 2v_2^H)[\eta^H + e_2^*(v_2^H) + C(e_2^*(v_2^H))]$$

$$+ v_2^H[\eta^L + e_2^*(v_2^H) + \varepsilon_2] - C(e_2^*(v_2^H))\}]\}]. \tag{B8}$$

The interpretation of equation (B8) is straightforward. High-ability venture capitalists maximize their utility in the first period, subject to the constraint that low-ability venture capitalists are indifferent between offering their optimal contract which reveals their type in period one and offering the contract that high types offer. The choice of contract for high-ability venture capitalists in the first period will not influence the form of their second-period contract, so their program for the first period is to maximize their first-period utility, assuming that low-ability venture capitalists will not find it in their interest to mimic the high type's offer. The high-ability venture capitalist is concerned only about first-period utility because we are ruling out two-period contracts.

Taking the expectation of equation (B8), and remembering from equation (B4) that $v_2^H = v_2^L = v_2$, yields the following:

$$\max - \exp\left\{ -r\left[\frac{1}{2}[\eta^H + e_1(v_1^H) - C(e_1)] - \frac{r}{2}(v_1^H)^2\sigma_\varepsilon^2 \right] \right\}$$

$$\text{s.t.} - \exp\left\{ -r\left[\frac{1}{2}[\eta^L + e_1^*(v_1^L) - C(e_1^*)] - \frac{r}{2}(v_1^L)^2\sigma_\varepsilon^2 \right. \right.$$

$$+ \delta\left\{ \frac{1}{2}[\eta^L + e_1^*(v_2) - C(e_2^*)] - \frac{r}{2}(v_2)^2\sigma_\varepsilon^2 \right\}\bigg]\bigg\}$$

$$= -\exp\left\{ -r\left[\frac{1}{2}[(1 - 2v_1^H)\eta^H + 2v_1^H\eta^L + e_1^*(v_1^H) - C(e_2(v_2))] \right. \right.$$

$$- \frac{r}{2}(v_1^H)^2\sigma_\varepsilon^2 + \delta\left\{ \frac{1}{2}[(1 - 2v_2)\eta^H + 2v_2\eta^L \right.$$

$$+ e_2^*(v_2^H) - C(e_2^*(v_2))] - \frac{r}{2}(v_2)^2\sigma_\varepsilon^2 \right\}\bigg]\bigg\}. \tag{B9}$$

Equation (B9) can be transformed into an equivalent optimization problem by removing the exponentials, to give the program in equation (B10):

$$\max \frac{1}{2}[\eta^H + e_1(v_1^H) - C(e_1)] - \frac{r}{2}(v_1^H)^2\sigma_\varepsilon^2$$

$$\text{s.t.} \frac{1}{2}[\eta^L + e_1^*(v_1^L) - C(e_1^*(v_1^L))] - \frac{r}{2}(v_1^L)^2\sigma_\varepsilon^2$$

$$+ \delta\left\{\frac{1}{2}[\eta^L + e_1^*(v_2) - C(e_2^*(v_2))] - \frac{r}{2}(v_2)^2\sigma_\varepsilon^2\right\}$$

$$= \frac{1}{2}\{(1 - 2v_1^H)\eta^H + 2v_1^H\eta^L + e_1^*(v_1^H) - C(e_2(v_2))\} - \frac{r}{2}(v_1^H)^2\sigma_\varepsilon^2$$

$$+ \delta\left\{\frac{1}{2}[(1 - 2v_2)\eta^H + 2v_2\eta^L + e_2^*(v_2^H) - C(e_2^*(v_2))] - \frac{r}{2}(v_2)^2\sigma_\varepsilon^2\right\}.$$

$$(B10)$$

Equation (B10) can be solved by forming the Lagrangian equation (B11), and taking the first-order conditions for v_1^H:

$$L = [\eta^H + e_1^*(v_1^H) - C(e_1^*)] - r(v_1^H)^2\sigma_\varepsilon^2$$

$$+ -\lambda\{(1 - 2v_1^H)\eta^H + 2v_1^H\eta^L + e_1^*(v_1^H) - C(e_2(v_2)) - r(v_1^H)^2\sigma_\varepsilon^2$$

$$+ \delta\{[(1 - 2v_2)\eta^H + 2v_2\eta^L + e_2^*(v_2) - C(e_2^*(v_1^H))] - r(v_2)^2\sigma_\varepsilon^2\}$$

$$- \{[\eta^L + e_1^*(v_1^L) - C(e_1^*(v_1^L))] - r(v_1^L)^2\sigma_\varepsilon^2$$

$$+ \delta[\eta^L + e_1^*(v_2) - C(e_2^*(v_2)) - r(v_2)^2\sigma_\varepsilon^2 r]\}\}$$

$$(B11)$$

The solution to these first-order conditions is shown in equations (B12) and (B13):

$$v_1^H = \frac{1 + 2\left(\dfrac{\lambda}{1 - \lambda}\right)(\eta^H - \eta^L)C''[e_1(v_1^H)]}{1 + 2r\sigma_\varepsilon^2 C''[e_1^*(v_1^H)]};$$

$$(B12)$$

$$\lambda = \frac{e_1' - C'(e_1)e_1' - 2rv_1^H\sigma_\varepsilon^2}{e_1' - C'(e_1)e_1' - 2rv_1^H\sigma_\varepsilon^2 + 2(\eta^L - \eta^H)}.$$

$$(B13)$$

Because the optimal v_1^H is above the unconstrained optimal v, both the numerator and the denominator in equation (B13) are less than 0. The absolute value of the denominator is greater than the absolute value of the numerator, and the Lagrangian multiplier is therefore between 0 and 1:

$$0 < \lambda < 1. \qquad\qquad (B14)$$

Appendix C: Assumptions Used in the Calculation of Variable and Base Compensation

The fixed fee in venture capital fund contracts, also known as the management fee, changes in many funds over time. For instance, the management fees will often be reduced in later years, reflecting the expectation that the partnership's costs will decline in the last years of a venture capital fund's life. The fees may contain provisions for inflation adjustments. The base used to calculate the fee also often varies. Although most agreements compute the annual fee as a percentage of invested capital, in some cases the partnership's net asset value is used as the base. Funds will also often limit the maximum or the minimum fee, or both. A number of funds do not charge a stated fee, but rather negotiate fees based on actual expenses. In most cases the contract will indicate a range in which fees are expected to fall; in other cases a budget is negotiated annually. Finally, a number of firms charge fees not only on the funds raised by the partnership but also on the indebtedness of the companies in which they invest. This fee structure was commonplace in the 1960s, when Small Business Investment Companies (SBICs), many of which were commercial bank affiliates, made equity investments in firms and arranged for their credit lines.

To address the problems that arise from the disparities in venture capital partnership agreements, we make the following assumptions:

• We do not include in the analysis cases where a budget is negotiated each year, or where fees are charged on the indebtedness of companies in which they invest. These cases represent only 6 percent of the observations.

• We assume that all funds last for eleven years. Most funds have a contractual life of ten years (a few have shorter lives). Most have provisions, however, for one or two extensions, each of which can extend the life of the contract for one or two more years, which venture capitalists frequently exercise. We repeat the analysis assuming that the partnerships have a thirteen-year life. Because most funds have fees in their final years that are considerably below the fees charged in earlier years, and the assets remaining in the funds at this point are typically quite small, we find that this change makes little difference.

• In some cases, the fixed fees stipulated in the private placement memoranda are conditional on the ultimate amount raised. For example, fees could be set at 2.5 percent of committed capital up to $20 million, and

2 percent of all committed capital above that amount. In these cases, we employ the ultimate amount raised by the partnership to compute the annual fee. If we do not know the ultimate amount raised, we use the midpoint between the minimum and maximum amount being sought. We know the actual amount raised for 94 percent of the funds.

• We assume that the venture fund's assets, before any deductions for fees, grow at one of three rates: 5, 20, or 35 percent. These values roughly correspond to the average returns and a one standard deviation range for funds active over the sample period. For instance, Venture Economics (1998) estimates that funds established prior to 1982 that were still active in 1989 had a mean return of 17.6 percent, with a standard deviation of 14.2 percent.

• We assume that the venture capitalist draws down funds from the limited partners in even amounts at the beginning of the year. Venture partnership agreements typically call for funds to be disbursed in a series of capital infusions. This structure reflects the staged nature of the venture investment process, wherein the bulk of the funds are not immediately needed. For example, if the contract calls for 40 percent of the funds to be disbursed at the close of the investment, and 30 percent to be disbursed at the first and second anniversaries, we treat these as three equal install-ments. If the contract only indicates a minimum and maximum time until the last investment will be required, we use the anniversary nearest the midpoint of this range. If no schedule of capital infusions is provided, we assume that the funds are drawn down in three equal amounts, at the closing and first and second anniversaries. For those funds in our sample with complete data, the mean time from the closing to the last drawdown is 2.4 years; the median, 2.0 years.

• We assume that distributions follow an identical pattern for all funds included in the sample. A major institutional investor has provided us with monthly valuation and distribution data through December 1992 for 140 domestic and foreign venture funds. For the 116 funds that we can confirm as independent U.S.-based venture partnerships, we compute the ratio of the distributions in each year of the fund's life to its valuation on the previous anniversary. We assume that each fund follows this average pattern in undertaking its distributions. In other words, since the average fund distributes 10 percent of the value of its assets between its fourth and fifth anniversary, each fund in our calculations does the same. If all distributions go to the limited partners prior to the return of committed capital, we replicate this pattern in our calculations, and if the fund specifies a hurdle based on net asset value, we employ such a test. We assume that the portfolios are completely liquidated on their eleventh anniversary. We explore the robustness of the results to other assumptions by repeating the calculations using two other rules. We alternatively assume that distributions, as a percentage of asset value, are twice as high as in the institutional investor's sample, and that no fund undertakes any distributions until the end of the eleventh year. The results in reported tables are robust to these assumptions.

• For those funds that compute fees on the basis of capital under management, less the cost basis of distributions and write-offs, we assume that the cost basis of distributions follows a pattern proportional to the distributions, such that if 10 percent of all distributions over the life of the partnership occur in one year, then 10 percent of the reduction in the cost basis occurs in that year. When we vary the pattern of distributions as described above, we vary the change in the cost basis accordingly.

• We assume that each year's fixed fees are paid in advance on each anniversary. These payments are almost always paid in advance on a quarterly basis, but this assumption simplifies the calculations considerably.

• If the fees are reduced after the fund is fully invested, we assume that this reduction occurs two years after the date of the last capital drawdown. If the fees are reduced after the fund is 75 percent invested, we assume that this reduction occurs one year after the date of the last capital infusion. We also assume that these events occur four and two years, respectively, after the last capital drawdown, and find that the changes have little impact.

• If the fees are reduced after the organization raises a new fund, we assume that this event occurs on the fund's sixth anniversary. We use this anniversary year because of historical patterns. Examining the venture funds raised before 1985, we find that the median organization raised its next fund four years and one month after the last closing. Because fundraising has become more difficult in recent years, we use a slightly longer interval for our calculations. We also assume that the next fund is raised four years after this fund's closing. We find that the change has little impact. If fees are indexed for inflation, we assume that they rise at a 4 percent annual rate.

• In our calculations, we do not consider whether the fixed fee covers the legal, accounting, brokerage, and consulting fees, or whether these additional costs are borne in whole or in part by the limited partners. These charges are generally modest. An analysis of recent annual reports in the files of Harvard Management Company, which include a total of 141 reporting years covering 44 funds, suggests that these fees average less than 0.1 percent of net asset value. Our reluctance to include these fees stems from the disparate information contained in the partnership agreements and private placement memoranda. Although the treatment of these fees is always addressed in the partnership agreements, such relatively minor considerations are often ignored in placement memoranda. Rather than introduce biases due to incomplete reporting, we ignore this factor entirely. This choice will lead to a slight understating of fees. Similarly, we ignore any reductions in fees due to the payment of board membership fees by portfolio companies to the general partners. This omission will lead to a slight overstating of fees.

• We alternately discount the venture capitalists' compensation at 10, 15, or 20 percent. We also discount fees that can be expected to be paid with relative certainty, including those based on committed capital, committed capital less the cost basis of distributions, or the minimum of committed capital and net asset value, at 10 percent, while applying a 20 percent discount rate to the more uncertain fees, based on net asset value or the maximum of asset value and capital under management. Distributions of capital gains are discounted at 20 percent.

5 Does the Venture Capital Structure Matter?

As noted in chapter 2, the structure of private equity organizations—in particular, the reliance on limited partnerships of finite life with substantial profit sharing—has been identified as critical to their success. These claims, however, have received little empirical scrutiny.

Chapter 5 addresses this omission by comparing investments made by traditional venture capital organizations with those of venture funds sponsored by corporations. These corporate funds have similar missions and are staffed by individuals with backgrounds resembling those in independent organizations. But the organizational and incentive structures in corporate funds are very different: most are structured as corporate subsidiaries and have much lower incentive-based compensation. In this respect, corporate funds differ dramatically from both independent venture organizations and funds associated with commercial and investment banks. Many bank-affiliated funds retain the autonomous partnership structure employed by independent venture organizations, albeit with a lower share of the profits accruing to the venture investors.

This provides a natural test case for examining the impact of organizational structure on investment performance. The arguments about the importance of the structure of independent, private-equity organizations suggest that corporate programs would prove less successful. Either their process of selecting or overseeing investments would be distorted or else the programs would prove unstable. It may be, however, that corporate programs enjoy benefits that offset some of these costs. A lengthy literature on complementarities in the strategy literature argues that corporations can benefit from closely related activities (for a review and formalization, see Athey and Stern 1997). Corporations may be able to select better ventures using the information from their related lines-of-business or may add greater value to the firms once the investments are made.

Before turning to the empirical analysis, we consider the experience of Xerox Technology Ventures, which illustrates both of these points. This corporate venture fund compiled excellent financial returns between 1988 and 1996 by aggressively exploiting the technology and knowledge of the corporate parent. Nonetheless, the corporate parent dissolved the fund before the ending date originally intended. The case highlights that—contrary to both popular wisdom and academic arguments—corporate venture programs can still be successful without the traditional partnership structure. The case also suggests, however, some of the difficulties that these efforts encounter, and the apparent importance of having a strong linkage between the fund's investment focus and the corporate parent's strategic focus.

We then consider the more general evidence. Using the VentureOne database of private equity financings, we examine over thirty thousand investments into entrepreneurial firms by venture capital programs. The evidence appears to underscore the importance the complementarities hypothesis outlined above. Portfolio companies that receive funds from corporate investors with a well-defined strategic focus enjoy greater success. Investments are made at a premium, but this may reflect the indirect benefits that the corporation receives. Corporate programs with a well-defined strategic focus also appear to be as stable as traditional independent venture organizations. Among the corporate funds without a strong strategic focus, we see significantly less success in the investments and less stability than among the focused funds.

We end with a more general discussion of the implications of these results for our understanding of the venture capital industry. It may be that—contrary to the emphasis in the finance literature—the structure of corporate venture funds is not a critical barrier to their success. Rather, the presence of a strong strategic focus may be critical for achieving a sustainable program. Alternatively, the corporate programs without a strong strategic focus may also have particularly weak incentive schemes and other problematic structural characteristics.

The organization of this chapter is as follows. In the next section, we briefly summarize the history of corporate venture capital funds. The third section discusses the case of Xerox Technology Ventures, and the fourth section describes the data set. The empirical analysis is presented in the fifth section and the sixth section concludes the chapter.

The History of Corporate Venture Capital Investment[1]

The first corporate venture funds began in the mid-1960s, about two decades after the first formal venture capital funds. The corporate efforts were spurred by the successes of the first organized venture capital funds, which backed such firms as Digital Equipment, Memorex, Raychem, and Scientific Data Systems. Excited by this success, large companies began establishing divisions that emulated venture capitalists. During the late 1960s and early 1970s, more than 25 percent of the Fortune 500 firms attempted corporate venture programs.

These efforts generally took two forms—external and internal. At one end of the spectrum, large corporations financed new firms alongside other venture capitalists. In many cases, the corporations simply provided funds for a venture capitalist to invest. Other firms invested directly in start-ups, giving them a greater ability to tailor their portfolios to their particular needs. At the other extreme, large corporations attempted to tap the entrepreneurial spirit within their organizations. These programs sought to allow entrepreneurs to focus their attention on developing their innovations, while relying on the corporate parents for financial, legal, and marketing support.

In 1973, the market for new public offerings—the primary avenue through which venture capitalists exit successful investments—abruptly declined. Independent venture partnerships began experiencing significantly less attractive returns and encountered severe difficulties in raising new funds. At the same time, corporations began scaling back their own initiatives. The typical corporate venture program begun in the late 1960s was dissolved after only four years.

As discussed in chapter 1, funds flowing into the venture capital industry and the number of active venture organizations increased dramatically during the late 1970s and early 1980s. Corporations were also once again attracted to the promise of venture investing in response. These efforts peaked in 1986, when corporate funds managed $2 billion, or nearly 12 percent of the total pool of venture capital.

After the stock market crash of 1987, however, the market for new public offerings again went into a sharp decline. Returns of and fundraising by independent partnerships declined sharply. Corporations scaled

---

1. This history is based in part on Fast (1978), Gee (1994), and Venture Economics (1986), among other sources.

back their commitment to venture investing even more dramatically. By 1992, the number of corporate venture programs had fallen by one-third and their capital under management represented only 5 percent of the venture pool.

Interest in corporate venture capital climbed once again in the mid-1990s, both in the United States and abroad. Once again, much of this interest was stimulated by the recent success of the independent venture sector: the rapid growth of funds and their attractive returns. These corporate funds have invested directly in a variety of internal and external ventures as well as in funds organized by independent venture capitalists. (Venture Economics estimates that corporate investors accounted for 30 percent of the commitments to new funds in 1997, up from an average of 5 percent in the 1990–1992 period.)

This brief discussion makes clear that corporate involvement in venture capital has mirrored (perhaps even in an exaggerated manner) the cyclical nature of the entire venture capital industry over the past three decades. At the same time, numerous discussions suggest that certain basic noncyclical issues also have a significant impact on corporate venture capital activity.

In particular, it appears that the frequent disillusion of earlier corporate venture programs was due to three structural failings. First, these programs suffered from a lack of well-defined missions (Fast 1978; Siegel, Siegel, and MacMillan 1988). Typically, they sought to accomplish a wide array of not necessarily compatible objectives, from providing a window on emerging technologies to generating attractive financial returns. The confusion over program objectives often led to dissatisfaction with the outcomes. For instance, when outside venture capitalists were hired to run a corporate fund under a contract that linked compensation to financial performance, management frequently became frustrated about their failure to invest in the technologies that most interested the firm.

A second cause of failure was insufficient corporate commitment to the venturing initiative (Hardymon, DiNino, and Salter 1983; Rind 1981; Sykes 1990). Even if top management embraced the concept, middle management often resisted. Research and development (R&D) personnel preferred that funds be devoted to internal programs; corporate lawyers disliked the novelty and complexity of these hybrid organizations. In many cases, new senior management teams terminated programs, seeing them as expendable "pet projects" of their predecessors. Even if they did not object to the idea of the program, managers were often concerned about its impact on the firm's accounting earnings. During periods of financial pressure, money-losing subsidiaries were frequently terminated in an effort to increase reported operating earnings.

A final cause of failure was inadequate compensation schemes (Block and Ornati 1987, Lawler and Drexel 1980). Corporations have frequently been reluctant to compensate their venture managers through profit-sharing ("carried interest") provisions, fearing that they might need to make huge payments if their investments were successful. Typically, successful risk taking was inadequately rewarded and failure excessively punished. As a result, corporations were frequently unable to attract top people (i.e., those who combined industry experience with connections to other venture capitalists) to run their venture funds. All too often, corporate venture managers adopted a conservative approach to investing. Nowhere was this behavior more clearly manifested than in the treatment of lagging ventures. As discussed in part II of this volume, independent venture capitalists often cease funding to failing firms because they want to devote their limited energy to firms with the greatest promise. Corporate venture capitalists have frequently been unwilling to write off unsuccessful ventures, lest they incur the reputational repercussions that a failure would entail.

The Case of Xerox Technology Ventures

These general observations can be illustrated through a case study. The Xerox Corporation originated as a photography-paper business called the Haloid Company.[2] The Haloid Company's entrance into what would later become its principal business came in 1947 when it and Battelle Memorial Institute, a research organization, agreed to produce a machine based on the recently developed process named xerography. Invented by patent lawyer Chester Carlson, xerography involved a process by which images were transferred from one piece of paper to another by means of static electricity. Rapid growth and a redirection of the company's emphasis toward xerography characterized the Haloid Company in the 1950s. In 1961, in recognition of the spectacular growth of sales engendered by the first plain paper copier, the firm was renamed the Xerox Corporation.

In response to IBM's entrance into the copier field in the late 1960s, Xerox experimented with computers and with designing an electronic office of the future. It formed Xerox Computer Services, acquired Scientific Data Systems, and opened its Palo Alto Research Center (PARC) in

---

2. The first sixteen paragraphs of this section are based on Hunt and Lerner (1995).

California. These efforts were only the beginning of the copier giant's effort to become a force in the computer industry. Throughout the 1970s, Xerox completed several acquisitions to further their project for an "architecture of information." Unfortunately, in assembling these non-copier companies and opening PARC, Xerox created a clash of cultures. Differences between its east coast operations and west coast computer people would severely affect the company.

The focus for much of this division was PARC. In the 1970s, PARC was remarkably successful in developing ingenious products that would fundamentally alter the nature of computing. The Ethernet, the graphical user interface (the basis of Apple Computer's and Microsoft's Windows software), the "mouse," and the laser printer were all originally developed at PARC. The culmination of much of PARC's innovation was its development of the Alto, a very early personal computer. The Alto's first prototype was completed in 1973, and later versions were placed into the White House, Congress, and various companies and universities. Nonetheless, the Alto project was terminated in 1980.

Inherent in the Alto's demise was Xerox's relationship with PARC. Xerox did not have a clear-cut business strategy for its research laboratory, and in turn many of PARC's technologies did not fit into Xerox's strategic objectives. For instance, the Alto's ability to adapt to large customer's computer systems was inconsistent with Xerox's strategy of producing work stations compatible only with its own equipment.

The establishment of Xerox Technology Venture (XTV) was driven by two events in 1988. First, several senior Xerox managers were involved in negotiating and approving a spin-off from Xerox, ParcPlace, which sought to commercialize an object-oriented programming language developed at PARC in the 1970s. The negotiation of these agreements proved to be protracted and painful, highlighting the difficulty that the company faced in dealing with these contingencies. More importantly, in 1988 a book documenting Xerox's failure to develop the personal computer, *Fumbling the Future*, appeared. Stung by the description in the book, Xerox Chairman David Kearns established the task force, with the mandate of preventing the repetition of such a failure to capitalize on Xerox innovations.

The task force reviewed Xerox's history with corporate venture programs. Xerox had invested since the early 1970s in venture-backed firms. For instance, it had joined a variety of venture capitalists in investing in Rolm, Apple, and a number of other firms. The investments, while successful financially, were made on an ad hoc basis. In the early 1980s, Xerox established two venture funds with an external focus. These did not prove particularly successful, largely due to disputes within the firm about appropriate investments. The task force, in member (and future XTV president) Robert Adams' words, rapidly "concluded that we needed a system to prevent technology from leaking out of the company" (Armstrong 1993). The committee focused on two options: (1) to begin aggressively litigating those who tried to leave with new technologies, and (2) to invest in people trying to leave Xerox. Due to variations in employee noncompetition law across states (and particularly the weak level of protection afforded by the California courts), it was unclear how effective a policy of aggressive litigation would be. Furthermore, such a policy might reduce Xerox's ability to recruit the best research personnel, who might not want to limit their future mobility.

Based on the task force's recommendation, chairman Kearns decided to pursue a corporate venture capital program. He agreed to commit $30 million to invest in promising technologies developed at Xerox. As he commented at the time, "XTV is a hedge against repeating missteps of the past" (Armstrong 1993). He briefly considered the possibility of asking an established venture capital firm to jointly run the program with Xerox, but he decided that the involvement of another party would introduce a formality that might hurt the fledgling venture.

Modeling XTV after venture organizations had several dimensions. The most obvious was the structure of the organization. While this was a corporate division, rather than an independent partnership like most venture organizations, the XTV partners crafted an agreement with Xerox that resembled typical agreements between limited and general partners in venture funds.

The spin-out process was clearly defined in the agreement to ensure that disputes did not arise later on and to minimize the disruption to the organization. The XTV officials insisted on a formal procedure to avoid the ambiguity that had plagued earlier corporate ventures. The agreement made clear that the XTV partners had the flexibility to respond rapidly to investment opportunities, as independent venture capitalists typically possess. They essentially had full autonomy when it came to monitoring, exiting, or liquidating companies. The partners were allowed to spend up to $2 million dollars at any one time without getting permission from the corporation. For larger expenditures, they were required to obtain permission from XTV's governing board, which consisted of Xerox's chief executive officer, chief financial officer, and chief patent counsel.

Similar to independent venture organizations, but unlike many corporate programs, the program also had a clear goal: to maximize return on investment. The XTV partners believed that the ambiguous goals of many of the 1970s corporate venture programs had been instrumental in their downfall. They hoped to achieve a return on investment that exceeded both the average returns of the venture capital industry and Xerox's corporate hurdle rate for evaluating new projects.

Not only was the level of compensation analogous to that of the 20 percent "carried interest" that independent venture capitalists received, and the degree of autonomy similar, but XTV operated under the same ten-year time frame employed in the typical partnership agreement. Under certain conditions, however, Xerox could dissolve the partnership after five years.

The analogy to independent venture organizations also extended to the companies in which XTV invested. These were structured as separate legal entities, with their own board and officers. XTV sought to recruit employees from other start-ups who were familiar with managing new enterprises. The typical CEO was hired from the outside, on the grounds that entrepreneurial skills, particularly in financial management, were unlikely to be found in a major corporation. XTV also made heavy use of temporary executives who were familiar with a variety of organizations.

The independence of management also extended to technological decision making in these companies. The traditional Xerox product—for instance, a copier—was designed so that it could be operated and serviced in almost any country in the world. This meant not only constraints on how the product was engineered but also the preparation of copious documentation in many languages. These XTV ventures, however, could produce products for "leading-edge" users, who emphasized technological performance over careful documentation.

Like independent venture capitalists, XTV intended to give up control of the companies in which they invested. Transferring shares to management and involving other venture capitalists in XTV companies would reduce Xerox's ownership of the firm. Over the long run, after several rounds of financing, Xerox's goal would be to hold from 20 to 50 percent equity stake. XTV sought to have under a 50 percent equity stake at the time a spin-out firm went public. In this way, it would not need to consolidate the firm in its balance sheet (i.e., it would not need to include the company's equity on its balance sheet, which would reduce Xerox's return on equity). The Xerox lawyers had originally only wanted employees to receive "phantom stock" (typically bonuses based on the growth in the new units' performance). Instead, XTV insisted that the employees receive options to buy real shares in the venture-backed companies, in line with traditional Silicon Valley practices. The partners believed that this approach would have a much greater psychological impact, as well as a cleaner capital structure to attract follow-on financings by outside investors.

Between 1988 and 1996, the organization invested in over one dozen companies. These covered a gamut of technologies, mostly involving electronic publishing, document processing, electronic imaging, workstation and computer peripherals, software and office automation. These not only successfully commercialized technology lying fallow in the organizations but also generated attractive financial returns.

One successful example of XTV's ability to catalyze the commercialization of technological discoveries was Documentum, which marketed an object-oriented document-management system. Xerox had undertaken a large number of projects in this area for over a decade prior to Documentum's founding but had not shipped a product. After deciding this was a promising area, XTV recruited Howard Shao and John Newton, both former engineering executives at Ingress Corporation (a relational database manufacturer) to lead up the technical effort.

Shao spent the first six months assessing the state of Xerox's knowledge in this area—including reviewing the several 300-plus page business plans prepared for earlier proposed (but never shipped) products—and assessing the market. He soon realized that while Xerox understood the nature of the technical problems, it had not grasped how to design a technologically appropriate solution. In particular, the Xerox business plans had proposed building document-management systems for mainframe computers, rather than for networked personal computers (which were rapidly replacing mainframes at many organizations). With the help of the XTV officials, Shao and Newton led an effort to rapidly convert Xerox's accumulated knowledge in this area into a marketable product. Xerox's substantial know-how—as well as XTV's aggressive funding of the firm during the Gulf War period, when the willingness of both independent venture capitalists and the public markets to fund new technology-based firms abruptly declined—gave Documentum an impressive lead over its rivals.

Documentum went public in February 1996 with a market capitalization of $351 million.[3] XTV was able to exit a number of other companies successfully, whether through an initial public offering, a merger with an outside firm, or a repurchase by Xerox (at a price determined through

---

3. The next two paragraphs are based on public security filings and press accounts.

arms-length bargaining). A conservative calculation (assuming that Xerox sold its stakes in firms that went public at the time of the initial public offering, rather than the substantially appreciated prices thereafter, and valuing investments that Xerox has not yet exited or written off at cost, less a 25 percent discount for illiquidity), indicates that the $30 million fund generated capital gains of $219 million. Given the 80–20 percent split established in the XTV agreement, the proceeds to Xerox should have been at least $175 million, those to the three XTV partners, at least $44 million.

Using the same assumptions, this suggests a net internal rate of return for Xerox (*i.e.*, after fees and incentive compensation) of at least 56 percent. This compares favorably to independent venture capital funds begun in 1989, which had a mean net return of 13.7 percent (an upper quartile fund begun in that year had a return of 20.4 percent) (Venture Economics 1998). These calculations of Xerox's internal rate of return (IRR) do not include any ancillary benefits generated by this program for the corporation. For instance, some observers argued that high expected value projects that might have otherwise not been funded through traditional channels due to their high risk were increasingly funded during this period, apparently out of the fear that they would otherwise be funded by XTV and prove successful.

Despite these attractive returns, Xerox decided to terminate XTV in 1996, well before the completion of its originally intended ten-year life.[4] The organization was replaced with a new one, Xerox New Enterprises (XNE), which did not seek to relinquish control of firms or to involve outside venture investors. The XNE business model called for a much greater integration of the new units with traditional business units. The autonomy offered to the XNE managers and their compensation schemes were much closer to those in a traditional corporate division. As such, XNE appears to represent a departure from the several of the key elements that the XTV staff believed were critical to their success, such as their considerable degree of autonomy and high-powered incentives.

The experience of XTV has several implications for corporate venture capital programs more generally:

• The case makes clear that corporate venture capital programs—contrary to the suggestions in writings by both venture capitalists and financial economists—need not be failures. Xerox's financial returns, as noted

---

4. This paragraph is based on www.xerox.com/xne and Turner (1997).

above, were exceedingly favorable when compared to returns from comparable independent venture funds.

• XTVs' successes—such as Document Sciences and Documentum—were concentrated in industries closely related to the corporate parent's core line-of-business (i.e., document processing). This suggests that the fund's strong strategic focus was important to its success.

• The Xerox Corporation was unable to commit to a structure akin to that of a traditional venture capital partnership. Despite efforts by XTVs' founders to model the fund as closely as possible after a traditional venture partnership, the fund was still dissolved early. This experience underscores the challenges that these hybrid organizational forms face.

The Analysis

We now turn to assessing the experience of corporate venture programs more systematically. In this analysis, we use the VentureOne database described in chapter 16. The investors in the VentureOne database are diverse. They include individuals, institutional investors such as pension funds, traditional independent venture funds (such as Kleiner, Perkins, Caufield & Byers), and funds sponsored by corporations, financial institutions, and government bodies. To understand the impact of organizational structure, we concentrate below on two types of funds: independent venture partnerships and corporate funds. By so doing, we sought to draw as sharp a contrast as possible between corporate and independent funds. We eliminated other hybrid venture funds, such as those affiliated with commercial and investment banks, because many of these closely resembled traditional venture organizations.

The procedure we employed is described in detail in chapter 16. It is worth emphasizing, however, that it is not always easy to ascertain whether an investor was a corporate venture organization. Some U.S. and several European companies invest in companies through traditional venture capital partnerships. For example, Eastman Kodak not only makes direct equity investments but also invests through a partnership called Aperture Partners in which it is the sole limited partner. While we are able to identify many of these cases, in some cases we may have missed such affiliations. In other cases, independent venture organizations also cater to corporate investors. A prominent example is Advent, a Boston-based organization that organizes comingled funds for financial investors and other funds for single corporate limited partners. From the VentureOne data, it is usually difficult to determine whether the private equity group is investing its traditional partnerships or one of its corporate funds.

Finally, for the corporate venture capital investments, we characterized the degree of fit between the corporation and the portfolio firm. To do this, we examined the corporate annual reports for the 1983, 1989, and 1994 fiscal years. We classified investments as to whether there was a direct fit between one of the corporation's lines-of-business during the period and the portfolio firm, whether there was an indirect relationship, or whether there was no apparent relationship at all. In the analyses below, we denoted investments as having a strategic fit only if there was a direct relationship between a line-of-business of the corporate parent and the portfolio firm. The results are robust to expanding the definition to include indirectly related transactions as well: for example, when a corporate fund invests in a firm that is a potential supplier to or customer of the corporate parent. Not all investments were classified. In some cases, we were not able to determine the relationship. In others, we could not obtain the proximate annual reports. In particular, it was difficult to obtain the 1983 and 1989 annual reports for many of the foreign firms.

Summary Statistics

Table 5.1 provides an overview of the sample by year. After the deletions noted above, the sample consists of 32,364 investments. Investments by independent venture funds represent over one-half of the total transactions in the sample. Corporate venture investments represent a much smaller share, about 6 percent. Because on average about four investors participate in each financing round, the number of rounds—8,506—is significantly smaller. In the discussion below, we will analyze patterns on both the investment- and round-level.

Table 5.2 provides a comparison of four categories of investments: the total sample, those by corporate and independent venture capital organizations, and corporate investments where there was a strategic fit between the parent and the portfolio firm. In general, the corporate investments closely resemble those of the other funds:

• *Status at time of investment.* Corporate funds tend to invest slightly less frequently in start-up and mature private firms. Instead, they are disproportionately represented among companies in the middle stages such as "development" or "beta."[5]

---

5. See the appendix to this chapter for definitions of stages, regions, and industries.

Table 5.1

Distribution of the sample, by year. The table depicts the number of venture capital investments in the VentureOne sample by year between 1983 and 1994 as well as the number of financing rounds (a round may consist of several investments by different investors) and the aggregate amount of funding disbursed (in millions of 1997 dollars). Similar tabulations of the number of investments are presented for corporate and independent venture funds.

Year	Number of investments			Number of rounds	Dollar amount
	Total	Corporate VC	Independent VC		
1983	1,841	53	1,013	436	2,386
1984	2,249	91	1,206	550	3,123
1985	2,593	139	1,382	625	3,128
1986	2,557	129	1,381	592	2,574
1987	2,675	152	1,397	642	3,295
1988	2,599	179	1,385	611	2,889
1989	2,866	202	1,490	720	3.299
1990	2,826	233	1,455	784	3,913
1991	2,890	249	1,472	757	3,448
1992	3,166	214	1,699	911	4,183
1993	3,118	198	1,586	931	4,872
1994	2,984	193	1,601	947	5,346
Total	32,364	2,032	17,067	8,506	42,457

• *Location of firm.* The sample disproportionately includes investments in firms based in California. This reflects VentureOne's greater coverage of this region, particularly in the early years. While corporate venture investments as a whole are slightly more common in California than other venture investments, corporate investments with a strong strategic fit are more frequent elsewhere.

• *Industry of the firm.* Venture capital investments tend to focus on a few high-technology industries. This is even more true for corporate venture investments with a strategic focus.

• *Maturity of firm and investment characteristics.* Corporate venture funds tend to invest in later and larger financing rounds and in slightly older firms than other venture funds.

Success of Investments

We now consider the success of the investments by the various types of venture organizations. The discussions of the importance of the independent

Table 5.2
Characteristics of firms at the time of investment. The sample consists of 32,364 investments in privately held venture-backed firms between 1983 and 1994. The table presents the stage of the firm's development at the time of the investment, the geographic location of the firm, the industry of the firm, the ordinal rank of the venture round, the age of the firm at the time of the investment (in years), and the amount of the investment in the financing round (in millions of 1997 dollars). Separate tabulations are presented for investments by corporate venture firms, corporate funds where there was a strategic fit between the parent and portfolio firms, and independent venture funds.

	Entire sample	Corporate VC only	Corporate VC and strategic fit	Independent VC only
Status at time of investment				
Start-up	9.8%	7.1%	6.4%	10.4%
Development	30.5	33.6	35.9	31.2
Beta	4.1	5.5	6.4	4.1
Shipping	45.5	44.4	42.9	44.8
Profitable	7.6	6.9	5.6	7.3
Restart	2.4	2.5	2.8	2.3
Location of firm				
All Western United States	59.7%	63.7%	59.6%	60.8%
California	51.6	53.7	51.3	52.7
All Eastern United States	24.1	25.2	29.1	23.4
Massachusetts	12.8	14.0	16.5	12.6
Industry of firm				
Medical	25.5%	25.9%	24.2%	24.2%
Computer hardware	16.7	17.0	16.2	16.8
Communications	14.5	14.2	22.1	15.5
Computer software/on-line services	15.1	15.1	14.0	16.2
Other	28.1	27.9	23.5	27.3
Round of investment				
Mean	2.4	2.8	2.9	2.4
Median	2	3	3	2
Age of firm at time of investment				
Mean	3.9	4.0	4.2	3.8
Median	3.0	3.3	3.4	2.8
Amount invested in venture round				
Mean	6.6	6.7	6.5	6.1
Median	4.6	4.8	5.1	4.5

venture organizations' partnership structure noted above suggest that these investors should have the greatest success. Meanwhile, the suggestion that corporate investors may benefit from complementarities with their existing lines-of-business suggest that corporate investments may also perform well, at least those where there is a strong strategic fit.

The measurement of returns presents some challenging issues. Ideally, we would capture the direct and indirect returns to each class of venture investor. Unfortunately, because VentureOne does not compile the stake held by each investor, we cannot compute the direct financial returns for particular investors. Furthermore, it is difficult to identify the indirect benefits—for example, an insight that leads to a redirected research program in a corporate laboratory—that corporate venture investors receive, much less quantify these benefits. As a result, we employ two less satisfactory, but more tractable measures.

The first is the success of the firm receiving the funds. This is likely to be a reasonable measure for traditional venture groups. As noted above, traditional venture capitalists generate the bulk of their profits from firms that go public. This measure is also likely to have some validity for corporate venture investors. If the venture fails, the key people and knowledge are likely to be scattered, and the benefits to the corporation are likely to be few. A more successful venture may or may not provide indirect benefits to the corporate parent, but at least should have attractive financial returns.

Table 5.3 presents the status of the firm in the spring of 1998 for four classes of investors as well as tests of the statistical significance of the differences between them. Firms backed by corporate venture groups are significantly more likely to have gone public than those financed by other organizations and are less likely to have been liquidated. These differences are particularly strong for the investments where there was a strategic tie between the corporate parent and the portfolio firm. These comparisons may be influenced, however, by differences among the firms backed by corporate and other venture investors.

To address this concern, we examine these patterns in a regression framework. We estimate logit regressions, alternatively using each investment and each financing round as observations. We seek to explain the probability that the investment had gone public by the spring of 1998 or the probability that the firm had gone public, filed a registration with the U.S. Securities and Exchange Commission (a preliminary step before going public), or been acquired for a valuation of at least twice the

Table 5.3
Status of firms in the spring of 1998. The sample consists of 32.364 investments in privately held venture-backed firms between 1983 and 1994. Panel A presents the status of the firms in the spring of 1998. Separate tabulations are presented for investments by corporate venture firms, corporate funds where there was a strategic fit between the parent and portfolio firms, and independent venture funds. Panel B presents the p-values from Pearson χ^2-tests of the equality of three outcomes (completion of an initial public offering; IPO or filing of a registration statement or acquisition at twice (in inflation-adjusted dollars) the post-money valuation at the time of the investment; and not being liquidated) in different subsamples.

Panel A: Status of firms in the spring of 1998

	Entire sample	Corporate VC only	Corporate VC and strategic fit	Independent VC only
Status in the spring of 1998				
Initial public offering completed	31.1%	35.1%	39.3%	30.6%
Registration statement filed	0.7	0.2	0.3	0.7
Acquired	29.0	29.0	27.5	30.3
Still privately held	20.6	21.1	18.3	19.7
Liquidated	18.7	14.6	14.7	18.7

Panel B: p-value, tests of equality of firm status in the spring of 1998

	Probability of IPO	Probability of IPO, registration, or acquisition at >2X Value	Probability of not liquidated
Corporate VC vs. all others	0.000	0.002	0.000
Independent VC vs. all others	0.043	0.557	0.796
Corporate VC vs. independent VC	0.000	0.005	0.000
Corporate VC and strategic fit vs. independent VC	0.000	0.000	0.006

post-money valuation[6] of the financing.[7] As independent variables, we use the age of the firm at the time of the investment and the ordinal rank of the investment round. We also employ dummy variables denoting investments by corporate and independent venture capital funds, corporate venture investments where there was a strategic fit with the portfolio firm, firms based in California and Massachusetts, the status of the firm

---

6. The post-money valuation is defined as the product of the price paid per share in the financing round and the shares outstanding after the financing round. In calculating the valuations, VentureOne converts all preferred shares into common stock at the conversion ratios specified in the agreements. Warrants and options outstanding are included in the total, as long as their exercise price is below the price per share being paid in the financing round.

7. The results are also robust to the use of a third dependent variable, the probability that the firm had not been liquidated by the spring of 1998.

Table 5.4
Logit regression analyses of firms in the spring of 1998. The sample in the first four regressions consists of 32,364 investments in privately held, venture-backed firms between 1983 and 1994; in the fifth and sixth regressions, 8,506 financing rounds of privately held, venture-backed firms between 1983 and 1994. The dependent variable in the first, second, fifth, and sixth regressions is a dummy variable that takes on the value of one if the firm had gone public by the spring of 1998. In the third and fourth regressions, the dummy takes the value of one if the firm had gone public, filed a registration statement, or been acquired at twice (in inflation-adjusted dollars) the post-money valuation at the time of the investment by the spring of 1998. Independent variables include the age of the firm at the time of the investment, the ordinal rank of the investment round, and dummy variables denoting investments by corporate and independent venture capital funds, corporate venture investments where there was a strategic fit with the portfolio firm, firms based in California and Massachusetts, the status of the firm at the time of the investment, the year of the investment (not reported), the industry of firm (not reported), and a constant (not reported). All dummy variables take on the value of one if the answer to the posed question is in the affirmative. Absolute t-statistics reported in brackets.

	Observations are investments				Observations are rounds	
	Did firm go public?		Did firm go public, register, or have favorable acquisition?		Did firm go public?	
Age of firm at time of financing	−0.02 [5.52]	−0.02 [0.50]	−0.02 [6.17]	−0.02 [6.13]	−0.02 [2.47]	−0.02 [2.50]
Round number	0.13 [11.39]	0.13 [11.18]	0.13 [11.48]	0.13 [11.29]	0.17 [7.13]	0.16 [6.95]
Corporate venture investment?	0.15 [2.54]	−0.19 [1.31]	0.12 [2.15]	−0.23 [1.64]	0.20 [2.87]	0.03 [0.31]
Independent venture investment?	−0.003 [0.09]	−0.002 [0.07]	0.07 [2.54]	0.07 [2.56]	0.14 [1.92]	0.13 [1.82]
Corporate investment and strategic fit?		0.52 [3.15]		0.57 [3.55]		0.40 [3.32]
Firm based in California?	0.30 [9.29]	0.29 [8.96]	0.23 [7.44]	0.22 [6.98]	0.25 [3.96]	0.26 [4.04]
Firm based in Massachusetts?	0.36 [7.83]	0.36 [7.75]	0.24 [5.26]	0.23 [5.04]	0.25 [2.77]	0.25 [2.71]
Firm is in development stage?	0.44 [7.73]	0.42 [7.27]	0.38 [6.99]	0.35 [6.41]	0.37 [3.70]	0.36 [3.68]
Firm is in beta stage?	0.25 [2.83]	0.22 [2.50]	0.14 [1.60]	0.11 [1.24]	0.13 [0.70]	0.13 [0.69]
Firm is in shipping stage?	0.38 [6.28]	0.36 [5.95]	0.30 [5.20]	0.28 [4.82]	0.33 [3.12]	0.34 [3.23]
Firm is in profitable stage?	1.32 [17.08]	1.30 [16.61]	1.10 [14.77]	1.08 [14.27]	1.44 [10.52]	1.46 [10.63]
Firm is in restart stage?	−0.56 [4.20]	−0.56 [4.19]	−0.43 [3.64]	−0.45 [3.71]	−0.45 [1.70]	−0.45 [1.68]
Log Likelihood	−14743.6	−14252.0	−15477.4	−14973.7	−3694.4	−3688.9
χ^2-statistic	2409.9	2362.4	2065.5	2025.7	609.0	620.1
p-value	0.000	0.000	0.000	0.000	0.000	0.000
Number of observations	24515	23740	24515	23740	6445	6445

at the time of the investment, the year of the investment, the industry of firm, and a constant.

The results are consistent with the univariate comparisons above. Corporate venture investments are significantly more successful than other investments. (In most of the regressions, independent venture investments are also more successful, though the effect is smaller in magnitude and statistical significance.) When the dummy variable denoting corporate venture investments with a strategic fit is added to the regressions, the corporate venture dummy variable becomes insignificant (and frequently negative). Corporate venture investments in general do not perform better, only those with a strategic fit do so. These results appear consistent with the complementarities hypothesis above.

Our second proxy for the direct and indirect returns for corporate and other investors is the valuation assigned to the firm at the time of the investment. All else being equal, the higher the valuation (i.e., the higher price paid per share), the lower the direct financial returns to the investor (subject to the caveats in the discussion below). For each investment round where the data was available (about one-half of the entire sample), we computed the pre-money valuation, the product of the price paid per share in the financing round and the shares outstanding before the financing round.[8]

Table 5.5 presents the pre-money valuations for four classes of investors tabulated above, as well as tests of the statistical significance of these differences. Corporate venture funds appear to pay significantly more, with a mean pre-money valuation of $28.5 million versus an average of $18.1 million for the independent venture firms. Corporate investments in which there is a strategic fit are also priced at a premium, but the average price ($26.9 million) is lower than the other corporate investments.

Once again, we seek to corroborate these patterns through a regression analysis. We estimate a hedonic regression, seeking to explain the logarithm of the pre-money valuations (see Gompers and Lerner (1997a) for a detailed discussion of this methodology). We once again use each investment and each financing round as observations. As independent variables, we use the logarithm of the age of the firm at the time of the investment and the logarithm of the ordinal rank of the investment round. We also employ dummy variables denoting investments by corporate and inde-

---

8. As discussed at length in Lerner (1994), the pre-money valuation is a more appropriate dependent variable than the post-money valuation because it is independent of the amount invested in the firm during the current financing round. As chapter 7 discusses, the amount invested may vary with many considerations, including the fundraising environment.

Table 5.5
Pre-money valuation at the time of financing. The sample consists of 32,364 investments in privately held venture-backed firms between 1983 and 1994. Panel A presents the mean and median pre-money valuation of the firms at the time of the financing in 1997 dollars. The pre-money valuation is defined as the product of the price paid per share in the financing round and the shares outstanding prior to the financing round. Separate tabulations are presented for investments by corporate venture firms, corporate funds where there was a strategic fit between the parent and portfolio firms, and independent venture funds. Panel B presents the p-values from t-tests and Wilcoxon rank-sum tests of the equality of the mean and median valuations in different subsamples.

Panel A: Pre-money valuation at time of financing

	Entire sample	Corporate VC only	Corporate VC and strategic fit	Independent VC only
Mean	21.5	30.5	28.8	19.4
Median	13.8	18.6	17.0	12.5

Panel B: p-value, tests of equality of pre-money valuations

	Mean	Median
Corporate VC vs. all others	0.000	0.000
Independent VC vs. all others	0.000	0.000
Corporate VC vs. independent VC	0.000	0.000
Corporate VC and strategic fit vs. independent VC	0.000	0.000

pendent venture capital funds, corporate venture investments where there was a strategic fit with the portfolio firm, firms based in California and Massachusetts, the status of the firm at the time of the investment, the year of the investment, the industry of firm, and a constant.

We find results similar to those in the univariate comparisons. Corporate venture investments are associated with between 18 and 30 percent higher valuations, while those by independent funds are associated with between 7 and 18 percent lower valuations. The dummy variable denoting corporate venture investments with a strategic fit is inconsistent in sign and never significant.

These results suggest two possible interpretations. First, traditional venture investors and entrepreneurs could be exploiting the relative inexperience of the corporate venture investors, persuading them to invest in overvalued transactions. (See, for instance, AbuZayyad, et al. 1996). Second, corporate investors are likely to enjoy some indirect benefits from their involvement with portfolio firms that independent venture firms do not enjoy. Standard bargaining models (Nash 1950) suggest that the additional surplus enjoyed by the corporation will lead to corporate venture capitalists investing at a higher prices than others. Some of this value

Table 5.6
Ordinary least squares regression analyses of pre-money valuation at the time of the financing. The sample in the first two regressions consists of 32,364 investments in privately held, venture-backed firms between 1983 and 1994; in third and fourth regressions, 8,506 financing rounds of privately held, venture-backed firms between 1983 and 1994. The dependent variable is the logarithm of the pre-money valuation of the firms at the time of the financing in 1994 dollars. The pre-money valuation is defined as the product of the price paid per share in the financing round and the shares outstanding prior to the financing round. Independent variables include the logarithm of the age of the firm at the time of the investment, the logarithm of the ordinal rank of the investment round, and dummy variables denoting investments by corporate and independent venture capital funds, corporate venture investments where there was a strategic fit with the portfolio firm, firms based in California and Massachusetts, the status of the firm at the time of the investment, the year of the investment (not reported), the industry of firm (not reported), and a constant (not reported). All dummy variables take on the value of one if the answer to the posed question is in the affirmative. Absolute t-statistics reported in brackets.

	Observations are investments		Observations are rounds	
Logarithm of age of firm	0.14 [11.32]	0.14 [11.26]	0.15 [6.01]	0.15 [6.00]
Logarithm of round number	0.68 [49.43]	0.49 [48.94]	0.68 [24.09]	0.68 [24.04]
Corporate venture investment?	0.18 [7.39]	0.26 [4.38]	0.30 [9.43]	0.27 [6.76]
Independent venture investment?	−0.07 [5.76]	−0.07 [5.75]	−0.18 [4.85]	−0.18 [4.91]
Corporate investment and strategic fit?		−0.09 [1.37]		0.07 [1.22]
Firm based in California?	0.20 [14.78]	0.20 [14.54]	0.14 [4.76]	0.14 [4.80]
Firm based in Massachusetts?	0.06 [2.79]	0.06 [2.82]	0.03 [0.61]	0.03 [0.59]
Firm is in development stage?	0.40 [14.08]	0.38 [13.30]	0.37 [7.01]	0.37 [6.99]
Firm is in beta stage?	0.51 [13.24]	0.50 [12.81]	0.48 [6.11]	0.48 [6.10]
Firm is in shipping stage?	0.58 [18.86]	0.57 [18.26]	0.60 [10.28]	0.60 [10.30]
Firm is in profitable stage?	1.10 [29.06]	1.09 [28.61]	1.15 [15.51]	1.15 [15.54]
Firm is in restart stage?	−0.85 [17.22]	−0.84 [17.00]	−0.72 [7.04]	−0.72 [7.04]
Adjusted R^2	0.39	0.39	0.43	0.43
F-statistic	397.1	371.5	102.03	98.32
p-value	0.000	0.000	0.000	0.000
Number of observations	15895	15406	3544	3544

created by the investment will be shared with the young firm and its investors.

Disentangling these interpretations is difficult. Nonetheless, we are struck by the lack of a relationship between the price premium paid and the degree of strategic fit. We suggest that this may reflect the fact that corporations are also more savvy investors in companies close to their existing lines-of-business. While the indirect benefits to the parent may be greater in these instances resulting in a willingness to pay more, its understanding of the market is also likely to be better. As a result, the corporation may be less likely to invest in overpriced transactions in these cases. In areas outside the corporation's experience, overpaying for investments may be a more common phenomenon. This appears to be supported by the data.

Duration of Programs

We finally consider the duration of the venture organizations. Table 5.7 presents several measures of the stability of these organizations. First, we examine the total number of investments in the sample. Similarly, we examine the timespan (in years) between the first and the last investment in the sample by each venture organization. (A venture organization that made a single investment would be coded as having a timespan of zero.)

Both of these measures, however, are somewhat problematic. Many corporate venture programs have begun in recent years. As a result, they may have made only a few investments to date. This does not imply, however, that they will not continue to exist for a long time in the future. To control for this "vintage effect," we create a third measure: the time between the first and last investments by the venture organization in the sample expressed as a percentage of the time from the first investment by the venture organization to December 1994. Using this approach, both a long-standing venture group and relatively recent program that remains active through the end of the sample period would be coded as 1.0.

Unlike the earlier analyses, we confine the analysis (and that in table 5.8) to independent and corporate venture funds. Some of the other investors are reported in an inconsistent manner, which would make this type of analysis potentially misleading. For instance, when only a small number of individuals invest, the more prominent ones are identified by name. When a large number invest, all are lumped together as "individuals."

Stark differences appear between the corporate and independent funds. The corporations make a mean of 4.4 investments over 2.5 years, while

Table 5.7
Duration of investment programs. The sample consists of 19,099 investments by 855 corporate and independent venture funds in privately held firms between 1983 and 1994. Panel A presents the mean and median number of investments during the sample period by each venture organization, the timespan between the first and last investments by the venture organization in the sample (in years), and the timespan between the first and last investments by the venture organization in the sample, expressed as a percentage of the timespan from the first investment by the venture organization to December 1994. Separate tabulations are presented for investments by corporate venture firms, corporate venture funds where there was a strategic fit with the portfolio firm in at least one-half of the investments, and independent venture funds. Panel B presents the p-values from t-tests and Wilcoxon rank-sum tests of the equality of the mean and median measures of duration in different subsamples.

Panel A: Duration of investment programs

	Entire sample	Corporate VC only	Corporate VC and strategic fit	Independent VC only
Number of investments				
Mean	22.3	4.4	9.8	43.5
Median	4	2	4	21
Timespan				
Mean	4.6	2.5	4.4	7.1
Median	3.8	1.0	4.2	8.0
Ratio of active to possible timespan				
Mean	51.7%	34.8%	55.6%	71.7%
Median	58.7	21.8	71.5	90.4

Panel B: p-value, tests of equality of investment program duration

	Number of investments		Time-span		Ratio of active to possible time-span	
	Mean	Median	Mean	Median	Mean	Median
Corporate VC vs. independent VC	0.000	0.000	0.000	0.000	0.000	0.000
Corporate VC and strategic fit vs. independent VC	0.000	0.000	0.000	0.000	0.001	0.000

the independent funds make 43.5 investments over 7.1 years. Even using the ratio of the active timespan to the possible timespan, the differences are dramatic: the average is 34.8 percent for the corporate funds as opposed to 71.7 percent for the independent funds. The differences are less extreme, but still significant, for the corporate programs where there was a strategic fit in at least one-half of the investments.

We then examine these patterns in a regression analysis. The first two regressions employ all corporate and independent venture organizations in the sample as observations; the second set, only those organizations

Table 5.8
Double-censored regression analyses of length of venture program. The sample consists of 855 corporate and independent venture funds that invested in privately held firms between 1983 and 1994. The dependent variable is the time between the first and last investments by the venture organization in the sample, expressed as a percentage of the time from the first investment by the venture organization to December 1994. The first two regressions employ all observations; the second set, only those organizations with four or more investments in the sample. Independent variables include the date of the venture organization's first investment (with an investment in May 1992 expressed as 1992.4, etc.), dummy variables denoting observations of corporate venture capital funds and of corporate venture funds where there was a strategic fit with the portfolio firm in at least one-half of the investments, and a constant. All dummy variables take on the value of one if the answer to the posed question is in the affirmative. Absolute t-statistics reported in brackets.

	All corporate and independent VC funds		Corporate and independent funds with ≥4 investments	
Date of first investment	−0.05 [10.15]	−0.05 [9.69]	−0.0003 [0.07]	0.001 [0.28]
Corporate venture fund?	−0.32 [8.98]	−0.39 [10.77]	−0.11 [4.55]	−0.16 [6.03]
Corporate investment and strategic fit?		0.35 [6.42]		0.15 [3.95]
Constant	103.85 [10.22]	96.77 [9.76]	1.47 [0.18]	−1.45 [0.18]
Log likelihood	−586.2	−566.1	−52.2	−59.9
χ^2-statistic	290.2	330.5	23.0	38.4
p-value	0.000	0.000	0.000	0.000
Number of observations	855	855	450	450

with four or more investments in the sample.[9] As a dependent variable, we use the ratio of the timespan that the fund was active to the timespan from its first investment to December 1994. Independent variables include the date of the venture organization's first investment, dummy variables denoting observations of corporate venture capital funds and of corporate venture funds where there was a strategic fit with the portfolio firms in at least one-half of the investments, and a constant. Reflecting the fact that the dependent variable must fall between 0 and 1, we employ a double-censored regression specification.

Once again, the corporate venture programs have a significantly shorter duration. The dummy variable for corporate venture programs in which at least one-half of the investments were strategic, however, has a positive coefficient of almost equal magnitude. While corporate programs without a strategic focus are very unstable, those with such a focus appear to have a longevity equivalent to more traditional independent funds, at least using this measure.

We consider two explanations for the shorter timespan of the corporate investments. One possibility is that this is a response to technological change. An extensive literature on the economics of innovation has high-lighted that new entrants often exploit technological breakthroughs in more innovative and aggressive ways than the established incumbents, and that these changes are often associated with dramatic shifts in market leadership.[10] In many cases, product leaders have rapidly lost their com-manding position after many years of dominance. Academics have attrib-uted these patterns to a rational reluctance on the part of existing industry leaders to jeopardize their current revenues and profits as well as the myopic reluctance of many successful organizations to recognize that their leadership is waning. (In many instances, the continuing financial success of mature product lines masks the organizations' failure to intro-duce new products.)[11] Corporate venture capital programs may be a response to these short-run periods of technological discontinuity.[12]

---

9. In this way, we seek to examine whether groups that dissolve after only one or two investments drive the results or whether this is a more general pattern. The results are also robust to the use of other cutoff points.

10. Two academic studies documenting these patterns (there are also many other more anecdotal accounts) are Henderson (1993) and Lerner (1997).

11. For an overview, see Reinganum (1989).

12. For instance, the pharmaceutical industry aggressively employed corporate venture pro-grams after being confronted with the biotechnology revolution in the 1980s. Henderson and Cockburn (1996) show that the more successful firms responded by aggressively estab-lishing outside relationships to access new ideas in response.

Once this transition period has passed, the corporation may dissolve the effort.

Alternatively, the instability may reflect the manner in which corporate programs are designed. One important argument in favor of the decade-long partnership structure typically employed by independent venture funds is that it allows venture capitalists to make long-run investments, without the fear of demands to liquidate their portfolios. (For a discussion of how such fears can affect the behavior of hedge fund managers, who typically do not have these protections, see Shleifer and Vishny 1997a.) Corporate venture funds are typically structured as corporate divisions or affiliates without the protections afforded by a legal partnership agreement. Furthermore, field research suggests that corporate venture groups are often plagued by defections of their most successful investors, who become frustrated at their low level of compensation. These defections may also affect the stability of the groups. This suggests that most corporate venture groups should be unstable.

The evidence is difficult to reconcile with either hypothesis. If programs were generally designed to address short-run technological discontinuities, it should be the strategic programs that were of the shortest duration. This is clearly not the case. The structural view suggests that most corporate venture programs should rapidly be terminated, which is hard to reconcile with the success of programs with strong strategic objectives. One possibility is that the organizations without a clear strategic focus also tend to be the ones with a low degree of autonomy and low levels of incentive compensation. Thus, the limited duration of the funds without a clear strategic focus may thus reflect the importance of the organizational structure employed by independent venture funds.

Conclusions

This chapter has compared investments by corporate venture organizations with those of independent and other venture groups. Corporate venture investments in entrepreneurial firms appear to be at least as successful (using such measures as the probability of the portfolio firm going public) as those backed by independent venture organizations, particularly when there is a strategic overlap between the corporate parent and the portfolio firm. Although corporate venture capitalists tend to invest at a premium to other firms, this premium appears to be no higher in investments with a strong strategic fit. Finally, corporate programs without a strong strategic focus appear to be much less stable, frequently ceasing operations after only a few investments, but strategically focused programs appear to be as stable as independent venture organizations. The evidence is consistent with the existence of complementarities that allow corporations to effectively select and add value to portfolio firms, but somewhat at odds with the suggestion that the structure of corporate funds introduces distortions and limits their effectiveness.

Chapter 5 suggests that the presence of a strong strategic focus is critical to the success of corporate venture funds. This subset of corporate funds appears to have been quite successful, despite having very different structures from traditional funds. This appears to challenge the emphasis in the finance literature on the importance of the partnership structure employed by independent private equity funds. But, as alluded to above, it may well be that corporate programs without a clear strategic focus are also the ones with a low degree of autonomy and low levels of compensation. To comprehensively distinguish between these hypotheses, we would need to have information on the compensation schemes and organization structures employed by these groups. While this chapter has only skimmed the surface of this issue, this is a rich area for further exploration, which we hope to explore in future research.

This chapter is related to an extensive corporate finance literature about the relationship between organizational structure and corporate performance (reviewed, for instance, in Jensen 1993). More specifically, a number of papers has examined the structure of financial institutions and investment performance. Among these are studies of the performance of initial public offerings underwritten by investment banks that are and are not affiliated with commercial banks (Kroszner and Rajan 1994), the performance of loans underwritten by savings and loan institutions structured as mutual and stock organizations (Cordell, MacDonald, and Wohar 1993), and the impact of mutual fund performance on investment choices and returns (Chevalier and Ellison 1997). As far as we are aware, however, no paper has analyzed the impact of the limited partnership structure on investment performance.

This chapter is also related to a body of literature on private equity partnerships more generally. These writings suggest reasons to be both positive and skeptical about the importance of the partnership structure. On the one hand, a set of articles document that investments by private equity organizations are associated with real changes in the firms that they fund, measured on both an accounting (Muscarella and Vetsuypens

1990) and a financial basis (see chapter 14). Moreover, the structure of private-equity groups—whether measured through the sensitivity of compensation to performance (see chapter 4) or the extent of contractual restrictions (see chapter 3)—appears to be responsive to the changing investment mix and characteristics of the funds. On the other hand, it appears that other factors (see chapter 3) can also affect the structure of partnerships. Furthermore, certain features of partnerships apparently can lead to pathological outcomes. For instance, policies allowing venture capitalists to distribute shares in stock, designed to maximize investors' choices regarding the liquidation of their positions, have been exploited by some private-equity groups to inflate returns and to boost their compensation (see chapter 13). This chapter raises questions about the necessity of the partnership structure employed by independent private-equity funds: a clear strategic orientation may be more important.

The analysis raises several puzzles that cannot be answered with the existing data. We end by highlighting two of these. First, why do corporations set up programs that appear likely to be unsuccessful? In the sample, for instance, we see repeated examples of funds being established that do not have a clear relationship to the corporate parent's lines-of-business. Certainly, in many cases, carefully thought-through proposals appear to have been modified during the review process in ways that are likely to substantially reduce their likelihood of success. Understanding these processes and placing them in the context of the broader literature on the problems that can beset corporate decision making is an interesting area for future research.

Second, is there an optimal mixture between internally funded corporate research and outside ideas accessed through initiatives such as corporate venture programs? Some high-technology corporations, such as AT&T and IBM, have historically funded internal research laboratories at high levels. Other high-technology giants, such as Cisco Systems, have relied on acquisitions and strategic investments to identify and access product and process innovations. The "make-or-buy" decisions that corporate R&D managers face is an important but little-researched issue.

Appendix: Definition of Firm Categorizations

Definition of Investment Stages

Start-up: Company with a skeletal business plan, product, or service development in preliminary stages.

Development: Product or service development is underway, but the company is not generating revenues from sales.

Beta: For companies specializing in information technology, the beta phase is when the product is being tested by a limited number of customers but not available for broad sales. For life sciences companies, beta is synonymous with a drug in human clinical trials or a device being tested.

Shipping: The product or service is being sold to customers and the company is deriving revenues from those sales, but expenses still exceed revenues.

Profitable: The company is selling products or services and the sales revenue yields a positive net income.

Restart: A recapitalization at a reduced valuation, accompanied by a substantial shift in the product or marketing focus.

Definition of Industry Groups

Computer hardware: Firms whose primary lines-of-business are personal computing, minicomputers or work stations, mainframe computers, CAD/CAM/CAE systems, data storage, computer peripherals, memory systems, office automation, source data collection, multimedia devices, and computer networking devices.

Computer software: Firms whose primary lines-of-business are compilers, assemblers, systems application, CAD/CAM/CAE/CASE, recreational and home, artificial intelligence, educational, and multimedia software, and on-line services.

Communications: Firms whose primary lines-of-business include modems, computer networking, fiber optics, microwave and satellite communications, telephone equipment, pocket paging, cellular phones, radar and defense systems, television equipment, teleconferencing, and television and radio broadcasting.

Medical: Firms whose primary lines-of-business include biotechnology, pharmaceuticals, diagnostic imaging, patient monitoring, medical devices, medical lab instruments, hospital equipment, medical supplies, retail medicine, hospital management, medical data processing, and medical lab services.

Definition of Regions

Eastern United States: Firms whose headquarters are located in Connecticut, Delaware, the District of Columbia, Maine, Maryland, Massachusetts, New Hampshire, New Jersey, New York, Pennsylvania, Rhode Island, Vermont, and West Virginia.

Western United States: Firms whose headquarters are located in Alaska, Arizona, California, Colorado, Hawaii, Idaho, Montana, New Mexico, Nevada, Oregon, Utah, Washington, and Wyoming.

Source: Adapted from VentureOne (1998).

II   Venture Capital Investing

An Overview of Venture Capital Investing

Before considering the mechanisms employed by venture capitalists, it is worth reviewing why firms backed by venture capitalists find it difficult to meet their financing needs through traditional mechanisms. Entrepreneurs rarely have the capital to see their ideas to fruition and must rely on outside financiers. Meanwhile, those who control capital—for instance, pension fund trustees and university overseers—are unlikely to have the time or expertise to invest directly in young or restructuring firms. Some might think that entrepreneurs would turn to traditional financing sources, such as bank loans or the issuance of public stock, to meet their needs.

But a variety of factors may limit access to capital for some of the most potentially profitable and exciting firms. These difficulties can be sorted into four critical factors: uncertainty, asymmetric information, the nature of firm assets, and the conditions in the relevant financial and product markets. At any time, these four factors determine the financing choices that a firm faces. As a firm evolves, however, these factors can change in rapid and unanticipated ways. In each case, the firm's ability to change dynamically is a key source of competitive advantage, but also a major problem to those who provide the financing.

The first of these four problems, uncertainty, is a measure of the array of potential outcomes for a company or project. The wider the dispersion of potential outcomes, the greater the uncertainty. By their very nature, young and restructuring companies are associated with significant levels of uncertainty. Uncertainty surrounds whether the firm's research program or new product will succeed. The response of firm's rivals may also be uncertain. High uncertainty means that investors and entrepreneurs cannot confidently predict what the company will look like in the future.

Uncertainty affects the willingness of investors to contribute capital, the desire of suppliers to extend credit, and the decisions of firms' managers. If managers are averse to taking risks, it may be difficult to induce them to make the right decisions. Conversely, if entrepreneurs are overoptimistic, investors want to curtail various actions. Uncertainty also affects the timing of investment. Should investors contribute all the capital at the beginning or should they stage the investment through time? Investors need to know how information-gathering activities can address these concerns and when they should be undertaken.

The second factor, asymmetric information, is distinct from uncertainty. Because of day-to-day involvement with the firm, an entrepreneur knows more about the company's prospects than investors, suppliers, or strategic partners. Various problems develop in settings where asymmetric information is prevalent. For instance, the entrepreneur may take detrimental actions that investors cannot observe: perhaps undertaking a riskier strategy than initially suggested or not working as hard as the investor expects. The entrepreneur might also invest in projects that build up a reputation at the investors' expense.

Asymmetric information can also lead to selection problems. Entrepreneurs may exploit the fact that they know more about the project or their abilities than investors do. Investors may find it difficult to distinguish between competent entrepreneurs and incompetent ones. Without the ability to screen out unacceptable projects and entrepreneurs, investors are unable to make efficient and appropriate decisions about where to invest.

The third factor affecting a firm's corporate and financial strategy is the nature of its assets. Firms that have tangible assets—for example, machines, buildings, land, or physical inventory—may find financing easier to obtain or may be able to obtain more favorable terms. The ability to abscond with the firm's source of value is more difficult when it relies on physical assets. When the most important assets are intangible, such as trade secrets, raising outside financing from traditional sources may be more challenging.

Market conditions also play a key role in determining the difficulty of financing firms. Both the capital and product markets may be subject to substantial variations. The supply of capital from public investors and the price at which this capital is available may vary dramatically. These changes may be a response to regulatory edicts or shifts in investors' perceptions of future profitability. Similarly, the nature of product markets may vary dramatically, whether due to shifts in the intensity of competition with rivals or in the nature of the customers. If there is exceedingly intense competition or a great deal of uncertainty about the size of the potential market, firms may find it very difficult to raise capital from traditional sources.

Related Research

Jensen and Meckling (1976) demonstrate that conflicts between managers and investors ("agency problems") can affect the willingness of both debt and equity holders to provide capital. If the firm raises equity from outside investors, the manager has an incentive to engage in wasteful expenditures (e.g., lavish offices) because he may benefit disproportionately from these but does not bear their entire cost. Similarly, if the firm raises debt, the manager may increase risk to undesirable levels. Because providers of capital recognize these problems, outside investors demand a higher rate of return than would be the case if the funds were internally generated.

Even if the manager is motivated to maximize shareholder value, informational asymmetries may make raising external capital more expensive or even preclude it entirely. Myers and Majluf (1984) and Greenwald, Stiglitz, and Weiss (1984) demonstrate that equity offerings of firms may be associated with a "lemons" problem (first identified by Akerlof 1970). If the manager is better informed about the investment opportunities of the firm and acts in the interest of current shareholders, then managers only issue new shares when the company's stock is overvalued. Indeed, numerous studies have documented that stock prices decline when equity issues are announced, largely because of the negative signal sent to the market.

These information problems have also been shown to exist in debt markets. Stiglitz and Weiss (1981) show that if banks find it difficult to discriminate among companies, raising interest rates can have perverse selection effects. In particular, the high interest rates discourage all but the highest risk borrowers, so the quality of the loan pool declines markedly. To address this problem, banks may restrict the amount of lending rather than increasing interest rates.

More generally, the inability to verify outcomes makes it difficult to write contracts that are contingent upon particular events. This inability makes external financing costly. Many of the models of ownership (Grossman and Hart 1986 and Hart and Moore 1990) and financing choice (Hart and Moore 1998) depend on the inability of investors to verify that certain actions have been taken or certain outcomes have occurred. While actions or outcomes might be observable, meaning that investors know what the entrepreneur did, they are assumed not to be verifiable: that is, investors could not convince a court of the action or outcome. Start-up firms are likely to face exactly these types of problems, making external financing costly or difficult to obtain.

If the information asymmetries could be eliminated, financing constraints would disappear. Financial economists argue that specialized financial intermediaries, such as venture capital organizations, can address these problems. By intensively scrutinizing firms before providing capital and then monitoring them afterwards, venture capitalists can alleviate some of the information gaps and reduce capital constraints. Thus, it is important to understand the tools employed by venture investors as responses to this difficult environment, which enable firms to ultimately receive the financing that they cannot raise from other sources. It is the nonmonetary aspects of venture capital that are critical to its success.

The mechanisms that venture capitalists use to mitigate agency conflicts among entrepreneurial firms and outside investors have been explored in depth in a series of theoretical studies. These include the active monitoring and advice that is provided (Cornelli and Yosha 1997, Marx 1994, Hellmann 1998), the screening mechanisms employed (Chan 1983), the incentives to exit (Berglöf 1994), the proper syndication of the investment (Admati and Pfleiderer 1994), or the staging of the investment (Bergemann and Hege 1998). In virtually all cases, a critical role of venture capitalists is generating information about the firm's prospects. This work has deepened our understanding of the factors that affect the relationship among venture capitalists and entrepreneurs.

One of the most common and potent features of venture capital is the meting out of financing in discrete stages over time. Prospects for the firm are periodically reevaluated. The shorter the duration of an individual round of financing, the more frequently the venture capitalist monitors the entrepreneur's progress and the greater the need to gather information. Staged capital infusion keeps the owner/manager on a "tight leash" and reduces potential losses from bad decisions. Because venture capital financings are costly to negotiate and structure, funding is provided in discrete stages.

Even though venture capitalists periodically "check-up" on entrepreneurs between capital infusions, entrepreneurs still have private information about the projects that they manage. Thus, it is important to employ other mechanisms as well. Two of these are informal monitoring and controls over the compensation of the entrepreneur.

Gorman and Sahlman (1989) explore venture capitalists' oversight of portfolio firms through a survey. They show that between financing rounds, the lead venture capitalist visits the entrepreneur once a month on average and spends four to five hours at the facility during each visit. Nonlead venture capitalists typically visit the firm once a quarter for an average of two-to-three hours. Venture capitalists also receive monthly financial reports. Gorman and Sahlman show, however, that venture capitalists do not usually become involved in the day-to-day management of the firm. Major reviews of progress and extensive due diligence are confined to the time of refinancing. The checks between financings are designed to limit opportunistic behavior by entrepreneurs between evaluations.

Another mechanism utilized by venture capitalists to avoid conflicts is the wide-spread use of stock grants and stock options. Managers and critical employees within a firm receive a substantial fraction of their compensation in the form of equity or options. This tends to align the incentives of managers and investors. The close link between investors' and managers' returns is a natural response to the special circumstances facing entrepreneurial firms. Jensen and Meckling (1976) show that if managers have little ownership in the firm, conflicts with investors' interests become likely. These conflicts are likely to be particularly problematic in young, start-up firms. Linking incentives of all parties is critical to success.[1]

The venture capitalist also employs additional controls on compensation to reduce potential gaming by the entrepreneur. First, venture capitalists usually require vesting of the stock or options over a multiyear period. In this way, entrepreneurs cannot leave the firm and take their shares. Similarly, the venture capitalist can significantly dilute the entrepreneur's stake in subsequent financings if the firm fails to realize its targets. This provides additional incentives for the entrepreneur. To maintain a stake, the entrepreneur will need to meet stated targets.

Why can other financial intermediaries (e.g., banks) not undertake the same sort of monitoring? First, because regulations limit banks' ability to hold shares, they cannot freely use equity to fund projects. Though several papers focus on monitoring by banks (James 1987; Petersen and Rajan 1994, 1995; Hoshi, Kashyap, and Scharfstein 1991), banks may not have the necessary skills to evaluate projects with few collateralizable assets and significant uncertainty. In addition, Petersen and Rajan (1995) argue that banks in competitive markets will be unable to finance high-risk projects because they are unable to charge borrowers rates high

---

1. By way of contrast, in Jensen and Murphy's (1990) examination of a large set of public companies, the typical sensitivity of pay for performance is quite low. Typically, a CEO's personal wealth increases by only a dollar or two for each $1000 increase in firm value. This may either reflect the diminished need for incentive compensation in this setting for the presence of agency problems.

enough to compensate for the firm's riskiness. Taking an equity position in the firm allows the venture capitalist to proportionately share in the upside, guaranteeing that the venture capitalist benefits if the firm does well. Finally, venture capital funds' high-powered compensation schemes examined in chapter 4 give venture capitalists incentives to monitor firms more closely because their individual compensation is closely linked to the funds' returns.

An Overview of Part II

The three chapters that follow examine the various roles played by venture capitalists in addressing these problems. Although they are not intended to be an exhaustive catalog of the interactions between venture capitalists and entrepreneurs, the chapters highlight the diversity and flexibility of the venture capitalist's role.[2]

Chapter 7 examines the staging of venture capital investments. The research on conflicts among investors and managers discussed above suggests several factors that should affect the duration and size of venture capital investments. Venture capitalists should weigh potential agency and monitoring costs when determining how frequently they should reevaluate projects and supply capital. The duration of funding should decline and the frequency of reevaluation should increase when the venture capitalist expects that conflicts with the entrepreneur are more likely. The nature of the firm's assets also has important implications for expected agency costs and the structure of staged venture capital investments. Intangible assets should be associated with greater agency problems. As assets become more tangible, venture capitalists can recover more of their investment in liquidation. This reduces the need to monitor tightly and should increase the time between refinancings. Industries with high levels of R&D should also have more frequent agency problems, and venture capitalists should shorten funding duration. Finally, a substantial finance literature argues that firms with high market-to-book ratios are more susceptible to these agency costs, thus venture capitalists should increase the intensity of monitoring of these firms.

These predictions are tested using a random sample of 794 venture capital-financed companies. The results confirm the predictions of agency theory. Venture capitalists concentrate investments in early stage com-

---

2. While Part II of this volume will focus on the venture investment process, we will also highlight the interconnections with other parts of the venture cycle. The strength of the fundraising environment and the characteristics of the public markets at the time will affect how the venture capitalists deploy their assets.

panies and high technology industries where informational asymmetries are significant and monitoring is valuable. Venture capitalists monitor the firm's progress. If they learn negative information about future returns, the project is cut off from new financing. Firms that go public (these firms yield the highest return for venture capitalists on average) receive more total financing, and a greater number of rounds than other firms (which may go bankrupt, be acquired, or remain private). Early stage firms receive significantly less money per round. Increases in asset tangibility increase financing duration and reduce monitoring intensity. As the role of future investment opportunities in firm value increases (higher market-to-book ratios or R&D intensities), firms are refinanced more frequently. These results suggest the important monitoring and information-generating roles played by venture capitalists.

The advice and oversight provided by venture capitalists is often embodied by their role on the firm's board of directors. Chapter 8 analyzes the decision of venture capitalists to provide this oversight. It examines whether venture capitalists' representation on the boards of the private firms in their portfolios is greater when the need for oversight is larger. This approach is suggested by Fama and Jensen (1983) and Williamson (1983), who hypothesize that the composition of the board should be shaped by the need for oversight. These authors argue that the board will bear greater responsibility for oversight—and consequently that outsiders should have greater representation—when the danger of managerial deviations from value maximization is high. If venture capitalists are especially important providers of managerial oversight, their representation on boards should be more extensive at times when the need for oversight is greater.

Chapter 8 also examines changes in board membership around the time that a firm's chief executive officer (CEO) is replaced, an approach suggested by Hermalin and Weisbach's (1988) study of outside directors of public firms. The replacement of the top manager at an entrepreneurial firm is likely to coincide with an organizational crisis and to heighten the need for monitoring. An average of 1.75 venture capitalists are added to the board between financing rounds when the firm's CEO is replaced in the interval; between other rounds, 0.24 venture directors are added. No differences are found in the addition of other outside directors. This oversight of new firms involves substantial costs. The transaction costs associated with frequent visits and intensive involvement are likely to be reduced if the venture capitalist is proximate to the firms in a portfolio. Consistent with these suggestions, geographic proximity is an important determinant of venture board membership: organizations with offices within five miles of the firm's headquarters are twice as likely to be board members as those more than 500 miles distant. Over half the firms in the sample have a venture director with an office within sixty miles of their headquarters.

Venture capitalists will usually make investments with other investors. One venture firm will originate the deal and look to bring in other venture capital firms. This syndication serves multiple purposes. First, it allows the venture capital firm to diversify its portfolio, thereby reducing the exposure to any single investment. If the venture capitalist were the sole investor in all the companies in a portfolio, then many fewer investments could be made. By syndicating investments, the venture capitalist can invest in more projects and diversify away some of the firm-specific risk.

For example, a venture capital firm may raise a fund of $100 million. In any one particular round, a portfolio company receives between $2 and $5 million. If the typical venture-backed company receives four rounds of venture financing, any one firm might require between $10 and $20 million of financing. If the venture capital firm originating the deal were to make the entire investment, the fund could only make five to ten investments. Hence, the value of bringing in syndication partners for diversification is large.

A second potential explanation for syndication patterns is that involving other venture firms provides a second opinion on the investment opportunity. There is usually no clear-cut answer as to whether any of the investments that a venture organization undertakes will yield attractive returns. Having other investors approve the deal limits the danger that bad deals will get funded. This is particularly true when the company is early stage or technology-based.

Chapter 9 tests this "second opinion" hypothesis in a sample of biotechnology venture capital investments. In the early rounds of investing, experienced venture capitalists tend to syndicate only with venture capital firms that have similar experience. The analysis argues that if venture capitalists were looking for a second opinion, then they would want to get a second opinion from someone of similar or better ability, certainly not from someone of lesser ability.

A Caveat

The research presented in part II highlights the ways in which venture capitalists can successfully address agency problems in portfolio firms. As discussed in chapters 1 and 2, however, the venture industry appears to have gone through periods when there were dramatic shifts in the supply of capital available from institutional and individual investors and the demand from entrepreneurs. These shifts appear to affect not only the terms of venture capital partnerships, but also the investments made by these funds. Understanding the venture cycle requires an understanding of the linkages among the various stages. The fundraising environment and the terms and conditions of venture partnerships can have profound effects on the efficiency of venture investing.

While discussions of these issues have appeared in the trade press since at least the 1960s, the first extended discussion was in Sahlman and Stevenson (1986). The authors chronicle the exploits of venture capitalists in the Winchester disk drive industry during the early 1980s. Sahlman and Stevenson assert that a type of "market myopia" affected venture capital investing in the industry. During the late 1970s and early 1980s, nineteen disk drive companies received venture capital financing. Two-thirds of these investments came between 1982 and 1984, the period of rapid expansion of the venture industry. Many disk drive companies also went public during this period. While industry growth was rapid during this period (sales increased from $27 million in 1978 to $1.3 billion in 1983), Sahlman and Stevenson question whether the scale of investment was rational given any reasonable expectations of industry growth and future economic trends.[3] Similar stories are often told concerning investments in software, biotechnology, and the Internet. The phrase "too much money chasing too few deals" is a common refrain in the venture capital market during periods of rapid growth.

We systematically examine one facet of these claims through a data set of over 4,000 venture investments between 1987 and 1995 developed by the consulting firm VentureOne (Gompers and Lerner 1997a). We construct a price index that controls for various firm attributes that might affect firm valuation, including firm age, stage of development, and industry, as well as macroeconomic variables such as inflow of funds into the venture capital industry. In addition, we control for public market valuations through indexes of public market values for firms in the same industries and average book-to-market and earnings-to-price ratios.

---

3. Lerner (1997) suggests, however, that these firms may have displayed behavior consistent with strategic models of "technology races" in the economics literature. Because firms had the option to exit the competition to develop a new disk drive, it may have indeed been rational for venture capitalists to fund a substantial number of disk drive manufacturers.

The results support contentions that a strong relation exists between the valuation of venture capital investments and capital inflows. While other variables also have significant explanatory power—for instance, the marginal impact of a doubling in public market values was between a 15 and 35 percent increase in the valuation of private equity transactions—the inflows variable is significantly positive. A doubling of inflows into venture funds leads to between a 7 and 21 percent increase in valuation levels.

These regression coefficients can be used to construct a price index, which controls for the shifting mixture of venture capital investments. Although prices rose somewhat in 1987, they declined and remained quite flat through the 1990s. Starting in 1994, however, prices steadily increased. This increase coincided with the rise in venture fundraising. The regression results show that this rise in fundraising is an important source of the increase in prices.

The results are particularly strong for specific types of funds and funds in particular regions. Because funds have become larger in real dollar terms, with more capital per partner, many venture capital organizations have invested larger amounts of money in each portfolio company. Firms have attempted to do this in two ways. First, there has been a movement to finance later stage companies that can accept larger blocks of financing. Second, venture firms are syndicating less. This leads to greater competition for making later stage investments. Similarly, because the majority of money is raised in California and Massachusetts, competition for deals in these regions should be particularly intense and venture capital inflows may have a more dramatic effect on prices in those regions. The results support these contentions. The effect of venture capital inflows is significantly more dramatic on later stage investments and investments in California and Massachusetts.

We also examine whether increases in venture capital inflows and valuations simultaneously reflect improvements in the environment for young firms. If shifts in the supply of venture capital are contemporaneous with changes in the demand for capital, the inferences may be biased. Success rates—whether measured through the completion of an initial public offering or an acquisition at an attractive price—did not differ significantly between investments made during the early 1990s, a period of relatively low inflows and valuations, and those of the boom years of the late 1980s. The results appear to indicate that the price increases reflect increasing competition for investment.

Thus, it appears that interactions among venture capitalists and entrepreneurs are subject to the same kind of disequilibria and pressures that have been discussed in part I (and will be discussed in part III). These pressures may affect the returns that venture capitalists and their investors benefit.

On a more speculative level, it may be possible that the tremendous concentration of the firms backed by venture capitalists is also problematic in terms of social welfare. Several models argue that institutional investors frequently engage in "herding", making investments that are too similar to one another. These models suggest that a variety of factors—for instance, when performance is assessed on a relative, not an absolute, basis—can lead to investors obtaining poor performance by making too similar investments. (Much of the theoretical literature is reviewed in Devenow and Welch 1996.) As a result, social welfare may suffer because value-creating investments in less popular technological areas may have been ignored.

Final Thoughts

The discussion above raises an important—and as yet unanswered—question: the real impact of venture capital on the economy. A key motivation for policymakers abroad, seeking to emulate the U.S. model, is the perception that venture capital organizations are a key factor in the rising leadership of U.S. firms in high-technology industries, whether measured through patent counts or more qualitative measures. Demonstrating a casual relationship between innovation and job growth on the one hand and the presence of venture capital investment on the other is, however, a challenging empirical problem.[4] To what extent are the mechanisms described above uniquely suited to addressing the needs of entrepreneurial high-technology firms? To what extent is venture capital just one of many financing alternatives for these firms, with its own set of strengths and limitations? This topic will reward creative researchers in the years to come.

---

4. Preliminary evidence in support of this claim can be found in Chapter 14, as well as in Hellmann and Puri (1998) and Kortum and Lerner (1998). Many research opportunities remain, however, in this arena.

7   Why Are Investments Staged?

Staged capital infusions are the most potent control mechanism a venture capitalist can employ. Prospects for the firm are periodically reevaluated. The shorter the duration of an individual round of financing, the more frequently the venture capitalist monitors the entrepreneur's progress and the greater the need to gather information. The role of staged capital infusion is analogous to that of debt in highly leveraged transactions, keeping the owner/manager on a "tight leash" and reducing potential losses from bad decisions.

This chapter examines the staging of capital infusions by venture capitalists. It explores not only how these investments are structured but also why this approach is employed. The evidence indicates that the staging of capital infusions allows venture capitalists to gather information and monitor the progress of firms, maintaining the option to abandon projects periodically.

This chapter develops predictions from agency theory that shed light on factors affecting the duration and size of venture capital investments. Venture capitalists weigh potential agency and monitoring costs when determining how frequently they should reevaluate projects and supply capital. Venture capitalists are concerned that entrepreneurs' private benefits from certain investments or strategies may not be perfectly correlated with shareholders' monetary return. Because monitoring is costly and cannot be performed continuously, the venture capitalist will periodically check the project's status and preserve the option to abandon. The duration of funding and hence the intensity of monitoring should be negatively related to expected agency costs. Agency costs increase as the tangibility of assets declines, the share of growth options in firm value rises, and asset specificity grows.

This chapter examines a random sample of 794 venture capital-financed companies. The results confirm the predictions of agency theory. Venture capitalists concentrate investments in early-stage companies and high-technology industries where informational asymmetries are significant and monitoring is valuable. Venture capitalists monitor the firm's progress and if they learn negative information about future returns, the project should be cut off from new financing. Firms that go public (these firms yield the highest return for venture capitalists on average) receive more total financing and a greater number of rounds than other firms (those that go bankrupt or are acquired). Early-stage firms also receive significantly less money per round. Increases in asset tangibility increase financing duration and reduce monitoring intensity. As the role of future investment opportunities in firm value increases (higher market-to-book ratios), duration declines. Similarly, higher R&D intensities lead to shorter funding durations.

Chapter 7 also provides evidence about the relationship between investment and liquidity in the venture capital market. In periods when venture capitalists are able to raise more capital for new investments, they invest more money per round and more frequently in the firms they finance. Greater commitments to new venture capital funds may measure entry of new, inexperienced venture capitalists or free cash-flow agency costs.

The chapter is organized as follows. The next section presents predictions about factors that should affect the structure of staged capital infusions. Factors affecting the staging of venture capital investments are analyzed in the third section. The fourth section examines alternative explanations, and the fifth section concludes the chapter.

Factors Affecting the Structure of Staged Venture Capital Investments

Agency and Monitoring Costs

Venture capitalists claim that the information they generate and the services they provide for portfolio companies are as important as the capital infused. Many entrepreneurs believe that venture capitalists provide little more than money. If the monitoring provided by venture capitalists is valuable, certain predictions can be made about the structure of staged capital infusions.

If monitoring and information gathering are important, venture capitalists should invest in firms in which asymmetric information is likely to be a problem. The value of oversight will be greater for these firms. Early-stage companies have short or no histories to examine and are difficult to evaluate. Similarly, firms in industries with significant growth opportunities and high R&D intensities are likely to require close monitoring. A significant fraction of venture investment should therefore be directed toward early-stage and high-technology companies.

Total venture financing and the number of financing rounds should also be higher for successful projects than for failures if venture capitalists utilize information in investment decisions. Venture capitalists monitor a firm's progress and discontinue funding the project if they learn negative information about future prospects. Firms going public—which, as discussed in chapter 2, yield the highest return for venture investors—should thus receive greater total funding and more rounds of financing than firms that are acquired or liquidated.

The positive relationship between going public and level of investment is not obvious unless venture capitalists use information during the investment process. If venture capitalists only provide capital, firms that go public might quickly turn profitable and would need less venture capital financing and fewer rounds than companies that are acquired or liquidated.

If asymmetric information and agency costs do not exist, the structure of financing is irrelevant. As Hart (1993) points out, if entrepreneurs pursue shareholder value-maximizing strategies, financing is simple. Venture capitalists would give entrepreneurs all the money they need and entrepreneurs would decide whether to continue the project based on their information. In the case of start-ups, entrepreneurs would derive stopping rules that maximized shareholder value using methods described in Roberts and Weitzman (1981) and Weitzman, Newey, and Rabin (1981). Based on their private information, they would decide whether to continue the project or not.

The private benefits from managing the firms they create, however, may not always be perfectly correlated with shareholders' monetary returns. Entrepreneurs may have incentives to continue running projects they know have negative net present value (NPV). Similarly, entrepreneurs may invest in projects that have high personal benefits but low monetary returns for investors. If venture capitalists could costlessly monitor the firm, they would monitor and infuse cash continuously. If the firm's expected NPV fell below the stopping point, the venture capitalist would halt funding the project.

In practice, venture capitalists incur costs when they monitor and infuse capital. Monitoring costs include the opportunity cost of generating reports for both the venture capitalist and entrepreneur. If venture capitalists need to "kick the tires" of the plant, read reports, and take time away from other activities, these costs can be substantial. Contracting costs and the lost time and resources of the entrepreneur must be imputed as well. Each time capital is infused, contracts are written and negotiated, lawyers are paid, and other associated costs are incurred. These costs mean that funding will occur in discrete stages.

Two well-known companies illustrate how venture capitalists use staged investment to periodically evaluate a firm's progress. Apple Computer received three rounds of venture capital financing. In the first round, venture capitalists invested $518,000 in January 1978 at a price of $0.09 per share. The company was doing well by the second round of venture financing in September 1978. Venture investors committed an additional $704,000 at a price of $0.28 per share, reflecting the progress the firm had made. A final venture capital infusion of $2.331 million was made in December 1980 at $0.97 per share. At each stage, the increasing price per share and the growing investment reflected resolution of uncertainty concerning Apple's prospects.

Federal Express represents a second example of how venture capitalists utilize staged capital infusions to monitor the firm. Federal Express also received three rounds of venture capital financing, but the firm's prospects developed in a much different manner. The first venture financing round occurred in September 1973 when $12.25 million was invested at a price of $204.17 per share. The firm's performance was well below expectations and a second venture financing round was necessary in March 1974. $6.4 million was invested at $7.34 per share, reflecting the poor performance of the company. Performance continued to deteriorate and a third round of financing was needed in September 1974. At this stage, the venture capital investors intervened extensively in the strategy of the company. The $3.88 million investment was priced at $0.63 per share. Ultimately, performance improved and Federal Express went public in 1978 at $6 per share, but the staged investment of the venture capitalist allowed the venture investors to intervene and price subsequent rounds so they could earn a fair rate of return.

Two related types of agency costs exist in entrepreneurial firms. First, entrepreneurs might invest in strategies, research, or projects that have high personal returns but low expected monetary payoffs to shareholders. For example, a biotechnology company founder may choose to invest in a certain type of research that brings great recognition in the scientific community but provides less return for the venture capitalist than other projects. Similarly, because entrepreneurs' equity stakes are essentially call options,[1] they have incentives to pursue high-variance strategies like rushing a product to market when further testing may be warranted.

Second, if the entrepreneur possesses private information and chooses to continue investing in a negative NPV project, the entrepreneur is undertaking inefficient continuation. For example, managers may receive initial results from market trials indicating little demand for a new product, but entrepreneurs may want to keep the company going because they receive significant private benefits from managing their own firm.

The nature of the firm's assets may have important implications for expected agency costs and the structure of staged venture capital investments. The capital structure literature motivates a search for those factors. Much of this literature (see Harris and Raviv 1991) has emphasized the role of agency costs in determining leverage. Asset characteristics that increase expected agency costs of debt reduce leverage and make monitoring more valuable. Therefore, factors reducing leverage should shorten funding duration in venture capital transactions.

Williamson (1988) argues that leverage should be positively related to the liquidation value of assets. Higher liquidation values imply that default is less costly. Liquidation value is positively related to the tangibility of assets because tangible assets (e.g., machines and plants) are on average easier to sell and receive a higher fraction of their book value than are intangible assets like patents or copyrights. In empirical research on capital structure, many researchers, including Titman and Wessels (1988), Friend and Lang (1988), and Rajan and Zingales (1995), use the ratio of tangible assets to total assets as a measure of liquidation value. All find that use of debt increases with asset tangibility.

In the context of staged venture capital investments, intangible assets would be associated with greater agency costs. As assets become more tangible, venture capitalists can recover more of their investment in liquidation, and expected losses due to inefficient continuation are reduced. This reduces the need to monitor tightly and should increase funding duration.

Shleifer and Vishny (1992) extend Williamson's model by examining how asset specificity might affect liquidation value and debt levels. They show that firms with assets that are highly industry- and firm-specific

---

1. The entrepreneurs' equity stakes are almost always junior to the preferred equity position of venture capital investors. The seniority of the venture capitalists' stake makes the entrepreneur's payoff analogous to levered equity, hence it is also equivalent to a call option. Similarly, if the firm is doing poorly and the option is "out of the money," entrepreneurs may have incentives to increase risk substantially.

would use less debt because asset specificity significantly reduces liquidation value. Firms that have high R&D intensities are likely to generate assets that are very firm- and industry-specific. Bradley, Jarrell, and Kim (1984) and Titman and Wessels (1988) use the ratio of R&D to sales to measure uniqueness of assets in investigating the use of debt. Both find a negative relationship between leverage and R&D intensity. Similarly, Barclay and Smith (1995) utilize the ratio of R&D to firm value to explore debt maturity.

Asset specificity would also influence the structure of staged venture capital investments. Industries with high levels of R&D intensity would be subject to greater discretionary investment by the entrepreneur and increase risks associated with firm- and industry-specific assets. These factors increase expected agency costs and shorten funding durations.

Finally, Myers (1977) argues that firms whose value largely depends on investment in future growth options would make less use of debt because the owner/manager can undertake investment strategies that are particularly detrimental to bondholders. Myers suggests that a firm's market-to-book ratio may be related to the fraction of firm value that is comprised of future growth opportunities. Empirical results support this prediction. Rajan and Zingales (1995) find a negative relationship between firm market-to-book ratios and leverage. Similarly, Barclay and Smith (1995) find that debt maturity declines with a firm's market-to-book ratio.

Entrepreneurs have more discretion to invest in personally beneficial strategies at shareholders' expense in industries where firm value largely depends on future growth opportunities. Firms with high market-to-book ratios are more susceptible to these agency costs, thus increasing the value of monitoring and reducing funding duration.

Venture Capital, Liquidity, and Investment

The growth of inflows to new venture capital funds may also have effects on the structure of investment. As discussed in the introduction, the venture capital industry has gone through several fundraising cycles. During periods of low fundraising, venture capitalists might be liquidity constrained. Liquidity constraints and their effects on investment have been examined in several contexts (Fazzari, Hubbard, and Petersen 1988; Hoshi, Kashyap, and Scharfstein 1991; Petersen and Rajan 1994). Venture capitalists would like to make more and bigger investments (which are positive NPV), but they are unable to raise enough money to invest in all of these projects. If constraints restrict investment, greater commitments to new funds lead venture capitalists to invest more money per round and to invest more often.

Free cash-flow theory (Jensen 1986) also predicts that increases in commitments to venture capital funds would lead to larger investments and shorter time between investments. Venture capitalists would try to put the increased level of commitments to use. Free cash-flow agency costs have been documented by Blanchard, Lopez de Silanes, and Shleifer (1994), who provide evidence that cash windfalls adversely affect companies' investment behavior. Lawsuit winners appear to invest in bad projects rather than give cash to shareholders. If free cash-flow problems affect venture capitalists, more frequent and larger investment implies venture capitalists may be overinvesting.

Similarly, growth of the venture capital pool may measure entry by inexperienced venture capitalists. These new entrants may overinvest and may not monitor companies as effectively as experienced venture capitalists. As in the case of free cash-flow agency costs, the increase in investment is excessive.

The Structure of Staged Investment

Summary Information and Statistics

A random sample[2] of 794 firms that received venture capital financing between January 1961 and July 1992 was gathered from the Venture Economics' Venture Intelligence Database (described in chapter 16). The firms were included in the sample if their first round of venture capital financing occurred prior to January 1, 1990.[3] This chapter utilizes a database of venture capital funds compiled by Venture Economics' Investors

2. The random sample was generated as follows: at the time the data were collected, approximately 7,000 firms were contained in the Venture Economics database. Each firm is given a number from 1 to 7,000 by Venture Economics. Then 800 unique random numbers were generated from 1 to 7,000 in a spreadsheet. These 800 numbers were used as firm reference numbers. Six firms were eliminated from the final sample because their data were suspect. The six firms had venture financing dates that were more than ten years apart. Apparently, for each of these six entries two firms with the same name had been venture financed and their records merged.

3. The current status of each firm was verified with Lexis/Nexis databases. COMPNY and NEWS databases were searched for all records concerning the firms. If no news stories or legal filings were found, the firm was assumed to be private. The data are limited in several respects. First, it is unclear how well each company is doing at each round of financing. Second, the data do not have information on other types of financing that the firms receive.

Services Group (described in chapter 16) to collect annual information on total venture capital funds under management, new capital commitments to the industry, and the amount of venture capital invested.

Because accounting data for private firms is unavailable, annual Standard Industrial Codes (SIC) industry averages from COMPUSTAT for each firm that received venture capital financing is used to control for industry effects. If the four-digit SIC group had fewer than four companies, the three-digit industry was used. Similarly, if the three-digit group had fewer than four companies, the two-digit SIC group averages is used. Variables were collected to calculate various measures of asset tangibility (the ratio of tangible assets to total assets), growth opportunities (market value of equity to book value), and research intensity (either the ratio of R&D expenditures to total assets or R&D expenditures to sales). The data were matched by date and industry to each firm and each round of financing. The inflation rate and real return on treasury bills and common stocks were collected for each month from 1961 to 1992 from Ibbotson Associates.

Table 7.1 provides summary information on the dates and amounts of total venture capital financing for the 794 firms. These 794 firms received 2,143 individual rounds of venture capital financing and represent roughly 15 percent of all venture capital over this period.[4] The coverage of the data appears to be better for the latter half of the sample period. This may reflect increasing completeness of the Venture Economics database over time.

Table 7.2 looks at the distribution of investments across various industries by the percentage of rounds invested. Industry trends can be discerned. Computer firms received significant amounts of financing from 1982 to 1984, but investment subsequently declined. After the oil embargoes of the 1970s, energy-related investments were popular, but these declined substantially after the early 1980s when domestic exploration declined. On the other hand, medical and health-related firms have been receiving increasing attention from venture capitalists.

What is evident from the industry results, however, is the focus on high-technology firms (e.g., communication, computers, electronics, biotechnology, and medical/health). The percentage of venture capital invested in high-technology firms never falls below 70 percent of annual investments. For firms in the sample, the average industry ratio of R&D to

---

4. The sample represents slightly more that 15 percent because certain data on financing amounts were missing.

Table 7.1
Time series of random sample from the Venture Economics database. The sample is
794 randomly selected companies from the set of firms that received their first venture capital investment prior to January 1, 1990. The table shows the number of rounds, total amount
invested, and the number of new firms in each year in the sample of random firms. Amount
of known investment is in thousands of 1997 dollars.

Year	Rounds of venture capital financing	Amount of venture capital investment	Number of new firms receiving venture capital
1961	1	$318	1
1962	1	$227	1
1968	1	$284	1
1969	3	$2,423	2
1970	6	$2,168	4
1971	8	$2,561	4
1972	4	$2,803	1
1973	9	$22,055	6
1974	9	$18,591	1
1975	14	$12,227	9
1976	17	$20,623	9
1977	23	$10,285	12
1978	35	$20,122	24
1979	44	$73,517	30
1980	55	$39,025	30
1981	77	$129,125	50
1982	126	$204,211	64
1983	170	$431,931	82
1984	208	$588,251	84
1985	179	$587,161	66
1986	204	$549,667	95
1987	219	$493,567	60
1988	225	$674,393	85
1989	234	$475,382	67
1990	142	$179,044	0
1991	109	$162,127	0
1992	16	$48,533	0

Table 7.2
Percentage of investment by industry and stage of development in each year. Data are 2143 financing rounds for a random sample of 794 venture capital-backed firms. Panel A shows the industry composition of venture investments in the sample through time. Industry classifications are reported by Venture Economics. Panel B shows how the stage of firm development for venture investments varies in the sample. Early-stage investments are seed, startup, early, first, and other early-stage investments. Late-stage financing is second, third, or bridge stage investments.

Panel A: Percentage of rounds invested by industry.

Industry	Year 1975	1976	1977	1978	1979	1980	1981	1982	1983	1984	1985	1986	1987	1988	1989
Communications	28.6	23.5	18.2	8.6	18.2	11.1	13.3	12.9	14.9	13.3	12.4	12.3	11.9	12.0	11.5
Computers	0.0	0.0	0.0	2.9	2.3	3.7	4.0	8.9	10.1	10.1	6.2	3.9	4.6	4.4	1.3
Computer related	0.0	5.9	4.5	11.4	15.9	11.1	13.3	21.8	19.6	16.1	17.5	14.2	14.2	11.1	15.8
Computer software	7.1	0.0	0.0	0.0	0.0	0.0	6.7	10.5	13.7	9.6	14.7	13.2	11.4	9.3	11.1
Electronic components	0.0	0.0	4.5	0.0	2.3	5.6	2.7	0.8	3.6	3.2	4.5	3.4	4.6	3.6	3.0
Other electronics	28.6	35.3	4.5	2.9	4.5	11.1	10.7	8.9	3.6	7.8	6.8	4.4	4.1	4.9	5.6
Biotechnology	7.1	0.0	0.0	2.9	6.8	3.7	2.7	5.6	3.6	3.7	1.1	4.4	5.0	6.7	6.4
Medical/health	0.0	0.0	9.1	20.0	4.5	9.3	2.7	6.5	10.1	11.0	16.4	13.2	14.6	15.6	12.0
Energy	14.3	0.0	31.8	5.7	6.8	7.4	4.0	3.2	3.0	0.0	0.6	1.5	0.5	1.3	0.9
Consumer products	0.0	11.8	4.5	17.1	13.6	18.5	10.7	4.8	6.0	11.9	9.6	9.3	11.4	15.1	13.7
Industrial products	7.1	17.6	4.5	14.3	9.1	9.3	17.3	9.7	4.2	6.0	4.0	7.8	7.8	9.8	8.5
Transportation	0.0	0.0	18.2	0.0	4.5	0.0	1.3	2.4	0.6	0.9	0.6	2.0	0.9	1.8	0.0
Other	7.1	5.9	0.0	14.3	11.4	9.3	10.7	4.0	7.1	6.4	5.6	10.3	9.1	4.4	10.3

Panel B: Percentage of rounds invested by stage of development

Stage	Year 1975	1976	1977	1978	1979	1980	1981	1982	1983	1984	1985	1986	1987	1988	1989
Early stage	69.2	92.9	85.7	63.3	70.6	66.7	52.3	59.5	54.9	55.3	47.7	43.1	39.7	40.0	34.5
Late stage	30.8	7.1	14.3	36.7	29.4	33.3	47.7	40.5	45.1	44.7	52.3	56.9	60.3	60.0	65.5

sales is 3.43 percent (median 3.82 percent). The average for all COM-
PUSTAT industries during the time period 1972–1992 was 1.30 percent
(median 2.66 percent). Asymmetric information and agency costs are a
major concern in R&D-intensive firms, which may require specialized
knowledge to monitor. Industry investment composition suggests that
venture capitalists specialize in industries in which monitoring and information evaluation are important.

Table 7.2 also examines the distribution of investment by stage.
(Rounds are classified as early stage if the investment is seed, startup, or
early stage. The investment is classified as late stage if it is expansion,
second, third, or bridge financing.) The table documents the relative
decline in early-stage financing and the growing importance of later stage
investments. This trend reflects the effects of a maturing industry. While
the venture capital industry was growing rapidly in the early 1980s, more
investment went to early-stage companies. As the industry matured, the
investment mix reflected previous investments. Early-stage investments in
the mid-1980s became late-stage investments in the late 1980s. Even with
the decline, a substantial fraction of investment is in early-stage companies where monitoring is important.

The distribution of outcomes for firms that received venture capital
financing is examined in table 7.3. Firms can go public (IPO), undergo a
merger or acquisition, file for bankruptcy, or remain private as of July 31,
1992. In table 7.3, only those firms that had not received a venture capital
infusion since January 1, 1988, are classified as venture-backed firms that
remain private. Other firms may yet receive another venture capital investment or may achieve some other exit (e.g., IPO, merger, etc.) While
this measure is imprecise, and it is impossible to be certain of the eventual
status of all projects, the present classification gives some indication of
relative outcomes. Such a determination is critical if research is to determine how investment structure affects a firm's success.

Table 7.3 shows that in the entire sample 22.5 percent of the firms go
public, 23.8 percent merge or are acquired, 15.6 percent are liquidated or
go bankrupt, and 38.1 percent remain private. In transportation, biotechnology, and medical/health, the proportion of firms that go public is
quite high. This may reflect either the relative success of companies in this
industry or their need for large capital infusions that an IPO provides. In
electronic components, industrial products, and other (services), the proportion of IPOs is quite low and many more firms remain private. These
results may understate the proportion of liquidations, however. First,
some of the acquisitions/mergers may be distressed firms that provide

Table 7.3
Outcomes for 794 venture capital-backed firms by industry. The number of firms that had performed an initial public offering, merged, went bankrupt, or remained private as of July 31, 1992. The first column is firms that went public. The second column is all firms that were acquired or merged with another company. The third column is all firms that filed for bankruptcy. The fourth column is all firms that are still private and have not received venture capital financing since January 1, 1988. Percentage of outcome classification for each industry are in parentheses.

Industry	IPOs	Mergers/ acquisitions	Liquidations/ bankruptcies	Private
Communications	17 (24.6)	17 (24.6)	9 (13.0)	26 (37.7)
Computers	5 (20.0)	7 (28.0)	9 (36.0)	4 (16.0)
Computer related	20 (29.0)	19 (27.5)	15 (21.7)	15 (21.7)
Computer software	11 (21.6)	9 (17.6)	11 (21.6)	20 (39.2)
Electronic components	2 (11.8)	6 (35.3)	0 (0.0)	9 (52.9)
Other electronics	6 (20.0)	9 (30.0)	6 (20.0)	9 (30.0)
Biotechnology	9 (50.0)	5 (27.8)	2 (11.1)	2 (11.1)
Medical/health	17 (30.4)	17 (30.4)	12 (21.4)	10 (17.9)
Energy	4 (20.0)	3 (15.0)	2 (10.0)	11 (55.0)
Consumer products	19 (27.9)	10 (14.7)	6 (8.8)	33 (48.5)
Industrial products	4 (7.0)	20 (35.1)	6 (10.5)	27 (47.4)
Transportation	5 (41.7)	2 (16.7)	1 (8.3)	4 (33.3)
Other	8 (11.1)	10 (13.9)	9 (12.5)	45 (62.5)
Total	127 (22.5)	134 (23.8)	88 (15.6)	215 (38.1)

little more than physical assets to their acquirer.[5] The return to the venture capitalist from these firms would be very low. Similarly, a number of the firms classified as private may have been liquidated, but no record of the event could be located. Firms without any debt would have no need to file for bankruptcy.

Funding statistics by industry and outcome are presented in table 7.4. Average total funding received, number of rounds, and age at first funding show considerable variability across industries. High-technology ventures receive more rounds and greater total financing than low-technology ventures. The four industries with the highest total funding per firm are communications, computers, computer related, and biotechnology. Four of the five industries with lowest total funding per firm are energy, industrial products, transportation, and other (primarily services). A firm's age at first funding does not appear to follow any clear pattern even though one might think that high-technology companies need access to venture capital soon after incorporation. Biotechnology, electronic components, and medical/health companies are relatively young. Firms in computers, consumer products, and transportation are substantially older on average. Most firms are not start-ups; they are typically well over one year old when they receive their first venture capital infusion. These firms received other funding (personal, "angel," or bank financing) prior to receiving venture capital.

Table 7.4 also stratifies funding data by outcome. Examining the structure of funding by outcome can determine whether venture capitalists periodically evaluate a firm's prospects. The total amount and number of rounds of financing are greater for the sample of IPO firms than for either the entire sample or the subsamples that go bankrupt or are acquired/merged. The data indicate that venture capitalists stage capital infusions to gather information and monitor the progress of firms they finance. New information is useful in determining whether or not the venture capitalist should continue financing the project. Promising firms receive new financing while others either are liquidated or find a corporate acquirer to manage the assets of the firm.

The Duration and Size of Financing Rounds

The analysis in this section classifies each financing according to the company's stage of development at the time of financing as reported by Ven-

---

5. Initial public offerings and acquisitions may also be viewed as one large financing round. Examining the amount of venture capital invested classifying firms by outcome is still important for understanding the venture capitalists' return.

Table 7.4
Number of investments, age at first funding, and total funding received by industry and outcome.
The sample is 794 venture capital-backed firms randomly selected from the Venture Economics database. The number of rounds, age at first funding, and total venture capital financing (in constant 1997 dollars) are tabulated for various industries and various outcomes. Firms can either go public in an IPO, go bankrupt, or be acquired. Average total funding is in thousands of dollars. Average age at first funding is in years. Median values are in parentheses.

Industry	Number of rounds				Age at first funding			
	Full	IPO	Bankrupt	Acquired	Full	IPO	Bankrupt	Acquired
Communications	2.78	3.41	2.44	2.47	3.46	3.29	2.56	5.11
	(2)	(2)	(2)	(2)	(0.92)	(1.34)	(1.87)	(1.34)
Computers	3.89	4.60	4.33	3.42	4.19	1.11	2.75	2.30
	(3)	(6)	(4)	(3)	(1.33)	(0.17)	(1.84)	(1.29)
Computer related	3.66	4.00	3.47	3.32	4.29	3.74	4.10	4.10
	(3)	(4)	(2)	(3)	(1.88)	(1.67)	(2.75)	(2.75)
Computer software	2.99	2.91	2.00	3.22	3.59	3.83	4.30	4.30
	(3)	(2)	(1)	(3)	(1.92)	(3.67)	(2.59)	(2.59)
Electronic components	3.27	4.00	na	3.50	0.86	0.53	na	0.77
	(2)	(4)		(3.5)	(0.00)	(0.53)		(0.00)
Other electronics	3.21	2.50	3.50	2.78	3.45	2.54	5.67	5.46
	(2)	(2)	(2.5)	(2)	(2.38)	(3.17)	(3.00)	(3.92)
Biotechnology	3.69	3.56	4.00	4.60	1.21	0.89	0.37	2.08
	(4)	(3)	(4)	(4)	(0.71)	(0.50)	(0.37)	(2.00)
Medical/health	2.98	3.94	1.91	2.53	1.97	2.30	0.58	1.59
	(2)	(3)	(1)	(2)	(1.00)	(1.41)	(0.12)	(0.71)
Energy	1.91	2.25	2.00	1.67	2.85	7.01	2.13	2.00
	(1)	(2)	(2)	(1)	(2.00)	(5.17)	(2.13)	(2.00)
Consumer products	2.14	2.16	2.33	1.20	5.90	7.63	0.98	17.92
	(1)	(2)	(2)	(1)	(1.67)	(4.41)	(0.75)	(17.35)
Industrial products	2.09	3.75	2.17	1.65	3.79	5.94	18.97	4.66
	(1)	(2)	(1.5)	(1)	(2.25)	(6.38)	(10.46)	(2.46)
Transportation	1.93	2.00	2.00	2.50	6.33	15.84	na	9.09
	(2)	(2)	(2)	(2.5)	(5.67)	(5.27)		(9.09)
Other	1.60	1.63	1.78	1.80	5.83	12.48	1.00	10.11
	(1)	(1)	(1)	(1)	(2.25)	(3.17)	(0.46)	(5.96)

Table 7.4 (continued)

Industry	Total Funding				Number of Firms			
	Full	IPO	Bankrupt	Acquired	Full	IPO	Bankrupt	Acquired
Communications	$8,399 ($3,745)	$7,962 ($4,962)	$3,224 ($2,269)	$5,325 ($1,642)	98	17	9	17
Computers	$18,399 ($8,794)	$23,243 ($23,243)	$17,596 ($6,808)	$6,086 ($2,828)	27	5	9	7
Computer related	$9,148 ($5,596)	$15,189 ($15,189)	$8,433 ($5,674)	$5,634 ($4,905)	90	20	15	19
Computer software	$5,148 ($2,374)	$8,606 ($8,606)	$3,379 ($1,702)	$6,931 ($1,820)	77	11	11	9
Electronic components	$11,891 ($3,953)	$14,099 ($14,099)	na	$7,845 ($2,818)	22	2	0	6
Other electronics	$5,932 ($4,539)	$7,229 ($7,183)	$7,690 ($7,690)	$3,586 ($2,128)	41	6	6	9
Biotechnology	$9,716 ($6,241)	$14,429 ($12,433)	$8,691 ($8,691)	$9,153 ($13,617)	29	9	2	5
Medical/health	$6,445 ($3,404)	$11,626 ($4,136)	$3,237 ($3,237)	$4,239 ($3,858)	90	17	12	17
Energy	$3,502 ($1,020)	$4,446 ($2,762)	$5,331 ($5,331)	$2,227 ($965)	22	4	2	3
Consumer products	$7,434 ($2,538)	$12,665 ($6,210)	$3,012 ($3,012)	$6,461 ($1,087)	103	19	6	10
Industrial products	$3,384 ($1,702)	$11,183 ($8,936)	$3,573 ($3,573)	$2,580 ($1,362)	89	4	6	20
Transportation	$5,654 ($3,690)	$7,339 ($2,837)	$4,539 ($4,539)	$6,667 ($6,667)	15	5	1	2
Other	$5,136 ($2,233)	$14,625 ($9,078)	$3,189 ($3,189)	$9,915 ($4,853)	96	8	9	10

ture Economics (e.g., seed, start-up, first stage, etc.) This information is self-reported by venture capital firms. There are no clear divisions among the definitions of each stage, so divisions should be seen as relative measures of firm development rather than absolute measures. To overcome some of the potential reporting biases in the regression results, various stages are grouped into early rounds, middle rounds, or late rounds. All seed and start-up investments are classified as early rounds. These investments are usually made in very young companies. First-stage and early-stage investments are classified as middle rounds because even though the firms are still relatively young, they are further developed than seed or start-up companies. Finally, second, third, expansion, or bridge stage funding is considered to be late stage financing.

Table 7.5 summarizes average duration, amount of venture capital funding, and the rate at which the firm uses cash during that particular round (in dollars per year) for various types of investment. In general, the duration of financing declines for late-stage companies and the average amount of financing per round generally rises. Venture capitalists may know more about late-stage firms and may therefore be willing to invest more money and for longer periods of time. Late-stage companies would be associated with lower agency costs. Similarly, the rate of cash utilization rises for late-stage firms. Cash utilization rates for later rounds might be higher because the need for investment in plant and working capital accelerates as the scale of the project expands.[6]

Regression results in table 7.6 present a clearer picture of the factors affecting venture capital staging patterns. The regressions include dummy variables to control for early and middle stage financings utilizing the Venture Economics classifications for type of investment. (The results are unchanged if firm development is measured by using round numbers— e.g., first investment, second investment, etc.—instead of dummies for early, middle, and late-stage firms.) The regressions also include industry accounting variables to control for the nature of the firm's assets and investment opportunities. Because private firm balance-sheet data is unavailable, industry averages from COMPUSTAT should be viewed as instruments for the private firms' true values. To the extent that any of the

---

6. A second possibility is that only poorly performing firms receive later rounds of financing (profitable firms generate their own cash). The higher cash utilization rate indicates a selection bias caused by selecting poor performers. Evidence from the sample of 127 firms going public indicates that the selection bias is not a problem. Successful firms have higher cash utilization rates.

Table 7.5

Duration, amount of investment, and cash utilization by stage of development. The sample is 794 venture capital-backed firms randomly selected from the Venture Economics database. Investment type is self-reported stage of development for venture capital-backed firms at time of investment. Median values are in parentheses. Time to next funding is the duration (in years) from one reported financing round to the next. Amount of funding is the average size of a given type of financing round (in thousands of 1997 dollars). Cash utilization is the rate at which the firm is using cash between rounds of financing (in thousands of 1997 dollars per year).

Type of funding	Time to next funding	Amount of funding	Cash utilization ($,000s per year)	Number
Seed	1.63	$1,045	$641	122
	(1.17)	($329)	($281)	
Start-up	1.21	$2,709	$2,255	129
	(1.00)	($1,246)	($1,246)	
Early stage	1.03	$1,196	$1,161	114
	(0.83)	($851)	($1,026)	
First stage	1.08	$2,188	$2,025	288
	(0.92)	($1,135)	($1,233)	
Other early	1.08	$2,476	$2,292	221
	(0.75)	($1,362)	($1,816)	
Expansion	1.26	$2,659	$2,111	377
	(0.88)	($1,135)	($1,289)	
Second stage	1.01	$2,845	$2,816	351
	(0.83)	($1,532)	($1,846)	
Third stage	0.86	$3,159	$3,673	181
	(0.75)	($1,362)	($1,816)	
Bridge	0.97	$3,066	$3,160	454
	(0.83)	($1,702)	($2,050)	

coefficients on the industry variables are significant, significance levels for firms' true values are probably even higher.

From the previous discussion, firms that are subject to greater agency costs should be monitored more often, and funding durations should be shorter. The ratio of tangible assets to total assets for the industry should be related to the liquidation value of the firm. The coefficient on the ratio of tangible assets to total assets should be positive in regressions for the duration of financing rounds. Tangible assets lower expected agency costs of inefficient continuation. The market-to-book ratio should rise as the fraction of growth options in firm value rises. Because potential agency costs associated with investment behavior rise with growth options, the

Table 7.6
Regressions for duration and amount funding per round controlling for firm and industry factors. The sample is 2,143 funding rounds for 794 venture capital-backed firms for the period 1961 to 1992. The dependent variables are the time in years from funding date to the next funding date and the logarithm of the round's funding amount in thousands of 1992 dollars. Independent variables include a dummy variable that equals 1 if the funding round is either seed or start-up (early stage) and a dummy variable that equals 1 if the round is either early, first, or other early (middle stage). Liquidity in the venture capital industry is controlled using new capital commitments to venture capital partnerships in the previous year in constant 1992 dollars. Tangibility of assets is measured by the average ratio of tangible assets to total assets for companies in the firm's industry. Market-to-book is the average industry ratio of market value of equity to book value of equity. Research and development intensity is proxied by the average industry ratios of R&D to sales or R&D to assets. The age of the venture capital-backed firm is months from incorporation to financing date. Panel A are maximum-likelihood estimates for Weibull distribution duration models. Panel B estimates are ordinary least squares. t-statistics for coefficients are in parentheses.

Panel A: Regressions for duration of financing round.

Independent variables	Dependent variable: Duration of financing round					
	(1)	(2)	(3)	(4)	(5)	(6)
Constant	−0.030	0.361	0.407	0.417	0.070	0.082
	(−0.19)	(2.50)	(2.86)	(2.93)	(0.39)	(0.42)
Investment was in an early-stage firm?	0.051	0.040	0.037	0.047	0.036	0.031
	(0.63)	(0.49)	(0.44)	(0.56)	(0.44)	(0.38)
Investment was in a middle-stage firm?	−0.054	−0.058	−0.103	−0.094	−0.102	−0.106
	(−0.93)	(−1.00)	(−1.72)	(−1.55)	(−1.71)	(−1.75)
Capital committed to new venture funds in previous year	−0.60xE-04	−0.56xE-04	−0.52xE-04	−0.55xE-04	−0.54xE-04	−0.56xE-04
	(−4.97)	(−4.56)	(−4.10)	(−4.41)	(−4.22)	(−4.36)
Industry ratio of tangible assets to total assets	0.405				0.400	0.398
	(4.01)				(3.84)	(3.23)
Industry market-to-book ratio		−0.047			0.000	−0.019
		(−1.87)			(0.00)	(−0.41)
Industry ratio of R&D expense to sales			−3.390		−2.268	
			(−2.52)		(−1.79)	
Industry ratio of R&D expense to total assets				−0.795		−0.194
				(−2.69)		(−1.67)
Age of the firm at time of venture financing round	0.016	0.016	0.016	0.017	0.016	0.017
	(3.58)	(3.68)	(3.49)	(3.56)	(3.52)	(3.60)
Logarithm of the amount of venture financing this round	0.011	0.012	0.016	0.011	0.010	0.009
	(0.71)	(0.73)	(0.68)	(0.65)	(0.59)	(0.52)
Pseudo-R²	0.045	0.037	0.045	0.046	0.053	0.051
Model χ^2	56.00	42.25	48.64	49.47	62.74	60.38

Panel B: Regressions for size of each financing round

Independent variables	Dependent variable: Logarithm of the financing amount in the round					
	(1)	(2)	(3)	(4)	(5)	(6)
Constant	6.580	6.756	6.902	6.929	6.379	6.108
	(38.00)	(39.02)	(46.39)	(46.27)	(26.97)	(22.39)
Investment was in an early-stage firm?	−0.635	−0.608	−0.703	−0.703	−0.748	−0.760
	(−4.14)	(−4.22)	(−4.83)	(−4.83)	(−5.14)	(−5.23)
Investment was in a middle-stage firm?	−0.224	−0.216	−0.308	−0.309	−0.314	−0.328
	(−2.29)	(−2.20)	(−3.06)	(−3.06)	(−3.13)	(−3.26)
Capital committed to new venture funds in previous year	0.0001	0.0001	0.0001	0.0001	0.0001	0.0001
	(3.94)	(4.21)	(3.91)	(3.98)	(3.10)	(3.08)
Industry ratio of tangible assets to total assets	0.352				0.612	0.810
	(2.23)				(3.64)	(4.16)
Industry market-to-book ratio		−0.051			0.041	0.084
		(−0.64)			(0.49)	(1.03)
Industry ratio of R&D expense to sales			1.578		3.618	
			(0.72)		(1.56)	
Industry ratio of R&D expense to total assets				−0.099		1.372
				(−0.21)		(2.43)
Age of the firm at time of venture financing round	−0.019	−0.019	−0.014	−0.014	−0.014	−0.014
	(−2.58)	(−2.58)	(−1.82)	(−1.86)	(−1.90)	(−1.89)
R^2	0.031	0.028	0.039	0.031	0.041	0.044
F-statistic	9.33	8.40	8.50	8.40	8.03	8.55

coefficient on the market-to-book ratio should be negative. Two measures of research and development intensity are included: R&D expenditure to sales and R&D expenditure to total assets. R&D intensive firms are likely to accumulate physical and intellectual capital that is very industry- and firm-specific. As asset specificity increases, so do expected losses in liquidation. Therefore, coefficients on R&D measures should be negative in the duration regressions.

Also included is firm age when it receives venture financing. Older firms may have more information available for venture capitalists to evaluate. Therefore, holding stage of development and all else constant, informational asymmetries are smaller and the funding duration should be longer (i.e., the coefficient on age should be positive in the duration regressions).

Finally, the effects of venture capital market growth on financing are measured through the amount of money (in constant dollars) raised by venture capital funds in the year prior to the financing of the firm. If venture capitalists cannot make all the investments they would like because they have insufficient capital, more liquidity should decrease the duration of financing (firms receive follow-on funding sooner) and increase the amount of funding per round.

The dependent variable in panel A is the duration of a particular venture financing round, the time in years from one particular financing to the next. The estimation of regressions with duration data introduces certain methodological issues. First, the data is right censored: we only observe the duration of financing when a subsequent financing occurs. A subsequent financing might not be observed for two reasons: firms may be in the middle of an ongoing financing round or firms might not receive another investment because they went bankrupt, went public, or were acquired. Models of unemployment (Lancaster 1979, 1985) deal with similar censoring. Duration data techniques are used, as in the unemployment estimation surveyed in Kiefer (1988).

A firm is assumed to have a certain probability of receiving financing in each period. The instantaneous probability of receiving financing is called the hazard rate, h(t). h(t) is defined as:

$$h(t) = \frac{\text{Probability of receiving funding between } t \text{ and } t + \Delta t}{\text{Probability of receiving funding after } t}. \qquad (7.1)$$

To estimate the duration model, assumptions about the distribution of the hazard rate must be made. The two most common distributions used

in duration models are the Weibull and exponential distributions. The
Weibull distribution offers two advantages. First, the time dependency of
the hazard rate can be estimated. Second, the likelihood function for the
Weibull model can be easily modified to allow for censored data. Other
distributional assumptions (e.g., exponential or normal) were estimated
and did not affect the qualitative results, although the Weibull model gave
better fit. The model estimated in tables 7.6 and 7.8 is:

$$h(t) = h_0(t)e^{\beta_0 + \beta_1 X_1 + \cdots + \beta_K X_K};$$

$$h_0(t) = t^{1/(\sigma-1)},$$
(7.2)

where $h_0(t)$ is the baseline hazard function.

Coefficients $\beta_0, \beta_1, \ldots$ are estimated via maximum likelihood estimators.
These coefficients yield estimates of the probability that the firm receives
financing in a particular month given values of the independent variables
(including time from last investment). The resulting estimates from the
Weibull regressions can be presented in multiple ways. Tables 7.6 and 7.8
present the model in log-expected time parameterization, that is, for given
values of the independent variables, the model gives the logarithm of the
expected time to refinancing. The interpretation of coefficients is straightforward, positive coefficients imply longer financing duration on average.
Conversely, negative coefficients imply shorter expected durations.

The results of table 7.6 are generally consistent with the implications of
an informational and agency-cost explanation for staged venture capital
infusions. In panel A, financing duration declines with decreases in the
industry ratio of tangible assets to total assets, increases in the market-to-
book ratio, and greater R&D intensity. The coefficients are significant between the 7 and 1 percent confidence levels. These factors are associated
with greater agency costs of investment and liquidation and therefore
lead to tighter monitoring.

The age of the venture-backed firm at the time of financing is positively
and significantly related to financing duration. More information may be
available for venture capitalists to evaluate older projects. One might also
expect that larger financing rounds lead to longer funding duration. That
is not the case. None of the coefficients on amount of venture financing
are significant. The results indicate that industry- and firm-specific factors
are important in determining the financing duration independent of the
investment size.

Finally, in regressions (5) and (6), all industry accounting variables are
used together to determine which of the asset measures are relatively

more important. The ratio of tangible assets to total assets remains the most significant variable, while market-to-book drops out completely. Higher R&D intensities still reduce funding duration, but size and significance of the coefficients are reduced when the other asset measures are included. The results indicate that tangible assets may be particularly important in lowering expected agency costs.

Panel B examines factors affecting size of the venture round. The dependent variable is the logarithm of the size of the financing round in thousands of 1992 dollars. The ratio of tangible assets to total assets has the greatest effect on the amount of financing. Increases in tangibility increase the amount of financing per round. More R&D intensive industries also appear to receive more financing per round controlling for tangibility.

Panel A also shows that the durations of early- and middle-stage financings are not significantly different from late-stage financings. The stage of development does, however, affect the amount of financing per round. Results from regressions in panel B show that average early-stage investments are between $1.30 and $2.03 million smaller than comparable late-stage investments. Similarly, middle-stage investments are on average $0.70 to $1.21 million smaller than late-stage investments. The increasing size of investment per round reflects the growing scale of a firm. Greater investment is needed to expand the firm.

The duration of financing and the amount of funding per round is also sensitive to the growth in the venture capital industry. Greater commitments of capital to new venture funds reduce duration of financing and increases financing amount per round. A one standard deviation increase in new commitments to venture capital funds decreases funding duration by two months and increases the average funding by almost $700,000.

If venture capitalists are capital rationed, larger cash commitments allow venture capitalists to invest more often in positive NPV projects and with larger cash infusions. If venture capitalists are susceptible to free cash-flow agency costs, they might waste the extra cash by investing more, and more often, in bad projects. Similarly, the growth in new and inexperienced fund managers during the mid-1980s could have led to a deterioration in investment quality and monitoring. Sahlman and Stevenson's (1986) case study of the computer disk drive industry shows that venture capital investment in certain industries during the early and mid-1980s might have been excessive. This period coincides with the dramatic increase in commitments to venture capital funds and might indicate that either free cash-flow agency costs or venture capitalist inexperience is a more likely explanation for the investment sensitivity to fundraising during this period of rapid entry.

Total Venture Financing and Number of Rounds

Data on total venture capital invested and the number of rounds provide another measure of monitoring intensity. Table 7.7 presents results for both variables. Included in the regressions are three dummy variables for the outcome of venture financing: a dummy variable that equals one if the firm went public, another dummy variable that equals one if the firm was liquidated or filed for bankruptcy, and a third dummy variable that takes the value one for all firms that are acquired or merge with another company. Coefficients on these dummies provide information about the impact of monitoring for projects of varying success.

The dependent variable in panel A is the logarithm of the total amount of venture financing that the firm received. Firms that go public, the results show, receive between $3.36 and $5.67 million more venture capital financing than firms that remain private. There is no difference in the total funding for those firms that are acquired and those that are liquidated compared to firms that remain private. Even controlling for the number of financing rounds, firms that eventually go public receive more total financing.

The results in panel B for the number of financing rounds confirm these results. Because the dependent variable is non-negative and ordinal, Poisson regressions are estimated for the number of rounds received. Firms that go public receive more financing rounds than those that remain private, while firms that are acquired or go bankrupt do not receive more rounds on average than those that remain private.

A plausible explanation for these results is that venture capitalists gather information about the potential profitability of projects over time. If venture capitalists receive favorable information about the firm and it has the potential to go public, the venture capitalist continues to fund the project. If the project is viable but has little potential to go public, the venture capitalist quickly searches for a corporate buyer. Firms that have little potential are liquidated.

Industry factors appear to have an important impact on total funding received. Panel A shows that firms in industries with more tangible assets receive less total financing. Firms in industries with high market-to-book ratios receive more total financing. Similarly, R&D intensive industries receive significantly greater amounts of financing.

Table 7.7
Regressions for total venture capital funding and number of rounds of financing. The sample is 794 venture capital-backed firms for the period 1961 to 1992. The dependent variables are the total venture capital funding that the firm received in thousands of 1992 dollars and the number of distinct rounds of venture financing. Independent variables include a dummy variable that equals 1 if the firm completed an initial public offering, a dummy variable that equals 1 if the firm filed for bankruptcy, and a dummy variable that equals 1 if the firm was acquired by or merged with another company. Tangibility of assets is measured by the average ratio of tangible assets to total assets for companies in the firm's industry. Market-to-book is the average industry ratio of market value of equity to book value of equity. Research and development intensity is proxied by the average industry ratios of R&D to sales or R&D to assets. Estimates in panel A are from ordinary least squares regressions. Estimates in panel B are from Poisson regressions. t-statistics for regression coefficients are in parentheses.

Panel A: Regressions for total funding

Independent variables	Dependent variable: Logarithm of total venture financing received					
	(1)	(2)	(3)	(4)	(5)	(6)
Constant	11.017	7.075	7.290	7.427	4.714	4.771
	(12.38)	(38.22)	(67.40)	(68.38)	(4.41)	(4.47)
Firm exited via an IPO?	1.043	1.018	0.882	0.905	0.664	0.666
	(6.18)	(6.01)	(4.88)	(4.96)	(4.31)	(4.32)
Firm went bankrupt or was liquidated?	−0.023	−0.024	−0.102	−0.047	−0.085	−0.077
	(−0.11)	(−0.12)	(−0.49)	(−0.22)	(−0.48)	(−0.44)
Firm exited via merger or acquisition?	−0.125	−0.129	−0.003	−0.009	0.124	0.123
	(−0.76)	(−0.78)	(−0.02)	(−0.05)	(0.84)	(0.83)
Industry ratio of tangible assets to total assets	−3.660				1.118	1.036
	(−3.90)				(1.12)	(1.04)
Industry market-to-book ratio		0.311			0.402	0.420
		(2.90)			(3.52)	(3.69)
Industry ratio of R&D expense to sales			13.033		3.600	
			(4.02)		(1.24)	
Industry ratio of R&D expense to total assets				5.709		2.540
				(1.95)		(1.02)
Number of rounds of venture financing received					0.396	0.399
					(15.19)	(15.43)
R^2	0.073	0.064	0.067	0.048	0.337	0.336
F-statistic	13.40	11.60	11.05	7.82	44.37	44.26

Table 7.7 (continued)

Panel B: Poisson regressions for number of rounds

Independent variables	Dependent variable: Number of financing rounds received			
	(1)	(2)	(3)	(4)
Constant	2.904	0.945	0.796	0.888
	(10.51)	(13.88)	(18.82)	(21.55)
Firm exited via an IPO?	0.255	0.239	0.186	0.203
	(4.35)	(4.06)	(2.91)	(3.18)
Firm went bankrupt or was liquidated?	0.054	0.052	0.017	0.052
	(0.71)	(0.68)	(0.23)	(0.68)
Firm exited via merger or acquisition?	0.027	−0.006	−0.010	−0.004
	(0.43)	(−0.09)	(−0.16)	(−0.06)
Industry ratio of tangible assets to total assets	−2.054			
	(−6.96)			
Industry market-to-book ratio		0.021		
		(0.54)		
Industry ratio of R&D expense to sales			7.416	
			(6.25)	
Industry ratio of R&D expense to total assets				2.907
				(2.73)
Pseudo-R^2	0.020	0.006	0.019	0.007
Model χ^2	60.25	18.55	50.07	18.81

The most important factor influencing total venture financing is the number of financing rounds the firm has received. In fact, when the number of financing rounds is included in regressions with industry variables, tangibility of assets and R&D intensity are no longer significant. The coefficient on industry market-to-book ratio is unchanged, however. Even controlling for the number of financing rounds, firms in industries with high market-to-book ratios receive more total venture funding. If market-to-book measures the potential profitability of investment and growth opportunities, investment should be relatively higher in industries that have more growth opportunities. Similarly, firms in high market-to-book industries may have less access to debt financing and may therefore rely more on venture capital.

Panel B shows that tangibility of assets and R&D intensity do indeed work through the number of financing rounds. Firms in industries with a greater fraction of tangible assets receive fewer rounds of venture financing. Similarly, firms in R&D intensive industries receive more rounds of financing.

Overall, the evidence suggests that venture capitalists are concerned about the lack of entrepreneurial incentive to terminate projects when it becomes clear that projects will fail. Venture capitalists minimize agency costs by infusing capital more often. As asset tangibility and liquidation value increase, venture capitalists can recover more of their money if liquidation occurs, and the need to monitor declines. By gathering information, venture capitalists determine whether projects are likely to succeed and continue funding only those that have high potential.

Alternative Explanations

While the results from the above section are consistent with predictions from agency theory, alternative explanations may explain the results. Cost of monitoring may affect investment structure through the efficacy of interim monitoring. Tangible assets may be easy to monitor without formal evaluation. A venture capitalist can tell if a machine is still bolted to the floor. If costs of monitoring are very low, the venture capitalist may choose to have long financing rounds to avoid costs of writing new contracts. At the same time, venture capitalists could monitor the firm more often between capital infusions. Easier interim monitoring would reduce expected agency costs between financing rounds and, hence, increase funding duration.

Both monitoring and agency costs are important. Conversations with practitioners, however, indicate that they normally make continuation decisions when a new financing round occurs. Venture capitalists evaluate a firm based upon performance progress, not whether a machine is still bolted down. Future work should examine the importance of monitoring costs in determining investment structure and the frequency of monitoring.

The relation between funding duration and the nature of firm assets may also be driven by differences between high-technology and low-technology firms. High-technology firms may naturally pass through more milestones. Because industry measures like the ratio of tangible assets to total assets, market-to-book, and R&D intensity are highly correlated with high-technology and low-technology status, shorter funding duration may be correlated with these measures. The coefficients in table 7.6 would measure the amount of information revealed over time and the number of benchmarks used to evaluate the firm. The more information that is revealed, the more often the project is reevaluated.

If the alternative of technology-driven milestones were true, then coefficients on asset measures would be driven by the difference between high-technology and low-technology industries. If we rerun the duration regressions within technology groups, the effect of asset tangibility, industry market-to-book ratios, and R&D intensities should be much less important. Table 7.8 presents Weibull distribution maximum likelihood estimates for each technology cohort. In panel A, the sample is high-technology firms, including communications, computers, computer related, software, electronic components, other electronics, biotechnology, and medical equipment companies. The sample in panel B is low-technology firms, including medical services, energy, consumer products, industrial products, transportation, and other (primarily services) companies.

The coefficients on industry-asset measures are surprisingly similar for the high-technology and low-technology cohorts, and both have estimates that are close to the estimates for the entire sample. It is impossible to reject the hypothesis that the coefficients for the tangibility of assets, market-to-book ratio, and the R&D intensity are equal across types of industries. The similarity of the coefficients shows that the relation between duration and asset measures is consistent within industrial classifications as well. In unreported regressions, finer industry divisions had no qualitative effect on the coefficients.

The one major difference between the two groups is the effect of firm age. The age of the firm receiving financing does not have an effect on the financing duration for high-technology firms but has a significantly positive effect in the low-technology cohort. Firm age may be more important in measuring potential asymmetric information for low-technology firms but may have only a small impact on asymmetric information for high-technology companies.

While alternative explanations may help explain some of the results, conversations with venture capitalists indicate that they are concerned about the entrepreneur's continuation decisions and strategy choices. Results in the section on staged investment are consistent with venture capitalists' stated concern that entrepreneurs have private information about the future viability of the firm, that they always want to continue the firm, and that entrepreneurs may want to enrich their reputation through activities at investors' expense.

Conclusions

Corporate control is a fundamental concern of investors. If individuals knew all potential outcomes, state-contingent contracts would be able to solve any potential agency cost. But such complete knowledge does not

Table 7.8

Regressions for duration controlling for firm and industry factors with the sample split into high-technology and low-technology companies.
The sample is 2,143 funding rounds for 794 venture capital-backed firms for the period 1961 to 1992. The dependent variable is the time in years from funding date to the next funding date. Independent variables include a dummy variable that equals 1 if the funding round is either seed or start-up (early stage) and a dummy variable that equals 1 if the round is either early, first, or other early (middle stage). Liquidity in the venture capital industry is controlled using new capital commitments to venture capital partnerships in the previous year in constant 1992 dollars. Tangibility of assets is measured by the average ratio of tangible assets to total assets for companies in the firm's industry. Market-to-book is the average industry ratio of market value of equity to book value of equity. Research and development intensity is proxied by the average industry ratios of R&D to sales or R&D to assets. The age of the venture capital-backed firm is months from incorporation to financing date. All regressions are maximum-likelihood estimates for Weibull distribution duration models. t-statistics for coefficients are in parentheses.

Panel A: Regressions for duration of financing round for high-technology industries

Independent variables	Dependent variable: Duration of financing round					
	(1)	(2)	(3)	(4)	(5)	(6)
Constant	-0.036	0.464	0.542	0.549	0.022	-0.056
	(-0.17)	(2.56)	(2.99)	(3.03)	(0.09)	(-0.22)
Investment was in an early-stage firm?	0.066	0.065	0.042	0.046	0.036	0.029
	(0.68)	(0.66)	(0.42)	(0.45)	(0.36)	(0.30)
Investment was in a middle-stage firm?	-0.022	-0.009	-0.085	-0.084	-0.101	-0.109
	(-0.32)	(-0.13)	(-1.15)	(-1.14)	(-1.38)	(-1.48)
Capital committed to new venture funds in previous year	-0.63xE-04	-0.59xE-04	-0.54xE-04	-0.57xE-04	-0.59xE-04	-0.61xE-04
	(-4.50)	(-4.01)	(-3.59)	(-3.82)	(-3.81)	(-3.93)
Industry ratio of tangible assets to total assets	0.514				0.553	0.633
	(3.47)				(3.60)	(3.55)
Industry market-to-book ratio		-0.059			0.037	-0.003
		(-0.66)			(0.39)	(-0.03)
Industry ratio of R&D expense to sales			-2.418		-0.986	
			(-1.83)		(-0.51)	
Industry ratio of R&D expense to total assets				-0.541		-0.315
				(-1.88)		(-1.68)
Age of the firm at time of venture financing round	-0.001	-0.001	-0.005	-0.005	-0.006	-0.005
	(-0.17)	(-0.09)	(-0.70)	(-0.70)	(-0.74)	(-0.64)
Logarithm of the amount of venture financing this round	0.001	0.003	-0.002	-0.002	-0.004	-0.005
	(0.07)	(0.13)	(-0.08)	(-0.08)	(-0.21)	(-0.22)
Pseudo-R^2	0.036	0.029	0.032	0.032	0.041	0.040
Model χ^2	31.07	20.75	21.85	21.99	33.63	33.81

Panel B: Regressions for duration of financing round for low-technology industries

Independent variables	Dependent variable: Duration of financing round					
	(1)	(2)	(3)	(4)	(5)	(6)
Constant	-0.078	0.399	0.382	0.400	0.130	0.208
	(-0.29)	(1.50)	(1.54)	(1.62)	(0.45)	(0.62)
Investment was in an early-stage firm?	-0.050	-0.095	-0.087	-0.068	-0.093	-0.098
	(-0.35)	(-0.66)	(-0.61)	(-0.48)	(-0.65)	(-0.69)
Investment was in a middle-stage firm?	-0.148	-0.194	-0.210	-0.179	-0.196	-0.195
	(-1.45)	(-1.88)	(-2.03)	(-1.72)	(-1.89)	(-1.88)
Capital committed to new venture funds in previous year	-0.43xE-04	-0.38xE-04	-0.37xE-04	-0.40xE-04	-0.38xE-04	-0.38xE-0_
	(-1.86)	(-1.89)	(-1.68)	(-1.72)	(-1.68)	(-1.62)
Industry ratio of tangible assets to total assets	0.433				0.393	0.337
	(2.90)				(2.55)	(2.17)
Industry market-to-book ratio		-0.076			-0.053	-0.078
		(-1.41)			(-0.91)	(-1.43)
Industry ratio of R&D expense to sales			-4.270		-2.006	
			(-2.18)		(-1.89)	
Industry ratio of R&D expense to total assets				-1.067		-0.388
				(-2.41)		(-1.66)
Age of the firm at time of venture financing round	0.026	0.028	0.030	0.031	0.029	0.030
	(4.07)	(4.34)	(4.44)	(4.54)	(4.34)	(4.41)
Logarithm of the amount of venture financing this round	0.022	0.018	0.017	0.014	0.019	0.017
	(0.79)	(0.63)	(0.61)	(0.50)	(0.66)	(0.59)
Pseudo-R^2	0.086	0.075	0.088	0.091	0.100	0.100
Model χ^2	39.27	33.29	39.38	40.34	46.19	45.82

exist, and investors must minimize potential agency costs. Mechanisms in financial contracts among venture capitalists and entrepreneurs directly account for potential agency costs and private information associated with high-risk, high-return projects.

This chapter has demonstrated that the staging of venture capital investments can be understood in an agency and monitoring framework. Results from a sample of venture capital-backed companies are consistent with the predictions presented. Venture capitalists are concerned that entrepreneurs with private information and large private benefits will not want to liquidate a project even if they have information that the project has a negative NPV for shareholders. Entrepreneurs may also pursue strategies that enrich their reputation at shareholders' expense. Agency costs increase with declining asset tangibility, increasing growth options, and greater asset specificity. Venture capitalists monitor entrepreneurs with increasing frequency as expected agency costs rise.

The evidence indicates that venture capitalists use their industry knowledge and monitoring skills to finance projects with significant uncertainty. Venture capitalists concentrate investment in early-stage companies and high-technology industries. Results also demonstrate that the duration of financing is related to the nature of the firm's assets. Higher industry ratios of tangible assets to total assets, lower market-to-book ratios, and lower R&D intensities are associated with longer funding duration. Firms that go public have received significantly more financing and a greater number of rounds than have firms that are acquired or liquidated.

This chapter raises several interesting questions for future research. Because large firms also engage in projects that compete with investments by venture capitalists, comparing the structure and timing of investment of large corporations with those of venture capitalists might shed light on the comparative advantage of each. What implication does the structure of venture capital investment have on the future performance of new business and established firms? Can the structure of investment increase the probability that an entrepreneurial project ends up like Apple Computer, Genentech, or Microsoft? Cross-sectional and time-series effects of firm- and industry-specific factors on the outcome of investment (e.g., IPO, merger, bankruptcy, or remaining private) need to be examined.

The effect of growth in the venture capital industry on investment should be investigated further. Do free cash-flow costs, liquidity constraints, or the entry of inexperienced venture capitalists better describe venture capitalists' response to changes in capital commitments to new funds through the 1980s? Does the fund raising ability of the venture capitalist affect only the size of the investment or does it lead to softer benchmarks as well?

The data in this chapter are limited because they examine only venture capital equity financing. Most venture capital-backed firms receive some financing before they tap venture capital. What are these sources and how significant are they? "Angels," wealthy individuals who invest in entrepreneurial ventures, are one source. Family and friends are also major contributors. Bank lending may be important in certain industries, but very high-risk companies might not have access to debt financing. Future work should examine appropriate sources of capital for new firms and how those sources change as the firm evolves. Determining the relationship among sources of capital for start-up enterprises would be pivotal in understanding the genesis of new firms.

This chapter examines another aspect of venture capitalists' role as overseers of private firms: their role on the boards of directors. Chapter 8 analyzes whether venture capitalists' representation on the boards of the private firms in their portfolios is greater when the need for oversight is larger. To do this, the analysis examines the periods when the need for oversight is likely to be particularly high: the transition between chief executive officers (CEOs) of the firm. The role of venture capitalists in the firm should be particularly sensitive to such events, with increasing involvement around such events.

Venture capitalists' oversight of new firms involves substantial costs. The transaction costs associated with frequent visits and intensive involvement are likely to be reduced if venture capitalists are proximate to the firms in their portfolios. Consistent with these suggestions, geographic proximity is an important determinant of venture board membership: organizations with offices within five miles of the firm's headquarters are twice as likely to be board members as those more than 500 miles distant. Over half the firms in the sample have a venture director with an office within sixty miles of their headquarters. This has important implications due to the uneven regional distribution of venture capitalists. Petersen and Rajan (1994, 1995) demonstrate that the concentration of bank credit can lead to highly different financing patterns across markets. The presence or absence of venture capitalists may likewise lead to significant differences in the availability and pricing of venture capital across regions.

The organization of the chapter is as follows. In the next section, the empirical analysis of board composition around CEO successions is presented. The third section examines how geographic considerations affect board involvement, and the fourth section concludes the chapter.

The Determinants of Board Composition

The Sample and Descriptive Statistics

This chapter—like chapters 9 and 11 that follow—focuses on a single industry, biotechnology. The approach allows the use of a variety of industry-specific information sources. Through these data sources, the behavior
of firms that ultimately went public can be more thoroughly analyzed and
many firms that were acquired or terminated before going public are included in the sample.[1]

This analysis is based on the database of venture capital financings
assembled by Venture Economics, which is discussed in chapter 16. This
section also describes the steps taken to correct the sample using other
data sources. Table 8.1 summarizes the sample, disaggregated by year and
round of investment. The table presents the number of financing rounds,
as well as the cumulative and average size of these transactions. (All size
figures are in millions of 1997 dollars.) Observations are concentrated in
the latter half of the sample. While no trend appears in the size of transactions over time, the greater size of later financing rounds is apparent.

Information about the boards of these firms is found in several loca-
tions. IPO prospectuses report board members at the time of the offering
and in many cases indicate former board members in the "certain transactions" and "principal and selling shareholders" sections. When these
listings do not mention former directors, the firm's original and amended
articles of incorporation, which are usually reproduced in its S-1 registration statement, are checked. Information is often available about the
boards of private firms that are acquired by public firms or file for an
abortive IPO in the acquirers' proxy, 10-K, or 10-Q statements, or in the
(ultimately withdrawn) registration statements. In addition, in the fall of

---

1. Although an industry sample allows the use of other data sources to verify and correct
the data set, it raises the concern that the investment patterns here are not representative of
venture capital as a whole. The IPOs of firms in the biotechnology sample closely resemble
the 433 venture-backed IPOs examined by Barry, Peavy, Muscarella, and Vetsuypens (1990)
in several critical respects. These include the inflation-adjusted IPO size, the length of venture capitalist involvement with the firm, and the number of venture capitalists serving as
directors of the firm. In the cross-sectional sample of venture-backed firms described in chapter 7, the cumulative venture funding received by biotechnology firms is near the mean: the
average funding of these firms is more than computer software and medical device companies, but considerably less than computer and electronic component manufacturers. The
mean firm in the sample went public 4.8 years after being established; the median, 4.3 years.
This can be contrasted with Megginson and Weiss's (1991) sample of 320 venture-backed
IPOs between 1983 and 1987, where the mean age was 8.6 years and the median 5.3 years.

Table 8.1

The corrected financings sample. The table presents the number of financing rounds of private biotechnology firms in the corrected Venture Economics sample, the total dollars disbursed, and the average size[a] of each round (in millions of 1997 dollars). The sample consists of 653 financing rounds of 271 biotechnology firms between 1978 and 1989. Financing rounds are segmented by year and by round number.

Panel A: Financing segmented by year

Year	Number of rounds	Aggregate size (1997 $ millions)	Average size (1997 $ millions)
1978	7	22.03	3.14
1979	8	69.58	8.69
1980	16	157.81	9.87
1981	41	180.10	4.61
1982	46	249.50	5.55
1983	62	291.31	4.86
1984	46	182.60	4.24
1985	55	190.65	3.89
1986	79	345.08	4.73
1987	102	460.18	4.84
1988	102	392.84	4.13
1989	89	430.12	5.51

Panel B: Financings segmented by round number

Financing round	Number of rounds	Aggregate size (1997 $ millions)	Average size (1997 $ millions)
First round	270	673.82	2.70
Second round	186	881.19	5.04
Third round	113	832.24	7.85
Later round	84	584.57	7.59

a. Because we could determine the size of some financing rounds, the aggregate size does not equal in all cases the product of the number of rounds and the average round size.

1990 we gathered material on these firms in the files of the North Carolina Biotechnology Center (NCBC). The NCBC has solicited information from public and private firms on an annual basis. Their files include promotional material (used to produce an industry directory) and surveys conducted for the U.S. Office of Technology Assessment. These materials detail both the firms' managements and their boards.

The IPO prospectuses provide biographies of directors. Other sources, however, often only list directors' names. Directors are identified using *Pratt's Guide to Venture Capital Sources* (Venture Economics 1992a), biographical material in other prospectuses (many individuals serve on more than one board), general business directories (Marquis's *Who's Who in Finance and Industry* 1993, *Standard and Poor's Register of Corporations, Directors and Executives* 1993), and BioVenture View's *BioPeople* (1993). These sources are supplemented with information from the NCBC "actions" (1990a) database (a compilation of trade magazine stories) and Mead Data Central's databases.

Panel A of table 8.2 presents the distribution of board members by round of investment. Each case where the board members at the time of the investment or within three months of the investment date are known is used. Following Baysinger and Butler (1985), directors are divided into quasi-insiders, outsiders, and insiders. Quasi-insiders are those parties who do not work directly for the firm, but have an ongoing relationship with the concern. Affiliated academic professionals who hold full-time teaching or clinical positions are counted as quasi-insiders rather than insiders, even if they hold an official title in the firm and draw substantial compensation. Outside directors include investors and disinterested outsiders. Included in this category are representatives of corporations who have invested in or financed research at the firm.[2] The analysis distinguishes between venture capitalists and other outsiders.[3]

The number of board members increases in each round, from a mean of four in the first round to just fewer than six in the fourth and later rounds. In the fourth and later rounds, venture capitalists control a mean of 2.12 board seats. This sample corresponds closely to the interindustry population of 433 venture-backed IPOs of Barry, et al. (1990). In their mean firm, venture capitalists control two out of six board seats. The distribution of the directors is presented in more detail in panel B. In table 8.2 only one observation of each firm is used: the directors at the time of the last round of venture financing in the sample period.

---

2. A number of corporations, rather than investing directly in smaller firms, channel their funds through a corporate venture capital subsidiary. In these cases, a corporate venture capitalist may sit on the board. These officials are counted as other outsiders rather than as venture capitalists. The analysis in the above section was repeated, with these individuals recorded as venture capitalists. Neither the magnitude nor the significance of the results changes markedly.

3. Venture capitalists are defined as individuals who are general partners or associates at partnerships focusing on venture capital investments (i.e., equity or equity-linked securities with active participation by the fund managers in the management or oversight of the firms). These individuals are counted as venture capitalists, even if they officially work for the firm. (Most partnership agreements between general and limited partners require that salaries be paid out of the management fee and not by the fund. Venture capitalists can get around this restriction by being paid by a firm in their portfolio.) The analysis includes venture organizations that are either unaffiliated with any other organization or else affiliated with a financial institution.

Table 8.2
The board membership of private biotechnology firms. The sample consists of 653 financing rounds of 271 biotechnology firms between 1978 and 1989. The board membership by round is presented for each of the 362 rounds where membership can be determined. Venture capitalists are defined as individuals who are general partners or associates at venture capital organizations that are either unaffiliated with any other organization or else affiliated with a financial institution. Full-time affiliates of a venture capital organization are counted as venture capitalists, even if they work for a venture-backed firm. Other outsiders include corporate investors, other investors (individuals who (1) (either alone or in a partnership) held a 5 percent stake in the organization at some time, (2) never were an officer of the firm, and (3) never were an affiliate of a company that signed a collaborative arrangement with the firm or of a venture investor), and individuals who do not have another relationship with the firm. Insiders are either senior (the chief executive officer, president, and chairman of the board) or junior managers employed directly by the firm. Quasi-insiders are those parties who do not work directly for the firm, but have an ongoing relationship with the concern. The second panel reports the professional affiliation of board members at the time of the last financing round in the sample.

Panel A: Board membership by round number

Mean number of board members

Financing round	Venture capitalists	Other outsiders	Insiders	Quasi-insiders
First round	1.40	0.86	1.28	0.52
Second round	1.87	0.86	1.40	0.56
Third round	2.09	1.02	1.61	0.67
Later round	2.12	1.27	1.73	0.54

Panel B: Professional affiliation of board members at time of last financing round (in percent)

Outside directors

Venture capitalist	36.2
Corporate partner	6.4
Other investor	3.1
Executive with other health-care or biotechnology firm	3.5
Retired health-care or high-technology executive	3.6
Academic without firm affiliation	0.9
Lawyer, consultant, or investment banker without firm affiliation	1.4
Other or unidentified	5.1

Inside directors

Senior manager	20.3
Junior manager	7.1

Quasi-inside directors

Academic affiliated with the firm	8.9
Lawyer affiliated with the firm	0.5
Investment or commercial banker affiliated with the firm	1.0
Former manager of the firm	0.6
Relative or other	1.3

Board Membership and Chief Executive Officer Turnover

This section follows an approach suggested by Fama and Jensen (1983) and Williamson (1983), who hypothesize that the composition of the board should be shaped by the need for oversight. These authors argue that the board will bear greater responsibility for oversight—and consequently that outsiders should have greater representation—when the danger of managerial deviations from value maximization is high. If venture capitalists are especially important providers of managerial oversight, their representation on boards should be more extensive at times when the need for oversight is greater.

This chapter examines changes in board membership around the time that a firm's CEO is replaced, an approach suggested by Hermalin and Weisbach's (1988) study of outside directors of public firms. The replacement of the top manager at an entrepreneurial firm is likely to coincide with an organizational crisis and to heighten the need for monitoring. The need for monitoring should be greater in these cases. As with public firms (Weisbach 1988), the replacement of the CEO frequently occurs when the firm is encountering difficulties. In addition, since the uncertainty about the new person's ability is likely to be high, the CEO's activity may be more intensively monitored.[4]

The analysis only uses as cases of CEO turnover instances where the firm's top executive was replaced. It is important to avoid instances that may generate a spurious correlation between the addition of board members and CEO turnover: for example, cases where neither a CEO has been hired nor a complete board assembled when the firm begins operations. Consequently, instances when a venture capitalist that originally held the title of "chairman and chief executive officer" relinquishes the second title are not included. Similarly eliminated are cases where a firm run by an "acting CEO" or by one or more vice presidents hires a full-time chief.

Cases of CEO turnover are identified using the sources described above. Forty cases of CEO turnover meeting these criteria are identified. Few of these changes are retirements: the median age of the exiting CEOs

---

4. Robert Kunze (1990) of Hambrecht and Quist notes that the replacement of the CEO "is the single most critical development in the life of a baby company. The time spent hiring the new chief executive officer, the shock to the organization when the changeover takes place, the lack of direction in the interim, the quality of the new person hired, and the speed with which he or she seizes command, all impact heavily on the health and potential of the company. In the best of circumstances replacing a chief executive officer is a wrenching experience and companies can easily fail at this juncture."

Table 8.3

The changes in board membership between financing rounds. The sample consists of 220 second or later financing rounds where the board membership at the time of the current and previous round can be determined. The first panel indicates the change in board membership since the last financing round, divided by whether CEO turnover occurred. Venture capitalists are defined as individuals who are general partners or associates at venture capital organizations that are either unaffiliated with any other organization or else affiliated with a financial institution. Full-time affiliates of a venture capital organization are counted as venture capitalists, even if they work for a venture-backed firm. Other outsiders include corporate investors, other investors (individuals who (1) (either alone or in a partnership) held a 5 percent stake in the organization at some time, (2) never were an officer of the firm, and (3) never were an affiliate of a company which signed a collaborative arrangement with the firm or of a venture investor), and individuals that do not have another relationship with the firm. Insiders are managers employed directly by the firm. Quasi-insiders are those parties who do not work directly for the firm, but have an ongoing relationship with the concern. The second panel presents p-values from t-tests and non-parametric Wilcoxon tests of whether the change in board membership differs in rounds with CEO turnover. The t-tests do not assume that the two distributions have the same variance.

Panel A: Changes in board membership between financing rounds

	Mean change in the number of board members since the last financing round			
	Venture capitalists	Other outsiders	Insiders	Quasi-insiders
180 rounds without CEO turnover	+0.24	+0.28	+0.10	+0.06
40 rounds with CEO turnover	+1.75	+0.33	+0.23	+0.25

Panel B: Tests of equality of changes in board membership between financing rounds

	p-value, test of null hypothesis of no difference between CEO turnover rounds and other rounds			
	Venture capitalists	Other outsiders	Insiders	Quasi-insiders
p-value, t-test	0.000	0.750	0.339	0.140
p-value, Wilcoxon test	0.000	0.519	0.094	0.297

at the time of the last financing round in which they are in office is 40. (The median age of the CEOs holding office at the time of the last financing round in the sample is 43.) Only one replaced CEO is between the ages of 64 and 66 at the time of exit, the criterion used by Weisbach (1988) to identify CEO retirements.

Table 8.3 summarizes the changes in board membership between venture rounds. First presented are the 180 second or later venture rounds where the board membership at the time of the current and previous financing round is known and there was no CEO turnover in this interval. (Also included are cases where there is an observation of board members up to three months after the financing.) There is a slight increase in the representation of each class of board member.

Then the forty rounds in the sample where the board membership at the time of the current and previous financing is known and there was CEO turnover in this interval are presented.[5] In these rounds, the representation of each class of board member increases at a greater rate than between rounds without CEO turnover. The increase in insiders and quasi-insiders is not surprising, as in some cases the departing CEO will remain a board member, whether the person continues as a lower-level employee or becomes an ex-employee (who are classified as quasi-insiders). By far the largest increase (1.75) is in the number of venture directors. The analysis presents t-tests and Wilcoxon tests of whether the change in the number of directors is the same in rounds with and without CEO turnover. Because in each case an F-test rejects the equality of variances, the t-tests do not assume that the distributions have the same variance. Nonparametric Wilcoxon tests are employed because the change in the number of board members is an ordinal number. Panel B presents the p-values from these tests. The increase in the representation of venture board members is significantly larger when there is CEO turnover. The differences in the changes of other directors are insignificant.

These patterns are then examined econometrically. Following Hermalin and Weisbach (1988), a Poisson specification is employed, with the number of new directors as the dependent variable. (In these regressions, a goodness-of-fit test cannot reject the Poisson specification.) Two separate regressions are run, using as dependent variables the number of new directors who are venture capitalists and other outsiders. All 216 second and later venture rounds where both the board membership and funds provided at the time of the current and previous rounds are used. As independent variables, the regression employs a dummy variable indicating if there was CEO turnover between the current and previous venture round (with 1.0 indicating such a change) and two control variables. The first controls for the difference between the funds provided in the current and previous venture round (expressed in millions of constant dollars). An increase in funding may lead to the involvement of new investors, who may be offered a board seat. The second controls for the number of directors

Table 8.4
Poisson regression analysis of the addition of board members between financing rounds. The sample consists of 216 second or later financing rounds where the board membership at the time of and the amount invested in the current and previous round can be determined. In the first panel, separate regressions are estimated using the number of new directors who are venture capitalists and other outsiders as the dependent variable. Independent variables include a dummy indicating if there was CEO turnover between the previous and current round, the difference in the amount invested in the current and previous round (expressed in millions of 1989 dollars), and the number of board members who departed the board between the previous and current round. Absolute t-statistics in brackets. The second panel tests whether the coefficients of the CEO turnover variable in the two regressions are equal.

Panel A: Poisson regression analysis of the addition of board members between financing rounds

	Dependent variable: Number of new board members who are	
	Venture capitalists	Other outsiders
CEO turnover	1.88 [8.86]	−0.04 [0.13]
Change in dollars invested	0.02 [0.89]	−0.06 [2.28]
Number of departing board members	0.15 [2.06]	0.19 [1.41]
Constant	−1.43 [8.94]	−1.13 [8.00]
Log likelihood	−175.29	−157.20
χ^2-statistic	112.50	7.56
p-Value	0.000	0.056
Number of observations	216	216

Panel B: Test of the equality of coefficients in the venture capitalist and other outsider regressions

p-Value, χ^2-test of null hypothesis that CEO turnover coefficients are equal	0.000

who have exited the board since the previous round. As Hermalin and Weisbach note, if firms routinely fill vacated board seats, a regression without such a control may be biased.

As panel A of table 8.4 reports, the coefficient of the CEO turnover variable in the venture capitalist regression, 1.88, is highly significant. At the mean of the other independent variables, the exit of the CEO increases the number of new venture directors from 0.25 to 1.59. This coefficient in the other outsiders regression is of the opposite sign and insignificant. In panel B, the coefficients of the CEO turnover variable in the venture capitalist and other outsider regressions are compared. Table 8.4 presents the p-value from the χ^2-test of the null hypothesis of no difference. The null hypothesis is rejected at the 1 percent level of confidence. This difference is robust to modifications of these regressions. For instance, an independent variable that controls for the time between the current and previous venture round is added, and separate independent variables for each class of director who leaves the board are created. Also the number of new investors is used as an independent variable instead of the increase in the funds provided.

Hermalin and Weisbach (1988) propose an alternative explanation for the addition of outside directors around a CEO succession. They suggest that corporate insiders who are passed over for the top position leave after a new CEO is selected. The firm—facing a shortage of qualified insiders—then fills the board seats with outsiders. This explanation is unlikely to apply here. Managers who depart private firms voluntarily often must pay a heavy financial penalty: selling their shares back to the firm at the same discounted price that they originally paid (typically a small fraction of the current value). Consequently, voluntary departures of senior executives from private venture-backed firms are infrequent.

Board Membership and Geographic Proximity

The distance between venture capitalists and the private firms on whose boards they sit is then examined. The cost of providing oversight is likely to be sensitive to the distance between venture capitalists and the firms in which they invest. If the provision of oversight is a significant and costly role for venture capitalists, then proximity should be an important determinant of which venture investors serve on the board.

First, the geographic proximity of venture directors is examined. To compute this measure, the zip codes in which the firm has its headquarters and the venture capital organization has its office nearest the firm are used. To determine the former, the specialized industry directories cited above and the records of Venture Economics are employed. The latter information is available for each venture organization in several sources (Clay 1991, National Register 1992, Venture Economics 1992a). If possible, the edition of *Pratt's Guide* published in the year of the firm's final financing round in the sample is used. (*Pratt's* information is gathered through a survey of venture organizations conducted in January of the year of publication.) Since the Venture Economics database lists the name of the fund, the associated venture organization must be determined. The name of the venture organization is often obvious. (For instance, Mayfield, VII, L.P., is managed by the Mayfield Fund.) In other cases, an unpublished Venture Economics database identifies the venture organization. To compute the distance between the zip codes, a computer program developed by the Center for Regional Economic Issues at Case Western Reserve University is used. The program computes the mileage between the center of pairs of zip codes.

Panel A of table 8.5 presents the distance from each firm's headquarters to its most proximate, furthest, and median venture director at the time of the last venture round in the sample. The results suggest that for the majority of the firms, the nearest venture director is quite close. More than half the firms have a venture director with an office within sixty miles of their headquarters, while 25 percent of the firms have a venture director within seven miles. Panel B examines the probability that a venture investor is a director at the time of the final round in the sample. The probability that a venture investor with an office within five miles of the firm serves as a director is 47 percent; for a venture capitalist whose nearest office is more than 500 miles away, the probability is 22 percent. An F-test examines whether these probabilities are equal. The null hypothesis of no difference is rejected at the 1 percent confidence level.

To correct for other determinants of board membership, a probit regression is estimated. As observations, the regression uses each venture investor in the firm as of the last round in the sample. The dependent variable is a dummy indicating whether a representative of the venture organization served on the firm's board at the time of the last round in the sample (with 1.0 denoting a board member). As independent variables, the distance from the investor's nearest office to the firm's headquarters (in thousands of miles) is used and several control variables. A venture organization with a larger equity stake in a firm should be more likely to have a director, as it has more at risk. The stake that venture organizations held in the firms is determined through the Venture Economics database, as well as information from Recombinant Capital and U.S. Securities and Exchange Commission filings. Larger and older venture capitalists may be more likely to serve as board members: experienced venture capitalists may either be more effective monitors or may more effectively certify the firm to potential investors. To determine the age and size of the venture organization, *Pratt's Guide* and several other sources (Clay 1991, National Register 1992, Venture Economics 1992a) are used. The age of each venture organization is expressed in years; size is the ratio of the capital committed to the venture organization at the time of the investment to the total pool of venture capital. A ratio is employed because the size of the venture pool changes dramatically over this period. Separate

Table 8.5
The relationship between proximity and board membership for venture investors. The distance (in miles) between the headquarters of the firm and the nearest office of each venture capitalist that served as a board member at the time of the last venture round in the sample. The sample consists of 700 pairs of venture capital organizations and private biotechnology firms. The second panel presents the relationship between probability of a venture investor serving as a board member and its distance to the firm, and the p-value from an F-test of this pattern. The final panel presents a probit regression analysis of the relationship between venture investor proximity and board membership. The dependent variable is a dummy indicating if a representative of the venture organization served on the board at the time of the last venture round in the sample. (1.0 denotes a director.) Independent variables include the distance from the venture organization's nearest office to the headquarters of the firm (in thousands of miles), the fraction of the firm's equity held by the venture organization, the age of the venture organization (in years), and its size (the ratio of its committed capital to the total venture capital pool). All variables are calculated at the time of the last venture round in the sample. Absolute t-statistics in brackets.

Panel A: Proximity of venture capitalist directors

	Distance from venture capitalist's nearest office to firm headquarters (in miles)			
	Mean	Median	First quartile	Third quartile
Nearest venture director	359	59	7	418
Median distance venture director	584	287	32	965
Furthest venture director	993	419	73	1951

Panel B: Relationship between proximity of venture investor and probability of board membership

	Distance from venture capitalist's nearest office to firm headquarters (in miles)			
	<5	5–50	50–500	>500
Probability of joining board	46.7%	30.7%	34.9%	21.8%
p-value, F-test of null hypothesis of no relationship				0.000

Panel C: Regression analysis of board membership

	Dependent variable: Venture investor served on board			
	Using venture capitalist age and stake	Using venture capitalist size and stake	Using venture capitalist age	Using venture capitalist size
Venture office to firm (000 miles)	−0.18 [3.72]	−0.20 [4.04]	−0.16 [4.16]	−0.20 [4.71]
Stake held by venture organization	4.21 [6.96]	4.19 [6.61]		
Age of venture organization (years)	0.01 [1.54]		0.01 [2.18]	
Organization's share of total venture pool		18.64 [2.17]		18.62 [2.77]
Constant	−0.86 [7.33]	−0.87 [7.57]	−0.51 [5.80]	−0.48 [6.07]
Log likelihood	−319.48	−297.36	−413.19	−384.85
χ^2-statistic	82.68	85.58	27.12	35.66
p-value	0.000	0.000	0.000	0.000
Number of observations	580	548	700	661

regressions use venture capitalist age and size as control variables, because these two measures are highly correlated.

Panel C of table 8.5 presents the results. The coefficient for distance is highly significant in explaining the service of venture capitalists on boards, even after controlling for ownership and experience. Since the venture organization's stake cannot always be computed, this variable is omitted in the third and fourth regressions. The results are robust to the use of the larger sample.[6]

Conclusions

This chapter examines the role of venture capitalists as directors of private venture-backed firms. The analysis examines whether the representation of venture capitalists increases around the time of CEO turnover, as might be expected if these individuals were intensively monitoring managers. Unlike other outside directors, the representation of venture capitalists increases around such events. The analysis also examines the geographic proximity of venture directors. Since the provision of oversight is costly, venture capitalists should seek to minimize this cost by overseeing local firms. Firms are likely to have a nearby director, and proximity is an important determinant of board membership. These findings complement earlier empirical studies of how venture capitalists address agency problems as well as analyses of the ties between banks and the firms to which they lend.

The results of this analysis suggest several avenues for future investigation. The first of these is the impact of venture capitalists' involvement in firms after going public. Barry, et al. (1990) and Lin and Smith (1995) document the continuing role of venture capitalists as directors and shareholders in the years after going public. In some cases, venture capitalists terminate their relationships with the firm quickly; but in a significant number of instances, venture capitalists retain a board seat even after distributing their holdings to the limited partners of their funds. If venture capitalists are specialized providers of oversight, it might be expected that these firms would be less prone to agency problems.[7]

---

6. In unreported regressions, the logarithm of distance is used as an independent variable, which proves to have even more explanatory power.

7. An alternative possibility is that a relationship between firm success and venture involvement exists, but that this pattern is driven by reverse causality. Venture capitalists may choose to remain on the boards of successful companies, whether out of the belief that board membership highlights their past accomplishments to outsiders or else out of hubris.

A second avenue for empirical analysis is suggested by the results concerning the importance of geographic proximity of venture capitalists. Regions differ dramatically in their concentration of venture capitalists (see table 1.4). Akin to Petersen and Rajan's (1994, 1995) finding of differences across credit markets with different degrees of lending concentration, firms located in regions where venture capital is relatively scarce may face different price schedules for or availability of this form of financing.

9   Why Do Venture Capitalists Syndicate Investments?

This chapter empirically examines the syndication of venture capital investments in privately held firms. It explores three hypotheses about why these investors share transactions with each other. The first two suggest that syndication may be a mechanism through which venture capitalists resolve informational uncertainties about potential investments:

• Syndicating first-round venture investments may lead to better decisions about whether to invest in firms. Sah and Stiglitz (1986) show that hierarchical organizations, in which investments are made only if several independent observers agree, may be superior to ones in which projects are funded after one affirmative decision. Another venture capitalist's willingness to invest in a potentially promising firm may be an important factor in the lead venture capitalist's decision to invest.

• Admati and Pfleiderer (1994) develop a rationale for syndication in later venture rounds, based on informational asymmetries between the initial venture investor and other potential investors. A venture capitalist involved in the firm's daily operations understands the details of the business. The venture capitalist may exploit an informational advantage, overstating the proper price for the securities in the next financing round. Under the model's assumptions, the only way to avoid opportunistic behavior is if the lead venture capitalist maintains a constant share of the firm's equity. This implies that later round financings must be syndicated.

The third hypothesis is different in emphasis. Syndication may also be a mechanism through which venture capitalists exploit informational asymmetries and collude to overstate their performance to potential investors:

• Lakonishok, Shleifer, Thaler, and Vishny (1991) suggest that pension funds "window dress." Because institutional investors may examine not only quarterly returns but also end-of-period holdings, money managers may adjust their portfolios at the end of the quarter by buying firms whose shares have appreciated and selling "mistakes." Venture capitalists may similarly make investments in the late rounds of promising firms, even if the financial returns are low. This strategy allows them to represent themselves in marketing documents as investors in these firms.

While these three hypotheses do not exhaust the rationales for syndication, they lend themselves to empirical examination.

This chapter examines these concepts using a sample of 651 investment rounds prior to going public at 271 biotechnology firms. Syndication is commonplace even in the first-round investments. Experienced venture capitalists primarily syndicate first-round investments to venture investors with similar levels of experience. In later rounds, established venture capitalists syndicate investments to both their peers and less-experienced capital providers. When experienced venture capitalists invest for the first time in later rounds, the firm is usually doing well (i.e., the firm's valuation has increased over the prior venture round). Finally, the ownership stake of venture capitalists frequently stays constant in later venture rounds. These results support the three hypotheses.

This is a topic of more general interest as well: cooperation between financial institutions is an enduring feature of the equity issuance process. Syndicated underwritings in the United States date back at least as far as an 1870 offering by Pennsylvania Railroad. By the 1920s, these arrangements were quite intricate: separate syndicates in many cases handled the purchase, inventory, and sale of securities (Galston 1925). Although the Securities Act of 1933 regulated these arrangements, comanaged offerings and selling syndicates continue to be prominent in equity issues to this day. Despite its persistence, syndication has been little scrutinized in the corporate finance literature. The neglect may be due to the complex motives for these arrangements as well as the difficulty of analyzing these patterns empirically. Venture capital syndications differ in two ways from public sales of registered securities, which suggest that securities sales by private firms are an attractive arena to study the economics of syndication. First, the process through which private firms sell securities is little regulated by the SEC. Thus, financial intermediaries have few constraints on their ability to work together. Second, the securities are purchased directly by the venture capital fund and must be held for at least one year under SEC Rule 144. By contrast, financial intermediaries take on relatively limited risks when they underwrite a public security issue: the underwriters ascertain the demand schedule for the new security before the price is determined.

This topic is of more general interest for another reason: corporate finance has devoted relatively little attention to interactions among incumbent and entrants. By way of contrast, industrial organization has long focused on relationships. Due to our ability to measure interactions and returns, finance is a natural testing ground. This chapter joins the relatively few studies of the relationship between incumbent and entrant financial institutions.[1]

The plan of this chapter is as follows. The next section discusses several suggestions from the industrial organization and finance literature about syndication. The third section presents the analysis, and the fourth section concludes the chapter.

Rationales for Syndication

This chapter focuses on three hypotheses. First, syndication may lead to a superior selection of investments. Sah and Stiglitz (1986) contrast decision making in hierarchies and polyarchies: that is, settings in which projects are undertaken only if two reviewers agree that the project is worthy and those in which the approval of either is sufficient. The authors show that it may be more efficient to undertake only those projects approved by two reviewers.

Venture capitalists, upon finding a promising firm, typically do not make a binding commitment to provide financing. Rather, they send the proposal to other investors for their review. Another venture capitalist's willingness to invest in the firm may be an important factor in the lead venture investor's decision to invest (Pence 1982). Practitioners often emphasize this motivation for syndication:

Venture capitalists prefer syndicating most deals for a simple reason—it means that they have a chance to check out their own thinking against other knowledgeable sources. If two or three other funds whose thinking you respect agree to go along, that is a double check to your own thinking (George Middlemas, Inco Securities, quoted in Perez 1986).

Most financing involves a syndicate of two or more venture groups, providing more capital availability for current and follow-on cash needs. Syndication also spreads the risk and brings together more expertise and support. These benefits pertain only to start-up financing requiring the venture capitalist's first investment decision. There are different strategies and motivations for syndication in follow-on financing (Robert J. Kunze, Hambrecht and Quist 1990).

---

1. Others include, for example, Beatty and Ritter (1986), Hayes, Spence, and Marks (1983), Lakonishok, Shleifer, and Vishny (1992), and Sirri and Tufano (1998).

If this is an important motivation for syndication, venture organizations should be careful in their choice of first-round syndication partners. Established firms should be unlikely to involve either new funds or small, unsuccessful organizations as coinvestors. The choice of syndication partners should be less critical in later rounds. Having decided to provide capital to the firm, venture capitalists should be much less concerned about confirming their judgment. This suggests that (1) experienced venture capitalists are likely to invest with one another in the first round and (2) seasoned venture capitalists should invest with both experienced and inexperienced investors in later rounds.[2]

Admati and Pfleiderer (1994) develop a rationale for syndication in later rounds. Syndication should occur, they argue, even when venture capitalists are risk neutral and without capital constraints. They begin by considering a situation where an informed entrepreneur raises funds from outside investors directly. In keeping with Brennan and Kraus (1987), the entrepreneur can communicate all private information with a set of contingent claims. If an unforeseen state of the world occurs, however, the signaling equilibrium breaks down. As a result, the entrepreneur may be unable to raise the full amount needed.

A lead venture capitalist, who becomes involved in the firm's operations, can solve this information problem. Other, less informed investors will invest if the venture capitalist does. The venture capitalist, however, may exploit an informational advantage. For instance, if one believes that the firm's prospects are particularly attractive, one may reserve fewer shares for outside investors. If troubled by the firm's prospects, one may allow outside investors to provide more of the capital. Under the assumptions of their model, Admati and Pfleiderer show that the only way to ensure optimal behavior in the face of this "adverse selection" problem is if the lead venture capitalist maintains a constant equity stake. Consider a case where the lead venture capitalist obtains one-half of a company's two million shares in the first round. (The entrepreneur retains the other 50 percent.) If the second round involves the issuance of another million shares, the venture capitalist should only buy one-half of these. The remaining half-million shares should be purchased by other venture capitalists. This model provides a rationale for syndication in later rounds, and it suggests that venture capitalists will hold a constant equity stake across rounds.

2. Another hypothesis that would generate a similar empirical pattern is Welch's (1992) model of "cascades" in equity sales. While Welch focuses on the sale of equity in IPOs, the same pattern could appear here: upon observing the decision of early venture capitalists to invest in the firm, less sophisticated venture investors rush in to invest in later rounds.

Lakonishok, Shleifer, Thaler, and Vishny's (1991) discussion of "window dressing" by money managers suggests a third rationale for venture syndication. They note that pension funds, which typically assess their money managers once a quarter, examine performance in several ways. Because market-adjusted performance is a noisy indicator of a money manager's skill, plan sponsors also examine the portfolio of securities held at the end of the quarter. In response, money managers may adjust their portfolios just before the quarter's end. This may include buying firms that have performed particularly well in that quarter or selling "mistakes" that incurred losses.

Venture capital funds may exhibit similar behavior. In their private placement memoranda for new funds, venture organizations discuss the performance of their previous funds. The performance data is often difficult for outsiders to confirm. For instance, in computing historical returns in these documents, venture capitalists may make generous assumptions about the valuation of securities.[3] Thus, potential investors also may examine venture organizations' prior investments. The private placement memoranda discuss successful past investments, often leaving ambiguous whether the venture organization was an early or late investor. (Similar listings of previous investments are found in marketing documents aimed at managers of new firms seeking financing.) An investment in a promising firm shortly before it goes public may consequently benefit a venture organization, even if the financial return is low. Early venture investors may curry favor with their colleagues by permitting them to invest in later-round financings of promising firms. The early-round investors may do so in the hope that the syndication partners will in turn offer them opportunities to invest in later rounds of their deals.

This hypothesis suggests that venture capitalists should offer shares in the best deals to those firms most able to reciprocate: well-established venture firms. Venture capitalists should be less likely to offer such opportunities to less established venture organizations.

---

3. Venture funds frequently do not sell shares of firms that have gone public, but rather distribute them to their limited partners. (Limited partners usually include tax-exempt and tax-paying entities, which may have different preferences on the timing of sales.) The transfer of the securities from the venture capitalist to the limited partners may take several weeks. During this period, the firm's share price may fall sharply, either because the venture capitalists themselves sell their shares of the thinly traded security or because the market anticipates forthcoming sales by the limited partners. In calculating returns, venture funds may employ not the price on the date that the shares reached the limited partners, but rather the price on the date that the distribution was announced (see chapter 13).

A final rationale for syndication that is not examined is diversification through risk sharing (Wilson 1968). Venture capitalists have much at stake in the performance of their funds. First, venture capitalists typically receive as compensation between 20 percent and 30 percent of their funds' profits. Fund performance also affects the ability to raise new funds. Under certain assumptions, venture capitalists may wish to diversify their holdings to ensure that they do not conspicuously underperform their peers. To address this behavior, many contracts establishing venture capital partnerships contain explicit prohibitions against investing in other venture funds (see chapter 3). By investing in many syndicated investments, however, a venture fund can achieve much the same effect.

It is unclear whether risk aversion will lead to a greater tendency to syndicate by less or more established funds. A new venture organization may believe that a follow-on fund is difficult to raise unless it performs very well (see chapter 12). The fund may make high-risk solo investments. Alternatively, an established venture organization may believe that its reputation will allow it to raise a later fund even after a disastrous performance. Its fund may thus be willing to invest alone in risky but promising projects. To analyze empirically the relationship between risk aversion and syndication, we would need to know about the utility functions of the venture capitalists, the status of their current funds, and their future fundraising plans.[4]

An Analysis of Syndication Patterns

The Sample

This chapter, like Chapter 8, examines financings between 1978 and 1989 by privately held biotechnology firms that received venture capital before going public in Venture Economics' Venture Intelligence Database. (For a detailed description of the database, see chapter 16.)

Table 9.1 describes the sample. Even in the first round, there is extensive syndication. In each later venture round, two or more new investors typically invest in the firm. The mean number of investors rises from 2.7

---

4. One test is to examine funds that specialize in start-ups, traditionally the most risky of venture investments. These venture capitalists, it might be anticipated, have relatively little risk aversion. Using a t-test, the number of syndication partners (by round of investment) are compared for these funds and all others. The specialist funds are identified using a database of funds assembled by Venture Economics (described in chapter 16). Although these funds have slightly fewer syndication partners, the differences are not statistically significant.

Table 9.1
Description of the sample. The sample consists of 651 financing rounds of privately held biotechnology firms between 1978 and 1989. The table indicates the number of observations, the mean number of venture and nonventure investors, and the mean number of such investors investing in the firm for the first time. The table also reports the mean amount invested by venture and nonventure investors, in millions of nominal dollars.

	Round of external financing		
	# 1	# 2	# 3+
Number of observations	269	184	198
Mean number of investors in each round			
Venture investors	2.2	3.3	4.2
Nonventure investors	0.5	0.9	1.1
Mean number of new investors in each round			
Venture investors	2.2	1.5	1.3
Nonventure investors	0.5	0.7	0.7
Amount invested per investor ($ million)			
Venture investors	0.5	0.6	0.6
Nonventure investors	0.9	0.9	1.3

Because some early round investors do not invest in subsequent rounds, the number of investors in a given round is often less than the sum of the investors in the previous round and the new investors.

(including nonventure investors[5]) to 5.3. Because some early round investors do not invest in subsequent rounds, the number of investors in a given round is often less than the sum of the number of investors in the previous round and the number of new investors.

The amount invested per venture and nonventure investor is quite stable. The size of each financing round increases (on an absolute and per investor basis) as the firm matures. This reflects the growing number of investors and the increasing representation of nonventure investors.

Syndication Partners in First and Later Rounds

The analysis next examines the choice of syndication partners in the sample. Established venture capitalists should disproportionately syndicate

---

5. Venture investors are defined as either (1) traditional limited partnerships where general partners invest the limited partners' capital and oversee these investments or (2) corporate venture capital programs that are established enough to be listed in Pratt's Guide (Venture Economics 1992a). Nonventure investments include private placements by other corporations or financial institutions as well as by partnerships established solely to invest in a single firm. Investments that are made by an agent and marketed to retail investors are also designated as nonventure investments.

first-round investments with other established firms. In later rounds, they should be much more willing to syndicate investments with less seasoned firms.[6]

There is no obvious way, however, to distinguish between established and marginal venture capital organizations. While many influential venture capital organizations such as Greylock and TA Associates date back to the 1960s, other of today's leading venture capitalists did not close their first fund until the 1980s. Meanwhile, a substantial number of venture organizations have had protracted lives without ever becoming major factors in the industry. The analysis does not thus simply characterize venture capitalists by age, but also by the relative size of the organization's fund. More established venture organizations should be able to access capital from investors for larger and more frequent funds. Venture capitalists generally prefer larger funds because of the substantial economies of scale in operating a large venture fund (or several large funds). The organization's size is expressed as a percentage of the total venture capital pool because venture capital expanded dramatically in the years after 1978: it is relative rather than absolute size that measures relative experience.[7]

Table 9.2 divides all venture capitalists into quintiles based on size. The ratio of venture organization's committed capital (the total amount provided by investors) to the total venture pool in the year of investment is computed. Venture organizations typically operate several funds (i.e., partnerships) at any given time. All funds sponsored by a venture capital organization are aggregated for the purpose of the analysis. The committed capital is used rather than the value of assets because venture capitalists follow divergent practices as to when they write up or write off their investments.

---

6. One question suggested by this analysis is which firms do not syndicate at all. The age and size of venture organizations investing alone are compared to those organizations investing jointly. Larger and older venture organizations are only slightly more likely to invest alone than others are. The t-tests comparing syndicating and solo investors are statistically insignificant and not reported in the tables.

7. Neither age nor relative size provides an indication of industry expertise. One might expect certain venture capitalists to develop special expertise in a complex industry such as biotechnology. While we might expect that many early round investments would involve a specialist in biotechnology, it is not obvious that these specialists will be particularly likely to coinvest with each other. In many cases, early round syndications between two established venture organizations will pair one group with industry-specific experience and another without such experience, which is expected to contribute general management and financial expertise. Established venture organizations can be expected to be involved as syndication partners, even when they do not have specialized industry expertise (Kunze 1990).

Table 9.2

Syndication partners in venture financings of privately held biotechnology firms. The sample consists of 651 financing rounds between 1978 and 1989. Venture organizations are divided into quintiles on the basis of committed capital, relative to all venture organizations active in biotechnology in the year of the investment. Each row of the table indicates, for one size quintile, the distribution of syndication partners (i.e., the percentage of syndication partners in each size quintile). First-, second- and later-round investments are considered separately.

First-round financings

Venture capital size quintiles	Size quintile of syndication partner				
	Largest	Second	Middle	Fourth	Smallest
Largest quintile	14%	35	20	17	14
Second quintile	27%	25	14	19	16
Middle quintile	22%	20	20	23	16
Fourth quintile	18%	25	21	16	20
Smallest quintile	12%	17	12	16	43

Second-round financings

Venture capital size quintiles	Size quintile of syndication partner				
	Largest	Second	Middle	Fourth	Smallest
Largest quintile	21%	22	24	18	15
Second quintile	25%	22	20	15	17
Middle quintile	26%	19	21	21	13
Fourth quintile	22%	18	23	21	18
Smallest quintile	18%	18	14	18	32

Later-round financings

Venture capital size quintiles	Size quintile of syndication partner				
	Largest	Second	Middle	Fourth	Smallest
Largest quintile	19%	23	26	18	14
Second quintile	20%	20	25	21	17
Middle quintile	19%	21	24	21	15
Fourth quintile	17%	21	25	20	17
Smallest quintile	15%	18	22	20	24

Rows may not add to 100 percent due to rounding. Because certain size quintiles undertook more or fewer syndicated investments, the table is not symmetric along the diagonal axis.

The syndication partners in each size quintile of venture organizations are then examined. First-, second- and later-round investments are considered separately. Were funds equally likely to syndicate with a venture organization of any size, each cell would be equal: 20 percent of the syndications will be with the largest quintile of organizations, 20 percent with the middle quintile, and so forth.

The analysis is presented figure 9.1 and table 9.2. There are an uneven number of observations for each quintile, so the tabulations are not symmetric around the diagonal axis. For instance, there are forty-four syndicated first-round investments between venture capitalists in the largest quintile and those in the middle quintile. The number of syndicated investments involving the largest quintile of organizations is slightly larger than the number involving the middle quintile. Thus, coinvestments with middle-quintile firms make up 20 percent of the joint investments by the largest quintile of organizations. These forty-four transactions with the largest quintile comprise 22 percent of the coinvestments by middle-quintile venture capitalists.

The smallest quintile of venture capitalists is disproportionately likely to undertake early round transactions with each other. The bottom quintile of venture organizations syndicates 43 percent of their first-round investments with other bottom-quintile venture capitalists. With each subsequent round, this pattern becomes less pronounced. The percentage of the bottom quintile's syndications with each other in second and later rounds was 32 percent and 24 percent. Some patterns, however, are not readily explicable. It is not obvious, for instance, why top-tier firms syndicate first-round investments more frequently with second-quintile organizations (35 percent) than other top-quintile firms (14 percent).

Table 9.3 examines the statistical significance of these patterns and tests the null hypothesis that the probability of each cell is 20 percent using a Pearson χ^2-test. For the first-round analysis reported in table 9.2, the null hypothesis is rejected at the 1 percent level of confidence. In the other rounds, the null hypothesis cannot be rejected at conventional confidence levels.

Similar results appear when venture organizations are segmented by age: 36 percent of the first-round syndication partners of the quintile of youngest firms are also in the youngest quintile. Although the full results are not reported for age, the pattern is similar. Table 9.3 tests for deviations from the equally likely distribution. Again, the null hypothesis of equal probabilities is rejected (at the 5 percent level of confidence) in the first round. In later rounds, the null hypothesis cannot be rejected.

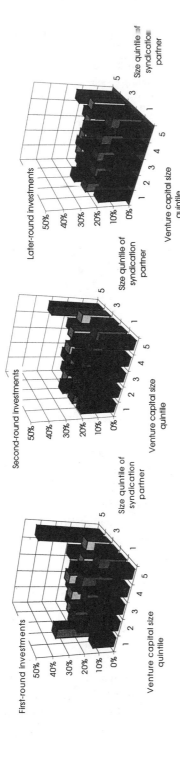

Figure 9.1
Syndication partners in venture financings of privately held biotechnology firms. The sample consists of 651 financing rounds between 1978 and 1989. Venture organizations are divided into quintiles on the basis of committed capital, relative to all venture organizations active in biotechnology in the year of investment. The quintile of the largest venture capital firms is denoted as 1; the smallest as 5. First-, second-, and later-round investments are considered separately. The vertical axis indicates, for each size quintile, the percentage of syndication partners in each of the five quintiles.

Table 9.3
Tests of the randomness of the distribution of syndication partners in venture financings of privately held biotechnology firms. The sample consists of 651 financing rounds between 1978 and 1989. Venture organizations are divided into quintiles on the basis of committed capital and age, relative to all venture organizations active in biotechnology in the year of the investment. The table indicates the test statistic and significance level for a Pearson χ^2-test, whose null hypothesis is that 20 percent of the observations are in each cell. Separate tests are performed for the first, second, and later investment rounds.

	Firms divided into quintiles by venture organization's	
	Size	Age
First-round financings		
Pearson χ^2-statistic	48.08	26.87
p-value	0.000	0.043
Second-round financings		
Pearson χ^2-statistic	18.93	7.83
p-value	0.273	0.954
Later-round financings		
Pearson χ^2-statistic	6.44	16.07
p-value	0.983	0.448

The analyses reported in tables 9.2 and 9.3 using the age and size proxies suggest sharp divisions between more and less established venture capitalists. If the unwillingness of experienced venture capitalists to invest with small and young organizations in the first round stems from a mistrust of inexperienced investors' judgment, then a second pattern should appear as well. Experienced venture capitalists should be reluctant to invest in the later rounds of deals begun by their less seasoned counterparts. Inexperienced venture investors should be brought into later round financings by experienced organizations, but not vice versa.

To assess this claim, venture organizations investing for the first time in the second or later venture rounds are examined. The characteristics of the new investors are contrasted with those of the venture organizations that invested previously in the firm. Funds are compared along three measures of experience: the size of the venture capital organization (committed capital in the year of the investment as a percentage of the total committed capital in the venture pool), age of the venture organization in years, and the number of biotechnology firms in which the organization had invested before this transaction.

The later-round venture investors should be less experienced than the previous investors. Table 9.4 compares the characteristics of the new investors to those of the previous venture financiers and presents the

Table 9.4

The experience of venture capitalists investing in the second and later rounds. The sample consists of 651 financing rounds between 1978 and 1989. The experience level of each venture organization investing in a firm for the first time in the second or later round is compared to the experience level of previous venture investors in the firm. Venture organizations are compared on the basis of size (committed capital in the year of the investment as a percentage of the total pool of venture capital), age (in years), and the number of biotechnology firms in which the organization had previously invested. The differences are expressed as the experience level of the new investor minus that of the previous investor.

Measures of venture experience	Average difference, experience of new investor and previous investor	p-value, t-test of no difference
Venture organization size as percent of total pool	−0.12%	0.008
Age of venture organization (in years)	−1.42	0.006
Prior biotech investments by venture organization	−0.76	0.001

Table 9.5

Equity stakes in privately held venture-backed biotechnology firms. The sample consists of 332 financing rounds between 1978 and 1989 where the size of the ownership stake for each investor can be determined. The table indicates the mean percentage of the firm's equity held by outside investors after each venture round as well as the percentage of the equity sold in the round purchased by previous investors in the firm.

	Round of external financing		
	#1	#2	#3
Total stake held by outside investors after investment round	33.9%	51.1%	57.0%
Share of equity sold in round purchased by previous investors		30.0%	52.7%

In computing the equity stake, all preferred shares are converted into common at the conversion ratios then in force. (These are typically stipulated in the amended by-laws prepared after each venture round.) Outstanding warrants and options are only counted if their exercise price is below the per-share price of the venture round.

p-values from t-tests comparing these firms. The results are consistent with the hypothesis and significant at the 1 percent confidence level. The typical later-round syndication involves less experienced venture capitalists investing in a deal begun by established organizations.

Changes in Equity Holdings across Venture Rounds

Next an empirical prediction of Admati and Pfleiderer's model is examined: that the stakes held by venture capitalists will be relatively constant across venture rounds. Table 9.5 examines investors' aggregate equity holdings and their equity purchases in financing rounds. In the second

Table 9.6
Changes in venture equity stakes in privately held biotechnology firms. The sample consists of 188 second or later financing rounds between 1978 and 1989 where the size of the ownership stake of each venture capitalist before and after the venture round can be determined. The table indicates the change in the equity ownership of each venture organization around each financing round: the difference between the new and old stake divided by the old stake is calculated (a total of 871 observations). All funds of a given venture organization are considered together.

Percent change in ownership	Number of observations	Percent
$< -25\%$	72	8.3
$< -5\%$ and $> -25\%$	298	34.2
$< 5\%$ and $> -5\%$	183	21.0
$< 25\%$ and $> 5\%$	134	15.3
$< 50\%$ and $> 25\%$	94	11.1
$< 75\%$ and $> 50\%$	23	2.6
$< 100\%$ and $> 75\%$	27	3.1
$> 100\%$	40	4.6

In computing the equity stake, all preferred shares are converted into common at the conversion ratios then in force. (These are typically stipulated in the amended by-laws prepared after each venture round.) Outstanding warrants and options are only counted if their exercise price is below the per-share price of the venture round.

round, first-round investors purchase 30 percent of the shares sold. New investors buy the remaining shares. The existing investors' purchase corresponds quite closely to their previous ownership position of 33 percent prior to the round. In the third round, when previous investors hold 51 percent of the equity, existing shareholders purchase about half the shares. In later rounds, current shareholders purchase over half the shares. These results confirm the prediction of Admati and Pfleiderer that venture shareholders strive to maintain a constant equity share.

Similarly, the equity ownership of individual venture organizations shows relatively little variation. Table 9.6 shows the change in equity held by each venture investor before and after each venture round, computing:

$$[(\textit{Stake after Round-Stake before Round})/\textit{Stake before Round}]. \tag{9.1}$$

In 21 percent of the cases, the share of the firm held by the venture capitalist changes by less than 5 percent after the venture round. In 70.5 percent of the cases, the change is less than 25 percent.[8]

---

8. That is, in 70 percent of the cases, a venture capitalist with a 10 percent stake in a company before a venture round would have an equity stake of between 7.5 and 12.5 percent thereafter.

Later-Round Syndications of Investments in Promising Firms

Finally, suggestions of "window dressing" in the syndication of venture investments are examined. An empirical implication of the hypothesis is that experienced venture capitalists will invest in the later rounds of deals particularly likely to go public.

Each second- and later-round venture investment is used as an observation. A pair of probit regressions is run. The pair uses the same independent variables but different dependent variables:

$$(INVEST?)_{ij} = \alpha_{0j} + (\Delta VALUE)_i \alpha_{1j} + (VCSIZE)_i \alpha_{2j} + \varepsilon_{ij}. \tag{9.2}$$

The dependent variables are dummy variables indicating if (1) one or more experienced venture capitalists invested in the firm for the first time in the round and (2) one or more inexperienced venture capitalists invested for the first time. In both cases, the dependent variable is coded as 1.0 when a new investor is present. Experienced and inexperienced firms are defined as those above and below the median size of those venture organizations investing in biotechnology in that year, using the amount of capital committed to the venture organization as a measure of size.

Two independent variables are used. To identify the most promising deals, the change in the per share valuation of the firm between the current and previous venture round is used. The firms whose valuations increase sharply should be superior performers and are most likely to go public. The size of the largest previous venture investor is also used as an independent variable to control for the reluctance of established firms to invest in deals begun by less established firms.

The partition of venture capitalists into experienced and inexperienced is crude: much of the information about their characteristics is discarded. In unreported regressions, the analysis is repeated with specifications that capture more detail. First, four separate regressions are run, examining if venture capitalists in each of four size quartiles invested for the first time in the transaction. Then, Poisson specification is used, where the dependent variable is the number of new venture capitalists in each size quartile who invested in the firm. The results are robust to these changes.

The robustness of the analysis to the use of venture organization age rather than relative size is also examined:

$$(INVEST?)_{ij} = \beta_{0j} + (\Delta VALUE)_i \beta_{1j} + (VCAGE)_i \beta_{2j} + \varepsilon_{ij}. \tag{9.3}$$

As before, two dependent variables are used, indicating if an experienced or an inexperienced venture capitalist joined as a new investor. Experi-

enced and inexperienced firms are now defined as those above or below
the median age of those venture organizations investing in biotechnology
in that year. Instead of size, the age of the oldest previous investor is used
as an independent variable.

The results in table 9.7 support suggestions of "window dressing." The
coefficients 0.14 and 0.15 in the first and third regressions show that
established venture capitalists are significantly more likely to invest for
the first time in later rounds when valuations have increased sharply.[9]
Valuation changes are insignificant (and actually negative) in explaining
the probability of investments by less established firms.

Conclusions

Chapter 9 examines the structure of private investments in the biotechnology industry. In the first round, established venture capitalists
tend to syndicate with one another. Later rounds involve less-established
venture organizations. These results are consistent with the view that
syndication is a device through which established venture capitalists
obtain information to decide whether to invest in risky firms. When established funds join as new investors in later rounds, the firm's valuation
has often increased sharply prior to the investment. This pattern supports
suggestions of "window dressing" in the syndication of later-round investments. The chapter also presents evidence consistent with Admati
and Pfleiderer's constant equity share hypothesis.

While this chapter has examined syndication in one particular environment, the results may be more broadly applicable. We see many of these
behaviors in public security issuances. For instance, in IPOs of firms specializing in complex technologies, the decision to go public and the terms

---

9. Although it could be argued that the price per share increases because other experienced
venture capitalists invested in the firm, there are strong arguments to the contrary. Venture
capital partnership agreements will frequently specify that new venture investors be
involved in situations where venture capitalists may be tempted to price investments at too
high valuations. An example is when a venture fund makes a later-round investment in a
company already held by the venture capitalist's earlier fund (Venture Economics 1992b).
Venture capitalists may be tempted to undertake a follow-on financing at a high valuation.
This is because they can then write up the value of their first fund's investment, in the hopes
of impressing potential investors in the third fund. (The potential investors will find it difficult to independently assess the value of a privately held firm.) The investors in the second
fund demand a coinvestment by another venture capitalist who does not stand to benefit
from the write-up of current holdings because they expect that such an investor will demand
a lower valuation.

Table 9.7
The probability of venture capitalists investing for the first time in a second or later financing round. The sample consists of 199 second or later financings of privately held biotechnology companies between 1978 and 1989 in which the valuations of the firm in the current and previous rounds are available. The dependent variable is a dummy variable indicating if one or more venture investors above or below the median size or age of venture organizations active in biotechnology in that year were first-time investors in this round. (Rounds with new investors are coded as 1.0.) The independent variables are the percentage change in the valuation of the firm from the previous to the current venture round, the age (or size) of the most experienced venture organization that had previously invested in the firm, and a constant. A probit regression is employed (absolute t-statistics in brackets).

	Dependent variable			
	Organization above median size invested	Organization below median size invested	Organization above median age invested	Organization below median age invested
Percent change in valuation between previous and current round	0.14 [2.21]	−0.04 [0.83]	0.15 [2.67]	−0.03 [0.5]
Size of oldest previous investor (as % of total venture pool)	21.86 [2.12]	12.33 [1.50]		
Age of oldest previous investor (in years)			0.03 [2.15]	0.02 [2.6]
Constant	0.33 [1.85]	−0.49 [3.15]	0.41 [1.12]	−0.62 [3.5]
Log likelihood	−101.9	−128.2	−110.6	−128.4
χ^2-statistic	8.86	2.86	6.99	7.79
p-value	0.01	0.24	0.03	0.02
# observations	199	199	199	199

The change in the firm value is computed using the price per share in the previous venture round and the price per share in the current round. Number of shares and valuation are corrected for any stock splits, reverse splits, and stock dividends.

of the offering are often decided in consultation with two colead invest-ment bankers. Decision sharing is an important motivation in many of these comanaged offerings (see, for instance, the description of Micro-soft's IPO in Wallace and Erickson 1992).

This analysis does not exhaust the important questions concerning syndication. One issue that has been acknowledged but not addressed is how reputation affects the risk aversion of venture capitalists and their consequent willingness to syndicate. For instance, more established ven-ture organizations may be willing to accept lower returns as long as the variance is lower. They may thus participate in many syndicated deals. A second research opportunity, suggested by the industrial organization lit-erature, is the response to entrants. The 1980s saw the entry of many new firms into venture capital. While a few entrants participated in many syn-dicated first-round transactions, many more were relegated to later-round syndications. The process through which some of the entrants joined the core of established venture organizations remains unclear. Nor is it clear whether the syndication of later-round investments by established ven-ture capitalists helped establish the stature of the new organizations. (One of the few empirical examinations of entry in the finance literature is Beatty and Ritter 1986.) Thus, several aspects of the syndication of both public and private securities would reward further scrutiny.

III Exiting Venture Capital Investments

Part 3 of this volume examines the process through which private equity investors exit their investments. Successful exits are critical to ensuring attractive returns for investors and, in turn, to raising additional capital. But private equity investors' concerns about exiting investments—and their behavior during the exiting process itself—can sometimes lead to severe problems for entrepreneurs.

While exiting is the last phase of the venture capital cycle that we discuss, it is extremely important to the health of the other parts of the cycle. The need to ultimately exit investments shapes every aspect of the venture capital cycle, from the ability to raise capital to the types of investments that are made.

Perhaps the clearest illustration of the relation between the private and public markets was seen during the 1980s and early 1990s. In the early 1980s, many European nations developed secondary markets. These sought to combine a hospitable environment for small firms (e.g., they allowed firms to be listed even if they did not have an extended record of profitability) with tight regulatory safeguards. These enabled the pioneering European private equity funds to exit their investments. A wave of fundraising by these and other private equity organizations followed in the mid-1980s. After the 1987 market crash, initial public offering activity in Europe and the United States dried up. But while the U.S. market recovered in the early 1990s, the European market remained depressed. Consequently, European private equity investors were unable to exit investments by taking them public. They were required either to continue to hold the firms or to sell them to larger corporations, often at relatively unattractive valuations. While U.S. private equity investors—pointing to their successful exits—were able to raise substantial amounts of new capital, European private equity fundraising during this period remained depressed. The influence of exits on the rest of the private equity cycle suggests that this is a critical issue for funds and their investors. Many European nations have again set up emerging stock exchanges in recent years in the hopes of promoting increased venture capital activity.

The exiting of venture capital investments also has important implications for social welfare. As discussed in part I, the typical private-equity fund is liquidated after about one decade. Thus, if private-equity investors cannot foresee how a company will be mature enough to take public or to sell at the end of a decade, they are unlikely to invest in the firm. If it was equally easy to exit investments of all types at all times, this might not be a problem. But interest in certain technologies by public investors appears to be subject to wide swings. For instance, in recent years "hot-issue markets" have appeared and disappeared for computer hardware, biotechnology, multimedia, and Internet companies. Concerns about the ability to exit investments may have led to too many private-equity transactions being undertaken in these "hot" industries. At the same time, insufficient capital may have been devoted to industries not in the public limelight. Promising technologies might not be developed if they are currently "out of favor."

Concerns about exiting may also adversely affect firms once they are financed by venture capitalists. Less scrupulous investors may occasionally encourage companies in their portfolio to undertake actions that boost the probability of a successful initial public offering, even if they jeopardize the firm's long-run health: for example, increasing earnings by cutting back on vital research spending. In addition, many private-equity investors appear to exploit their inside knowledge when dissolving their stakes in investments. While this may be in the best interests of the limited and general partners of the fund, it may have harmful effects on the firm and the other shareholders.

As discussed in part I, some institutions and features have evolved to improve the efficiency of the venture capital investment process, while others have sprung up primarily to shift more of the economic benefits to particular parties. Many of the features of the exiting of private-equity investments can be understood as responses to environmental uncertainties. An example is the "lock-up" provisions that prohibit corporate insiders and private equity investors from selling at the time of the offering. This helps avoid situations in which the officers and directors exploit their inside knowledge that a newly listed company is overvalued by rapidly liquidating their positions.

At the same time, other features of the exiting process can be seen as attempts to transfer wealth between parties. An example may be the instances in which private-equity funds distribute shares to their investors immediately prior to a drop in price. Even if the price at which the investors ultimately sell the shares is far less, the private-equity investors use the share price before the distribution to calculate their fund's rate of return and to determine when they can begin profit sharing.

The efficiency and attractiveness of exiting venture capital investments will be determined by the relative strength of these two forces. Over time, an attractive environment for exits can exist only when formal or informal safeguards prevent opportunitistic behavior.

Related Literature

Venture-backed offerings were the focus of much of the initial empirical research into IPOs. Much of this research focused on the structure of IPOs, contrasting differences between venture-backed and nonventure IPOs.

Barry, Muscarella, Peavy, and Vetsuypens (1990) focus on establishing a broad array of facts about the role of venture capitalists in IPOs, using a sample of 433 venture-backed and 1123 nonventure IPOs between 1978 and 1987. Barry, et al., document that venture capitalists hold significant equity stakes in the firms they take public (on average, the lead venture capitalist holds a 19 percent stake immediately prior to the IPO, and all venture investors hold 34 percent), and they hold about one-third of the board seats. They continue to hold their equity positions in the year after the IPO. Finally, venture-backed IPOs have less of a positive return on their first trading day. The authors suggest that this implies that investors need less of a discount to purchase these shares (i.e., the offerings are less "underpriced"), because the venture capitalist has monitored the quality of the offering. In their paper, however, they explicitly eschew undertaking formal hypothesis testing, preferring to generate a broad array of facts about venture investments.

Megginson and Weiss (1991) argue that because venture capitalists repeatedly bring firms to the public market, they can credibly stake their reputation on the quality of the issuing firm. Put another way, they can certify to investors that the firms they bring to market are not overvalued. Certification requires that venture capitalists possess reputational capital, that the acquisition of such a reputation is costly, and that the present value of lost reputational capital by cheating is greater than the one-time gain from behaving in a duplicitous manner.

The certification model yields several empirical implications. First, because venture capitalists repeatedly take firms public, they build relationships with underwriters and auditors. These relationships may lead to the average venture-backed IPO having higher quality underwriters and auditors than nonventure IPOs. Megginson and Weiss also argue that these relationships and the existence of reputation should lead to greater institutional holdings of the venture-backed firm after IPO. Megginson and Weiss claim that the retention of large stakes of equity both before and after the IPO is a "bonding mechanism" that increases the effectiveness of the venture capitalist's certification. Any benefit to issuing overpriced shares would be minimized because the venture capitalist sells few or no shares at IPO.

Megginson and Weiss test these ideas using a matched set of 320 venture-backed and 320 nonventure IPOs between 1983 and 1987. First, they examine the quality of the underwriters who bring the firms to market. They show that the underwriters of venture-backed firms are significantly more experienced than the underwriters of comparable nonventure offerings. Megginson and Weiss also find that institutional holdings of venture-backed firms after the IPO are higher than comparable nonventure companies. Third, Megginson and Weiss gather evidence on expenses associated with going public. Venture-backed IPOs have significantly lower fees than nonventure IPOs. Fourth, Megginson and Weiss demonstrate that venture capitalists retain a majority of their equity after the IPO. Megginson and Weiss argue that this is a commitment device. Finally, Megginson and Weiss present evidence that the underpricing of venture capital-backed IPOs is significantly less than the underpricing of nonventure IPOs.

The exiting of venture capital investments has attracted very little theoretical attention. (The few exceptions include Berglöf 1994, and Black and Gilson 1998.) The complex institutional features and the many conflicting incentives suggest that this would be a rich environment for such analyses.

An Overview of Part III

The four chapters that follow examine the timing of the decision to take firms public and to liquidate the venture capitalists' holdings (which frequently occurs well after the IPO), as well as the relative performance of venture-backed and nonventure offerings. Consistent with discussion above, it suggests that venture capitalists can add significant value to the firms in which they invest. At the same time, distortions may affect the timing of decisions to exit venture capital investments.

Several potential factors affect when venture capitalists choose to bring firms public. One of these is the relative valuation level of publicly traded securities. Chapter 11 examines when venture capitalists choose to finance a sample of biotechnology companies in another private round versus taking the firm public. Using a sample of 350 privately held venture-backed firms, the analysis shows that venture capitalists take firms public at market peaks, relying on private financings when valuations are lower. Seasoned venture capitalists appear more proficient at timing IPOs. The results are robust to the use of alternative criteria to separate firms and controls for firms' quality. The results are not caused by differences in the speed of executing the IPOs or in the willingness to withdraw the proposed IPOs.

Another consideration may be the reputation of the venture capital firm. Chapter 12 argues that young venture capital firms have incentives to "grandstand": that is, they take actions that signal their ability to potential investors. Specifically, young venture capital firms bring companies public earlier than older venture capital firms in an effort to establish a reputation and successfully raise capital for new funds. For example, the effect of recent performance in the IPO market on the amount of capital raised is stronger for young venture capital firms, providing them with a greater incentive to bring companies public earlier. Young venture capital firms have been on the IPO company's board of directors fourteen months less and hold smaller percentage equity stakes at the time of IPO than the more established venture firms. The IPO companies that they finance are nearly two years younger and more underpriced when they go public than companies backed by older venture capital firms. Much of the difference in underpricing and the venture capitalists' percentage equity stake is associated with a shorter duration of board representation, indicating that rushing companies to the IPO market imposes costs on the venture firm. The results suggest that the relation between performance and capital raising affects the incentives and actions of venture capitalists.

The typical venture capital firm, however, does not sell their equity at the time of the IPO. The negative signal that would be sent to the market by an insider "cashing out" would prevent a successful offering. In addition, most investment banks require that all insiders, including the venture capitalists, do not sell any of their equity after the offering for a pre-specified period (usually six months). Once that lock-up period is over, however, venture capitalists can return money to investors in one of two ways. They can liquidate their position in a portfolio company by selling shares on the open market after it has gone public and then paying those proceeds to investors in cash. More frequently, however, venture capitalists make distributions of shares to investors in the venture capital fund. Many institutional investors have received a flood of these distributions during the past several years and have grown increasingly concerned about the incentives of the venture capitalists when they declare these transfers.

Chapter 13 examines how investors might be affected by these distributions of equity. From the records of four institutions, we construct a representative set of over 700 transactions by 135 funds over a decade-long period. We use the features of the venture funds making the distributions, the firms whose shares are being distributed, and the changes associated with the transactions in a way that can discriminate between the various alternative explanations for these patterns.

The results are consistent with venture capitalists possessing inside information and of the (partial) adjustment of the market to that information. After significant increases in stock prices prior to distribution, abnormal returns around the distribution are negative and significant, comparable to the market reaction to publicly announced secondary stock sales. The sign and significance of the cumulative excess returns for the twelve months following the distribution appear to be negative in most specifications, but are sensitive to the benchmark used. Distributions that occur in settings where information asymmetries may be greatest—especially where the firm has been taken public by a lower tier underwriter and the distribution is soon after the IPO—have larger immediate price declines. Post-distribution price performance is related to factors that predict event window returns.

Whatever the short-run behavior around the time of IPO and distribution, the ultimate question is whether the transition from venture capital financing to the public marketplace is good for the company and the new investors. As one of the quotes reproduced in the introduction suggests, many popular discussions of venture capitalists and the decision to go public suggest that public investors are consistently taken advantage of during this process. These issues are examined in the final chapter of this section.

Chapter 14 investigates the long-run performance of over 4,000 venture-backed and nonventure IPOs between 1972 and 1992. The analysis shows that venture-backed firms do not underperform the market after going public. The poor performance of IPOs relative to market benchmarks appears to be confined to the smallest non-venture offerings. In fact, venture backed offerings appear to earn positive risk-adjusted returns subsequent to going public. Far from duping the public, venture capitalists appear to bring companies public that have considerable staying power.

Final Thoughts

Part III thus paints two depictions of the IPO process. First, it is clear that the decision to go public is influenced by a wide variety of factors, including the need to impress potential investors and relative valuation levels. Venture investors do not appear averse to exploiting their superior information at certain times. But as we step back and take a broader view, a somewhat different picture emerges. When the evolution of venture-backed firms over the half-decade after the offering is viewed, there is no evidence that the transition is one with persistent inefficiencies.

The relationship between venture capital and the public markets is a rich area that will reward further exploration. We have already highlighted the need for theoretical analyses of the role that venture capitalists play in the decision to go public. Two empirical opportunities should also be highlighted.

The first of these is the assessment of venture capital as a financial asset. Many institutions, primarily public and private pension funds, have increased their allocation to venture capital and private equity in the belief that the returns of these funds are largely uncorrelated with the public markets. It is natural to see how they come to this conclusion. Firms receiving capital from private equity funds very often remain privately held for a number of years after the initial investment. These firms have no observable market price. To present a conservative assessment of the portfolio valuation, private equity managers often refrain from marking portfolio firm values to market, preferring to maintain the investments at book value. But as discussed throughout this volume, there appear to be many linkages between the public and private equity market values. Thus, the stated returns of private equity funds may not accurately reflect the true evolution of value and the correlations reported by Venture Economics (1998) and other industry observers may be deceptively low. To ignore the true correlation is fraught with potential dangers.[1]

---

1. In a preliminary analysis using data from one venture group, we (1997b) find that the correlation between venture capital and public market prices increases substantially when the underlying venture portfolio is "marked-to-market." An alternative approach is to examine the relatively modest number of publicly traded venture capital funds, as is done by Martin and Petty (1983).

Second, as the discussion at the beginning of this chapter and in chapter 2 suggested, policymakers in many nations have postulated that healthy domestic IPO markets will stimulate venture capital investments in their countries. Assessing these claims requires disentangling a complex web of interconnected events. Nonetheless, careful analyses of the evolution of venture capital activity across a wide range of nations would be a valuable exercise.

This chapter examines the ability of venture capitalists to time initial public offerings (IPOs) by going public when equity values are high and using private financings when values are lower. As discussed above, venture capitalists generate the bulk of their profits from firms that go public. Successful timing of the IPO market provides significant benefits to venture capitalists, even through they rarely sell shares at the time of the offering (Barry, Muscarella, Peavy, and Vetsuypens 1990). Taking companies public when equity values are high minimizes the dilution of the venture investors' ownership stake. Models of sequential stock sales (Allen and Faulhaber 1989, Grinblatt and Hwang 1989, Welch 1989) suggest a second rationale for timing the IPO. The deliberate underpricing of a new issue, which may be easier to accomplish in a hot market, "leaves a good taste" with investors. These investors are then more willing to purchase shares in follow-on offerings.

Venture capitalists have several mechanisms to ensure that firms go public at times that they perceive as optimal. Venture investors usually have several board seats and powerful control rights, including the right to put their shares to the firm's management (Barry, Muscarella, Peavy, and Vetsuypens 1990; Sahlman 1990). Probably more important is their activity as informal advisors to managers. Since 30 percent of the firms backed by venture capitalists over the past two decades have gone public, the venture investors have usually experienced many more IPOs than the firm's managers. Consequently, the venture capitalists may take the lead in deciding when and how a firm should go public.

The chapter uses a sample of 350 privately held biotechnology firms financed by venture capitalists between January 1978 and September 1992. Not only is the timing of their IPOs examined but also that of their private financings. Venture capitalists successfully time IPOs by being more likely to take companies public when their valuations are at their absolute and short-run peaks. Experienced venture capitalists appear to be more proficient in timing IPOs than their less experienced counterparts.

The chapter focuses on the biotechnology industry because the development of a bio-engineered pharmaceutical or agricultural product typically takes more than a decade. Biotechnology firms remain in a R&D phase until well after going public. These firms mature slowly and do not incur large up-front costs in building manufacturing facilities. Venture capitalists provide funds in stages, with each financing round accompanied by a formal review of the firm's status. Each round involves an explicit decision to go public or remain private. Therefore, venture investors in biotechnology firms have the flexibility to try to time their IPOs according to market conditions. For IPOs in other industries, the demand for capital and the changing need for oversight by active investors may be more important to the decision to go public than market conditions. Thus, the sample provides an opportunity for a more precise test of the ability to time IPOs.[1] The analysis suggests that the positive correlation between IPO volume and public equity market valuations is due not only to greater financing activity when investment opportunities are good but also to the substitution of public for private equity.

The sample also enables us to isolate the impact of investor characteristics on IPO timing. The 1978–1992 period was characterized by diverse venture investors. Freed by a 1979 Department of Labor policy statement to enter into venture partnerships, pension funds invested heavily during the sample period. This led to extensive entry on the part of new venture partnerships. The pool of venture capital under management increased six-fold from 1978 to 1990 (adjusted by the gross domestic product deflator). The wide range of experience among venture capitalists during the sample period makes it easier to identify the influence of venture experience.

The structure of this chapter is as follows. The next section presents the empirical results and checks their robustness. The third section examines two alternative hypotheses, and the fourth section concludes the chapter.

---

1. Ibbotson and Jaffe (1975) and Ritter (1984) document "hot issue" markets, while Ritter (1991) and Loughran and Ritter (1995) show that the poor long-run returns from investments in IPOs are due both to their poor performance relative to the market and their concentration around equity market peaks. The "impresario hypothesis" of Shiller (1990) and Shiller and Pound (1989) suggests that IPOs are subject to fads, which underwriters exploit by rushing firms to the market.

Table 11.1

Distribution of the sample. The table indicates by year the number and cumulative size (in millions of 1997 dollars) of public and private financings by privately held biotechnology firms that had already received venture capital. The gross amount raised is reported for both public and private financings before any deductions for offering costs.

Year	Public financings (IPOs) by private venture-backed firms		Private financings by private venture-backed firms	
	Number of IPOs	Total $ raised	Number of rounds	Total $ raised
1978	0	0	4	11
1979	1	7	4	35
1980	1	67	8	106
1981	4	249	9	66
1982	4	100	18	154
1983	18	414	40	247
1984	2	40	30	146
1985	2	9	36	138
1986	17	519	52	280
1987	12	231	61	382
1988	1	26	68	379
1989	6	65	75	413
1990	4	74	87	503
1991	34	1,252	86	458
1992[a]	30	993	36	201
Total	136	4,044	614	3,521

a. Through September 30 only.

Empirical Analysis

The Sample and Summary Statistics

In contrast to earlier studies of IPO timing and performance, both public and private financings are examined. Venture Economics' Venture Intelligence Database (described in chapter 16) is used to identify a sample of 750 financings by privately held firms that had already received venture capital. As table 11.1 indicates, these include 136 IPOs and 614 private financings. The public financings raised a total of $4.0 billion in 1997 dollars; the private financings, $3.5 billion. (Both figures are gross amounts, before deducting expenses associated with the equity sales.) The firms in this sample went public after as few as one venture financing round or as many as eight.

To assess the ability of venture capitalists to time public and private financings, the equity values of publicly traded biotechnology firms around these transactions are examined. This section describes the construction of the index.

Ideally, publicly traded biotechnology companies would be used as a benchmark throughout this period. Because companies dedicated to biotechnology did not begin going public until the late 1970s, however, "comparable" companies must be employed in the early years. For the 1978–1982 period, thirteen companies identified in the 1977 business press (primarily the analyst reports summarized in *Wall Street Transcript*, but also the *Wall Street Journal, Business Week*, and *Fortune*) as well-positioned to capitalize on the then current developments in biological science are employed. Beginning on January 1, 1983, the index uses thirteen "dedicated" biotechnology firms that went public between 1979 and 1982. The pre-1983 sample has the same distribution as the dedicated biotechnology firms: seven firms specialize in human pharmaceuticals or diagnostics, three firms whose products relate to agricultural or animal science, two producers of research equipment, and one specialty chemical producer.

The portfolio is invested equally in the comparable firms on January 1, 1978. At the end of each year, the portfolio is rebalanced so that an equal dollar amount of each security is held. The portfolio is not rebalanced daily, because for many securities the spread between the bid and ask prices is significant relative to the share price. An index with daily rebalancing would be biased upward because of the "bid-ask bounce" documented by Blume and Stambaugh (1983). On January 1, 1983, the investment in the comparable portfolio is liquidated and the proceeds used to buy equal dollar amounts of the dedicated portfolio. As companies are acquired or delisted, the most seasoned, publicly traded dedicated biotechnology company is added to the index. The indices constructed using the comparable and dedicated portfolios are highly correlated. During 1982 and 1983 (the year before and after the switch), the correlation coefficient of the daily returns is over 0.96.

Figures 11.1 and 11.2 display the number of IPOs and private financings in each month and the biotechnology equity index. The IPOs coincide with the peaks in equity valuations, while no clear pattern appears in the private financings. In particular, the high valuations of 1983, 1986, and 1991–92 were accompanied by intense IPO activity. The level of private financing activity, however, changed little. These patterns suggest

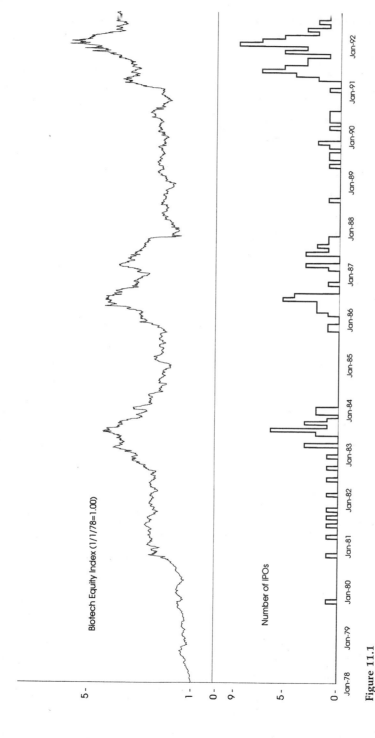

Figure 11.1
The timing of initial public offerings by privately held venture-backed biotechnology companies, January 1978 through September 1992. The top graph depicts an index of biotechnology equity, computed using the value of an investment in (between 1978 and 1982) 13 companies identified in the 1977 business press as well-positioned to capitalize on biotechnology developments and (from 1983 onward) 13 biotechnology companies. Acquired or delisted firms are replaced with the most seasoned publicly traded biotechnology firm. January 1, 1978, is normalized as one. The lower plot represents the number of biotechnology IPOs in each month. The data are compiled from Venture Economics, Recombinant Capital, U.S. Securities and Exchange Commission (SEC) filings and company contracts, as well as the Center for Research in Security Prices.

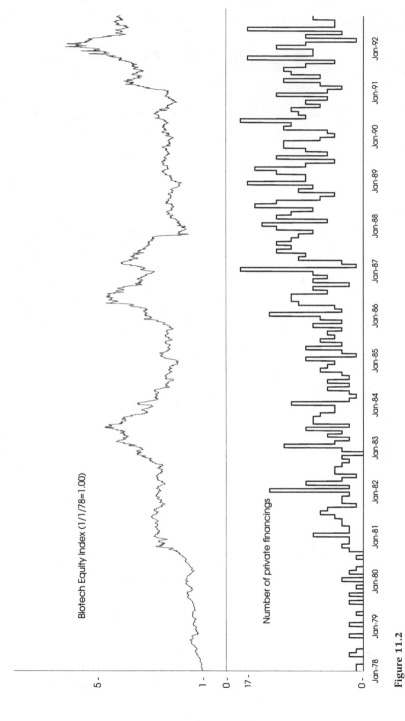

Figure 11.2

The timing of private financings by privately held venture-backed biotechnology companies, January 1978 through September 1992. The top graph depicts an index of biotechnology equity, computed using the value of an investment in (between 1978 and 1982) 13 companies identified in the 1977 business press as well-positioned to capitalize on biotechnology developments and (from 1983 onward) 13 biotechnology companies. Acquired or delisted firms are replaced with the most seasoned publicly traded biotechnology firm. January 1, 1978 is normalized as one. The lower plot represents the number of biotechnology private financings in each month. The data are compiled from Venture Economics, Recombinant Capital, SEC filings and company contacts, as well as the Center for Research in Security Prices.

Table 11.1

Biotechnology equity prices around public and private financings by privately held venture-backed biotechnology companies. The sample consists of 750 IPOs and private financings between January 1978 and September 1992 by firms that had already received venture capital. The table presents the level of a biotechnology equity index,[a] and the mean return from biotechnology equities in the three months before and after the financing. The table also compares the means and medians of these variables.

Panel A: Biotechnology equity prices

| | | Mean raw "buy-and-hold" return from biotechnology equities around financing date | |
	Mean level of biotechnology index	Trading days −60 to −1	Trading days 0 to 59
136 initial public offerings	4.05	9.9%	−4.6%
614 private financings	3.05	4.6%	6.1%

Panel B: Tests of differences in means and medians

Test	p-value
Wilcoxon test, median equity index on date of IPO = median equity index on date of private financing	0.00
t-test, mean return in $[-60, -1]$ window before IPO = mean return in $[-60, -1]$ window before private financing	0.00
t-test, mean return in $[0, 59]$ window after IPO = mean return in $[0, 59]$ window after private financing	0.00
t-test, mean return in $[-60, -1]$ window before IPO = mean return in $[0, 59]$ window after IPO	0.00
t-test, mean return in $[-60, -1]$ window before private financing = mean return in $[0, 59]$ window after private financing	0.27

a. The index and change in equity values are computed for the period 1978 to 1982 using thirteen companies identified in the 1977 business press as well-positioned to capitalize on biotechnology developments and (from 1983 onwards) thirteen biotechnology companies. Acquired or delisted firms are replaced with the most seasoned publicly traded biotechnology firms. The index is normalized to one on January 1, 1978. For the private financings where only the month and year of the transaction are known, the twelfth trading day of the month is used.

that venture capitalists are able to time the market, taking companies public at times when industry valuations are highest.

The Timing of Financings

First, the timing of all external financings in the sample is examined. Panel A of table 11.2 presents the main results. As figures 11.1 and 11.2 suggest, IPOs are far more likely to occur when the equity values are high. The mean equity index at the time of IPOs is 4.05, as opposed to 3.05 at the time of private financings. (The index is normalized as one on January

1, 1978.) Using a nonparametric Wilcoxon test, panel B of table 11.2 shows that the difference is statistically significant at the 1 percent level of confidence.

This test is repeated (as are the others shown below), adjusting the index in two ways. The increase in the equity index is partially due to inflation, and also to the need to provide a return to investors in excess of inflation. The index is detrended by the gross domestic product (GDP) deflator and by inflation plus a 5 percent annual premium. The differences in the index around IPOs and private financings remain significant. In the case of the inflation-adjusted series, the mean index at the time of the IPOs is 2.10; the mean index at the time of private financings, 1.69. (January 1, 1978 is once again normalized as one.) In the case of the inflation-adjusted series with the 5 percent annual premium, the mean index at the time of the IPOs is 1.26, the mean index at the time of private financings, 1.03. In both cases nonparametric Wilcoxon tests reject the null hypotheses of the equality of the distributions at the 1 percent level of confidence. The modified indices remain significant at the one percent level of confidence when used in probit regressions akin to that reported in table 11.3.

An IPO is also likely to coincide with a short-term maximum in equity values. The buy-and-hold returns from an equal-weighted investment in thirteen biotechnology securities are examined in the three months before and after the financing. The thirteen comparable securities are used prior to 1983 and thirteen publicly traded dedicated firms thereafter. The index is extended back into late 1977 and forward to the end of 1992 to be able to use observations that are near the beginning and the end of the sample period. If a firm is acquired or delisted during the period, the investment is rolled over into the most seasoned publicly traded dedicated biotechnology firm.

Such an investment gains an average of 9.9 percent in the event window $(-60, -1)$ before an IPO. (The event window of sixty trading days is chosen to be consistent with Mikkelson and Partch 1988 and several other studies.) An identical investment made at the close of the IPO date has lost 4.6 percent of its value by day 59. Panel B indicates that the mean returns differ significantly at the 1 percent level of confidence.

Private financings display no such differences in the months before $(+4.6$ percent) and after $(+6.1$ percent) the transaction. Panel B shows that the mean returns in the three months prior to the IPOs are significantly greater than in the three months prior to the private financings. The mean returns are also significantly lower in the three months after IPOs. In some older entries in the database where the firm did not subsequently go public, only the month and year of the private financings are known. In these cases, the twelfth trading day of the month is used. The results are robust to alternative approaches, including the assumption that the undated private financings took place on the first or last trading date of the month. They also are robust to using the changes in the index in the three months before and after the public and private financings, but not including the returns from the month of the financing.

One concern with the tests of the equality of means is their assumption of independence. The bunching of the IPOs and private financings implies that many of the sixty trading-day windows over which returns are calculated overlap. To address concerns about whether the bunching of returns may lead to an overstating of significance levels, the t-tests in table 11.2 are examined in a regression framework. The return is regressed on a constant and a dummy variable to indicate if the observation is from one of the two classes being compared: for example, if this is an observation of the returns in the sixty trading days prior to a private financing. Instead of assuming independence, however, a generalized least squares (GLS) approach is employed, akin to that used by Hansen and Hodrick (1980) and Meulbroek (1992a). In their analyses these authors employ monthly observations of forward and futures prices several months ahead. Through the use of GLS estimation, they correct their standard errors for the degree of overlap in the observations. Though the overlap here rises from the clustering of observations rather than the sampling procedure, a similar approach is used to examine the robustness of the results. A variance-covariance matrix Ω is created, and standard errors computed from the matrix $(X'\Omega^{-1}X)^{-1}$. The off-diagonal elements of the variance-covariance matrix Ω are constrained to be zero if the sixty trading day windows over which the equity index is calculated do not overlap and to be proportional to the extent of the overlap otherwise. In this way, nearby observations are assigned less weight in the analysis. Returns in the sixty trading days before and after IPOs remain significantly different at the 1 percent level of confidence. Returns in the sixty trading days prior to public and private financings do not differ at conventional confidence levels. Returns in the sixty trading days after public and private financings differ at the 5 percent level of confidence. In another analysis, the sixty trading-day returns are detrended for inflation and inflation plus a 5 percent annual premium. These corrections make little difference.

These patterns are then examined using the probit regression shown in table 11.3. Each financing by a privately held firm that has already

Table 11.3
Estimated probit regressions of the decision of privately held venture-backed biotechnology firms to employ public or private financing. The sample consists of 750 IPOs and private financings between January 1978 and September 1992 by firms that had already received venture capital. The dependent variable is 1 for firms that went public and 0 for firms that employed private financings. Independent variables include three alternative measures of market timing: the level of a biotechnology equity index[a] at the time of the financing, the changes in equity prices in the three months before the financing, and the changes in equity prices in the three months after the financing (absolute t-statistics in brackets).

	Dependent variable: Did firm go public? Regressions use alternative measures of market timing		
Level of biotechnology index	0.50 [9.33]		
Raw return from biotech equities in [−60, −1] window		0.74 [2.80]	
Raw return from biotech equities in [0, 59] window			−0.65 [3.64]
Constant	−2.65 [13.16]	−0.96 [16.78]	−0.90 [16.71]
Log likelihood	−307.55	−351.14	−348.23
χ^2-statistic	95.00	7.83	13.66
p-value	0.00	0.00	0.00
Number of observations	750	750	750

a. The index and change in equity values are computed for the period 1978 to 1982 using thirteen companies identified in the 1977 business press as well-positioned to capitalize on biotechnology developments and (from 1983 onwards) thirteen biotechnology companies. Acquired or delisted firms are replaced with the most seasoned publicly traded biotechnology firms. The index is normalized to one on January 1, 1978. For the private financings where only the month and year of the transaction are known, the twelfth trading day of the month is used.

received venture capital is employed as an observation. The dependent variable is a dummy indicating whether the firm received public or private financing (where 1 denotes an IPO, and zero a private financing):

$$IPO_{it} = \alpha_{0j} + \alpha_{1j}TIMING_{ijt} + \varepsilon_{ijt}. \tag{11.1}$$

The three measures of timing are the value of the biotechnology index at the time of the financing, the raw returns from an investment in biotechnology securities in the three months before the financing, and the raw returns in the three months after the financing.

Each of the variables is significant in explaining the decision to go public. As the coefficient of 0.50 suggests, a higher level of the equity index increases the probability of a public financing. The magnitude of this coefficient can be assessed by examining the effect of a 10 percent increase in the level of the equity index on the predicted probability that a public financing is employed. At the mean of all independent variables, the regression coefficients imply that the probability of an IPO is 15 percent. A 10 percent increase in the level of the equity index (i.e., from the mean of 3.23 to 3.56) boosts the probability of an IPO to 19 percent, or an increase of 27 percent. Increases in biotechnology equity values in the three months prior to the financing boost the chance of an IPO (the coefficient of 0.74) as do decreases in the three months after an IPO (-0.65).

The Impact of Venture Capitalist Experience

Next the analysis examines whether seasoned and inexperienced venture capitalists differ in their proficiency in taking firms public at market peaks. To examine this, the analyses in tables 11.2 and 11.3 were repeated. The firms were divided into those financed by more or less seasoned venture capitalists.

The age of the oldest venture capital partnership having financed the firm was used as a proxy for venture capitalist experience. This approach differs slightly from Barry, Muscarella, Peavy, and Vetsuypens (1990). Those authors used the venture capitalist with the largest equity stake in the firm at the time of the IPO to characterize the venture investors. Since the relative valuation of each round is not always known, however, the largest shareholder cannot always be determined. In a section below, alternative measures of venture capital experience are used. In point of fact, these measures show little difference. Venture capitalists tend to syndicate investments either to their peers or to their less experienced counterparts. They are not likely to invest in deals begun by their less seasoned counterparts (see chapter 9). The lead venture capitalist is usually the oldest one.

To establish that this is an economically meaningful partition of firms, the 136 IPOs in the sample are divided by the age of the oldest venture capital organization investing in the firm. Venture capital organizations are characterized by using several reference volumes (Clay 1991, National Register 1992, Venture Economics 1992a). If the name of the venture capital fund recorded in the Venture Economics database does not match an entry in these directories of venture organizations, then to establish a match an unpublished database from Venture Economics that lists venture capital funds and organizations is used. Data about the IPOs is collected from prospectuses, S-1 registration statements, and the Securities Data Company (SDC) Corporate New Issues database (1992).

IPOs divided in this manner differ in several respects. Table 11.4 shows that the reputation of the underwriter differs significantly at the 1 percent

Table 11.4
Characteristics of IPOs by venture-backed biotechnology firms, divided by the age of the oldest venture investor in the firm. The sample consists of 136 IPOs between January 1978 and September 1992. The table compares the underwriter ranking,[a] the presence of a "Big Six" accounting firm as the firm's auditor, and the most frequently represented underwriters, law firms, and accounting firms. The remaining columns describe these offerings: the share of equity retained by employees and management after the IPO,[b] the mean inflation-adjusted offering size,[c] the percentage of offerings in which units rather than common stock were sold, and the percentage change from the offering price to the first-day close.[d] The table also compares the means of these variables for firms whose oldest venture capitalist is above and below the median age.

	Firms divided by age of oldest venture capital provider		p-value, t-test of difference of means
	Above median	Below or equal to median	
Underwriter characteristics			
Carter-Manaster ranking	6.6	4.8	0.00
Most frequent firm (number)	Hambrecht and Quist (6)	D.H. Blair (14)	
Auditor characteristics			
Percent of firms in "Big Six"	98.5%	96.1%	0.56
Most frequent firm (number)	Ernst and Young (26)[e]	Ernst and Young (21)[e]	
Issuer's law firm characteristics			
Most frequent firm (number)	Cooley, Godward, Castro, Huddleston and Tatum (11)	Bachner, Tally, Polevoy and Misher (5)	
Offering characteristics			
Percent of equity retained by employees and management	7.2%	11.8%	0.00
Funds raised (millions of 1997 dollars)	33.7	25.6	0.08
Percent of IPOs which are unit offerings	4.4%	25.0%	0.00
Initial return	10.3%	15.4%	0.31

a. Carter and Manaster's (1990) ranking of lead underwriter prestige is employed, with nine representing the most prestigious underwriters, and zero the least. If the book underwriter is not included in the Carter-Manaster ratings, the ranking of the comanaging underwriter is used. If there is no comanaging underwriter, or it is also not ranked, these underwriters are assigned a rank of zero.
b. This measure includes all shareholdings by full-time managers and employees, but not venture capitalists or other financiers working as consultants at the firm.
c. This is the gross amount paid by the public, before allowance for direct and indirect underwriting fees. The GDP deflator is used.
d. The closing price, when not available, is calculated as the mean of the bid and ask.
e. Includes predecessor entities Ernst and Whinney and Arthur Young.

level of confidence, using the Carter Manaster (1990) rankings of under writer prestige. In this scheme, nine denotes the most prestigious under writers and zero the least prestigious. They determine these rankings through the positioning of companies in "tombstones," the advertise ments that underwriters use to publicize offerings. If the book under writer is not included in the Carter-Manaster ratings, the ranking of the comanaging underwriter is used. For twelve cases, there is no comanaging underwriter, or else it is not ranked. These are all small regional invest ment banks with limited underwriting experience (National Register 1992). These underwriters are assigned a rank of zero. Although Ham brecht and Quist is the most frequent underwriter for firms backed by ex perienced venture capitalists, D. H. Blair dominates the less experienced group.

Also presented are the other intermediaries involved in the offering. A partition frequently used to divide accounting firms in underpricing studies is the "Big Six" (previously the "Big Eight"), the largest U.S. accounting firms as measured by revenue (Balvers, McDonald, and Miller 1988; Beatty 1989). While the firms backed by more experienced venture capitalists are more likely to have a "Big Six" accounting firm, the differ ence is not significant. The most frequently used accountants and law firms are also reported.

The offerings also differ in magnitude. The equity stake retained by managers and employees after the offering is significantly larger for firms backed by the less experienced venture capitalists. In addition, the dollars raised in the IPOs by firms with seasoned venture investors is larger (though only at the 10 percent level of confidence). Both results are con sistent with Leland and Pyle (1977), who argue that lower quality man agers must retain larger equity stakes and raise less money to obtain any external financing.

Firms backed by seasoned venture capitalists are significantly less likely to employ a unit offering. These bundled offerings include at least one share of stock and one warrant. Schultz (1993) shows that unit offerings are usually employed by small firms with uncertain prospects. He sug gests that by providing only some of the funding up front, unit offerings limit the danger of managers squandering invested capital. The remaining funds are provided only if the warrants are exercised. Because the war rants are typically "out-of-the-money" at the time of the IPO (i.e., they can be exercised at a price higher than the per-share price of the IPO), the exercise of the warrants is usually conditional on the stock price rising. The first-day returns from the IPOs are lower for the firms backed by experienced venture capitalists, consistent with Barry, Peavy, Muscarella, and Vetsuypens (1990), but the difference is not significant.

After separating firms whose oldest venture investor is above or below the median age, the analysis in table 11.2 is repeated. Panel A of table 11.5 examines the choice between private and public equity. Both classes of firms appear to time IPOs. The effectiveness of this timing, however, appears greater for the more experienced venture capitalists, as the tests in panel B confirm. The average firm backed by experienced venture capitalists went public when the index was at 4.31; for the firms below the median, the level was 3.80. Similarly, the index run-up in the three months before the IPO and the run-down in the three months after are both larger.

Table 11.6 repeats the probit regression estimation of the decision to go public. Firms backed by venture capitalists above or below the median age are separated. Again, the probability of the firm that went public is the dependent variable, with the three measures of market timing as independent variables. In each of the three pairs of regressions, the timing variable is greater in magnitude and significance in the seasoned venture capital regression.

Panel C examines whether the regression coefficients differ significantly. First a pooled regression is estimated, allowing firms above and below the median to have distinct coefficients for the timing variable and constant. Then the coefficient of the timing variable is constrained to be the same in both regressions. The table presents the p-values from χ^2-tests of this constraint. In two of the three cases, the null hypothesis of no difference at the 5 percent level of confidence is rejected. These findings suggest that firms backed by established venture capitalists are more successful at timing their IPOs.

Robustness to Alternative Measures and Control Variables

Several analyses assess the robustness of the results to alternative measures of venture experience and the presence of control variables. They have little effect on the qualitative and quantitative results.

First, the results may be an artifact of the criteria used to divide the venture capitalists. As an alternative, size is used to divide venture capitalists into experienced and inexperienced investors. In this way, venture capitalists who raise new (but large) partnerships are counted as seasoned investors. The ratio of funds under management by the partnership to the total pool of venture capital under management in the year of the investment is computed, using the annual values reported in *Pratt's Guide* (Venture Economics 1992a). When this information is incomplete, the unpublished Venture Economics database is used. The results using this partition are consistent with the ones reported earlier.

A related set of regressions divide firms by relative, rather than absolute, age and size. The mean age and size of the venture partnerships that financed biotechnology firms dipped in the mid-1980s, reflecting the extensive entry into venture capital. The analysis identifies the age of the oldest venture capitalist providing funds to each biotechnology firm in each year, and it then divides the firms by whether their oldest investor was older or younger than the oldest investor in the median firm in that year. (The procedure for size is similar.) There appears to be little difference between these results and those in tables 11.5 and 11.6. These tests are not independent: relatively older venture partnerships are often the older ones on an absolute scale as well. The analysis shows, however, that these results are not an artifact of a particular approach to dividing firms.

The independent variables are also recast, using the change in the market index over two- and four-month windows. Using the longer window tends to slightly strengthen the results; the shorter window tends to weaken them. Although there are only a small number of cases in the sample where venture capitalists exited viable firms through mergers or sales, nevertheless the impact of including these cases is examined. The dependent variable is recast to measure IPOs and acquisitions of firms at prices higher than that of the last venture round. This change has little impact.

Finally, controls are added for the quality of the firms going public. More experienced venture capitalists are likely to fund higher quality firms, which may bias the results. Three sets of control variables for firm quality are used:

1. The age of the firm. In order of preference, the incorporation date reported in SEC filings, the self-reported founding date in industry directories (Corporate Technology (1996), Mega-Type (1992), Oryx (1992)), a questionnaire response (NCBC 1990b), or the date reported by Venture Economics are used.

2. A private placement from a corporation with a related line of business. Strategic investments are frequently used in high-technology industries, particularly biotechnology, to cement long-run agreements (Pisano 1989). Related lines of business are defined as those with any of the following Standard Industrial Classification identifiers in the *Million Dollar Directory*

Table 11.5
Biotechnology equity prices around public and private financings for privately held venture-backed biotechnology companies, divided by the age of the oldest venture investor in the firm. The sample consists of 750 IPOs and private financings between January 1978 and September 1992 by firms that had already received venture capital. The table presents the level of a biotechnology equity index,[a] and the changes in equity prices in the three months before and after the financing. The table also compares the means and medians of these variables for firms whose oldest venture capitalist is above and below the median age.

Panel A: Biotechnology equity prices

	Mean level of biotechnology index	Mean raw "buy-and-hold" returns from biotech equities around financing date	
		Trading days −60 to −1	Trading days 0 to 59
136 initial public offerings			
Firms whose oldest venture investor is above the median age	4.31	12.5%	−6.8%
Firms whose oldest venture investor is below the median age	3.80	7.4%	−2.4%
614 private financings			
Firms whose oldest venture investor is above the median age	3.08	5.1%	6.6%
Firms whose oldest venture investor is below the median age	3.03	4.0%	5.1%

Panel B: Tests of differences in means and medians

	p-value
Tests using firms whose oldest venture investor is above the median age	
Wilcoxon test, median equity index on date of IPO = median equity index on date of private financing	0.00
t-test, mean return in [−60, −1] window prior to IPO = mean return in [−60, −1] window prior to private financing	0.00
t-test, mean return in [0, 59] window after IPO = mean return in [0, 59] window after private financing	0.00
Tests using firms whose oldest venture investor is below the median age	
Wilcoxon test, median equity index on date of IPO = median equity index on date of private financing	0.00

t-test, mean return in $[-60, -1]$ window prior to IPO = mean return in $[-60, -1]$ window prior to private financing	0.20
t-test, mean return in $[0, 59]$ window after IPO = mean return in $[0, 59]$ window after private financing	0.01
Tests comparing firms whose oldest venture investor is above and below the median age	
Wilcoxon test, median equity index on date of IPO is same for both sets of firms	0.00
t-test, mean return in $[-60, -1]$ window prior to IPO is same for both sets of firms	0.03
t-test, mean return in $[0, 59]$ window after IPO is same for both sets of firms	0.07

a. The index and change in equity values are computed for the period 1978 to 1982 using thirteen companies identified in the 1977 business press as well-positioned to capitalize on biotechnology developments and (from 1983 onwards) thirteen biotechnology companies. Acquired or delisted firms are replaced with the most seasoned publicly traded biotechnology firms. The index is normalized to one on January 1, 1978. For the private financings where only the month and year of the transaction is known, the twelfth trading day of the month is used.

Table 11.6
Estimated probit regressions of the decision of privately held venture-backed biotechnology firms to employ public or private financing, with observations are divided by the age of the oldest venture investor in the firm. The sample consists of 750 financing rounds between January 1978 and September 1992 by firms that had already received venture capital. The dependent variable is 1 for firms that went public and 0 for firms that employed private financings. Independent variables include three alternative measures of market timing: the level of a biotechnology equity index[a] at the time of the financing, the changes in equity prices in the three months before the financing, and the changes in equity prices in the three months after the financing. (Absolute t-statistics in brackets). The table also compares the regression coefficients for firms whose oldest venture capitalist is above and below the median age.

Panel A: Estimated probit regressions using firms whose oldest venture investor is above the median age

	Dependent variable: Did firm go public? Regressions use alternative measures of market timing		
Level of a biotechnology index	0.65 [7.75]		
Raw return from biotech equities in [−60, −1] window		0.93 [2.53]	
Raw return from biotech equities in [0, 59] window			−1.44 [3.94]
Constant	−2.79 [10.10]	−0.87 [10.89]	−1.04 [12.90]
Log likelihood	−160.40	−191.14	−187.52
χ^2-statistic	67.95	6.48	9.11
p-value	0.00	0.01	0.00
Number of observations	375	375	375

Panel B: Estimated probit regressions using firms whose oldest venture investor is below the median age

	Dependent variable: Did firm go public? Regressions use alternative measures of market timing		
Level of biotechnology index	0.31 [4.92]		
Raw return from biotech equities in [−60, −1] window		0.48 [1.23]	
Raw return from biotech equities in [0, 59] window			−0.54 [2.32]
Constant	−2.39 [8.09]	−1.07 [12.84]	−0.78 [10.65]
Log likelihood	−145.46	−157.32	−155.58
χ^2-statistic	25.33	1.52	5.60
p-value	0.00	0.29	0.02
Number of observations	375	375	375

Panel C: χ^2-tests of differences in regression coefficients

	p-value
Tests comparing firms whose oldest venture investor is above and below the median age	
Coefficient of "level of biotechnology index" variable is identical in both regressions	0.01
Coefficient of "change in biotech equity values in $[-60, -1]$ window" variable is identical in both regressions	0.21
Coefficient of "change in biotech equity values in $[0, 59]$ window" variable is identical in both regressions	0.03

a. The index and change in equity values are computed for the period 1978 to 1982 using thirteen companies identified in the 1977 business press as well-positioned to capitalize on biotechnology developments and (from 1983 onwards) thirteen biotechnology companies. Acquired or delisted firms are replaced with the most seasoned publicly traded biotechnology firms. The index is normalized to one on January 1, 1978. For the private financings where only the month and year of the transaction is known, the twelfth trading day of the month is used.

(Dun's 1996) in the year of the transaction: SIC 283, Drugs; SIC 287, Agricultural Chemicals; and SIC 384, Medical Instruments and Supplies.

3. The firm's intellectual property position. Intellectual property protection was a critical focus of biotechnology firms in the 1980s. (See Lerner 1994 for an overview.) Product market competition was embryonic, and the alternative methods of protecting intellectual property ineffective. The disposition of a single patent could shift the valuation of a biotechnology firm by as much as 50 percent. Patents associated with these 350 firms are identified by using U.S. Patent and Trademark Office databases (USPTO/ OPDLP 1989, 1990), as well as those assigned to their wholly owned subsidiaries and their research and development limited partnerships. Awards to joint ventures and spin-offs are counted to the extent that the firm had an interest in the venture. The analysis uses two alternative variables. The first indicates the number of the patents awarded at the time of the financing round. The second indicates the number of successful patent applications awarded and in progress at the time. Because patent applications are held confidential by USPTO until the time of award, only observations made prior to 1990 are used in the second analysis.

In unreported regressions, while the age and patents variables have significant explanatory power, the timing variables remain significantly larger in the regressions that employ the firms backed by seasoned venture capitalists.

Alternative Explanations

Speed of IPO Execution

One alternative explanation for established venture capitalists' apparent superiority in timing IPOs is better execution. The failure of less experienced venture capitalists to take their firms public at market peaks may reflect their limited skill in planning and executing an offering, not their inability to perceive when the market is hot. In particular, SEC reviews of proposed IPOs can be protracted. Similarly, organizing a selling syndicate and assuring demand for the offering may be time consuming.

This claim is tested by examining the time from the receipt of the original S-1 statement by the SEC to the effective date of the IPO. The filing date is found in SDC's Corporate New Issues database (1992). When it is not available from this source, the date of the "received" stamp on the original S-1 filing is used.

Table 11.7
Time from the filing of the original S-1 statement to the effective date of initial public offering, divided by the age of the oldest venture provider. The sample consists of 136 IPOs by venture-backed biotechnology firms between January 1978 and September 1992. The table also compares the mean and median time for firms whose oldest venture capitalist was above and below the median age.

Panel A: Months from S-1 filing to IPO effective date

	Mean	Median
Firms whose oldest venture investor is above the median age	2.0	1.6
Firms whose oldest venture investor is below the median age	1.9	1.7

Panel B: Tests of differences in means and medians

	p-value
Tests comparing firms whose oldest venture investor is above and below the median age	
t-test, mean months from S-1 filing to IPO effective date is same for both sets of firms	0.52
Wilcoxon test, median months from S-1 filing to IPO effective date is same for both sets of firms	0.54

Table 11.7 summarizes the results. The mean time from filing to offering does not differ significantly for the firms financed by seasoned or inexperienced venture capitalists (2.0 months for more experienced; 1.9 months for the less experienced), nor do the medians differ appreciably. The results provide no support for the claim that the superior timing of the IPO market by seasoned firms is due to better execution.

Willingness to Withdraw Offerings

A second explanation relates to withdrawn offerings. The legal procedure for canceling a proposed IPO is straightforward. Firms may write a letter to the SEC to withdraw proposed security offerings before their effective date. Often firms do not withdraw failed IPOs. When a registration statement has been on file at the SEC for nine months, the SEC writes a letter to the firm and then declares the offering abandoned (17 Code of Federal Regulatory §230.479).

Although the formalities associated with an IPO withdrawal are few, the repercussions may be severe. A firm that withdraws its IPO may later find it difficult to access the public marketplace. Even if the stated reason for the withdrawal is poor market conditions, the firm may be lumped with other businesses whose offerings did not sell because of questionable accounting practices or gross mispricing. These reputational considerations may be less severe for a firm associated with a major venture capitalist. A greater willingness to withdraw IPOs in the face of deterio-

234   Chapter 11

rating market conditions may explain the apparent superiority of experienced venture capitalists in timing offerings.

To analyze these claims, withdrawn or abandoned IPO filings are examined. These offerings are identified using the SDC Corporate New Issues database. (SDC employs a data collection procedure similar to the *Investment Dealers' Digest* listings used by Mikkelson and Partch 1988 to identify withdrawn seasoned security offerings.) Because the coverage of abandoned IPOs is less than comprehensive, these records are supplemented with the "no go IPOs" section of *Going Public* (Howard 1992) and a database of failed IPOs compiled by a federal agency. (The official responsible for the creation of this database has requested anonymity.) Fourteen withdrawn or abandoned IPOs by these firms in this period were found.

In table 11.8, the probability that an IPO filing is completed successfully is examined. As observations, the analysis uses all filings of S-1

Table 11.8
Estimated probit regressions of the successful completion of an IPO by privately held venture-backed biotechnology firms who filed S-1 registration statements. The sample consists of 150 filings between January 1978 and September 1992. The dependent variable is 1.0 for firms that went public and 0.0 for firms that withdrew or abandoned their offerings. Independent variables include the age of the oldest venture investor, the age of the firm at the time of the filing, the number of patents awarded to the firm at the time of the filing,[a] and a dummy variable indicating whether the firm had previously received a private placement from a corporation with a related line-of-business at the time of the filing[b] (absolute t-statistics in brackets).

	Dependent variable: Did firm go public?	
Age of oldest venture investor (in years)	0.01 [0.46]	0.01 [0.76]
Age of firm at time of filing (in years)		−0.08 [1.48]
Patents awarded at time of filing		0.10 [1.04]
Did firm receive private placement from related corporation?		−0.32 [1.08]
Constant	1.22 [4.63]	1.58 [4.44]
Log likelihood	−46.62	−44.67
χ^2-statistic	0.21	3.71
p-value	0.64	0.44
Number of observations	150	150

a. All patents assigned to firms, their wholly owned subsidiaries, and their research and development limited partnerships are included. Awards to joint ventures and spin-offs are counted to the extent that a firm had an interest in the venture.
b. Corporations with related lines of business are defined as those with any of the following Standard Industrial Classification identifiers in the *Million Dollar Directory* (Dun's, 1992) in the year of the transaction: SIC 283, drugs; SIC 287, agricultural chemicals; and SIC 384, medical instruments and supplies.

registration statements by privately held firms in the Venture Economics sample. (These include the 136 successful IPOs and the fourteen withdrawn offerings.) A probit regression is estimated:

$$COMPLETE_{it} = \beta_0 + \beta_1 MAXAGE_{it} + \varepsilon_{it}. \qquad (11.2)$$

The dependent variable is a dummy, which takes on the value of 1 if the offering was successfully completed. The independent variable measures the age (in years) of the oldest venture capitalist to have financed the firm. No evidence that older venture capitalists are more willing to withdraw IPOs is found: the coefficient, 0.01, is of the opposite sign and insignificant.

The right-hand column in table 11.8 reports the results when the regression is rerun, controlling for the quality of the firm. Superior quality offerings may be less likely to be withdrawn, no matter whom the venture investor. The same independent variables discussed below are used: the age of the firm, the presence of a private placement from a related corporation, and the number of patent awards at the time of the financing. There is no evidence that firms backed by seasoned venture capitalists are more likely to withdraw offerings, even after controlling for quality.

Also examined are equity valuations after the filing of S-1 statements. Mikkelson and Partch (1988) examine stock prices after the announcement of seasoned security issues. In the weeks after the announcement of an ultimately withdrawn seasoned issue, both the market returns and the issuer's net-of-market returns are negative. No such pattern appears after the filing of successful offerings. The returns from an equally weighted investment in thirteen biotechnology securities between the close of the S-1 filing date and the close of the twentieth trading day thereafter are examined, using the same procedure as above. The index rises by 2 percent after the filing of successful offerings and declines by 9 percent after the filing of ultimately withdrawn offerings. The difference is significant at the 1 percent level of confidence, as are those computed using other windows.

Conclusions

In this chapter, the choice between private and public equity is explored. Both the private and public financings of a sample of 350 privately held venture-backed firms are examined. Venture capitalists take firms public at market peaks, relying on private financings when valuations are lower.

Seasoned venture capitalists appear more proficient at timing IPOs. The results are robust to the use of alternative criteria to separate firms and controls for firms' quality. The results are not caused by differences in the speed of executing the IPOs or in the willingness to withdraw the proposed IPOs.

Two limitations deserve further discussion. The first reflects the design of this study, which examined a setting particularly conducive to the empirical identification of market timing. In other industries, the need for oversight, or lumpy demands for capital, as the firm matures may affect the decision to go public more dramatically. In other periods, the heterogeneity between new and seasoned venture capitalists may not be as pronounced. Practitioner accounts, however, underscore the importance of IPO timing across industries and time. An example is an investment manager's discussion (McNamee 1991) of market conditions around peak periods for computer and electronics IPOs:

The whole problem can be summed up in the phrase "IPO window." The IPO window occurs when sellers try to bail out and buyers try to get rich without doing any work.... It is when the AEA (American Electronics Association) puts up a billboard on Highway 101 near Great America that says, "The buy side has lost its mind, let's bag them quick, before they catch on." Sometime late in the IPO window, we get to watch venture capitalists behave like Keystone Kops.

Nor are such narratives confined to the 1980s and 1990s. For instance, Jeffery (1961) describes similar patterns in the market for new securities of high-technology firms in the 1950s. In the business press, Stern and Pouschine (1992) discuss the timing of "reverse LBOs" (IPOs of firms that have previously undergone leveraged buyouts) by LBO funds. Venture capitalists may also time the market when they sell or distribute shares in firms that have gone public, as discussed in chapter 13.

A second concern relates to the results' interpretation. The seasoned venture capitalists' more effective timing of IPOs may reflect their superior proficiency. They may be better at recognizing when valuations are at a peak. There remain, however, several alternative interpretations. Less experienced venture capitalists may also wish to take firms public at market peaks, but may be unable to command the attention of investment bankers. This assertion may be plausible if underwriting services are rationed in key periods. Alternatively, chapter 12 suggests that inexperienced venture capitalists may not wait until the market is optimal to take firms public, because they need to signal their quality to potential investors in follow-on funds. The mechanisms through which managers and venture capitalists decide to go public and obtain access to investment bankers deserve further study.

A second opportunity for further research relates to the implications of the timing of the decision to go public. IPOs have been shown to coincide with declines in operating performance (Jain and Kini 1994) and broad shifts in the incentives offered managers (Beatty and Zajak 1994). Do early initial public offerings affect the subsequent performance of the firm? To what extent are these factors related to the maturity of the firm and the market conditions at the time of the IPO? The interactions among these financing choices and operational performance deserve further scrutiny.

12   Does Reputation Affect the Decision to Go Public?

This study analyzes venture capital organizations to provide new evidence about the relation between performance and capital raising and its implications for fund managers' incentives. Young venture capital firms have incentives to grandstand, that is, they take actions that signal their ability to potential investors.[1] Specifically, young venture capital firms bring companies public earlier than older venture capital firms in an effort to establish a reputation and successfully raise capital for new funds.

Empirical tests for a sample of 433 venture-backed initial public offerings (IPOs) from January 1, 1978, through December 31, 1987, and a second sample consisting of the first IPO brought to market by 62 venture capital funds support predictions of the grandstanding hypothesis. For example, the effect of recent performance in the IPO market on the amount of capital raised is stronger for young venture capital firms, providing them with greater incentive to bring companies public earlier. Similarly, young venture capital firms raise new funds closer to the IPO. Young venture capital firms have been on the IPO company's board of directors fourteen months less than older venture firms, hold smaller percentage equity stakes at the time of IPO than the stakes held by established venture firms, and the IPO companies they finance are nearly two years younger and more underpriced when they go public than companies backed by older venture capital firms. Much of the difference in underpricing and the venture capitalists' percentage equity stake is associated with a shorter duration of board representation, indicating that rushing companies to the IPO market imposes costs on the venture firm. The results suggest that the relation between performance and capital raising affects the incentives and actions of venture capitalists.

---

1. Webster's *Third New International Dictionary* defines the verb "to grandstand" as "to act or conduct oneself with a view to impressing onlookers."

Reputation and its effect on attracting capital are important topics in recent corporate finance research. Theoretical work by Diamond (1989) shows that reputation can be important in accessing debt and equity markets. Empirical research by Sirri and Tufano (1998) and Chevalier and Ellison (1997) demonstrates that past performance is a strong indicator of the ability to attract investors. The venture capital industry is particularly well suited for examining reputation and capital raising because most venture capital organizations raise money in limited partnerships. These partnerships have finite lifetimes so that a venture firm must periodically completely recapitalize itself by raising a new limited partnership. A venture capital organization would cease operations without raising a new fund. This puts pressure on young venture capital firms to establish a reputation and raise a new fund within a short, predetermined time.

Incentives to Grandstand

As discussed above, over 80 percent of venture capital funds are organized as limited partnerships with predefined lifetimes, usually ten years with an option to extend the fund for up to three years. Venture capitalists must therefore liquidate investments and distribute proceeds to investors within that time. Consequently, no new investments are made after the first four or five years of a fund. The predetermined lifetime of a particular fund means that venture capital firms must periodically raise follow-on partnerships to remain active in venture capital financing. Venture capital firms may have two or three overlapping funds, each starting three to six years after the previous fund.

As chapter 3 documents, most limited partners in venture capital funds are institutional investors whose role in the day-to-day operations of the fund is restricted by law if they are to retain limited liability. Limited partners receive periodic updates about the status of projects and new investment activity within the portfolio managed by the venture capitalist, but they do not participate in policy decisions. Evaluating a venture capitalist's ability is therefore difficult. Investors search for signals of ability when evaluating venture capitalists.

Theoretical and empirical research on other types of investment funds demonstrates the importance of reputation and fund performance in raising capital. Lakonishok, Shleifer, Thaler, and Vishny (1991); Patel, Zeckhauser, and Hendricks (1991); and Sirri and Tufano (1998) examine fundraising and investment patterns of various types of institutional fund managers and find that past performance influences fundraising ability. Stein (1988,

1989) and Rajan (1993) develop models in which investors' horizons
lead to managerial decisions that do not maximize shareholder value.
Incentives to boost performance in the short run lead to activities that
lower firm value. Chevalier and Ellison (1997) show that the relative performance of mutual fund managers affects growth in capital contributions
to their funds. Funds that underperform the market in the first nine
months of a year have an incentive to increase the riskiness of their portfolio. This incentive is particularly strong for new mutual funds.

A formal model of grandstanding developed by Gompers demonstrates
that new venture capital firms are willing to incur costs by taking companies public earlier than would maximize the return on those individual
companies and earlier than would an established venture capital firm. It is
assumed that venture capitalists have different abilities to select or create
companies that have a high probability of going public. The most effective way of signaling ability or the value of portfolio companies might
therefore be to bring one of the portfolio companies public in an IPO.[2] As
discussed in chapter 2, almost all of the returns for investors in venture
capital are earned on companies that eventually go public.

If investors believe that high-ability venture capitalists are more likely
to fund companies that eventually go public, then taking a portfolio company public would be interpreted as a sign that the venture capitalist is
skilled at financing start-up companies. After an IPO, investors increase
their assessment of the venture capitalist's ability. Because investors know
more about older venture capital firms, an additional IPO will not affect
their beliefs about an old firm's ability as much as it would their beliefs
about a young venture firm's ability.

If the amount of capital that venture capitalists can raise is an increasing
function of their perceived ability and the costs of earlier IPOs (e.g.,
greater underpricing or smaller equity stakes) are not trivial, then only
young venture capital firms are willing to incur those costs. Old venture
capital firms with good reputations do not need to signal, because investors have evaluated their performance over many years and believe in their
high ability. Only new venture capital firms will benefit from signaling in
the IPO market. Firms that are believed to be of low quality (through

---

2. By convention, most investments in a venture capital portfolio are held at book value until the next round of financing or an IPO occurs. Limited partners are often concerned that a
venture capital fund may make a small investment in a company at a higher price to write-up
the value of all previous investments in that company to the new price even though that
price may not be justified. For most investors the only meaningful price is therefore one established in the public market.

their inability to bring companies public) are unable to raise new funds. Diamond (1989) shows how reputation can similarly affect the debt market. In his model, young borrowers choose risky projects. If they survive for a certain length of time and acquire reputations as reliable borrowers, their investment behavior changes and they choose safe projects. Age becomes a proxy for reputation. Reputation can work in a similar way in the venture capital industry.

The grandstanding hypothesis predicts that the relation between bringing companies public and fundraising ability should be stronger for young venture capital firms. Each additional IPO attracts relatively more capital from investors for a young venture capital firm than for an old venture capital firm. An additional IPO changes investors' estimates of a young venture capitalist's ability more than it does their estimate of an old venture capitalist's ability. Therefore, if we compare the fundraising activity of venture capital firms, each additional IPO for a young venture capital firm attracts significantly more capital than each additional IPO for an older venture capital firm. Because the reputation of established venture capital firms is affected less by doing an IPO, the incentive to raise new funds immediately following an IPO should be smaller. If we compare the average time from an IPO to the closing of the venture capital firm's next fund, young venture firms will raise money sooner than older venture firms will.

The relation between reputation and capital raising is consistent with industry wisdom. Established venture capital firms with long track records raise large funds quickly and with little effort. When Greylock Management Company, one of the nation's oldest and most prestigious firms, began their eighth venture fund early in 1994, they collected more than $175 million in only a few months ($150 million had originally been targeted). All of the investors in Greylock's new fund were previous Greylock investors.

Venture capital firms in their first fund, which have shown no returns, find it difficult to raise new money. These firms may have strong incentives to grandstand. For example, Hummer Winblad Venture Partners formed its first venture capital fund in 1989. When Hummer Winblad tried to raise a second fund in 1992, it found it extremely difficult to attract investors despite nearly a half-year of marketing. This lack of interest stemmed largely from the lack of successes; Hummer Winblad had never taken a firm public. After Powersoft, one of their investments, went public on February 3, 1993, Hummer Winblad raised a $60 million second fund in a few months.

An additional prediction of the grandstanding hypothesis is that companies brought to market by young venture capital firms should be less mature. Two measures of IPO maturity are examined. The age of the offering company at the time of issue is one measure of an early IPO. If new venture capital firms grandstand, companies they back will be younger at the offering date than companies backed by older venture firms. Similarly, if young venture capital firms rush companies to market (compared to older venture capital firms), they will have shorter relationships and will have served on the boards of IPO companies for less time.

One cost incurred by new venture capital firms doing early IPOs is greater underpricing. Muscarella and Vetsuypens (1989) show that the older the firm at IPO (controlling for various factors), the lower the underpricing. As in Rock's (1986) IPO model, older firms have longer track records, reducing asymmetric information and underpricing. Models of IPO underpricing (Welch 1989, Grinblatt and Hwang 1989, Allen and Faulhaber 1989) view underpricing as a costly signal of a company's quality. The greater the uncertainty surrounding a company, the greater the underpricing. A company that goes to market earlier is younger and has less information available for evaluation by potential investors and so is underpriced to a greater degree. Underpricing is a real loss for the venture capital firm because it transfers wealth from existing shareholders, including the venture capitalist, to new shareholders. Companies brought to market by young venture capital firms should therefore be more underpriced at the IPO.

Additional costs that occur when bringing a company to market early reduce prospects for future growth. The venture capitalist may bear much of the cost of taking companies public early by receiving a smaller equity stake. A comparison of the equity stakes of young and old venture capital firms should reveal that venture capitalists investing in a company with a young lead venture capital firm should hold a smaller percentage of the offering company's equity at the IPO date.

The grandstanding hypothesis predicts that young venture capital firms incur the costs of signaling because the company goes public earlier than if it had been financed by a more established venture capitalist. When the costs associated with an IPO are examined in regressions, the age of the IPO company and the length of the venture capitalist's board service should explain some of the difference in underpricing and percentage equity stakes at IPO between young and established venture capital providers. It is not the presence of a young venture backer that increases underpricing and reduces equity stakes but rather the early timing of the

IPO. The age of the offering company and the length of board service should be negatively related to underpricing and positively related to the size of the venture capitalist's equity stake.

Empirical Results

Data Set and Descriptive Statistics

Two samples are used to test the predictions of the grandstanding hypothesis. The first sample, collected and described by Barry, Muscarella, Peavy, and Vetsuypens (1990), consists of 433 venture-backed IPOs taken public between January 1, 1978, and December 31, 1987. Kemper Financial Services and Brinson Partners, two investment advisors, supplied a second data set that includes all IPOs for sixty-two venture capital funds between August 1, 1983, and July 31, 1993. This second, supplemental data set is useful for addressing potential selection biases in the first sample. These two data sets are described in more detail in chapter 16.

Dates and sizes of new funds are from Venture Economics, a consulting firm that tracks investments and fundraising by venture capital firms. Venture capitalists most often syndicate their investments with other venture capitalists. When this occurs, one investor usually takes the role of lead venture capitalist. This investor ordinarily has significant control over the decisions of the firm and more actively monitors the company through board service. The firm that has been on the board the longest is classified as the lead venture capitalist; this classification differs from that of Barry et al. (1990) who classify the lead venture capitalist as the firm that owns the largest equity stake and has a board seat. If two firms have been on the board the same length of time, the larger equity holder is designated as the lead. Gorman and Sahlman (1989) find that the venture capital firm originating the investment is usually the firm that acquires a board seat first and has the most input into the decisions of the offering company. The originating firm does not always end up owning the largest stake at IPO.

To test the grandstanding hypothesis, the sample of venture-backed companies is divided into two groups: those backed by experienced venture capital firms and those backed by young venture capital firms. The age of the lead venture capital firm at IPO serves as a proxy for reputation, although it is an imperfect measure of reputation because experienced partners sometimes leave to start new venture capital firms. This effect would tend to bias the results away from seeing any difference between new and old venture capital firms. All lead venture capital firms that are under six years old at the IPO date are classified as young and those that are six years old or more as old. The results are not sensitive to cutoffs between four and ten years.[3]

Table 12.1 presents summary information for the IPOs backed by young and old venture capital firms. Younger venture capital firms bring companies public closer to the firms' next fund, an average (median) of sixteen months (twelve) prior to the next fund for young venture capital firms and twenty-four (twenty-four) months prior for old venture capital firms. The Venture Economics funds database shows that experienced venture capital firms raise new funds every two to four years, while young venture capital firms raise new money only every five or six years. If IPOs occur randomly, the average IPO for an old venture capital firm should be closer to its next fund than the average IPO for a new venture capital firm. Because it takes approximately one year to solicit money and close a new fund, the eight-to-twelve-month difference implies that young venture capital firms could be bringing companies public in the period immediately preceding or during the time they are raising money, while established firms are not. The average size of a new venture capital firm's next fund ($87.9 million) is also smaller than the size of an old venture firm's next fund ($136.6 million).

Summary statistics in table 12.1 for the maturity of the IPO company also support the predictions of the grandstanding hypothesis. The average (median) age of the offering company is 56 (42) months for IPOs backed by young venture capitalists and 80 (64) months for IPOs backed by old venture capitalists. Similarly, young venture capital firms sit on the board of directors for a shorter period of time. For these firms, the average (median) is 25 (20) months versus 39 (28) months for established venture firms.

Table 12.1 also shows that unseasoned venture capital firms bring to market IPOs that are more underpriced. The average (median) underpricing at the IPO date is 13.6 percent (6.7 percent) for IPOs brought to market by young venture capital firms compared to 7.3 percent (2.7 per-

---

3. The use of a dummy variable addresses potential nonlinearities in the reputation measure. Typical funds invest all their capital in the first five years and harvest investments during the last five. The firm is likely to run out of cash in the fifth year and must raise a new fund before then. After a second fund has been raised, the pressure to grandstand is greatly reduced or eliminated. To check the robustness of the results, regressions are run using the natural logarithm of the venture capital firm's age instead of the dummy variable. Results are qualitatively similar using the logarithm of age specification.

Table 12.1
Comparison of the characteristics for initial public offerings backed by young and old venture capital firms. Sample is 433 venture-backed companies that went public between January 1, 1978, and December 31, 1987. Medians are in brackets. Significance tests in the third column are p-values of t-tests for difference in averages and p-values of two-sample Wilcoxon rank-sum tests for difference in medians in brackets.

	Venture capital firms less than six years old at IPO	Venture capital firms six years old or greater at IPO	p-value test of no difference
Average time from IPO date to next follow-on fund in months	16.0 [12.0]	24.2 [24.0]	0.001 [0.002]
Average size of next follow-on fund in millions of 1997 dollars	87.9 [68.0]	136.6 [113.4]	0.018 [0.024]
Average age of venture-backed company at IPO date in months	55.1 [42.0]	79.6 [64.0]	0.000 [0.000]
Average duration of board representation for lead venture capital firm in months	24.5 [20.0]	38.8 [28.0]	0.001 [0.000]
Average underpricing at the IPO date	0.136 [0.067]	0.073 [0.027]	0.001 [0.036]
Average offering size in millions of 1997 dollars	18.3 [13.0]	24.7 [19.1]	0.013 [0.000]
Average Carter and Manaster underwriter rank	6.26 [6.50]	7.43 [8.00]	0.000 [0.000]
Average number of previous IPOs	1 [0]	6 [4]	0.000 [0.000]
Average fraction of equity held by all venture capitalists prior to IPO	0.321 [0.287]	0.377 [0.371]	0.025 [0.024]
Average fraction of equity held by lead venture capitalist after IPO	0.122 [0.100]	0.139 [0.120]	0.098 [0.031]
Average market value of lead venture capitalist's equity after IPO in millions of 1997 dollars	9.5 [4.3]	14.7 [8.7]	0.033 [0.000]
Average aftermarket standard deviation	0.034 [0.030]	0.030 [0.028]	0.080 [0.324]
Number	99	240	

cent) for older venture capital firms. The average offering size is also sig-nificantly smaller for IPOs brought to market by young venture capital firms. Old venture capital firms tend to use higher quality underwriters (the established venture capital firms may have contacts with more repu-table underwriters through previous IPOs or other business dealings). As expected, on average, old venture capital firms have financed more com-panies that have gone public (6.0) than have unseasoned venture capital firms (1.0).

The summary statistics in table 12.1 show that venture capitalists re-ceive a significantly smaller share of the equity in companies that go pub-lic when the lead venture capital firm is under six years old. The average (median) equity stake of all venture capital investors is 32.1 percent (28.7 percent) of the equity prior to the IPO when the lead venture capital firm is under six years old compared to 37.7 percent (37.1 percent) when the lead venture capital firm is older.

The market value of the lead venture capitalist's equity stake is also significantly lower for new venture capital organizations. IPO prospec-tuses indicate the number of shares sold in the IPO and the number of shares held after IPO by the lead venture capitalist. In calculating the market value of shares sold, the venture capitalist is assumed to receive the IPO offering price for all shares sold in the IPO. Shares held after IPO are valued at the first price listed on the Center for Research in Security Prices (CRSP) data tapes. The first price listed on CRSP is usually (but not always) on the IPO date, but it is never more than several days from the listed IPO date. Table 12.1 shows that the average (median) market value of a young lead venture capital firm's equity stake is $9.5 ($4.3) million while the market value of an established lead venture capital firm's equity stake is $14.7 ($8.7) million. These summary statistics are consistent with the grandstanding hypothesis. Young venture capital firms bring com-panies public early and bear real costs through greater underpricing and lower valued equity stakes, although the company going public also bears some of the cost.

An alternative explanation for the differences in firm age and board service is a selection bias caused by classifying young venture capital firms as all firms that are under six years old. The age of the venture capi-tal firm might be correlated with the age of the IPO company without a causal relationship. By definition, no young venture capital firm will have been on the board of the IPO company for more than 71 months. This would cause companies brought to market by young venture capital firms to have shorter venture capitalist board representation on average even though the IPO process was the same for young and old venture capital firms.

This potential selection bias should not be important because the length of time that the typical investment is held from first funding to IPO is significantly less than 71 months. Chapter 7 shows that the average (median) time from first-round venture financing to IPO date for a sample of 127 venture-backed IPOs is 34 (31) months. While the date of initial funding is unknown for the sample, in virtually all cases of first-round financing the venture capital firm receives a seat on the board of directors.[4] Old venture capital firms are on the board for an average (median) of 39 (28) months, while new venture capital firms are on the board 25 (20) months.

To determine the extent of the selection bias, the second set of IPOs provided by Kemper Financial Services and Brinson Partners is used. (This sample, for the period August 1, 1983, to July 31, 1993, is also described in chapter 16.) The sample consists of nineteen venture capital firms in their first fund and forty-three venture capital firms in their second fund or later. Funds that had not performed an IPO prior to July 1993 are excluded. From the complete fund histories, the first IPO brought to market by each fund is identified. The characteristics of the first IPO for first-fund venture capital firms are compared to the first IPO of second-or-later-fund venture capital firms. Because a successful venture fund may have only two or three IPOs, the first IPO is a strong signal of ability to take companies public. Comparing first IPOs for various funds eliminates any selection bias but sacrifices sample size.

Table 12.2 presents summary statistics for the sixty-two IPOs. The results support conclusions from the larger sample and are consistent with the grandstanding hypothesis. First IPOs for first-fund venture capital firms are significantly younger (32 vs. 54 months) and more underpriced (18.5 percent vs. 7.8 percent) than first IPOs for second-or-later-fund venture capital firms. First-fund venture capital firms have also been on the board for a shorter period of time and they raise money significantly sooner following the IPO (13 vs. 29 months). Neither the offering size nor average underwriter rank differs significantly. Average after-market standard deviation, however, is higher for the first-fund sample. Selection biases do not appear to drive the results.

---

4. Gompers (1995) examines conversion features and covenants in fifty venture capital convertible preferred private placements. Every contract included provisions for board representation by the syndicate of venture capital investors.

Table 12.2
Comparison of the characteristics for initial public offerings backed by young and old venture capital firms. Sample is the first IPO for each of sixty-two venture capital funds for two institutional investors from August 1, 1983, through July 31, 1993. Medians are in brackets. Significance tests in the third column are p-values of t-tests for difference in averages and p-values of two-sample Wilcoxon rank-sum tests for difference in medians in brackets.

	First-fund venture capital firms	Second-or-later-fund venture capital firms	p-value test of no difference
Average age of venture-backed company at IPO date in months	31.6 [33.5]	53.5 [50.0]	0.001 [0.001]
Average duration of board representation for lead venture capital firm in months	25.8 [30.0]	40.2 [40.0]	0.005 [0.005]
Average time from IPO date to next follow-on fund in months	12.9 [6.0]	29.0 [24.0]	0.028 [0.001]
Average underpricing at the IPO date	0.185 [0.215]	0.078 [0.038]	0.004 [0.005]
Average offering size in millions of 1997 dollars	37.2 [29.0]	36.9 [29.5]	0.949 [0.943]
Average Carter and Manaster underwriter rank	8.19 [8.00]	8.16 [9.00]	0.939 [0.329]
Average aftermarket standard deviation	0.036 [0.035]	0.031 [0.028]	0.884 [0.245]
Number	19	43	

Regression Results

Regressions are performed on the following variables: (1) the size of the lead venture capitalist's next fund, (2) the time from IPO to the lead venture capitalist's next fund, (3) length of board service, (4) the age of the offering company at IPO, (5) underpricing, and (6) the equity stake of all venture capitalists prior to IPO.

Mundlak (1961, 1978) demonstrates that if industry effects are present in the IPO sample, fixed-effects regression models are appropriate:

$$Y_{i,j} = \beta' X_{i,j} + \alpha_i + \varepsilon_{i,j}. \tag{12.1}$$

If firm j in industry i goes public, the dependent variable $Y_{i,j}$ (e.g., underpricing, age at IPO, or time to next fund) is a function of the independent variables $X_{i,j}$ (e.g., offering size, IPO market liquidity, underwriter rank, etc.) and α_i, a term that represents industry effects. The sample is divided into nineteen industries based on SIC codes, with dummy variables for each industry to control for unmeasured industry effects.

Size of Next Fund and Time to Next Fund

Results from regressions for the size of the lead venture capitalist's next fund and the length of time from the IPO to the firm's next fund are presented in table 12.3. The dependent variable in the first set of regressions is the logarithm of the amount of capital raised in the lead venture capitalist's next fund in constant dollars. The grandstanding hypothesis predicts that the amount of capital a venture firm can raise should be positively related to the number of companies the firm has taken public. Capital raising should also be more sensitive to IPOs for young venture capital firms.

Table 12.3 shows that the number of companies that the lead venture capitalist has taken public is positively related to the amount of capital raised. In the first regression, the coefficient of 0.039 means that each additional IPO translates into roughly $8 million more capital committed to the firm's next fund. Underwriter rank for the most recent IPO is also positively related to the amount of capital raised. Higher quality underwriters tend to take larger, more promising companies public. If underwriter rank is related to the quality of the IPO company, then the relation between rank and capital raised should be positive. Taking higher quality firms public is a stronger signal of ability. Industry reports and fund offering memoranda touting recent IPO successes clearly indicate that venture capitalists understand this relation.

The second regression includes interaction terms between the young venture capital firm dummy variable, the number of IPOs brought to market, and underwriter rank. The significantly positive coefficients on both interaction terms show that the amount of capital raised by young venture capital firms is more sensitive to both the number of IPOs they have financed and the underwriter rank of the most recent IPO, consistent with the predictions of the grandstanding hypothesis. Because older venture capital firms have established reputations, beliefs about their ability are not very sensitive to an additional IPO or the quality of the underwriter for that IPO. New venture capital firms have considerably more to gain (in terms of reputation and fundraising ability) by doing an IPO. The limited lifetime of venture funds and the strong relation between recent IPO performance and fundraising provide powerful incentives for young venture capital firms to bring companies to market earlier than older venture firms. The third and fourth regressions in table 12.3 show that the results are robust to using the logarithm of age specification for venture capital firm reputation.

The second set of regressions in table 12.3 indicates that new venture capital firms raise money for follow-on funds significantly sooner after the date of the IPO (between five and nine months sooner) despite the fact that the older venture capital firms started more funds during the time period. The results also indicate that larger venture capital firms wait longer to raise a new fund. Firms with more capital have less incentive to grandstand because they have more money in reserve for future investment opportunities. Although five to nine months may not seem like a large difference between young and established venture firms, the evidence is consistent with the existence of reputational concerns and the predictions of the grandstanding hypothesis. Reputation affects fundraising in the venture capital market.

Length of Board Service and Age at IPO

The regressions in table 12.3 indicate that the sensitivity of fundraising to recent IPO performance is stronger for young venture capital firms than it is for older ones. This relation provides an incentive for young firms to rush companies to the IPO market. Table 12.4 examines the effects of venture capital firm reputation on two measures of IPO timing. The first is the length of time that the lead venture capital firm has served on the board of directors. If young venture capital firms take companies public earlier, they will have served on the board of directors for a shorter length of time. The second measure of early IPOs is age of the issuing company. The first two regressions indicate that young venture capital firms (those under six years old) have served on the board of directors between 12 and 14 months less than established venture capital firms. Similarly, companies backed by a new venture capital firm are between 26 and 28 months younger than companies backed by more established venture capital firms. These results are consistent with the grandstanding hypothesis that companies backed by young venture capital firms go public sooner, controlling for other factors.

Table 12.4 also presents results from the sample of first IPOs for the sixty-two funds to examine potential selection biases. The results show that first-fund venture capitalists have been on the board of their first IPO 13 to 14 months less than second-or-later-fund venture capitalists. The

Table 12.3
Regressions for the size of the lead venture capitalist's next fund and the time from IPO until the firm raises its next fund. The sample is 433 venture-backed IPOs from 1978 to 1987. The dependent variables are the time from the IPO until the lead venture capital organization raises its next fund (in years) and the logarithm of the size of that next fund (in millions of 1992 dollars). Independent variables include a dummy variable that equals one if the lead venture capital organization is less than six years old, the logarithm of the venture capital firm's age in months, the cumulative number of IPOs (both venture- and nonventure-backed) in the previous four months, the capital under management at the lead venture capital firm, the number of previous IPOs in which the lead venture capital firm was an investor, the Carter and Manaster (1990) underwriter rank, and the first-day return on the IPO (t-statistics are in brackets).

Independent variables	Dependent variable							
	Logarithm of the size of next fund				Years until venture firm raises next fund			
Venture firm less than six years old	0.036 [0.17]	−1.925 [−2.38]			−0.70 [−3.12]	−0.44 [−1.76]		
Logarithm of venture firm age			0.092 [0.76]	0.836 [1.83]			0.310 [2.43]	0.286 [1.76]
Number of IPOs in previous four months	0.0013 [0.89]	0.0018 [1.04]	0.0014 [0.80]	0.0013 [0.69]	−0.0014 [−0.67]	−0.0013 [−0.28]	−0.0029 [−1.26]	−0.0021 [−0.85]
Venture capital under management					0.0018 [2.51]		0.004 [0.51]	
Number of IPOs for lead venture firm	0.039 [2.70]	0.037 [2.61]	0.033 [2.20]	0.036 [1.74]				
Number of IPOs for lead venture firm if under six years old		0.189 [1.86]						
Number of IPOs for lead venture firm multiplied by log of venture firm age				−0.015 [−0.41]				

Underwriter rank	0.0985 [1.93]	0.0171 [0.27]	0.896 [1.79]	0.295 [2.20]				
Underwriter rank if lead venture firm is under six years old		0.2297 [2.23]						
Underwriter rank times log of venture firm age				-0.106 [-1.68]				
First-day return (underpricing)	-0.216 [-0.46]	-0.225 [-0.48]	-0.175 [-0.37]	-0.242 [-0.51]				
Constant	3.307 [7.18]	3.914 [7.27]	3.219 [7.15]	1.809 [1.91]	2.14 [9.58]	1.77 [6.93]	1.34 [3.83]	1.9 [6.9]
R^2	0.121	0.169	0.125	0.147	0.083	0.081	0.042	0.0_6
p-value of F-test	0.011	0.004	0.009	0.012	0.007	0.011	0.032	0.1_6
Number	119	119	119	119	181	171	164	154

Table 12.4
Regressions for the length of board service and age of issuing company at IPO. The first sample is 433 venture-backed IPOs from 1978 to 1987. The second sample consists of the first IPOs for sixty-two venture capital funds from two institutional investors. The dependent variables are the length of time that the lead venture capitalist has been on the IPO company's board of directors (in months) at the time of IPO and the age of the offering company at the time of the IPO (in months). Independent variables include a dummy variable that equals 1 if the lead venture firm is less than six years old, a dummy variable that equals 1 if the lead venture capital organization has only raised one venture capital fund at the time of the IPO, the cumulative number of IPOs (both venture-backed and nonventure-backed) in the previous four months, the logarithm of IPO offering size, the Carter and Manaster (1990) underwriter rank, the percentage of the IPO company's equity held by all venture investors immediately prior to IPO, and the capital under management at the lead venture capital firm. Regressions for the sample of 433 IPOs include industry dummy variables to control for any fixed effects. Coefficients on industry dummies are not reported (t-statistics are in brackets).

	Dependent variable							
	Full sample of 433 IPOs				Sample of first IPOs for 62 funds			
Independent variables	Duration of board service (months)	Duration of board service (months)	Age of IPO firm (months)	Age of IPO firm (months)	Duration of board service (months)	Duration of board service (months)	Age of IPO firm (months)	Age of IPO firm (months)
Venture firm less than six years old	-14.35 [-3.26]	-12.59 [-2.95]	-26.83 [-3.91]	-28.81 [-3.43]	-13.00 [-2.58]	-14.94 [-2.55]	-20.76 [-3.25]	-19.40 [-2.85]
First-fund venture firm					0.77 [0.01]			
Number of IPOs in previous four months	0.037 [0.95]	0.091 [2.23]	-0.030 [-0.48]	0.106 [1.55]	-0.082 [-1.47]	-0.045 [-0.71]	-0.037 [-0.53]	-0.018 [-0.24]
Logarithm of IPO offering size	-4.630 [-1.87]	-0.781 [-0.28]	-15.20 [-3.81]	-16.92 [-3.38]	2.718 [0.64]	4.736 [1.04]	6.475 [1.22]	6.674 [1.25]
Underwriter rank		1.059 [0.75]		2.816 [1.15]		2.466 [1.10]		3.312 [1.25]
Equity stake of all venture firms prior to IPO		0.265 [2.71]		0.035 [0.22]				
Venture capital under management		-0.020 [-1.41]		-0.037 [-1.41]		-0.004 [-0.19]		0.075 [3.31]
Constant	109.13 [2.66]	24.46 [0.57]	326.65 [4.90]	319.15 [4.15]	-55.65 [-0.68]	-54.84 [-0.61]		-96.81 [1.01]
R^2	0.171	0.232	0.207	0.235	0.168	0.192	0.189	0.351
p-value of F-test	0.004	0.004	0.000	0.000	0.018	0.078	0.007	0.001
Number	245	191	332	191	58	51	61	53

first company brought public by a new fund is 19 to 20 months younger on average than the first IPO of a second-or-later-fund venture firm. These results are nearly identical to the results for the entire sample, indicating that selection bias is not a problem.

The differences in board service (14 months) and IPO firm age (28 months) are important. They represent a 30 percent difference in firm age and board service between the new venture capital firm sample and the old venture capital firm sample. Moreover, these companies are very young, and 14 to 28 months is a substantial fraction of their existence. Because young companies often grow by 50 to 100 percent per annum in their first years of operation, the small differences in board service and IPO company age mean that new venture-backed companies have only half the level of sales and earnings of old venture-backed companies have when they go public. This is a significant reduction in firm size. (As seen below, the effect of board service on the size and market value of equity stakes is quite large in economic terms.)

Underpricing

Table 12.5 presents underpricing regressions. Muscarella and Vetsuypens (1989) and Ritter (1987) view underpricing as a cost that companies bear when they go public because of the uncertainty surrounding the true value of the offering. Younger companies have more uncertainty and hence greater underpricing. Two specifications are used to control for the reputation of the venture capital firm. In all regressions, IPOs backed by young venture capital firms are associated with greater underpricing (whether new venture capital firms are defined as firms less than six years old or using the logarithm of venture firm age). When the logarithm of the length of board service and the age of the offering company at IPO are included, the size and significance of the reputation coefficients change very little. Of the two variables that represent early IPOs, length of board service has the larger impact on underpricing although it is only marginally significant. When underwriter rank is included in the regressions (third and sixth columns), the size and significance of the coefficients on the reputation variables are greatly reduced. Although companies brought to market by established venture firms are less underpriced, the difference is largely due to higher underwriter reputation. Finally, greater IPO market liquidity, smaller offering sizes, and less uncertainty reduce underpricing.

Table 12.5
Regressions for underpricing of the IPO. The sample is 433 venture-backed IPOs from 1978–1987. The dependent variable is underpricing of the IPO (i.e., the first-day return on the IPO firm). Independent variables include a dummy variable that equals one if the venture organization is less than six years old, the logarithm of the lead venture capital firm's age in months, the cumulative number of IPOs (both venture-backed and nonventure-backed) in the previous four months, the logarithm of IPO offering size, the standard deviation of the stock returns from day two to day twenty after the IPO, the logarithm of the IPO company's age in months, the logarithm of the number of months that the lead venture capitalist has been on the company's board of directors, the Carter and Manaster (1990) underwriter rank, and the capital under management at the lead venture capital firm. All regressions include industry dummy variables to control for any fixed effects. Coefficients on industry dummies are not reported (t-statistics are in brackets).

Independent variables	Dependent variable					
	First-day return—underpricing					
Venture firm less than six years old	0.076 [3.82]	0.088 [3.49]	0.031 [0.98]			
Logarithm of venture firm age				−0.040 [−3.89]	−0.052 [−4.07]	−0.020 [−1.18]
Number of IPOs in previous four months	−0.001 [−4.91]	−0.001 [−4.90]	−0.001 [−3.70]	−0.001 [−4.82]	−0.001 [−4.78]	−0.001 [−3.70]
Logarithm of IPO offering size	0.037 [3.26]	0.062 [4.49]	0.072 [4.05]	0.036 [3.19]	0.061 [4.50]	0.071 [4.03]
Standard deviation of stock return	1.77 [3.28]	2.22 [3.35]	1.40 [1.95]	1.75 [3.24]	2.15 [3.29]	1.37 [1.94]
Logarithm of IPO company age		0.002 [0.15]	−0.008 [−0.49]		0.002 [0.17]	−0.007 [−0.45]
Logarithm of length of board service		−0.015 [−1.64]	−0.004 [−1.23]		−0.018 [−1.69]	−0.005 [−1.31]
Underwriter rank			−0.022 [−2.50]			−0.22 [−2.51]
Venture capital under management			−0.0001 [−1.68]			0.0001 [1.94]
Constant	−0.548 [−2.89]	−0.910 [−3.66]	−0.861 [−2.97]	−0.424 [−2.29]	−0.744 [−3.15]	−0.767 [−2.80]
R^2	0.248	0.339	0.363	0.249	0.352	0.365
p-value of F-test	0.000	0.000	0.000	0.000	0.000	0.000
Number	337	241	190	337	241	190

Venture Capitalists' Equity Stakes

Table 12.6 reports results for regressions by examining a direct measure of the cost of grandstanding: the fraction of the company's equity held by all venture capitalists prior to the IPO. If young venture firms incur costs by rushing companies to the IPO market, then the percent of equity held by venture capital investors should be lower.

The regressions show that young venture capital firms (using either firms that are under six years old or the logarithm of age to control for reputation) receive a significantly smaller fraction of the company's equity. The offering size has little impact on the venture capitalists' equity stake. The most important factor in the percentage of equity held prior to the IPO is the length of board service for the lead venture capital firm. In fact, when length of board service is included, the size and significance of the venture capital reputation variables are reduced, indicating that shorter relationships (and hence earlier IPOs) are the cause of reduced equity stakes as predicted by the grandstanding hypothesis. The longer the venture capital firm has been on the board of directors, the larger is its equity stake. The results in table 12.6 indicate that the 12 to 14 month shorter board service by young lead venture capital firms estimated in table 12.4 accounts for more than half of the smaller equity stake of young venture firms (nearly 3 percent of the 4.7 percent difference).

The evidence on equity stakes is consistent with young venture capital firms incurring costs by bringing IPOs to market earlier than established venture capital providers. Much of the difference between young and old venture capital firms in percentage equity stakes is explained by the length of board service, an indication that young venture capital firms incur costs by taking companies public earlier. To test whether early IPOs have differential costs on young and old venture firms, interaction terms between reputation measures and IPO maturity are included in the regressions of tables 12.5 and 12.6, but these interaction terms are insignificant.

Alternative Explanations

Megginson and Weiss (1991) and Barry, Muscarella, Peavy, and Vetsuypens (1990) offer evidence that venture-backed firms go public earlier than nonventure firms because venture capitalists certify the quality of offerings. Venture capitalists repeatedly bring companies to the IPO market and can credibly commit not to offer overpriced shares. Their

Table 12.6
Regressions for the percentage equity held by all venture capital firms prior to IPO.
The sample is 433 venture-backed IPOs from 1978 to 1987. The dependent variable is the percentage of the offering company's equity held by all venture capital investors prior to the IPO (as listed in the IPO prospectus). Independent variables include a dummy variable that equals 1 if the lead venture organization is less than six years old, the logarithm of the venture capital firm's age in months, the cumulative number of IPOs (both venture-backed and nonventure-backed) in the previous four months, the logarithm of IPO offering size, the logarithm of IPO company age in months, the logarithm of the number of months that the lead venture capitalist has been on the IPO company's board of directors, the Carter and Manaster (1990) underwriter rank, and the capital under management at the lead venture capital firm. All regressions include industry dummy variables to control for any fixed effects. Coefficients on industry dummies are not reported (t-statistics are in brackets).

	Dependent variable			
Independent variables	Percentage of equity held by all venture firms prior to IPO			
Venture firm less than six years old	−4.73	−2.83		
	[−2.27]	[−0.70]		
Logarithm of venture firm age			0.973	0.536
			[1.70]	[0.24]
Number of IPOs in previous four months	0.010	0.008	0.009	0.006
	[0.44]	[0.25]	[0.40]	[0.019]
Logarithm of IPO offering size	2.918	0.144	3.266	0.256
	[1.96]	[0.06]	[2.14]	[0.12]
Logarithm of IPO company age		−2.65		−2.39
		[−1.25]		[−1.13]
Logarithm of length of board service		8.14		8.27
		[4.04]		[4.12]
Underwriter rank		0.784		0.797
		[0.71]		[0.73]
Venture capital under management		0.010		0.011
		[0.85]		[0.92]
Constant	−7.93	16.65	−17.08	11.44
	[−0.31]	[0.45]	[0.68]	[0.32]
R^2	0.125	0.270	0.118	0.268
p-value of F-test	0.005	0.003	0.005	0.002
Number	338	190	338	190

conclusions are similar to Carter and Manaster's (1990) findings about the reputation of underwriters and the underpricing of public offerings. Certification by venture capitalists is potentially consistent with grandstanding. Megginson and Weiss examine venture-backed versus nonventure IPOs, but they do not directly test for differences between types of venture capitalists. The grandstanding hypothesis has important implications for the IPO timing of young and old venture capital firms. Venture capital certification could lower underwriting costs and underpricing on average, but young venture capital firms may still have incentives to bring IPOs to market earlier than established venture capital firms to establish a track record and raise new capital.

Another explanation of earlier venture-backed IPOs is that investors recycle money within asset classes. Venture capitalists bring companies public to provide liquidity for previous investments. If investors reinvest the profits from previous venture capital investments into new venture capital funds, the venture capital firm can receive capital sooner by returning cash to investors.

Only the grandstanding hypothesis, however, implies that young venture capital firms have an incentive to perform early IPOs. The certification predicts that older venture capital firms should be associated with IPOs that are earlier or at least not later than those of new venture firms. If certification affects the cost but not the timing of IPOs, then there should be no difference between the two groups. The recycling hypothesis also predicts no difference in IPO timing between old and young venture capital firms. The results above, however, show that young venture firms do take companies public earlier, supporting the existence of grandstanding.

Grandstanding also predicts that young venture capital firms have an incentive to incur the costs of early IPOs because their fundraising is significantly more sensitive to performance than is an older firm's fundraising. Consequently, the duration of board service or the age of the offering company should explain a portion of the differences in underpricing and equity stakes. Certification implies that older venture capital firms have more reputational capital and hence lower costs of going public early. Neither the certification nor recycling hypothesis predicts that the length of board service at IPO explains the differences in underpricing and equity stakes between young and old venture firms. The results shown above establish that a portion of the underpricing and equity stake differences is explained by length of board service, supporting the predictions of the grandstanding hypothesis.

Conclusions

Reputational concerns affect the IPO timing decisions of young venture capital fund managers. Young venture capital firms raise money for a new fund sooner after an IPO, and the size of a young firm's next fund is more dependent on the number of IPOs it has financed previously than is the size of an old venture firm's next fund. Companies backed by new venture capital firms are younger at IPO than those backed by established venture capital firms, and the young venture capitalists have been on their boards for a shorter time. Young lead venture firms bear the costs of early IPOs, however, by receiving smaller equity stakes. These differences are consistent with the predictions of grandstanding.

The issues addressed by the grandstanding hypothesis and the empirical results provide insights for the venture capital industry. Signaling appears to cause real wealth losses. Limited partners bear a large fraction of the costs from early IPOs. More than 400 new venture capital firms entered the industry after 1978. The tremendous entry of new venture capital firms and the incentives to grandstand potentially explain some of the declining returns on venture capital in the 1980s.

Because the venture capitalist typically receives a fixed fee compensation based on the size of the fund (2 to 3 percent of assets under management per annum) in addition to 20 percent of the fund's profits from investing, the venture capitalist has incentives to grow the firm's capital under management by starting large follow-on funds. Chapter 4 shows that the present value of the annual fee is typically as large as the present value of the profits. Annual fixed fees are four to six times larger than the fees received by public market money managers documented by Lakonishok, Shleifer, and Vishny (1992). The desire to increase the size of the funds in turn increases the incentive to grandstand. Reduced fixed fees and increased profit sharing in large funds might better align the incentives of venture capitalists with the goals of investors.

Future research should examine the effects of venture capital on the long-run prospects of entrepreneurial projects and its relation to underpricing and investment characteristics. Entrepreneurs have little information on the IPO market in general or venture capitalists' role in that process in particular. While this chapter does not address the reasons entrepreneurs seek financing from young venture capital firms who then rush them to the IPO market, the issue deserves greater attention by examining the following: the relation between venture capitalists and entrepreneurs, the decision to accept venture financing, the process of deciding to go public, and the long-term impact of venture capital financing in general and grandstanding in particular on the life cycle and performance of companies. For example, what is the impact of venture capital financing on pre- and post-IPO sales, earnings, and asset growth rates? Mikkelson, Partch, and Shah (1997) examine accounting performance in a sample of venture-backed and nonventure IPOs and find no long-run differences, but costs of early IPOs could exist. Assessing these other costs would be an important addition not only to the literature on venture capital investments but also to the knowledge about the decision to go public.

13 Why Do Venture Capitalists Distribute Shares?

An enduring issue in the corporate finance literature has been the impact of trading by informed insiders on securities prices. Two cases initiated by the U.S. Securities and Exchange Commission (SEC) in the early 1960s[1] stimulated an interest in this relationship and its implications for social welfare (e.g., Manne 1966) that continues to this day.

An extensive body of research has examined trading by corporate insiders. Most notably, Seyhun (e.g., 1986, 1988) has documented the short- and long-run price impacts of trading by officers, directors, and other insiders. But as Meulbroek (1992b) notes:

Self-reported corporate transactions data [are] less appropriate for addressing [the impact of informed traders on stock prices]. The corporate transactions are by definition not based on material, nonpublic information. Because corporate insiders cannot legally trade on such information, they would most likely refrain from reporting their violative transactions to the SEC.

This chapter attempts to address the problem by examining the stock price reaction to a set of transactions by informed parties that are not affected by these legal constraints. But rather than focusing on illegal trades, as Meulbroek does, we examine a class of legal transactions that are largely exempt from SEC oversight—the distribution of shares in public companies by venture capital funds to their limited partners. Venture capitalists raise money from investors and make equity investments in young, high-risk, high-growth companies. Most successful venture capital-backed companies eventually go public in an underwritten initial public offering (IPO). Venture capitalists can liquidate their position in the company by selling shares on the open market and then paying those

---

1. *In the Matter of Cady, Roberts and* Co., SEC Release No. 6668, CCH Federal Securities Law Reporter par 76,803 (1961); *SEC v. Texas Gulf Sulphur Co.*, 401 F. Supp. 262 (S.D.N.Y. 1966), 401 F.2d 833 (2d Cir. 1968), 312 F. Supp. 77 (S.D.N.Y. 1970).

proceeds to investors in cash. More frequently, however, venture capitalists make distributions of shares to investors in the venture capital fund.

These distributions have several features that make them an interesting testing ground for an examination of the impact of transactions by informed insiders on securities prices. Because they are not considered to be "sales," the distributions are exempt from the antifraud and antimanipulation provisions of the securities laws. The legality of distributions provides an important advantage. Comprehensive records of these transactions are compiled by institutional investors and intermediaries who invest in venture funds, addressing concerns about sample selection bias. Like trades by corporate insiders, transactions are not revealed at the time of the transaction. Venture capitalists can immediately declare a distribution, send investors their shares, and need not register with the SEC or file a report under Rule 16(a). Rather, the occurrence of such distributions can only be discovered from corporate filings with a lag, and even then the distribution date cannot be precisely identified. To identify the time of these transactions, one needs to rely (as we do) on the records of the partners in the fund. We can also characterize in detail the features of the venture funds making the distributions, the firms whose shares are being distributed, and the changes associated with the transactions in a way that can discriminate among various alternative explanations for these patterns.

From the records of four institutions, we construct a representative set of over 700 transactions by 135 funds over a decade-long period. The results are consistent with venture capitalists possessing inside information and of the (partial) adjustment of the market to that information. After significant increases in stock prices prior to distribution, abnormal returns around the distribution are a negative and significant −2.0 percent, comparable to the market reaction to publicly announced secondary stock sales. The sign and significance of the cumulative excess returns for the twelve months following the distribution are sensitive to the benchmark used. The market's ability to discern and react to the information content of distributions is consistent with Seyhun (1986) and Meulbroek (1992b).

Significant differences appear in the returns for some subsamples. Distributions that occur in settings where information asymmetries may be greatest—especially where the firm has been taken public by a lower-tier underwriter and the distribution is soon after the IPO—have larger immediate price declines. Post-distribution price performance is related to factors that predict event window returns.

At the same time, we must acknowledge some important limitations to the analysis. Many of the recipients of these distributions (e.g., pension funds and endowments) will not desire to hold the distributed securities. Because distributions are not illegal, the limited partners will have no reason to disguise their sales (aside from reasons of strategic trading). In this sense, the distributions resemble the legal insider transactions that have been extensively examined by Seyhun (1986) and others. Furthermore, at least two other factors may cause the share price to drop at the time of distribution: the ending of the venture capitalists' value-added monitoring (since they often resign from the board at the time of the distributions) and the large increase in the public supply of shares after distribution (if demand for the company's stock is not perfectly elastic). To test these alternatives, we seek to explain the size of the short- and long-run reactions to these distributions. Variables that are consistent with these alternative hypotheses have little explanatory power.

In addition to works on insider trading, this study is related to several strands in the corporate finance literature. First, we draw upon the methodological studies on the measurement of long-run returns of securities. Recent works include Ball, Kothari, and Shanken (1995), Barber and Lyon (1997), Kothari and Warner (1997), and Barber, Lyon, and Tsai (1999). Second, an extensive literature (e.g., Mikkelson and Partch 1985) has shown that announcements of firms' intentions to undertake secondary issues and sales of shares by corporate insiders lead to immediate negative market reactions. More recently, Kahle (1996) has shown that firms issuing securities after insider sales experience significant negative excess returns, but other securities issuers do not. Another related strand is studies of the long-run performance of IPOs (e.g., Loughran and Ritter 1995). This analysis is closely related to chapter 14, which contrasts the post-IPO stock returns of venture-backed and nonventure firms. Although there certainly is overlap between the two analyses (most of the firms we examine had gone public relatively recently, on average one-and-a-half years prior to the distribution), our focus here is different. In particular, rather than studying the long-run returns of a particular class of securities, we seek to understand how rapidly transactions by informed insiders are incorporated into the stock price. At the same time, our finding of greater efficiency in the market for venture-backed securities (when contrasted with Kahle's results) is reminiscent of that chapter's conclusions.

The rest of this chapter is organized as follows. The next section provides an overview of venture capital distributions. The third section analyses stock price performance around distributions, and the fourth section concludes the chapter.

Venture Capitalists and Distribution Policy

As discussed above, venture capitalists typically exit successful investments by taking them public. They usually do not sell shares at the time of the IPO, but rather undertake a "lockup" agreement with the investment banker underwriting the offering in which they promise to refrain from selling their shares for several months.[2] Even after the lockup expires, venture capitalists will often continue to hold the shares in the company for months or even years. Once they decide to liquidate their positions, there are two alternatives. First, venture capitalists can sell the shares they hold on the open market and distribute cash to limited partners. More often, venture capitalists distribute shares to each limited partner and frequently to themselves.

A number of reasons are responsible for the preponderance of distributions in kind. First, SEC rules restrict sales by corporate insiders. Insiders, including the venture capitalist, are only allowed to sell shares each quarter up to the greater of 1 percent of the outstanding equity or the average weekly trading volume. The venture capital fund may hold a large fraction of the company's equity and selling the entire stake may take a long time. By distributing shares to limited partners, who are usually not considered insiders,[3] the venture capitalist can dispose of a large block of shares more quickly.

Second, tax motivations may also provide an incentive for the venture capitalist to distribute shares. If venture capitalists sell shares and distribute cash, taxable limited partners (e.g., individuals and corporations) and the venture capitalists themselves are subject to immediate capital gains taxes. These investors might prefer to postpone these taxes by receiving

---

2. Lin and Smith (1995) show that the shares sold by venture capitalists at the time of 497 venture-backed IPOs from 1979 to 1990 (representing 77 percent of the total number of venture-backed IPOs in this period) totaled less than $400 million. This represents about 1 percent of the total amount raised by venture capital funds in this period.
3. Limited partners in a venture capital fund would not be considered insiders unless they had board representation or some other affiliation with the portfolio company, or held 10 percent of the company's equity. While the venture capitalist might hold 10 percent, once the distribution is made, it is unlikely that any limited partner would. It is extremely improbable that a limited partner would have board representation because it would risk losing its limited liability status.

distributions in kind and selling the shares at a later date. These considerations will be unimportant to tax-exempt limited partners (e.g., pension funds and endowments). By distributing stock, venture capitalists provide limited partners with the flexibility to make their own decisions about selling the stock.

Third, if selling the shares has a large negative effect on prices, venture capitalists may want to distribute shares. The method of computing returns employed by limited partners and outside fund trackers (e.g., Venture Economics) uses the closing price of the distributed stock on the day the distribution is declared. The actual price received when the limited partners sell their shares may be lower. If prices decline after the distribution, actual returns to limited partners could be substantially less than calculated returns. Venture capitalists care about stated returns on their funds because they use this information when they raise new funds.

Finally, the venture capitalist's compensation can be affected by distribution policy. If the venture capital fund has not returned committed capital to its limited partners, most funds distribute shares of portfolio companies in proportion to the partners' actual capital commitments (usually 99 percent to limited partners and 1 percent to general partners). By distributing overvalued shares prior to the return of committed capital, the venture capitalist moves closer to the point where general partners collect a larger share of the profits. Once committed capital has been returned, venture capitalists still have an incentive to distribute overvalued shares. They may be able to sell their portions at a high valuation before limited partners receive their shares and the market discerns that a distribution has occurred. This problem is exacerbated if the venture partnership agreement allows, as many do, venture capitalists to receive distributions at their discretion prior to the return of the investors' committed capital. In these instances, the venture capitalist has even greater flexibility in choosing whether to be included in the distribution.

A venture capitalist's reputational concerns may not overcome the incentive to distribute overvalued shares. First, many institutional investors and advisors also care about stated return. They may be compensated based on how well the venture funds that they select do relative to a benchmark (calculated using the distribution price). This is particularly true if the shares are transferred immediately on receipt of the distribution to its public-equity managers. Any price decline may be attributed to the public-equity group. Second, certain investors may be unaware of the problem. Investors may not track stock price performance against an appropriate benchmark. Similarly, record keeping of the price at which the shares were sold is often incomplete.

Few SEC regulations cover distributions by private equity investors. Rule 16(a) states that individuals who are affiliates of a firm, such as directors, officers, and holders of 10 percent of the company's shares, must disclose any transactions in the firm's stock on a monthly basis. Provision 16(a)-7, however, explicitly exempts distributions of securities that (1) were originally obtained from issuers and (2) are being distributed "in good faith, in the ordinary course of business." An interpretation widely accepted within the industry is that venture capitalists distribute investments in the normal course of business, and that they do not convey any information unless the venture capitalist makes an explicit recommendation to hold or sell the shares at the time. Venture capital lawyers have applied the same principles when considering the applicability of Rule 10(b)-5, the most general prohibition against fraudulent activity in the purchase or sale of any security.

Analysis of Distributions

Sample and Summary Statistics

We collect data on the date, size, and sources of all distributions received by two institutional investors in venture funds and three investment advisors. We eliminate distributions from funds that primarily invested in leveraged buyouts and from publicly traded Small Business Investment Companies because the nature of these funds' investments and the incentives introduced by their compensation schemes and structures were quite different. In the relatively modest number of cases where contradictory information was recorded about the same distribution, we check with the organizations to reconcile the discrepancies. These deletions and corrections leave 731 distributions of shares in 259 firms by 135 venture capital limited partnerships.

The first panel of table 13.1 summarizes the IPOs and distributions in our sample. The increasing trend in distributions reflects two factors. First, the IPO market has hot and cold periods. The early 1990s saw a prolonged "hot issue" market with many IPOs. Second, venture capital under management grew substantially during this period: the venture pool was twelve times larger (in inflation-adjusted dollars) in 1993 than in 1980.

Table 13.1
Sample summary statistics. In the first panel, the venture capital stake of initial public offerings (IPOs) is the value of all shares held by venture capital (VC) limited partnerships in firms that went public in that year valued at the IPO price. The distribution series is the value of shares distributed by all venture capital limited partnerships to their investors, and is based on the records of Shott Capital Management (including distributions not in our sample). The first panel also presents the number of IPOs and distributions in each year of the sample. In the second panel, the first two columns compare the characteristics of the funds in our sample with those within the Venture Economics funds database whose first closing was in December 1992 or earlier but are not in our sample. We present both the mean and the median (in brackets) of several measures. The third column presents the p-values of t-tests and Wilcoxon signed-rank tests (in brackets) of the null hypotheses that these distributions are identical. The third panel presents some key characteristics of the distributions, as well as of some important independent variables.

Panel A: Summary of IPO and distribution activity

Year	All activity (billions of 1997 dollars)		Number of IPOs in our sample	Number of distributions in our sample
	Venture stake in IPOs	Venture distributions		
1978			1	0
1979			0	0
1980	0.06	0.10	2	0
1981	0.43	0.13	3	0
1982	0.24	0.33	3	0
1983	2.42	0.58	18	1
1984	0.41	0.30	11	0
1985	0.40	0.36	8	19
1986	1.58	0.39	27	33
1987	1.42	0.68	22	55
1988	0.82	0.29	16	21
1989	0.70	0.44	15	51
1990	1.29	0.76	20	80
1991	3.48	1.63	55	134
1992	3.52	1.57	44	195
1993	3.89	1.88	14	142
Total	20.63	9.44	259	731

Panel B: Comparison of funds included and not included in the sample

	Included in our sample	Not in our sample, but in Venture Economics database	p-value, test of no difference
Number of observations	135	1139	
Date of fund's first closing	Mar. 1984 (Jan. 1984)	Oct. 1983 (Apr. 1984)	0.143 (0.908)
Size of fund (millions of 1997 $s)	109.5 (76.5)	47.3 (31.9)	0.000 (0.000)
Size of venture firm (millions of 1997 $s)	227.8 (130.2)	120.4 (56.1)	0.000 (0.000)
Age of venture firm at time of fund's first closing (years)	5.63 (4.17)	3.65 (1.17)	0.000 (0.000)
Ordinal rank of fund	3.20 (3)	2.65 (2)	0.000 (0.000)

Table 13.1 (continued)

Panel C: Characteristics of distributions

	Mean	Median	Stan. dev.
All distributions			
Time from IPO (years)	1.78	1.02	1.90
Percent of VC's holdings distributed	67.2	68.9	33.6
First distributions only			
Time from IPO (years)	1.69	0.90	1.87
Percent of VC's holdings distributed	81.0	100	29.4
Fifth distributions only			
Time from IPO (years)	2.57	2.60	1.45
Percent of VC's holding distributed	26.0	24.4	16.6
Key independent variables			
Age of venture capital firm at time of distribution (years)	5.41	4.09	5.07
Underwriter rank	8.53	8.875	1.11
Market value of firm's equity at time of IPO (millions of 1997 $s)	174.5	153.7	102.9

The panel also shows how the aggregate number of venture-backed IPOs and distributions by venture capitalists increased over this period.

In panel B of table 13.1, we examine the representativeness of the venture funds for which we are able to collect distribution data. We compare the venture partnerships in our sample with all the partnerships identified by Venture Economics that closed prior to 1993 (for an overview of the database and our emendations to it, see chapter 16) on several dimensions: the age of the venture organization sponsoring the fund (the span between the date when the venture organization's first fund closed and the first closing of this fund), the size of the venture organization (the sum of funds in 1997 dollars that the venture organization has raised in the decade prior to the distribution), and the ordinal rank of the fund (the count of this fund among those raised by the venture organization). While our sample is representative in terms of closing date, it is biased toward larger, older venture capital firms that have raised more previous funds.

More information about the distributions is presented in the third panel of table 13.1. The typical distribution occurs nearly twenty months after the firm goes public. This distribution is skewed, with the median distribution occurring little more than one year after the IPO. Only 1 percent of the distributions occur in the three months immediately after going public: the lockup agreements that restrict insiders from selling shares after an IPO (typically for 40 to 180 trading days) preclude stock distributions as well.[4]

In many cases, there are multiple distributions for each firm. These are primarily due to the presence of several venture investors in the firm rather than multiple distributions of shares in the company by the same venture capitalist. Venture capitalists tend to distribute the entirety of their holdings at once: the third panel of table 13.1 reports that the average distribution involves 67 percent of shares that the venture capitalist holds. The table also provides summary data on two representative distributions: the first and fifth distributions of shares in a company. Not surprisingly, fifth distributions tend to occur later and involve a smaller percent of the venture capitalist's original holdings. (If there are many distributions, it is more likely that the venture capitalists are distributing their shares in several installments.) We discuss the issues posed by multiple distributions below.

Framework for the Analysis

We have already noted an important distinction between venture distributions and illegal insider trading: the limited partners may have few incentives to disguise the fact that a distribution has occurred. Additional differences stem from the fact that unlike an illegal insider trade, other events occur at the time of the distribution. First, venture capitalists hold large equity stakes and board seats even after the IPO. When the venture capitalist declares a distribution, an active, large-block shareholder is essentially dissolved. Theoretical and empirical work by Jensen and Meckling (1976), Shleifer and Vishny (1986), and others have shown that large block shareholders, who are often willing to incur the costs of monitoring management, can play an important role in increasing firm

---

4. We do not present summary statistics about the time from share purchase to ultimate distribution. Because venture capitalists typically invest in successful firms in multiple rounds, it is difficult to determine how long the distributed shares have been held. Venture partnership agreements typically bar the distribution of shares covered by SEC Rule 144, which during the period under study prohibited sales for two years after the purchase of restricted stock and limited the pace of sales between the second and third year after the purchase. These restrictions applied not only to the venture investor but also to the limited partners in their funds. Cases involving distributions of shares held for less than two years appear to comprise at most only a few distributions in the sample, and those of less than three years under 10 percent. Conversations with practitioners similarly suggest that such distributions are very rare. For a discussion, see Denning and Painter (1994).

value. The unanticipated dissolution of a large block holding provides an alternative explanation for stock price declines at the time of the distribution.

The increased number of publicly tradable shares associated with distributions suggests a second explanation. While their findings are not uncontroversial, a number of studies (e.g., Harris and Gurel (1986) and Shleifer (1986)) have suggested that demand curves for shares may slope downwards. If the demand for shares is not totally elastic, then increasing the supply of publicly tradable shares would decrease their price. The median lead venture capitalist controls 11.8 percent of the shares of the company subsequent to the IPO (Barry, et al. 1990). Since a typical venture-backed IPO has only about 30 percent of the shares in the initial public float, the distribution and subsequent sale of these securities represents a substantial increase in the number of publicly traded shares and may trigger a price decline.

Liquidity may play a role in price movements even if long-run demand curves for shares are not downward sloping. Bid-ask spreads or temporary price movements may be related to abnormal volume in the market. For example, a large block of shares may trade at a lower price because the market for the company's equity is not very liquid. If liquidity is the primary reason for price movements, stock prices should decline around distributions but quickly recover thereafter.

One way to address these alternative explanations is to examine how stock price reactions to distributions are associated with the characteristics of the venture capitalist and the firm. While many of these individual items can be criticized for their imprecision, if the evidence is consistent with a considerable majority of one set of predictions, we will be more comfortable with that view. We first examine the impact of the age of the venture organization making the distribution. If the markets are reacting to insider trading by the venture capitalists, distributions by more experienced venture capitalists should produce more negative price reactions. The corporate control alternative also predicts a negative relationship, because older venture firms may be better monitors and the elimination of their oversight reduces firm value more. We determine venture firm age from the Venture Economics database.[5]

---

5. We might anticipate that this relationship would be nonlinear: venture firms that were about to disband might behave differently from ongoing organizations. This, however, is difficult to predict in advance. Many venture firms raise series of successful funds, while others never raise a follow-on to their first fund.

The size of the equity stake held by the venture firm may be related to the incentive to monitor and the quality of information about the company. Both our central insider trading hypothesis and the corporate control alternative predict a negative relationship between the size of the equity stake and the price reaction to the distribution. The downward-sloping demand curve suggestion predicts that only the size of the equity stake actually distributed should affect prices. The stock price reaction should be independent of total equity stake held (but not distributed) by the venture capital firm. (If the market can forecast future distributions at the time of the first distribution, stock price reaction to the first distribution may be related to the size of the equity stake held.) This information is obtained from the parties receiving the distributions.

Underwriters may also play a role in limiting asymmetric information. The number and quality of analysts are often correlated with the reputation of the underwriter. If the market is reacting to insider trading by the venture capitalists, then companies going public with higher quality underwriters should have less negative price reactions because there are fewer information asymmetries. The characteristics of the IPOs of the distributed companies are found in SDC's Corporate New Issues database. We denote the quality of the underwriters using their relative standing in the period from 1985 to 1991 (Carter, Dark, and Singh 1998).

The level of asymmetric information between the venture capitalists and the market may be considerably higher for companies that have been public for a short time. These firms are likely to have less analyst coverage as well as a shorter track record over which the firms' management and prospects can be assessed. If venture capitalists have access to inside information, suggesting that these firms are severely overvalued, they may quickly distribute recent IPOs. On average, the market should interpret distributions soon after IPO as a sign of relatively greater overvaluation, and the length of time from IPO to distribution should be positively related to abnormal returns. The corporate control and downward-sloping demand alternatives suggest that the price response should be independent of the length of time that the shares have been held. If the market is reacting to insider trading or the corporate control alternative holds, then most of the negative information will be conveyed in the first distribution of a company's shares. Later distributions should have much smaller price responses because the first distribution revealed that the venture capitalist considers the firm overvalued or intends to exit the investment.

The availability of information may also be related to the size of the firm. Larger firms are likely to be tracked by more and better analysts. They are also more likely to be scrutinized in the media, which also reduces asymmetric information. The ability to trade on inside information should therefore be reduced for larger firms and price declines at distribution should be smaller. The alternative views have no clear predictions about the relation between the price reaction and firm size. We employ the valuation at the close for the first trading day for this analysis.

Board representation may also be associated with greater access to inside information. Consequently, if the market is reacting to insider trades, there should be more negative price reactions to distributions by board members. The corporate control alternative would also predict that the stock price of companies declines more when venture capitalists leave the board at distribution. Not only is a large block dissipated, but also venture capitalists no longer have the same control rights or information flows once they leave the board. Board membership and share ownership at and after the IPO date are obtained from prospectuses and annual proxy statements.

Contracts governing venture partnerships can also specify whether venture capitalists must distribute or sell shares soon after the IPO. If distributions within a certain time are mandatory, the market should not infer any negative information from the distribution event. If the alternative corporate control or downward-sloping demand curves views explain price reactions, then distribution restrictions should not affect the magnitude of the price decline at distribution. Unfortunately for our empirical tests, the bulk of the distribution restrictions (which we collect from partnership agreements provided by the four institutions who contribute distribution data) are quite weak: the partnership agreements of funds with restrictions almost invariably allow distributions to be deferred with the approval of the majority (or super-majority) of the fund's advisory board. In practice, it appears that these distribution restrictions have a relatively limited effect on behavior: for the twenty venture-backed IPOs in the sample where distributions were made both by funds with and without distribution restrictions, the distribution dates were not significantly different from each other. In fact, the average distribution by a fund without such a restriction occurred two weeks before that by a fund with a restriction. (This result was not driven by a single outlier among the restricted distributions. There was actually a lower variance in the time from IPO to distribution among the restricted distributions, though the difference was not significant.) Thus, the extent to which this measure can help us distinguish between hypotheses seems limited.

Stock Price Reaction to Distributions during the Event Window

The stock price response to distributions is estimated using a two-factor market model employing daily Center for Research in Security Prices (CRSP) stock price data. The two-factor market model utilizes $R_{m,t}$, the return on the CRSP value-weighted NASDAQ index, and $R_{s,t}$, the return on the NASDAQ smallest decile, to determine daily abnormal returns. Equation (1) is estimated for each firm using daily data:

$$R_{j,t} = \alpha_j + \beta_{j,m}R_{m,t} + \beta_{j,s}R_{s,t} + \varepsilon_t. \tag{13.1}$$

The regression coefficients (factor loadings) are calculated from trading day -260 to day -61 and from trading day $+160$ to day $+360$ relative to the distribution (or for the available subsets of these periods). We designate day 0 the day that the venture capitalist declared the distribution.[6] The coefficients are then used to calculate predicted returns. The difference between the predicted and actual return is labeled an abnormal return (AR), as shown in equation (2):

$$AR_{j,t} = R_{j,t} - (\alpha_j + \beta_{j,m}R_{m,t} + \beta_{j,s}R_{s,t}). \tag{13.2}$$

Table 13.2 documents the large price appreciation before the distribution. The cumulated ARs (CARs) for the twenty days prior to distribution are $+3.7$ percent. The abnormal returns for the three trading days following the distribution are all negative and significant. From day 0 to day $+3$, the CAR is -2.0 percent. The next seventeen trading days show little price movement. Figure 13.1 plots the CARs for all distributions. After a major rise of $+7.4$ percent from day -60 to day -1, the three days after the distribution date have negative CARs. Over the next three weeks the stock price reacts very little. From day $+20$ to $+100$, the CAR is once again significantly negative, -5.5 percent. This overall pattern is only suggestive of long-run returns. Cumulating daily returns over long time

6. Of the original 731 distributions, 726 distributions have at least sixty trading days on CRSP in the estimation period. Events that have less than sixty days to calculate factor loadings are not used. The inclusion of these five observations in the sample, using the average coefficients from the other regressions, has little impact on the results. The results are also robust to one-factor market models (i.e., omitting the small firm return proxy) and to substituting other market indices for the NASDAQ indices used in the results.

Table 13.2
Abnormal returns, cumulative abnormal returns, and trading volume around distributions. The sample is 731 distributions by 135 venture capital funds between January 1983 and December 1993. The abnormal returns (ARs) are derived from a market model using both the CRSP value-weighted NASDAQ index and the NASDAQ smallest decile as factors. Cumulative abnormal returns (CARs) are calculated by summing the ARs for the period specified. t-statistics calculated from the cross section of abnormal returns or cumulative abnormal returns are in brackets. Average daily trading volume is in thousands of shares.

Day from distribution	AR	t-statistic	CAR	t-statistic	Volume (000s)	Day from distribution	AR	t-statistic	CAR	t-statistic	Volume (000s)
Day −20	+0.11%	(0.71)	+0.11%	(0.71)	149	Day 0	−0.18%	(−1.18)	−0.18%	(−1.18)	214
Day −19	+0.39%	(2.63)	+0.50%	(2.46)	154	Day 1	−1.03%	(−7.89)	−1.21%	(−6.72)	225
Day −18	+0.41%	(3.31)	+0.91%	(3.85)	150	Day 2	−0.33%	(−2.41)	−1.54%	(−6.76)	191
Day −17	+0.22%	(1.48)	+1.13%	(4.06)	161	Day 3	−0.43%	(−3.41)	−1.97%	(−7.79)	177
Day −16	+0.20%	(1.48)	+1.32%	(4.43)	147	Day 4	+0.18%	(1.36)	−1.79%	(−6.54)	176
Day −15	−0.03%	(−0.20)	+1.30%	(4.11)	146	Day 5	−0.37%	(−2.82)	−2.16%	(−7.18)	175
Day −14	+0.07%	(0.52)	+1.36%	(4.10)	154	Day 6	−0.03%	(−0.23)	−2.19%	(−6.83)	169
Day −13	+0.01%	(0.09)	+1.38%	(3.86)	136	Day 7	−0.05%	(−0.43)	−2.24%	(−6.87)	162
Day −12	+0.28%	(1.88)	+1.66%	(4.40)	152	Day 8	−0.03%	(−0.19)	−2.27%	(−6.69)	167
Day −11	+0.23%	(1.79)	+1.88%	(4.70)	139	Day 9	+0.01%	(0.09)	−2.25%	(−6.36)	162
Day −10	+0.32%	(2.30)	+2.21%	(5.32)	153	Day 10	+0.05%	(0.40)	−2.21%	(−5.73)	161
Day −9	+0.07%	(0.54)	+2.28%	(5.22)	160	Day 11	+0.06%	(0.41)	−2.15%	(−5.31)	168
Day −8	−0.20%	(−1.57)	+2.08%	(4.59)	172	Day 12	+0.30%	(2.26)	−1.84%	(−4.43)	171
Day −7	+0.22%	(1.60)	+2.29%	(4.80)	166	Day 13	−0.12%	(−0.85)	−1.96%	(−4.41)	176
Day −6	+0.19%	(1.43)	+2.48%	(5.10)	166	Day 14	+0.14%	(1.01)	−1.82%	(−3.94)	171
Day −5	+0.40%	(2.99)	+2.88%	(5.84)	155	Day 15	−0.07%	(−0.43)	−1.89%	(−3.73)	175
Day −4	−0.01%	(−0.04)	+2.87%	(5.75)	160	Day 16	−0.15%	(−1.10)	−2.04%	(−3.95)	180
Day −3	+0.36%	(2.49)	+3.23%	(6.25)	167	Day 17	+0.02%	(0.15)	−2.02%	(−3.75)	181
Day −2	+0.07%	(0.49)	+3.30%	(6.09)	173	Day 18	+0.06%	(0.45)	−1.96%	(−3.63)	185
Day −1	+0.42%	(2.71)	+3.72%	(6.62)	185	Day 19	−0.31%	(−2.15)	−2.27%	(−4.01)	179
						Day 20	+0.14%	(0.93)	−2.13%	(−3.74)	187

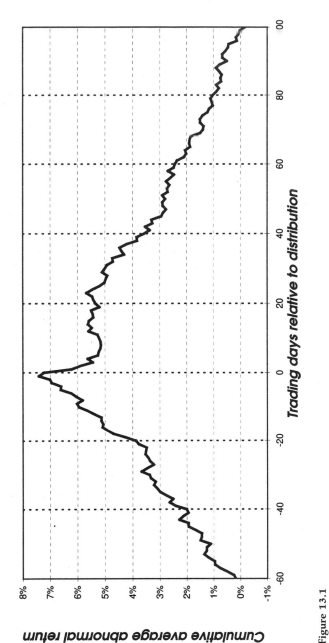

Figure 13.1
Cumulative average abnormal returns for the entire sample of distributions. The abnormal returns are derived from a market model using both the CRSP value-weighted NASDAQ index and the NASDAQ smallest decile as factors. Cumulative abnormal returns are calculated by summing the abnormal returns. The sample is 731 distributions by 135 venture capital funds between January 1983 and December 1993.

horizons may introduce biases. The section below explores long-run returns using buy-and-hold excess returns.

The first panel of table 13.3 summarizes the short-run reactions to distributions. CARs are calculated from day 0 to day +3 (the event window).
This is somewhat different from many event studies, which examine the
CARs from the day before the event to the day after. Unlike many phe-
nomena examined in event studies (e.g., takeover bids) it was unlikely that
there would be any "leakage" of news prior to the event: the decision to
distribute is usually made solely by the venture group without consultation with outside advisors or financial intermediaries. Thus, we believe it
is inappropriate to include the day prior to the distribution. (Indeed, as
table 13.2 indicates, the abnormal volume in the day before the offering
was little different from the other days prior to the distribution.) Because
distributions are not publicly announced, we think that the market would
incorporate the information into the stock price more slowly. Many distributions also occur after the market closes. Since it might take several
days for investors to receive their certificates, we consequently employ a
four-day window. The table also presents p-values from t-tests, comparing
differences in the mean CARs for the various subsets of firms. The only
significant differences are among the underwriter ranking: issues brought
public by less reputable underwriters experienced greater declines. As
discussed above, the presence of a high-quality underwriter suggests
reduced asymmetric information.[7]

7. One concern about this analysis is that the use of four-day event windows increases the
probability of correlation between the observations. While we are examining market- and
size-adjusted returns, the clustering of distributions in particular industries may mean that the
observations are not completely independent and that test-statistics are potentially overstated. We address this concern in two ways. First, we repeat the tabulations and regressions
in table 13.3 using two- and three-day windows. Although the magnitude of some of the
differences and coefficients are slightly smaller, the differences that are significant in the reported analyses remain so at conventional confidence levels. In these shorter windows, there
is less overlap across distributions and consequently less concern about inflated significance
levels. Second, we calculate an upper bound for the impact of the effect, following the generalized least squares methodology of Hansen and Hodrick (1980). In particular, we create a
variance-covariance matrix Ω, where each element is constrained to be zero if the two distribution windows do not overlap, 0.5 (a degree of correlation in the size- and market-adjusted
abnormal returns of different distributed firms that was considerably higher than that actually
observed) if the distributions occurred on the same day, and proportional to the degree of
overlap otherwise. We then computed the standard errors from the matrix $(X'\Omega^{-1}X)^{-1}$.
(Were there no overlap, Ω would be an identity matrix and the earlier results would be unchanged.) In this way, overlapping distributions are assigned less weight. Using various
specifications, we find that this correction increases the standard errors on average by just
under 10 percent.

The second panel of table 13.3 presents regression analyses of these patterns. The dependent variable is the CAR from day 0 to day +3. All regressions are weighted least squares, where the weight is the inverse of the variance of stock returns for the firm in the estimation period. While the regressions are very noisy and the goodness-of-fit low, the significant coefficients are consistent with the insider trading hypothesis.[8] First, companies going public with higher quality underwriters have less negative price declines at distribution. Second, as predicted by the hypothesis that the market is reacting to insider trading, distributions that occur soon after the IPO lead to more negative price reactions.

These variables are not only statistically significant, they are also economically meaningful. Consider the left-most regression in the second panel. At the mean of the independent variables, the predicted net-of-market return in the distribution window is −1.8 percent. A one-standard deviation reduction in the Carter-Manaster ranking of the book underwriter (i.e., by 1.1 rank) led to a predicted event window return of −2.8 percent. A one-standard deviation increase in the time from IPO to distribution (that is, by twenty-two months) generated a predicted return of −1.0 percent. Neither the corporate control nor the liquidity alternative receives much support from the regression results.

Long-Run Excess Returns

While figure 13.1 provides some evidence of long-run price appreciation before distribution and price declines after distribution, the pattern is only suggestive. The magnitude of the price movements may be biased by cumulating abnormal returns over long horizons. To compute long-run returns, we use monthly returns from CRSP. Figure 13.2 plots the nominal buy-and-hold returns for the firms from twelve calendar months prior to twelve calendar months after distribution. For comparison, the return on the CRSP value-weighted NASDAQ index is plotted as well. The graph displays that returns increase sharply starting four months prior to the

---

8. A natural question relates to the correlation of the independent variables. All correlation coefficients are under 0.35. We explore the impact of deleting one of these pairs of variables with correlation coefficients that are statistically significant: e.g., either the logarithm of firm market value or the market value of the stake held by the venture capitalist. These deletions have little impact on the results in this set of regressions, or those reported below. Results are little changed when we use substitutes for several independent variables such as ordinal rank of the venture fund for fund age, the market value of the company holdings by the venture capitalist for the percentage stake, and a dummy variable indicating whether the venture capitalist left the board for the board seat dummy.

Table 13.3
Returns around and after distributions. The sample is 731 distributions by 135 venture capital funds between January 1983 and December 1993. The distribution window abnormal returns (ARs) are derived from a market model using both the CRSP value-weighted NASDAQ index and the NASDAQ smallest decile as factors. Cumulative abnormal returns (CARs) are calculated by summing the ARs for the period from the day of distribution to three days after the distribution. The post-distribution excess returns (ERs) are for months +1 to +12 relative to the distribution month. The ERs are the difference between the firms' returns and the buy-and-hold return on the CRSP value-weighted NASDAQ index times the mean beta for the entire sample (in the first panel), and the buy-and-hold return from a portfolio matched by size and book-to-market ratio and the matching Fama-French industry portfolio (in the second panel). In the first panel, we report the sample means for observations where the variable is above the median or where the answer to the posed question is "yes"; the sample means for observations where the variable is below the median or where the answer to the posed question is "no"; and the p-values from t-tests of the difference in means. The second panel presents four regressions: the distribution window regressions are weighted least squares where the weight is the inverse of the variance of stock returns for the firm in the estimation period, while the post-distribution ones are ordinary least squares. Net-of-market returns before the distribution are the CARs from day −20 to Day 0 in the second regression; and ERs from Month −6 to Month −1 in the fourth regression. Absolute t-statistics are in brackets.

Variable	Mean CAR in distribution window			Mean ER in year after distribution		
	Above median or yes	Below median or no	p-value from t-test	Above median or yes	Below median or no	p-value from t-test
Venture firm age (in years)	−2.38%	−1.55%	0.104	−6.70%	−3.86%	0.544
Distributions as a percentage of equity	−1.97%	−1.97%	0.995	−6.01%	−4.77%	0.791
Underwriter ranking	−1.45%	−2.88%	0.006	1.19%	−10.82%	0.015
First distribution for firm?	−2.01%	−1.90%	0.844	−6.18%	−4.51%	0.734
Market value of IPO firm's equity at IPO (in millions of 1993 $s)	−1.57%	−2.37%	0.115	0.62%	−11.42%	0.010
Venture capitalist on board at IPO?	−2.15%	−1.74%	0.418	−5.64%	−5.09%	0.907
Venture capitalist leaves board?	−2.18%	−1.95%	0.790	−4.56%	−5.48%	0.910
Distribution restriction on venture fund?	−3.18%	−2.10%	0.235	−6.15%	−9.15%	0.712

	Dependent variable: CAR in distribution window	Dependent variable: ER in year after distribution	
		Size and book-to-market adjusted	Fama-French industry adjusted
Venture firm age (in years)	−0.0002 (0.45)	−0.0039 (0.71)	−0.0009 (0.1)
Share of IPO company's equity distributed	−0.0004 (0.64)	0.0036 (0.62)	−0.0030 (0.5)
Underwriter ranking	0.0090 (3.11)	0.683 (2.38)	0.0267 (0.8)
Time from IPO to distribution (in years)	0.0042 (2.41)	0.020 (1.20)	0.0108 (0.6)
First distribution for IPO company?	−0.0001 (0.01)	−0.0317 (0.53)	−0.0500 (0.84)
Share of equity held by venture firm at time of IPO	−0.0001 (0.25)	−0.0040 (0.94)	0.0037 (0.8)
Venture capitalist on board at IPO?	−0.0003 (0.01)		−0.0476 (0.84)
Logarithm of the market value of firm's equity at IPO (in millions of 1993 $s)	0.0074 (1.57)		0.0987 (2.05)
Net-of-market returns before distribution	−0.0054 (0.30)		0.0500 (0.7)
Constant	−0.1000 (3.74)	−0.4918 (1.87)	−0.6428 (2.10)
Adjusted R^2	0.022	0.006	0.005
F-statistic	3.34	1.56	1.35
p-value	0.003	0.157	0.208
Number of observations	628	573	602

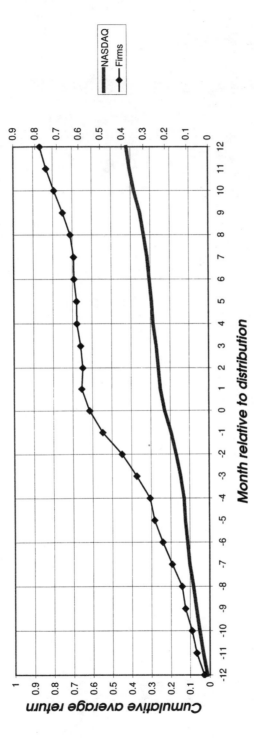

Figure 13.2
Cumulative average nominal buy-and-hold returns for the entire sample of distributions. For reference, the return on the CRSP value-weighted NASDAQ index is included. The sample is 731 distributions from 135 venture capital funds between January 1983 and December 1993.

distribution. From the month after the distribution to month +8, nominal returns are quite modest. These are computed using calendar months. For a distribution occurring in January, we designate the firm's February stock return as that of month +1, whether the transfer occurred on January 2 or 31. The predistribution runup is not biased upwards by first-day returns of IPOs. Venture-backed firms, like other IPOs, are typically underpriced, and gain on average 8.4 percent on their first day (Barry, Muscarella, Peavy, and Vetsuypens 1990). To avoid this bias, we exclude from this and subsequent analyses any firms completing an IPO in a given month: firms are included in the sample only in their second and later calendar months of trading.

We employ three approaches to calculating excess returns. First, we estimate a standard market-adjusted return. The appropriate measure of expected returns for these companies must be calculated outside the sample period. Because many of the companies went public less than one year prior to distribution, some distributions have little out-of-sample data. To overcome this problem, we estimate the beta from monthly data for all firms that have fifteen trading months of returns outside of the window from six months before to twelve months after the distribution. (We use all available monthly observations on the CRSP tapes through December 1995.) The mean beta is 1.596; the median, 1.511; and the interquartile range from 1.26 to 1.94. Excess returns (ERs) are calculated by subtracting 1.596 times the buy-and-hold return of the CRSP value-weighted NASDAQ index from the buy-and-hold return of the company,[9] as shown in equation (3):

$$ER_{i,(a,b)} = \prod_{t=a}^{b}(1 + R_{i,t}) - 1.596^* \prod_{t=a}^{b}(1 + R_{NASDAQ,t}). \tag{13.3}$$

A second approach is to calculate returns net of benchmark portfolios comprised of firms matched by size and book-to-market equity values. Comparing performance to size and book-to-market portfolios appears reasonable given the work of Fama and French (1992), which shows that size and book-to-market are important determinants of stock returns. We

---

9. One question that this procedure poses is whether we should also employ the alpha from the regression in computing our benchmark returns. The mean coefficient on the constant term, 0.0035, or 0.35 percent per month, is positive and significant. Nonetheless, we do not include it, even though omitting it may bias our benchmark downward and make our excess returns appear more positive than they would be otherwise. Our concern is that some of the predistribution runup might be occurring in the estimation period (e.g., in the seventh month prior to the distribution), thereby biasing our estimate of alpha upward.

form the size and book-to-market portfolios as described in Brav, Geczy, and Gompers (1996). We use all New York Stock Exchange (NYSE) stocks to create quintiles of firms based on market capitalization, with an equal number of NYSE firms in each quintile. We obtain our accounting measures from the COMPUSTAT quarterly and annual files and define book value as book common equity plus balance sheet deferred taxes and investment tax credits for the fiscal quarter ending two quarters before the sorting date, the same definition as in Fama and French (1992). Within each size quintile we form five book-to-market portfolios (with an equal number of NYSE firms in each book-to-market quintile) for a total of twenty-five (5 × 5) size and book-to-market portfolios.[10] Value-weighted returns are calculated for each portfolio for the next three months. We repeat the above procedure for April, July, and October of each year. To avoid comparing distributed firms to themselves, we eliminate firms undertaking initial or follow-on public offerings from the various portfolios for five years after their equity issue. Each issue is matched to its corresponding benchmark portfolio. Each quarter the matching is repeated, thus controlling for the time-varying firm risk characteristics of each distribution.

Finally, we calculate returns net of an industry benchmark. We match the firms to the forty-nine value-weighted industry portfolios developed by Fama and French (1997). For each distribution we compute the difference between the firm's returns and the return on the relevant industry benchmark. The sample sizes are somewhat smaller: certain firms cannot be matched to an industry portfolio due to the incompleteness of the Fama-French industry classification scheme.

If prices fully reacted to the informational content of the distribution, long-run excess returns should be zero on average in the months after the distribution. If the market underreacts or it takes time to learn that the venture capitalist has distributed shares, then long-run drifts in prices may occur. Table 13.3 explores the long-run excess returns for the twelve months after the distribution. The results are sensitive to the benchmark used. Using market-adjusted returns, the distributed shares lose 5.4 percent of their value in the next year. The use of portfolios matched by book-to-market and size or industry groupings as a benchmark, however,

---

10. If the book value is missing from the quarterly statements, we search for it in the annual files. For firms that are missing altogether from the quarterly files, we use the annual files. Following the convention of Fama and French (1992) and Barber, Lyon, and Tsai (1998), we exclude all firms with negative book values from the analyses.

leads to positive excess returns.[11] Long-run excess returns are positively correlated with underwriter rank, just as in analysis of abnormal returns in the event window. Sorting firms based on valuation at the close of the first trading day reveals that smaller firms have lower returns than their larger counterparts.

Multivariate examinations of the long-run returns are presented in the second panel. The dependent variable is the excess return from month $+1$ to month $+12$. Independent variables are the same as the ones used in the short-run analysis. Once again, the regression results are noisy. Factors that predict the short-run reaction to distributions also appear to have at least some power to explain the long-run price response. In the left regression (and several unreported ones), underwriter ranking is positively related to performance in the months after the offering. The magnitude of the effect declines when firm size (also positively associated with returns) is used as an independent variable. Overall, the market appears to quickly incorporate the information contained in the distribution into the stock price.

A major concern relates to the independence of observations. Although the magnitude of the distribution runup and rundown is similar throughout the sample period, correlations across the observations may lead to an understating of the standard errors. This problem has two dimensions. First, the data set includes distributions of shares of the same firm by different venture capital funds. In addition, venture capitalists may distribute shares of different firms in particular industries, such as computers and biotechnology, around the same time. Since the returns of these young firms may be quite correlated, the observations may not be truly independent.

We address the concerns about the nonindependence of the observations in two ways. First, we calculate all the long-run returns using only the first distribution for each firm. Results are qualitatively similar, although significance levels fall in the regressions reflecting the smaller sample sizes. We also address the correlation across different firms. Bernard (1987) discusses this problem and demonstrates that the primary

---

11. In unreported analyses, we examine excess returns in the six months prior to distribution. Using the various market benchmarks, the returns are significantly different from zero ($+15$ percent and $+21$ percent). Distributions of shares of smaller companies are associated with significantly greater price appreciation: excess returns for companies that were smaller than the median at the end of their first trading day vary from $+20$ to $+25$ percent, as opposed to $+10$ to $+17$ percent for large companies. Smaller companies may give venture capitalists more opportunity to exploit private information.

source of bias in such settings is intraindustry cross-correlations as opposed to correlations across industries. One way to address this problem is to compute returns for firms net of the appropriate industry benchmark rather than a general market index. As discussed above, the results using this approach are broadly consistent with the other analysis. These anxieties are also addressed by Barber, Lyon, and Tsai (1998). These authors find that forming excess returns using size and book-to-market matched portfolios eliminates many of the biases in long horizon returns, including the skewness of the test statistics as well as much of the cross-sectional correlation induced by the clustering of observations in calendar time. At the same time, it is important to acknowledge that there may still be significant cross-sectional correlations in the residuals, leading to understated standard errors and overstated t-statistics.

In a supplemental analysis, we examine trading volume, which an extensive literature (e.g., Easley and O'Hara 1987) suggests is a key mechanism through which the market discovers trades by informed insiders. Table 13.2 shows that the distribution window is associated with considerably larger trading volumes than other times.[12] We examine abnormal volume by estimating an ordinary least squares regression. Following earlier work, we use the logarithm of firm trading volume as the dependent variable and control for such variables as day of the week, news events, and NASDAQ market volume. Abnormal volume is significantly higher during the distribution window. In supplemental analyses, we show that the higher volume is associated with greater price movements, but the effect is not significantly stronger in the distribution window.

Conclusions

This chapter examines the distribution of venture capital investments to the investors in venture capital funds by the funds' general partners. This is a unique environment where transactions by informed insiders are exempt from antifraud provisions. The legality of these transactions allows us to build a systematic database. The evidence is consistent with the market reacting to the inside information of the venture capitalist: the 2

---

12. The average volume on the distribution day and the two subsequent days is 207 thousand shares; elsewhere in the forty days around distributions, the average volume is 165 thousand. This comparison is limited to days without any news events. News days are defined as those on which a story about the firm (excluding routine earnings announcements) appeared in the *Wall Street Journal* (and was included in the *Wall Street Journal Index*), as well as the trading days immediately before and after the day the story appeared.

percent drop around the distribution is akin to the reaction to public announcements of secondary stock sales even though venture capital distributions are not publicly disclosed.

When we disaggregate the market reactions, the patterns appear to be consistent with the view that this is a reaction to insider trading rather than the two other explanations we offer. In particular, distributions by firms backed by higher quality underwriters also appear to lower asymmetric information and reduce the negative cumulative abnormal returns at distribution. Distributions of less seasoned firms, which may be associated with greater asymmetric information, also trigger larger immediate price declines. The long-run, post-distribution returns are more ambiguous. Although the extent and significance of the market reaction appears to vary with the benchmark employed, at least some evidence suggests that the market does not fully incorporate information at the time of distribution.

14   How Well Do Venture-Backed Offerings Perform?

One of the central puzzles of finance—documented by Ritter (1991) and Loughran and Ritter (1995)—is the severe underperformance of initial public offerings (IPOs) during the past twenty years. These findings suggest that investors may systematically be too optimistic about the prospects of firms that are issuing equity for the first time. Recent work has shown that underperformance extends to other countries as well as to seasoned equity offerings (i.e., offering of companies whose shares are already traded).

We address three primary issues related to the underperformance of new issues. First, we examine whether the involvement of venture capitalists affects the long-run performance of newly public firms. We find that venture-backed firms do indeed outperform nonventure IPOs over a five year period, but only when returns are weighted equally.

The second set of tests examines the effects of using different benchmarks and different methods of measuring performance to gauge the robustness of IPO underperformance. We find that underperformance in the nonventure sample is driven primarily by small issuers, that is, those with market capitalizations less than $50 million. Value weighting returns significantly reduces underperformance relative to the benchmarks we examine. In Fama-French (1993) three-factor time-series regressions, portfolios of venture-backed IPOs do not underperform. Partitioning the nonventure sample on the basis of size demonstrates that underperformance primarily resides in small nonventure issuers. Fama-French's three-factor model cannot explain the underperformance of these small, nonventure firms.

Finally, this chapter provides initial evidence on the sources of underperformance. We find that returns of IPO firms are highly correlated in calendar time, even if the firms go public in different years. Because small nonventure IPOs are more likely to be held by individuals, bouts of investor sentiment are a possible explanation for their severe underperformance. Individuals are arguably more likely to be influenced by fads or lack complete information. We also provide initial evidence that the returns of small, nonventure companies covary with the change in the discount on closed-end funds. Lee, Shleifer, and Thaler (1991) argue that this discount is a useful benchmark for investor sentiment. Alternatively, unexpected real shocks may have affected small, growth firms during this time period. We find, however, that underperformance is not exclusively an IPO effect. When issuing firms are matched to size and book-to-market portfolios that exclude all recent firms that have issued equity, IPOs do not underperform. Underperformance is a characteristic of small, low book-to-market firms regardless of whether they are IPO firms or not.

The rest of the chapter is organized as follows. The next section presents relevant aspects of the venture capital market that are important in public firm formation. A discussion of behavioral finance and rational asset pricing explanations for long-run pricing anomalies is presented in the third section. Underperformance is examined in the fourth section, and the fifth section concludes the papers and discusses some possible explanations for the underperformance of small, nonventure IPOs.

Venture Capitalists and the Creation of Public Firms

As discussed in the second part of this book, venture capital firms specialize in collecting and evaluating information on start-up and growth companies. These types of companies are the most prone to asymmetric information and potential capital constraints discussed in Fazzari, Hubbard, and Petersen (1988) and Hoshi, Kashyap, and Scharfstein (1991). Because venture capitalists provide access to top-tier, national investment and commercial bankers and may partly overcome informational asymmetries that are associated with startup companies, we expect the investment behavior of venture-backed firms would be less dependent upon internally generated cash flows. Venture capitalists stay on the board of directors long after the IPO and may continue to provide access to capital that nonventure firms lack. Additionally, the venture capitalist may put management structures in place that help the firm perform better in the long run.

If venture-backed companies are better on average than nonventure companies, the market should incorporate these expectations into the price of the offering and long-run stock price performance should be similar for the two groups. Barry, Muscarella, Peavy, and Vetsuypens (1990) and Megginson and Weiss (1991) find evidence that markets react favorably to the presence of venture capital financing at the time of an IPO.

If the market underestimates the importance of a venture capitalist in the pricing of new issues, long-run stock price performance may differ. (Conversely, the market may not discount the shares of nonventure companies enough.) Such underestimation may result because individuals (who are potentially more susceptible to fads and sentiment) hold a larger fraction of shares after the IPO for nonventure firms (Megginson and Weiss 1991).

Venture capitalists may affect who holds the firm's shares after an IPO. Venture capitalists have contacts with top-tier, national investment banks and may be able to entice more and higher quality analysts to follow their firms, thus lowering potential asymmetric information between the firm and investors. Similarly, because institutional investors are the primary source of capital for venture funds, institutions may be more willing to hold equity in firms that have been taken public by venture capitalists with whom they have invested. The greater availability of information and the higher institutional shareholding may make venture-backed companies' prices less susceptible to investor sentiment.

Another possible explanation for better long-run performance by venture-backed IPOs is venture capitalists' reputational concerns. Chapter 12 demonstrates that reputational concerns affect the decisions venture capitalists make when they take firms public. Because venture capitalists repeatedly bring firms public, if they become associated with failures in the public market they may tarnish their reputation and ability to bring firms public in the future. Venture capitalists may consequently be less willing to hype a stock or overprice it.

Initial Public Offerings and Underperformance

Behavioral Finance

Behavioral economics demonstrates that individuals often violate rational choice theories when making decisions under uncertainty in experimental settings (Kahneman and Tversky 1982). Financial economists have also discovered long-run pricing anomalies that have been attributed to investor sentiment. Behavioral theories posit that investors weigh recent results too heavily or extrapolate recent trends too much. Eventually, overoptimistic investors are disappointed and subsequent returns decline.

DeBondt and Thaler (1985, 1987) demonstrate that buying past losers and selling past winners is a profitable trading strategy. Risk, as measured by beta or the standard deviation of stock returns, does not appear to explain the results. Lakonishok, Shleifer, and Vishny (1994) show that many "value" strategies also appear to exhibit abnormally high returns. They form portfolios based on earnings-to-price ratios, sales growth, earnings growth, or cash flow-to-price and find that "value" stocks outperform "glamour" stocks without appreciably affecting risk. In addition, La Porta (1996) shows that selling stocks with high forecasted earnings growth and buying low projected earnings growth stocks produces excess returns. These studies imply that investors are too optimistic about stocks that have had good performance in the recent past and too pessimistic about stocks that have performed poorly.

In addition to accounting or stock market-based trading strategies, researchers have examined financing events as sources of potential trading strategies. Ross (1977) and Myers and Majluf (1984) show that the choice of financing strategy can send a signal to the market about firm valuation. Event studies around equity or debt issues (e.g., Mikkelson and Partch 1986, Asquith and Mullins 1986) assume that all information implied by the financing choice is fully and immediately incorporated into the company's stock price. The literature on long-run abnormal performance assumes that managers have superior information about future returns and utilize that information to benefit current shareholders, and the market under-reacts to the informational content of the financing event.

Ritter (1991) and Loughran and Ritter (1995) show that nominal five year buy-and-hold returns are 50 percent lower for recent IPOs (which earned 16 percent) than they are for comparable size-matched firms (which earned 66 percent). Teoh, Welch, and Wong (1998) show that IPO underperformance is positively related to the size of discretionary accruals in the fiscal year of the IPO. Larger accruals in the IPO year are associated with more negative performance. Teoh et al. believe that the level of discretionary accruals is a proxy for earnings management and that the boosted earnings systematically fool investors.

If investor sentiment is an important factor in the underperformance of IPOs, small IPOs may be more affected. Individuals are more likely to hold the shares of small IPO firms. Many institutions like pension funds and insurance companies refrain from holding shares of very small companies. Taking a meaningful position in a small firm may make an institution a large blockholder in the company. Because the SEC restricts trading by 5 percent shareholders, institutions may want to avoid this level of ownership. Individual investors may also be more subject to fads (Lee, Shleifer, and Thaler 1991) or may be more likely to suffer from asymmetric information. These researchers use the discount on closed-end funds as a measure of investor sentiment. If investor sentiment affects returns and if closed-end fund discounts measure investor sentiment, then the returns on small IPOs would be correlated with the change in the average closed-end fund discount. Decreases in the average discount imply that investors are more optimistic and should be correlated with higher returns for small issuers.

Rational Asset Pricing Explanations

Recent work claims that multifactor asset pricing models can potentially explain many pricing anomalies in the financial economics literature. In particular, Fama and French (1996) argue that the "value" strategies in Lakonishok, Shleifer, and Vishny (1994) and the buying losers-selling winners strategy of DeBondt and Thaler (1985, 1987) are consistent with their three-factor asset pricing model.

Fama (1996) and Fama and French (1996) argue that their three-factor pricing model is consistent with Merton's (1973) Intertemporal Capital Asset Pricing Model. While the choice of factor mimicking portfolios is not unique, sensitivities to Fama and French's three factors (related to the market return, size, and book-to-market ratio) have economic interpretations. Fama and French claim that anomalous performance is explained by not completely controlling for risk factors.

Tests of underperformance, however, suffer from the joint hypothesis problem discussed by Fama (1976). The assumption of a particular asset pricing model means that tests of performance are conditional on that model correctly predicting stock price behavior. If we reject the null hypothesis, then either the pricing model is incorrect or investors may be irrational. Similarly, if factors like book-to-market explain underperformance, it does not necessarily verify the model. The results may just reflect that investor sentiment is correlated with measures like book-to-market. We do not wish to argue whether factors like book-to-market reflect rational market risk measures or investor sentiment. The tests we perform are consistent with either interpretation. Another problem with long-run performance tests, however, is the nonstandard distribution of long-run run returns. Both Barber and Lyon (1997) and Kothari and Warner (1997) show that typical tests performed in the literature suffer from potential biases. Although Barber and Lyon show that size and book-to-market adjusted returns give unbiased test estimates of underperformance for random portfolios (which we report in figures 14.5 and 14.6), neither paper addresses the cross-sectional or time-series correlation in returns when tests are predicated on an event.

Analysis of Performance

Constructing the Sample

Our sample of initial public offerings is collected from various sources. The venture-backed companies are taken from three primary sources. First, firms are identified as venture-backed IPOs in the issues of the *Venture Capital Journal* from 1972 through 1992. Second, firms that are in the sample of distributions analyzed in chapter 13, but not listed in the *Venture Capital Journal*, are added to the venture-backed sample. Finally, if offering memoranda for venture capital limited partnerships used in chapters 3 and 4 list a company as being venture financed but it is not listed in either of the previous two sources, it is added to the venture-backed sample. Jay Ritter provides data on initial public offerings from 1975 to 1984. IPOs are identified in various issues of the *Investment Dealers' Digest of Corporate Financing* from 1975 to 1992. Any firm not listed in the sample of venture-backed IPOs is classified as nonventure. The data include name of the offering company, date of the offering, size of the issue, issue price, number of secondary shares, and the underwriter.[1]

For inclusion in our sample, a firm performing an initial public offering must be followed by the Center for Research in Security Prices (CRSP) at some point after the offering date. Our final sample includes 934 venture-backed IPOs and 3,407 nonventure IPOs. 81.3 percent of the venture-backed sample are still CRSP-listed five years after their IPO. A slightly smaller fraction of nonventure IPOs, 76.7 percent, is CRSP-listed after five years. The frequency of mergers appears low. Only 11.2 percent of the venture-backed IPOs and 9.7 percent of the nonventure sample merge within the first five years. The number of liquidations, bankruptcies, and other delisting events is small for both groups as well. Only 7.5 percent of the venture-backed IPOs are delisted for these reasons in the first five years, while 13.3 percent of nonventure IPOs are.

---

1. Our sample differs from Loughran and Ritter's in two respects. First, our sample period is not completely overlapping. Loughran and Ritter look at IPOs from 1970 to 1990 and measure performance using stock returns through December 31, 1992. We look at IPOs conducted over the period 1975 to 1992 using stock returns through December 31, 1994. The different sample period does not change the qualitative results because we replicate Loughran and Ritter's underperformance in our sample period as well. Second, we eliminate all unit offerings from our sample. Unit offerings, which contain a share of equity and a warrant, tend to be made by very small, risky companies. Calculating the return to an investor in the IPO is difficult because only the share trades publicly. Value-weighted results would change very little because unit offering companies are usually small.

We also examine the size and book-to-market characteristics of our sample. Each quarter we divide all New York Stock Exchange (NYSE) stocks into ten size groups. An equal number of NYSE firms are allocated to each of the ten groups and quarterly size breakpoints are recorded. Similarly, we divide all NYSE stocks into five book-to-market groups each quarter with an equal number of NYSE firms in each group. The intersection of the ten size and five book-to-market groups leads to fifty possible quarterly classifications for an IPO firm.[2]

Our sample of venture-backed IPOs is heavily weighted in the smallest and lowest book-to-market firms. 38.5 percent are in the lowest size decile with another 27.2 percent in the second decile, while 84.0 percent of the venture-backed IPOs are in the lowest book-to-market quintile. Most venture-backed firms are young, growth companies. These firms may have many good investment opportunities for which they need to raise cash. On the other hand, their low book-to-market ratios may just be indicators of relative overpricing. Loughran and Ritter (1995) and chapter 11 present evidence that issuers time the market for new shares when their firms are relatively overvalued. Most nonventure firms are also small and low book-to-market, but a substantial number of firms fall in larger size deciles or higher book-to-market quintiles: 58.6 percent of firms are in the lowest size decile, 20 percent more than are in the lowest decile for the venture-backed sample. 73.2 percent of the nonventure firms fall in the lowest book-to-market quintile. 7.3 percent, however, are in the two highest book-to-market quintiles. The differences between venture and nonventure IPOs may result from greater heterogeneity in nonventure IPOs.

Full Sample Results

Ritter (1991) and Loughran and Ritter (1995) document underperformance of IPO firms using several benchmarks. Our approach is an attempt to replicate their work and extend it along several dimensions. Several benchmarks are utilized throughout this chapter. First, as in Loughran and

---

2. We calculate the market value of equity at the first CRSP-listed closing price. For book value of equity, we use COMPUSTAT and record the first book value after the IPO as long as it is within one year of the offering date. The bias in book value should not be too great because the increment in book value due to retained earnings in the first year is likely to be very small. When we match firms on the basis of book-to-market values, we lose 778 firms because they lack COMPUSTAT data within one year of the offering. For most results, this is unimportant because tests do not rely on book values. Where book-to-market ratios are used to either sort firms or match firms, the 778 firms are excluded.

Ritter, the performance of IPO firms is matched to four broad market indexes: the Standard & Poors' (S&P) 500, NASDAQ value-weighted composite index, NYSE/AMEX (American Stock Exchange) value-weighted index, and NYSE/AMEX equal-weighted index (all of which include dividends). Performance of IPOs is also compared to Fama-French (1997) industry portfolios and size and book-to-market matched portfolios that have been purged of recent IPO and seasoned equity offering (SEO) firms.[3]

Matching firms to industry portfolios avoids the noise of selecting individual firms and we can control for unexpected events that affect the returns of entire industries. We use the forty-nine industry portfolios created in Fama and French (1997). Industry groupings sort firms into the similar lines of business.

Comparing performance to size and book-to-market portfolios appears reasonable, given the effects documented by Fama and French (1992, 1993) which show that size and book-to-market are important determinants of the cross-section of stock returns. We form twenty-five (5 × 5) value-weighted portfolios of all NYSE/AMEX and NASDAQ stocks on the basis of size and the ratio of book equity to market equity. We match each IPO on those two dimensions to the corresponding portfolio for comparison.

We form the size and book-to-market portfolios as described in Brav, Geczy, and Gompers (1996). Starting in January 1964, we use all NYSE stocks to create size quintile breakpoints with an equal number of NYSE firms in each size quintile.[4] Within each size quintile we form five book-to-market portfolios with an equal number of NYSE firms in each book-to-market quintile to form twenty-five (5 × 5) size and book-to-market portfolios. (We do not include stocks with negative book values.) Value-weighted returns are calculated for each portfolio for the next three months. We repeat the above procedure for April, July, and October of each year. To avoid comparing IPO firms to themselves, we eliminate

---

3. We purge SEO firms from our benchmark portfolios as well since it has been argued (Loughran and Ritter (1995)) that these firms underperform after they make a seasoned offering.

4. Fama and French (1992) use only NYSE stocks to ensure dispersion of the number of firms across portfolios. Size is measured as the number of shares outstanding times the stock price at the end of the preceding month. We obtain our accounting measures from the COMPUSTAT quarterly and annual files, and we define book value as book common equity plus balance sheet deferred taxes and investment tax credits for the fiscal quarter ending two quarters before the sorting date. This is the same definition as in Fama and French (1992). If the book value is missing from the quarterly statements, we search for it in the annual files. For firms that are missing altogether from the quarterly files, we use the annual files.

IPO and SEO firms from the various portfolios for five years after their equity issue. Each issue is matched to its corresponding benchmark portfolio. Each quarter the matching is repeated, creating a separate benchmark for each issue. We then proceed to equal (value) weight IPO firm returns and the individual benchmark returns which results in equal (value) weighted portfolios adjusted for book-to-market and size. We thus allow for time-varying firm risk characteristics of each IPO and each matching firm portfolio.

We do not, however, replicate Loughran and Ritter's size-matched firm adjustment for several reasons. Matching on the basis of size alone ignores evidence that book-to-market is related to returns. Book-to-market appears particularly important for small firms (Fama and French 1992). Matching to small nonissuers makes it likely that firms in the matching sample are disproportionately long-term losers, that is, high book-to-market firms. IPO firms tend to be small and low book-to-market. The delisting frequency is low for the IPO sample and their risk of financial distress in the first five years may be small. A similar sized small firm that has not issued equity in the previous five years is probably a poorly performing firm with few growth prospects and not an appropriate risk match for the IPO firm if book-to-market is important. These firms may have higher returns because their risk of financial distress is higher. They are likely to be the DeBondt and Thaler (1985) underperformers that we know have high returns. This bias is especially strong prior to 1978 because NASDAQ returns only start in December 1972. Therefore, all size-matched firms would come from the NYSE and AMEX, potentially biasing the matched firms even more toward long-term losers, that is, very high book-to-market firms.

Tests in this chapter calculate returns in two ways, although we only report buy-and-hold results. First, as in Ritter (1991) and Loughran and Ritter (1995), we calculate buy-and-hold returns. No portfolio rebalancing is assumed in these calculations. We also calculate full five year returns assuming monthly portfolio rebalancing. While the absolute level of returns changes, qualitative results are unchanged if returns are calculated using monthly rebalancing.

Table 14.1 presents the long-run buy-and-hold performance for our sample. We follow each offering event using both the CRSP daily and monthly tapes. Compound daily returns are calculated from the offering date until the end of the offering month. We then compound their returns using the monthly tapes for the earlier of fifty-nine months or the delisting date. Firms that drop out will have IPO returns and benchmark

Table 14.1
Five-year post-initial public offering (IPO) returns and wealth relatives versus various bench-marks. The sample is all venture-backed IPOs from 1972 through 1992 and all nonventure-backed IPOs from 1975 through 1992. Five-year equal-weighted returns on IPOs are compared with alternative bench-marks. For each IPO, the returns are calculated by compounding daily returns up to the end of the month of the IPO and from then on compounding monthly returns for fifty-nine months. If the IPO is delisted before the fifty-nineth month we compound the return until the delisting date. Wealth relatives are calculated as $\Sigma(1 + R_{i,T})/\Sigma(1 + R_{bench,T})$, where $R_{i,T}$ is the buy and hold return on IPO i for period T and $R_{bench,T}$ is the buy-and-hold return on the benchmark portfolio over the same period. Size and book-to-market benchmark portfolios are formed by intersecting five size quintiles and five book-to-market quintiles (5×5) and removing all firms which have issued equity in the previous five years in either an IPO or a seasoned equity offering. All IPO and benchmark returns are taken from the Center for Research in Security Prices files.

Panel A: Five-year equal-weighted buy-and-hold returns

Benchmarks	Venture-backed IPOs			Nonventure-backed IPOs		
	IPO return	Benchmark return	Wealth relative	IPO return	Benchmark return	Wealth relative
S&P 500 index	44.6	65.3	0.88	22.5	71.8	0.71
NASDAQ composite	44.6	53.7	0.94	22.5	52.4	0.80
NYSE/AMEX value-weighted	44.6	61.4	0.90	22.5	66.4	0.75
NYSE/AMEX equal-weighted	44.6	60.8	0.90	22.5	55.7	0.79
Size and book-to-market (5×5)	46.4	29.9	1.13	21.7	20.8	1.01
Fama-French industry portfolio	46.8	51.2	0.97	26.2	60.0	0.79

Panel B: Five-year value-weighted buy-and-hold returns

Benchmarks	Venture-backed IPOs			Nonventure-backed IPOs		
	IPO return	Benchmark return	Wealth relative	IPO return	Benchmark return	Wealth relative
S&P 500 index	43.4	64.5	0.87	39.3	62.4	0.86
NASDAQ composite	43.4	50.4	0.95	39.3	51.1	0.92
NYSE/AMEX value-weighted	43.4	60.0	0.90	39.3	57.6	0.88
NYSE/AMEX equal-weighted	43.4	56.4	0.92	39.3	47.7	0.94
Size and book-to-market (5×5)	41.9	37.6	1.03	33.0	38.7	0.96
Fama-French industry portfolio	46.0	45.0	1.01	45.2	53.2	0.95

returns that are calculated over a shorter time period. Where available, we include the firm's delisting return. Our interval is set to match Loughran and Ritter's results (1995). In panel A we weight equally the returns for each IPO and their benchmark. As in Loughran and Ritter (1995), we calculate wealth relatives for the five year period after IPO by taking the ratio of one plus the IPO portfolio return over one plus the return on the chosen benchmark. Wealth relatives less than one mean that the IPO portfolio has underperformed relative to its benchmark.

The results weighting returns equally show that venture-backed IPOs outperform nonventure IPOs by a wide margin. Over five years, venture-backed IPOs earn 44.6 percent on average while nonventure IPOs earn 22.5 percent.[5] The five year equal-weighted wealth relatives show large differences in performance as well. Wealth relatives for the venture capital sample are all close to 0.9. Wealth relatives for the nonventure capital sample are substantially lower and range as low as 0.71 against the S&P 500 index.

Controlling for industry returns leaves performance differences as well. Using Fama-French (1997) industry portfolios, the venture capital sample shows little underperformance. The five year wealth relative is 0.97. Nonventure IPOs show substantial underperformance relative to their industry benchmarks—0.79 for the five year wealth relative.

Two interpretations of the industry results are possible. First, the benchmark industry returns for the venture-backed sample are lower than the industry returns for the nonventure sample. Thus, venture-backed IPOs may be concentrated in industries that have lower risk and therefore expected returns should be lower. Second, the relatively lower industry returns may reflect the venture capitalist's ability to time industry overpricing.

Wealth relatives versus size and book-to-market portfolios demonstrate that underperformance is not an IPO effect. When IPOs and SEOs are excluded from size and book-to-market portfolios, we find that venture-backed IPOs significantly outperform their relative portfolio returns (average wealth relative of 1.13) while nonventure IPOs perform as well

---

5. The five year buy-and-hold returns are not true five year returns because the average holding period is less than sixty months. Firms may take several months to be listed on the CRSP data tapes and so the first several return observations may be missing. Similarly, firms are delisted and so are only traded for some shorter period of time than the sample period. Finally, IPOs in the last two years have truncated returns because observations on returns only run through December 1994. The average holding period is approximately forty-seven months.

as the benchmark portfolios. The poor performance documented by Loughran and Ritter (1995) is not due to sample firms being initial public offering firms but rather results from the types of firms they are, that is, primarily small and low book-to-market firms.

Although the time frame of our sample is slightly different from Loughran and Ritter, our wealth relatives for NYSE/AMEX value and equal-weighted indexes, the NASDAQ value-weighted composite, and the S&P 500 are virtually identical to theirs. For example, five year performance versus the NYSE/AMEX equal-weighted and S&P 500 indexes produces wealth relatives of 0.78 and 0.84 in Loughran and Ritter's sample, while (in unreported results) our entire sample (venture and nonventure IPOs) produces wealth relatives of 0.78 and 0.82. Nonventure IPOs perform worse than Loughran and Ritter's results.

Panel B of table 14.1 presents results in which returns of IPOs and their reference benchmarks are weighted by the issuing firm's first available market value. If we are concerned about how important IPO underperformance affects investors' wealth, then value-weighted results may be more meaningful. Five year, value-weighted nominal returns on nonventure IPOs are higher than when returns are weighted equally. Value-weighted returns on the benchmark portfolios are similar to the equally weighted benchmark returns. This increases wealth relatives at five years for the nonventure capital sample and leaves venture capital wealth relatives relatively unchanged. Value-weighted performance looks similar for the two groups with little overall underperformance. Five year wealth relatives are closer to one. Large nonventure IPOs perform substantially better than smaller nonventure firms do.

Yearly Cohort Results

Ritter (1991) and Loughran and Ritter (1995) document clear patterns in the underperformance of IPOs. In particular, years of greatest IPO activity are associated with the most severe underperformance. Results in panel A of table 14.2 present equal-weighted, buy-and-hold cohort results versus the NYSE/AMEX equal-weighted index.[6] Nominal returns and wealth rel-

---

6. We use the NYSE/AMEX equal-weighted index because it produces wealth relatives that are somewhere in the middle of all benchmarks utilized. Replacing the NYSE/AMEX equal-weighted index with the S&P 500, NASDAQ composite index, or industry portfolios does not affect the time-series pattern of underperformance in any significant manner. Similarly, monthly portfolio rebalancing yields qualitatively similar results.

atives are high in the late 1970s but fall sharply in the early and mid-1980s. While five year returns increase in the late 1980s and early 1990s, they increase more in the venture-backed sample. Our five year return patterns closely follow Loughran and Ritter's results. For the venture-backed IPOs, underperformance is concentrated in the 1979 to 1985 cohorts; while for the nonventure sample, five-year underperformance is prevalent from 1978 forward. These results are largely consistent with the results of Ritter (1991) and Loughran and Ritter (1995) who find similar time-series patterns of underperformance.

We also investigate how value weighting affects yearly cohort buy-and-hold patterns in panel B. Each IPO is given a weight proportional to its market value of equity using the first available CRSP-listed closing price. Value weighting has different effects on the venture capital and nonventure capital samples. Value weighting the venture capital IPOs has little impact on the pattern of performance. Value weighting returns of the nonventure capital sample improves their nominal performance and wealth relatives in most cohorts. There is still some evidence of underperformance in the early 1980s, but it is much smaller. Most five-year nonventure capital wealth relatives are closer to one.

The yearly cohort results suggest several patterns that we examine more deeply. The level and pattern of underperformance previously documented appear to be sensitive to the method of calculating returns. When returns are value weighted, underperformance of nonventure IPOs is reduced in most years.

Calendar-Time Results

Event time results that are presented above may be misleading about the pervasiveness of underperformance. Cohort returns in table 14.2 may overstate the number of years in which IPOs underperform because the returns of recent IPO firms may be correlated. If firms that have recently gone public are similar in terms of size, industry, or other characteristics, then their returns will be highly correlated in calendar time. For example, if a shock to the economy in 1983 substantially decreased the value of firms that issued equity, then it makes the cohort years from 1979 through 1983 underperform, even though all the underperformance is concentrated in one year. Similarly, as discussed in De Long, Shleifer, Summers, and Waldmann (1990), investor sentiment is likely to be marketwide rather than specific to a particular firm and may cause returns to be correlated in calendar time.

To address this correlation we calculate the annual return on a strategy that invests in recent IPO firms. In panel A of table 14.3 we calculate the monthly return on portfolios which buy equal amounts of all IPO firms that went public within the previous five years. We calculate the annual return by compounding monthly returns on the IPO portfolios starting in January and ending in December of each year. These calendar-time returns are presented and compared to calendar-time returns on the NYSE/AMEX equal-weighted index and the NASDAQ composite index. The wealth relatives on the venture capital IPO portfolio are above one in nine of nineteen years and are higher than the nonventure capital portfolio

Table 14.2
Long-run performance of initial public offerings (IPOs) by cohort year versus NYSE/ AMEX equal-weighted index. The sample is all venture-backed IPOs and all nonventure-backed IPOs from 1976 through 1992. For each IPO, the returns are calculated by compounding daily returns up to the end of the month of the IPO and from then on compounding monthly returns for fifty-nine months. If the IPO is delisted before the fifty-ninth month we compound the return until the delisting date. Wealth relatives are calculated as $\Sigma(1 + R_{i,T})/\Sigma(1 + R_{bench,T})$, where $R_{i,T}$ is the buy-and-hold return on the IPO i for period T and $R_{bench,T}$ is the buy-and-hold return on the benchmark portfolio over the same period. All IPO and benchmark returns are taken from the Center for Research in Security Prices files.

Panel A: Equal-weighted five-year buy-and-hold returns

	Venture-backed IPOs				Nonventure-backed IPOs			
Year	Number	IPO return	NYSE/ AMEX	Wealth relative	Number	IPO return	NYSE/ AMEX	Wealth relative
1976	16	310.2	193.2	1.40	14	192.8	189.8	1.01
1977	13	253.1	128.9	1.54	9	103.0	119.0	0.93
1978	8	525.0	226.9	1.91	24	99.6	160.8	0.77
1979	8	71.1	164.4	0.65	44	51.0	141.8	0.62
1980	27	48.8	115.1	0.69	107	−23.4	107.0	0.37
1981	63	24.4	121.0	0.56	241	5.9	114.0	0.49
1982	25	32.8	142.8	0.55	75	110.8	128.9	0.92
1983	117	−14.7	51.1	0.56	507	3.6	50.7	0.69
1984	52	2.1	71.0	0.60	258	46.7	66.1	0.88
1985	46	12.6	40.4	0.80	253	5.3	41.5	0.74
1986	94	79.0	30.1	1.38	505	4.0	30.3	0.80
1987	78	25.3	27.1	0.99	379	12.3	26.0	0.89
1988	35	120.6	59.4	1.38	183	95.4	63.3	1.20
1989	33	141.1	58.3	1.52	129	48.9	58.2	0.94
1990	40	−14.3	67.8	0.51	116	30.7	66.5	0.79
1991	111	38.2	49.3	0.93	208	26.3	49.6	0.84
1992	147	17.7	28.3	0.92	343	15.0	27.7	0.90

Table 14.2 (continued)

Panel B: Value-weighted five-year buy-and-hold returns

	Venture-backed IPOs				Nonventure-backed IPOs			
Year	Number	IPO return	NYSE/ AMEX	Wealth relative	Number	IPO return	NYSE/ AMEX	Wealth relative
1976	16	166.8	208.0	0.87	14	228.7	183.0	1.16
1977	13	438.1	152.1	2.14	9	200.4	118.6	1.37
1978	8	529.4	218.1	1.98	24	141.8	181.7	0.86
1979	8	7.1	156.7	0.42	44	87.9	150.7	0.75
1980	27	1.3	115.6	0.47	107	−32.4	108.6	0.32
1981	63	37.6	127.1	0.61	241	22.6	122.6	0.55
1982	25	−25.7	125.3	0.33	75	81.1	108.2	0.87
1983	117	−26.0	53.3	0.48	507	21.8	54.7	0.79
1984	52	0.00	75.2	0.57	258	67.6	71.4	0.98
1985	46	26.5	43.3	0.88	253	13.9	39.4	0.82
1986	94	201.6	32.5	2.28	505	25.3	32.0	0.95
1987	77	20.1	29.8	0.93	379	39.2	25.4	1.11
1988	35	120.5	58.9	1.39	183	72.0	68.5	1.03
1989	33	130.6	59.0	1.45	129	65.4	61.5	1.02
1990	40	7.9	66.1	0.65	116	45.8	65.9	0.88
1991	111	46.9	48.3	0.99	208	49.8	50.7	0.99
1992	145	25.4	28.2	0.98	343	29.2	27.5	1.01

wealth relative in eleven of nineteen years. Underperformance for the venture capital sample is primarily concentrated from 1983 through 1986, and it is concentrated from 1981 through 1987 for the nonventure capital portfolio.

In panel B, the calendar-time portfolio is formed by investing an amount that is proportional to the market value of the IPO firm's equity in a given month. Value weighting the calendar-time portfolio does not have a major impact on the pattern of underperformance for venture-backed IPOs, but reduces underperformance in the nonventure sample.

The cross-sectional correlation between cohort years can be seen graphically in figures 14.1 and 14.2. The cumulative wealth relative is calculated for each IPO cohort year from 1979 through 1982 by taking the ratio of one plus the compound return on the portfolio that invests in each IPO that went public in a given year divided by the compound return on the NASDAQ composite index. Figure 14.1 plots the cumulative wealth relative for venture-backed IPOs and figure 14.2 plots the cumulative wealth relative for nonventure IPOs. All cohort years move in almost identical time-series patterns. Relative returns decline sharply for all cohorts in mid-1980, rise in parallel from January 1982 through the end of 1982, and then decline in 1983. The time-series correlation of the yearly cohorts illustrates the need to be concerned about interpretation of test statistics. Viewing each IPO as an independent event probably overstates the significance of estimated underperformance. Knowing that underperformance is concentrated in time may also help determine its causes.

Table 14.3
Calendar time initial public offering (IPO) performance. Annual performance of initial public offerings from 1976 through 1992 relative to the NYSE/AMEX value-weighted index and the NASDAQ value-weighted composite index. The sample is all venture capital (VC) IPOs from 1972 through 1992 and all nonventure-backed (nonVC) IPOs from 1975 through 1992. Each month, the return on all IPOs that went public within the past five years is calculated. The annual return in each year is the compound return from January through December of these average monthly returns. The annual benchmark returns are the compounded monthly returns on either the NYSE/AMEX value-weighted or NASDAQ composite index. IPO and benchmark returns are taken from the Center for Research in Security Prices files.

Panel A: Equal-weighted IPO calendar-time portfolio returns

Year	VC-IPOs	NonVC-IPOs	NYSE/AMEX	VC wealth relative	NonVC wealth relative	NASDAQ	VC wealth relative	NonVC wealth relative
1976	48.9	14.6	26.5	1.18	0.91	29.3	1.15	0.89
1977	32.3	22.2	−4.2	1.38	1.28	10.5	1.20	1.11
1978	44.7	10.5	7.8	1.34	1.03	16.1	1.25	0.95
1979	43.8	53.9	23.6	1.16	1.25	32.3	1.09	1.16
1980	78.0	89.7	32.7	1.34	1.43	37.7	1.29	1.38
1981	−7.1	−20.9	−4.3	0.97	0.83	−0.7	0.94	0.80
1982	34.6	5.8	20.2	1.12	0.88	22.4	1.10	0.87
1983	10.5	28.5	23.1	0.90	1.04	21.3	0.91	1.06
1984	−34.4	−21.1	5.1	0.62	0.75	−9.1	0.72	0.87
1985	30.1	23.5	31.2	0.99	0.94	33.8	0.97	0.92
1986	−8.9	3.4	16.9	0.78	0.88	8.0	0.84	0.96
1987	−11.4	−19.9	2.8	0.86	0.78	−4.6	0.93	0.84
1988	23.9	20.1	17.5	1.05	1.02	18.4	1.05	1.01
1989	7.9	11.4	29.4	0.83	0.86	21.1	0.89	0.92
1990	−15.0	−27.3	−4.8	0.89	0.76	−15.3	1.00	0.86
1991	97.4	50.5	30.6	1.51	1.15	60.0	1.23	0.94
1992	8.1	19.1	8.0	1.00	1.10	16.3	0.93	1.02
1993[1]	5.3	16.1	11.0	0.95	1.05	14.5	0.92	1.01
1994[1]	−3.1	−10.5	−0.3	0.97	0.90	−2.3	0.99	0.92

Table 14.3 (continued)

Panel B: Value-weighted IPO calendar-time portfolio returns

Year	VC-IPOs	NonVC-IPOs	NYSE/AMEX	VC wealth relative	NonVC wealth relative	NASDAQ	VC wealth relative	NonVC wealth relative
1976	1.1	2.7	26.5	0.80	0.81	29.3	0.78	0.79
1977	13.3	−5.9	−4.2	1.18	0.98	10.5	1.03	0.85
1978	44.9	12.7	7.8	1.34	1.05	16.1	1.25	0.97
1979	27.8	49.6	23.6	1.03	1.21	32.3	0.97	1.13
1980	67.3	99.3	32.7	1.26	1.50	37.7	1.22	1.45
1981	−7.6	−21.7	−4.3	0.97	0.82	−0.7	0.93	0.79
1982	29.6	14.6	20.2	1.08	0.95	22.4	1.06	0.94
1983	2.2	16.9	23.1	0.83	0.95	21.3	0.84	0.96
1984	−30.2	−19.4	5.1	0.66	0.77	−9.1	0.77	0.89
1985	21.4	30.5	31.2	0.93	0.99	33.8	0.91	0.97
1986	−7.0	8.9	16.9	0.80	0.93	8.0	0.86	1.01
1987	5.5	−11.3	2.8	1.03	0.86	−4.6	1.11	0.93
1988	14.0	15.4	17.5	0.97	0.98	18.4	0.96	0.97
1989	32.4	20.8	29.4	1.02	0.93	21.1	1.10	1.00
1990	0.1	−12.6	−4.8	1.05	0.92	−15.3	1.18	1.03
1991	78.6	38.3	30.6	1.37	1.06	60.0	1.12	0.86
1992	7.5	10.9	8.0	1.00	1.03	16.3	0.92	0.95
1993[1]	10.48	38.3	11.0	1.00	1.25	14.5	0.97	1.21
1994[1]	−4.7	10.9	−0.3	0.96	1.11	−2.3	0.98	1.14

[1] Returns for 1993 and 1994 only include IPOs that went public prior to December 31, 1992.

Risk-Adjusted Performance of the IPOs

If IPOs underperform on a risk-adjusted basis, portfolios of IPOs should consistently underperform relative to an explicit asset pricing model. Recent work by Fama and French (1993) indicates that a three-factor model may explain the cross-section of stock returns. Their three factors are: RMRF, which is the excess return on the value-weighted market portfolio; SMB, the return on a zero investment portfolio formed by subtracting the return on a large firm portfolio from the return on a small firm portfolio;[7] and HML, the return on a zero investment portfolio calculated as the return on a portfolio of high book-to-market stocks minus the return on a

7. The breakpoints for small and large firms are determined by NYSE firms alone, but the portfolios contain all firms traded on NYSE, AMEX, and NASDAQ exchanges.

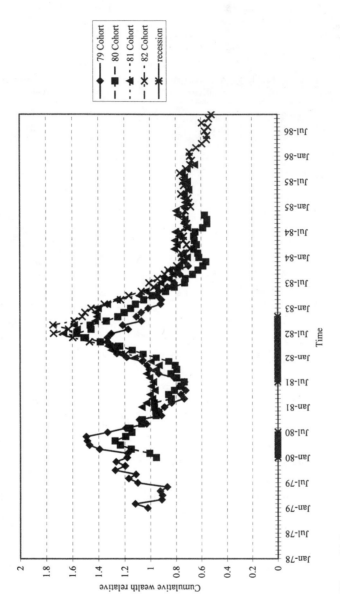

Figure 14.1
Time series of wealth relatives for selected venture-backed initial public offering (IPO) yearly cohorts. The sample is all venture-backed IPOs from 1979 through 1982. Performance of the portfolio of IPO firms is compared to the NASDAQ composite benchmark. The cumulative wealth relative from issue date through the calendar month is plotted by taking the ratio of one plus the equal-weighted buy-and-hold return for the portfolio of issuing firms in a cohort year starting from the beginning of the cohort year up to the given month divided by one plus the compounded NASDAQ return over the same time period.

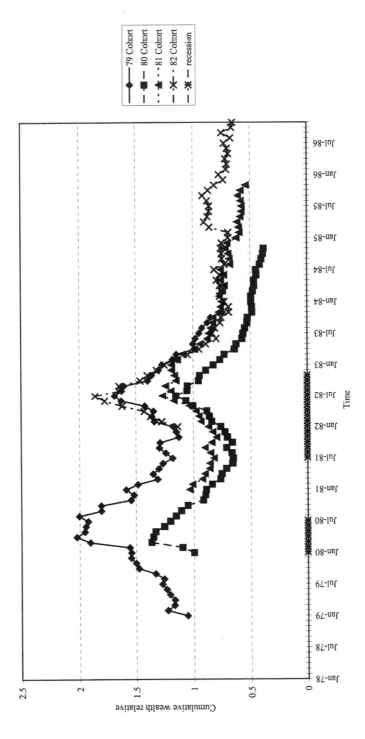

Figure 14.2
Time series of wealth relatives for selected nonventure-backed initial public offering (IPO) yearly cohorts. The sample is all nonventure-backed IPOs from 1979 through 1982. Performance of the portfolio of IPO firms is compared to the NASDAQ composite benchmark. The cumulative wealth relative from issue date through the calendar month is plotted by taking the ratio of one plus the equal-weighted buy-and-hold return for the portfolio of issuing firms in a cohort year starting from the beginning of the cohort year up to the given month divided by one plus the compounded NASDAQ return over the same period.

portfolio of low book-to-market stocks.[8] We use the intercept from time-series regressions as an indicator of risk-adjusted performance to determine whether the results documented by Ritter (1991) and Loughran and Ritter (1995) are consistent with the Fama-French model. The intercepts in these regressions have an interpretation analogous to Jensen's alpha in the Capital Asset Pricing model (CAPM) framework. This approach has the added benefit that we can make statistical inferences given the assumption of multivariate normality of the residuals. This was not possible in our previous analysis due to the right skewness of long horizon returns. The disadvantage of this approach is that it weights each month equally in minimizing the sum of squares. This point can be appreciated by noting that a monthly observation in mid-1976 (the average of a few IPOs) gets the same weight as a monthly observation in mid-1986 (the average of a large number of IPOs). If underperformance is correlated with the number of IPOs in our portfolios, the Fama-French results will reduce the measured underperformance.

Table 14.4 presents the three-factor time-series regression results. IPO portfolio returns are regressed on RMRF, SMB, and HML. For the equal- and value-weighted venture-backed IPO portfolios presented in panel A, results cannot reject the three-factor model. The intercepts are 0.0007 and 0.0015. Panel B presents results for nonventure IPOs. When the nonventure returns are weighted equally, the intercept is −0.0052 (52 basis points per month) with a t-statistic of −2.80 indicating severe underperformance. Value weighting nonventure capital returns produces a smaller intercept, −0.0029 with a t-statistic of −1.84.[9]

The coefficients on HML for venture-backed IPOs (−0.6807 and −1.0659) indicate that their returns covary with low book-to-market (growth) firms. When returns are value weighed, loadings on SMB decline but the loadings on HML become more negative for both IPO groups. The returns on larger IPO firms (in market value) tend to covary more with the returns of growth companies.

---

8. The high book-to-market portfolio represents the top 30 percent of all firms on COMPUSTAT, while the low book-to-market portfolio contains firms in the lowest 30 percent of the COMPUSTAT universe of firms.

9. Loughran and Ritter (1995) also run Fama-French three-factor regressions and find negative intercepts for all issuer portfolios. Loughran and Ritter's regressions, however, combine IPO and SEO firms. Their regressions are therefore not directly comparable to our results. Loughran and Ritter also sort issuing firms into large and small issuers, but use the median firm on NYSE/AMEX to determine the size breakpoint. This cutoff would leave very few IPO firms in the large issuing firm portfolio.

Table 14.4
**Fama-French (1993) three-factor regression on initial public offering (IPO) portfolios
for the whole sample and sorted on the basis of size.** The sample is all venture capital
IPOs from 1972 through 1992 and all nonventure-backed IPOs from 1975 through 1992.
Portfolios of IPOs are formed by including all issues that were done within the previous five
years. RMRF is the value weighted market return on all NYSE/AMEX/NASDAQ firms (RM)
minus the risk-free rate (RF) which is the one-month Treasury bill rate. SMB (small minus
big) is the difference each month between the return on small firms and big firms. HML
(high minus low) is the difference each month between the return on a portfolio of high
book-to-market stocks and the return on a portfolio of low book-to-market stocks. The first
two columns present results for the entire sample. The next three columns show portfolios
sorted by size. Every six months an equal number of stocks are allocated to one of three
size portfolios. Size breakpoints are the same for both the venture and nonventure-backed
samples. Portfolio returns are the equal-weighted returns for IPOs within that tercile. IPOs
are allowed to switch allocation every six months. All regressions are for January 1977
through December 1994 for a total of 216 observations (t-statistics are in brackets).

Panel A: Venture-backed IPOs

| | Full sample equal-weighted | Full sample value-weighted | Equal-weighted size terciles | | |
			Small	Two	Large
Intercept	0.0007	0.0015	0.0001	−0.0004	0.0023
	[0.35]	[0.55]	[0.02]	[−0.20]	[0.93]
RMRF	1.0978	1.2127	0.9481	1.1096	1.2333
	[22.97]	[17.64]	[11.28]	[19.41]	[19.46]
SMB	1.2745	1.1131	1.6841	1.3237	1.1373
	[18.57]	[10.37]	[12.91]	[14.83]	[11.49]
HML	−0.6807	−1.0659	−0.2765	−0.6734	−1.1373
	[−8.24]	[−8.96]	[−1.90]	[−6.81]	[−9.95]
Adjusted R^2	0.889	0.821	0.687	0.846	0.849

Panel B: Nonventure-backed IPOs

| | Full sample equal-weighted | Full sample value-weighted | Equal-weighted size terciles | | |
			Small	Two	Large
Intercept	0.0052	0.0029	0.0056	−0.0056	0.0004
	[−2.80]	[−1.84]	[−1.63]	[−2.72]	[−0.27]
RMRF	0.9422	1.0486	0.8073	0.9900	1.0312
	[19.94]	[26.12]	[9.24]	[18.74]	[26.40]
SMB	1.1450	0.6612	1.3870	1.2245	1.8322
	[15.52]	[10.55]	[10.17]	[14.85]	[13.65]
HML	−0.1069	−0.3405	−0.1909	−0.1906	−0.3229
	[−1.31]	[−4.90]	[1.26]	[−2.08]	[−4.77]
Adjusted R^2	0.825	0.868	0.544	0.813	0.879

Every six months we divide the sample into three size portfolios based on the previous month's IPO size distribution using all IPOs to determine the breakpoints. The portfolios are rebalanced monthly and IPOs are allowed to switch portfolios every half year. We estimate equal-weighted regressions within each size group. The venture capital terciles never underperform. No intercept is below −0.0004 and none are significant. The pattern for nonventure IPOs verifies our earlier results. Underperformance is concentrated in the two smallest terciles. Intercepts for the smallest two size terciles in the nonventure sample are large, −0.0056, with t-statistics of −1.63 and −2.72. Coefficients on SMB decline monotonically from the portfolio of smallest issuers to largest issuers. Returns of the smallest IPOs covary more with returns on small stocks.

Coefficients on HML show two interesting patterns. Coefficients for venture-backed IPO portfolios decline monotonically. The larger the firm, the more it covaries with low book-to-market firms. Venture-backed firms are similar in age and amount of capital invested (book value of assets). Venture-backed firms become large by having high market values. Large firms (in market value) will have low book-to-market ratios and hence covary with growth companies.

This pattern is not as clear in the nonventure sample. First, the smallest tercile has a positive coefficient on HML and the largest two portfolios have negative coefficients. Similarly, venture-backed IPOs load more negatively on HML than nonventure firms which indicates that venture-backed returns covary more with the returns of growth companies.

The results indicate that IPO underperformance is driven by nonventure IPOs in the smallest decile of firms based on NYSE breakpoints. Over 50 percent of nonventure firms are in the smallest size decile when breakpoints are determined by NYSE-listed firms. Therefore, all firms in the nonventure capital smallest portfolio of table 14.4 are from the smallest size decile.

Table 14.5 presents the results sorting firms on the basis of book-to-market ratios.[10] Panel A shows that for the equal-weighted venture-backed IPO portfolio, no book-to-market portfolio underperforms. Nonventure firms, however, show substantial underperformance in all terciles. Underperformance ranges from −0.0042 to −0.0055.

---

10. Results for the whole sample are not the same as in table 14.4 because sorting by book-to-market is predicated on having book equity data from COMPUSTAT. Some firms are on CRSP but not on COMPUSTAT, so the number of firms in table 14.4 is larger than the number of firms in table 14.5 by 778 observations.

Table 14.5
Fama-French (1993) three-factor regression on initial public offering (IPO) portfolios for the whole sample and sorted on the basis of book-to-market ratio. The sample is all venture capital IPOs from 1972 through 1992 and all nonventure-backed IPOs from 1975 through 1992. Portfolios of IPOs are formed by including all issues that were done within the previous five years. RMRF is the value weighted market return on all NYSE/AMEX/NASDAQ firms (RM) minus the risk-free rate (RF) which is the one-month Treasury bill rate. SMB (small minus big) is the difference each month between the return on small firms and big firms. HML (high minus low) is the difference each month between the return on a portfolio of high book-to-market stocks and the return on a portfolio of low book-to-market stocks. The first column presents results for the entire sample. The next three columns show portfolios sorted by book-to-market ratio. Every six months an equal number of stocks are allocated to one of three book-to-market portfolios. Book-to-market breakpoints are the same for venture and nonventure-backed samples. Portfolio returns are either equal-weighted or value-weighted returns for IPOs within that tercile. IPOs are allowed to switch allocation every six months. All regressions are for January 1977 through December 1994 for a total of 216 observations (t-statistics are in brackets).

Panel A: Venture-backed IPOs—equal-weighted portfolios

		Book-to-market terciles		
	Full sample	Low	Two	High
Intercept	0.0029	−0.0009	0.0026	−0.0007
	[0.15]	[−0.36]	[0.89]	[−0.23]
RMRF	1.0893	1.1128	1.1154	1.0400
	[20.94]	[16.51]	[14.75]	[13.70]
SMB	1.3416	1.2160	1.2801	1.5242
	[16.52]	[11.56]	[10.83]	[12.86]
HML	−0.6864	−0.9806	−0.8044	−0.2760
	[−7.63]	[−8.41]	[−6.15]	[−2.10]
Adjusted R^2	0.868	0.812	0.766	0.730

Panel B: Nonventure-backed IPOs—equal-weighted portfolios

		Book-to-market terciles		
	Full sample	Low	Two	High
Intercept	−0.0051	−0.0042	−0.0055	−0.0054
	[−2.90]	[−1.61]	[−2.60]	[−2.33]
RMRF	0.9762	1.0394	0.9881	0.9017
	[21.71]	[15.47]	[18.16]	[15.08]
SMB	1.1946	1.2839	1.1803	1.1264
	[17.02]	[12.24]	[13.90]	[12.07]
HML	−0.1667	−0.4977	−0.2641	0.2575
	[−2.14]	[−4.28]	[−2.81]	[2.49]
Adjusted R^2	0.852	0.770	0.805	0.703

Table 14.5 (continued)

Panel C: Venture-backed IPOs—value-weighted portfolios

| | Full sample | Book-to-market terciles | | |
		Low	Two	High
Intercept	0.0012	0.0036	0.0029	−0.0030
	[0.42]	[1.09]	[0.86]	[−1.01]
RMRF	1.1991	1.1814	1.1772	1.1664
	[16.89]	[13.82]	[13.58]	[15.38]
SMB	1.0283	0.9384	1.2043	1.3184
	[9.28]	[7.03]	[8.90]	[11.13]
HML	−1.0470	−1.2152	−0.9706	−0.5252
	[−8.52]	[−8.22]	[−6.47]	[−4.00]
Adjusted R^2	0.804	0.744	0.734	0.756

Panel D: Nonventure-backed IPOs—value-weighted portfolios

| | Full sample | Book-to-market terciles | | |
		Low	Two	High
Intercept	−0.0012	0.0021	−0.0015	−0.0039
	[−0.59]	[0.66]	[−0.71]	[−1.81]
RMRF	1.0438	1.0771	1.0631	1.0269
	[20.59]	[13.55]	[20.03]	[18.86]
SMB	0.6870	0.8899	0.7483	0.5189
	[8.68]	[7.17]	[9.03]	[6.10]
HML	−0.4282	−0.7053	−0.3632	−0.0090
	[−4.88]	[−5.12]	[−3.96]	[−0.10]
Adjusted R^2	0.813	0.698	0.802	0.732

Panels C and D show that value weighting again reduces the influence of small firm underperformance. The lowest book-to-market portfolio for the venture-backed IPOs now has a positive intercept of 0.0036 (36 basis points per month). No other venture or nonventure IPO tercile has significant underperformance relative to the Fama-French three-factor model. The Fama-French results provide evidence that underperformance remains even after controlling for size and book-to-market in time-series regressions. Venture-backed IPOs do not underperform whether the results are run on the entire sample or sortings based on size or book-to-market. Nonventure-backed IPOs exhibit severe underperformance (primarily concentrated in the smaller issuers) even relative to the Fama-French model.

To address the source of underperformance, we rerun the Fama-French three-factor regressions including an index that measures the change in the average discount on closed-end funds. We construct the index as seen in Lee, Shleifer, and Thaler (1991). The discount on a closed-end fund is the difference between the fund's net asset value and its price divided by the net asset value. We value weight the discount across funds in a particular month and then calculate the change in the level of the index from the previous month. Lee, Shleifer, and Thaler argue that the average discount reflects the relative level of investor sentiment. If this is the case, we expect the change in the discount to be related to returns of firms that underperform relative to the Fama-French three-factor model. When the change in discount is positive, that is, the average discount increases, individual investors may be more pessimistic and returns on firms affected by investor sentiment should fall. Conversely, when the change in average discount is negative, individual investors become more optimistic and returns should rise.

Table 14.6 confirms our predictions. The change in discount is negatively related to returns of the smallest group of firms, the smallest venture-backed companies and the smallest two terciles of nonventure firms. These firms are potentially most affected by investor sentiment. The negative relation between changes in the closed-end fund discount and returns of small IPO firms indicates that investor sentiment might be an important source of underperformance. Sophisticated investors may not enter this market because the cost of gathering information about these firms may outweigh the potential returns from correcting the mispricing. Informed investors may also not want to bet against noise traders if prices can move further out of line in the short run. Finally, short selling may be constrained because shares cannot be borrowed.

Cross-Sectional Results

Given the results from the Fama-French (1993) three-factor regressions, we explore how raw returns and wealth relatives vary with size and book-to-market. In table 14.7 we present summary statistics for size and book-to-market quintiles of the full sample and the subsets of venture-backed and nonventure IPOs. In panel A, we sort the entire sample of IPOs by their real (constant dollar) market value at the first available CRSP listed closing price. Equal numbers of IPOs are allocated to each size quintile. We impose the same cut offs for venture-backed and nonventure IPOs. Size increases from an average of $13.0 million in the first

Table 14.6
Fama-French (1993) three-factor regression on initial public offering (IPO) portfolios including the change in the average closed-end fund discount. The sample is all venture capital IPOs from 1972 through 1992 and all nonventure-backed IPOs from 1975 through 1992. Portfolios of IPOs are formed by including all issues that were done within the previous five years. RMRF is the value weighted market return on all NYSE/AMEX/NASDAQ firms (RM) minus the risk-free rate (RF) which is the one-month Treasury bill rate. SMB (small minus big) is the difference each month between the return on small firms and big firms. HML (high minus low) is the difference each month between the return on a portfolio of high book-to-market stocks and the return on a portfolio of low book-to-market stocks. ΔDiscount represents the change in the average discount on closed-end fund from the end of last month to the end of this month. The first two columns present results for the entire sample. The next three columns show portfolios sorted by size. Every six months an equal number of stocks are allocated to one of the three size portfolios. Size breakpoints are the same for both venture and nonventure-backed samples. Portfolio returns are the equal-weighted returns for IPOs within that tercile. IPOs are allowed to switch allocation every six months. All regressions are for January 1977 through May 1992 for a total of 185 observations. [t-statistics are in brackets.]

Panel A: Venture-backed IPOs

	Full sample equal weighted	Full sample value weighted	Equal-weighted size terciles		
			Small	Two	Large
Intercept	0.0009	0.0018	0.0011	−0.0008	0.0024
	[0.44]	[0.59]	[0.31]	[−0.34]	[0.89]
RMRF	1.0934	1.2043	0.9145	1.1258	1.2377
	[21.10]	[15.85]	[10.08]	[18.34]	[18.06]
SMB	1.3855	1.1071	1.7154	1.2986	1.1406
	[17.28]	[9.41]	[12.22]	[13.67]	[10.75]
HML	−0.7104	−1.0881	−0.4078	−0.6400	−1.0818
	[−7.51]	[−7.85]	[−2.47]	[−5.71]	[−8.65]
ΔDiscount	−0.0002	0.0018	−0.0038	0.0001	0.0031
	[−0.22]	[1.24]	[−2.18]	[0.06]	[2.34]
Adjusted R^2	0.891	0.819	0.701	0.850	0.853

quintile to $505.2 million in the biggest. Comparing average book-to-market ratios for the two subgroups demonstrates that venture-backed IPOs have substantially lower average book-to-market ratios within any given size quintile. The smallest two-size quintiles have disproportionately more nonventure IPOs. This reflects the larger average size of venture-backed IPO firms.[11] Differences in book-to-market ratios might

11. No time series bias is imparted by sorting the entire sample by the total sample breakpoints. No trend or pattern in real size or book-to-market ratios is evident that would lead to dramatic differences in the yearly representation in size or book-to-market quintiles.

Table 14.6 (continued)

Panel B: Nonventure-backed IPOs

	Full sample equal weighted	Full sample value weighted	Equal-weighted size terciles		
			Small	Two	Large
Intercept	−0.0049	−0.0032	−0.0050	−0.0053	−0.0004
	[−2.38]	[−1.80]	[−1.28]	[−2.32]	[−0.52]
RMRF	0.9121	1.0271	0.7801	0.9480	1.0096
	[17.61]	[23.28]	[8.03]	[16.66]	[23.50]
SMB	1.1650	0.6853	1.3910	1.2554	0.8581
	[14.53]	[10.04]	[9.25]	[14.26]	[12.91]
HML	−0.2155	−0.4172	0.0862	−0.3313	−0.4045
	[−2.28]	[−5.18]	[0.48]	[−3.19]	[−5.16]
ΔDiscount	−0.0022	−0.0000	−0.0030	−0.0031	−0.0005
	[−2.23]	[−0.06]	[−2.62]	[−2.87]	[−0.64]
Adjusted R^2	0.8290	0.871	0.543	0.824	0.882

reflect different industry compositions between the two groups. Venture capitalists back more firms in high-growth, low book-to-market industries.

In panel B IPOs are sorted into book-to-market quintiles. Average book-to-market ratios increase from 0.053 in the lowest quintile to 3.142 in the highest. Once again, significant differences are apparent across the two samples. The average size of the venture-backed IPOs is higher in the first through third quintiles, but lower in the fourth and fifth quintiles. Venture-backed growth (low book-to-market) firms tend to be larger and venture capital value (high book-to-market) firms tend to be smaller than comparable nonventure IPOs. Except for the highest book-to-market quintile, the quintiles have roughly constant proportions of venture and nonventure IPOs. The highest book-to-market quintile has substantially more nonventure IPOs than venture-backed IPOs. This may indicate that venture capitalists avoid investment in industries that have high book-to-market ratios (value industries) or that the nonventure firms simply have lower growth expectations.

Figure 14.3 plots the average equal-weighted nominal five year, buy-and-hold return for each size quintile classifying IPOs as venture or nonventure. Venture-backed IPOs show no size effect. Performance of the smallest quintile of venture-backed IPOs looks very similar to performance of the largest. A pronounced size effect is apparent in the nonventure firms, however. Average nominal returns on nonventure IPOs in size quintile 1 are negative.

Table 14.7
Summary statistics for size and book-to-market quintiles. The sampie is all venture capital initial public offerings (IPOs) from 1972 through 1992 and all nonventure-backed IPOs from 1975 through 1992. IPOs are divided into quintiles based on size (market value of equity at the first Center for Research in Security Prices (CRSP) listed closing price in constant 1997 dollars) or book-to-market at the time of IPO. The first book value of equity after the IPO is taken from COMPUSTAT as long as it is within one year of the offering date. An equal number of IPOs from the entire sample are allocated to each quintile. Breakpoints are the same for venture and nonventure-backed samples. Size is in millions of 1992 dollars. (Medians are in brackets.)

Panel A: Summary data for size quintiles

		Venture-backed IPOs		Nonventure-backed IPOs	
Size quintile	Average size	Average book-to-market	Number of firms	Average book-to-market	Number of firms
Small	$13.0	0.465 [0.323]	58	1.901 [0.295]	806
2	$29.6	0.360 [0.326]	132	0.531 [0.286]	732
3	$59.3	0.326 [0.286]	220	0.892 [0.305]	648
4	$114.9	0.248 [0.097]	285	0.907 [0.310]	579
Large	$505.2	0.187 [0.235]	237	0.709 [0.280]	622

Panel B: Summary data for book-to-market quintiles

		Venture-backed IPOs		Nonventure-backed IPOs	
Book-to-market quintile	Average book-to-market	Average size	Number of firms	Average size	Number of firms
Low	0.053	$228.5 [142.7]	198	$131.2 [49.7]	404
2	0.167	$166.9 [117.8]	182	$170.0 [58.8]	420
3	0.277	$133.0 [92.0]	181	$115.6 [51.9]	422
4	0.400	$102.4 [77.8]	157	$117.3 [44.5]	447
High	3.142	$82.2 [55.4]	92	$227.5 [55.6]	510

Equal-weighted nominal five year, buy-and-hold returns for book-to-market quintiles are shown in figure 14.4. Returns show an increase from lowest to highest quintile. The increase across book-to-market quintiles is substantially larger for nonventure firms. On an equal-weighted basis, all nonventure book-to-market quintiles underperform the venture-backed quintiles.

Figures 14.5 and 14.6 show that underperformance of small, low book-to-market IPO firms is not due to their status as equity issuers. We sort the IPO firms into their appropriate twenty-five (5 × 5) size and book-to-market portfolio based on the NYSE breakpoints that are discussed above. The five year, buy-and-hold return on the IPO firms is compared to the five year, buy-and-hold return on the size and book-to-market portfolio

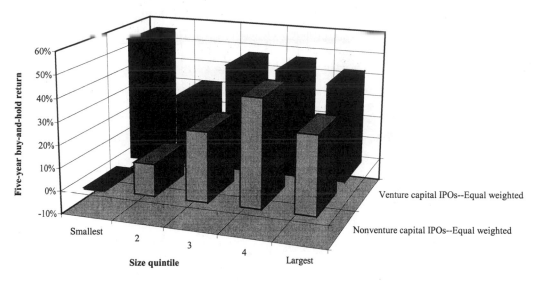

Figure 14.3
Five year equal-weighted buy-and-hold returns for venture and nonventure-backed initial public offerings (IPOs) by size quintile. The sample is 3,407 nonventure-backed IPOs from 1975 through 1992 and 934 venture-backed IPOs from 1972 through 1992. Each sample of IPOs is sorted into size quintiles based on the real size at the first closing price listed by the Center for Research in Security Prices. Size breakpoints are the same for the venture- and nonventure-backed samples. Quintile returns are the average buy-and-hold return for IPOs in that quintile.

that excludes IPO and SEO firms for five years after issue. Figure 14.5 plots the average excess returns of the venture capital-backed IPO sample by portfolio. Adjusting for size and book-to-market returns, no strong pattern of performance is seen. Small, low book-to-market venture-backed IPOs (380 of 934 firms) outperform the small, low book-to-market benchmark by 42 percent.

Figure 14.6 plots size and book-to-market excess returns for nonventure capital-backed IPO firms. The small, low book-to-market nonventure IPO firms (which make up 1,465 of the 3,407 firms) outperform similar nonissuing firms by 12 percent. This positive relative performance is not the result of large returns by the IPO firms, they only earn an average of 5 percent over five years. Small, low book-to-market nonissuing firms, however, earn an average of -7 percent over the same time period. Portfolios further from the small, low book-to-market portfolio have far fewer issuing firms. Standard errors for the estimates of mean excess returns would be much larger and hence little emphasis should be placed on

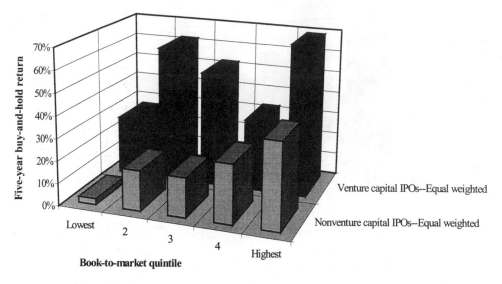

Figure 14.4
Five year equal-weighted buy-and-hold returns for venture and nonventure-backed
initial public offerings (IPOs) by book-to-market quintile. The sample is 3,407 nonventure-backed IPOs from 1975 through 1992 and 934 venture-backed IPOs from 1972
through 1992. Each sample of IPOs is sorted into book-to-market quintiles based on the real
size at the first closing price listed by the Center for Research in Security Prices and first
available book value of equity. Book-to-market breakpoints are the same for both samples.
Quintile returns are the average buy-and-hold return for IPOs in that quintile.

their significance. For the majority of the sample—that is, the corner of
the figure near the small, low book-to-market portfolio—relative performance is close to 0.

These results indicate that IPO underperformance is not an issuing firm
effect. It is a small, low book-to-market effect. Similar size and book-to-
market nonissuing firms perform just as poorly as IPO firms do. This does
not imply that returns are normal on a risk-adjusted basis. In fact, small,
low book-to-market firms appear to earn almost zero nominal returns
over a five-year period that starts with IPO issuance. It may be difficult to
explain this low return with a risk-based model.

In table 14.8, we present cross-sectional estimates of the determinants
of five-year, buy-and-hold wealth relatives using the NASDAQ composite index as the benchmark.[12] The dependent variable is the logarithm of
the five-year wealth relative. The independent variables are the logarithm

---

12. Because of the large cross-section that we employ, the standard 5 percent significance
level should be reduced.

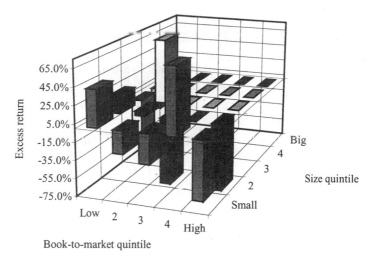

Figure 14.5
**Five year excess returns for venture capital-backed initial public offerings (IPOs) by
size and book to market profiles.** The sample is 934 venture-backed IPOs from 1972–
1992. 25 (5 × 5) size and book-to-market portfolios are formed based on the NYSE breakpoints. IPO firms are assigned to their appropriate size and book-to-market portfolio at issue.
The five year excess return is calculated by subtracting the five year buy-and-hold return on
the size and book-to-market portfolio that excludes all IPO and SEO firms for five years after
issue from the five year buy-and-hold return on the IPO firm. The average excess return is
plotted for each size and book-to-market portfolio.

of the firm's market value of equity (in constant dollars) at the first available CRSP listed closing price, a dummy variable indicating if the firm was
venture-backed, the logarithm of the firm's book value of equity to market
value, and the lagged dividend price ratio for the entire market. We include the dividend price ratio to determine whether overall market pricing
affects long-run returns.

The results demonstrate that size is an important determinant of relative returns. Across all specifications, the coefficient on logarithm of IPO-
firm size is positive and highly significant. This result captures the essence
of value-weighting returns. The presence of a venture capitalist is positively related to a firm's wealth relative, although the coefficient is only
marginally significant.[13] The coefficients on lagged dividend price ratio
are negative and significant. If the dividend price ratio captures the gen-

---

13. If the regressions are run on firms below the median size, the coefficient on the venture
capital dummy variable is positive and significant indicating that returns are significantly different for small venture and nonventure companies.

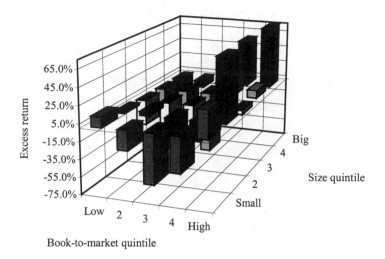

Figure 14.6
**Five year excess returns for nonventure capital-backed initial public offerings (IPOs)
by size and book to market portfolio.** The sample is 3,407 nonventure-backed IPOs from
1975-1992. 25 (5 × 5) size and book-to-market portfolios are formed based on the NYSE
breakpoints. IPO firms are assigned to their appropriate size and book-to-market portfolio
at issue. The five year excess return is calculated by subtracting the five year buy-and-hold
return on the size and book-to-market portfolio that excludes all IPO and SEO firms for five
years after issue from the five year buy-and-hold return on the IPO firm. The average excess
return is plotted for each size and book-to-market portfolio.

eral level of market prices, IPOs that go public during periods of higher
market valuation perform worse over the subsequent five years relative to
the market as a whole. Finally, book-to-market has an important impact
on returns at five year horizons. The coefficient on the book-to-market
ratio is positive and highly significant. The positive relationship between
book-to-market ratio and relative performance is consistent with both
Fama-French's interpretation of book-to-market as a priced risk factor and
Loughran and Ritter's belief that it proxies for relative overpricing.

Conclusions

The underperformance documented in Ritter (1991) and Loughran and
Ritter (1995) comes primarily from small, nonventure IPOs. We replicate
Loughran and Ritter's results and show that returns on nonventure IPOs
are significantly below those of venture-backed IPOs and below relevant
benchmarks when returns are weighted equally. We test performance

Table 14.8
Cross-sectional regressions on buy-and-hold returns and wealth relatives. The sample of initial public offerings (IPOs) is all venture-backed IPOs that went public between 1972 and 1992 and all nonventure-capital-backed IPOs that went public between 1975 and 1992. The dependent variable is the logarithm of the five year wealth relatives using the NASDAQ composite index as the benchmark. The independent variables are the logarithm of the market value of the firm's equity in billions of 1992 dollars valued at the closing price on the first day for which a price from the Center for Research in Security Prices database is available, a dummy variable that equals one if the firm was venture backed, the natural logarithm of the book-to-market ratio when the firm goes public, and the lagged-dividend price ratio for the market (t-statistics are in brackets.)

Independent variables	Dependent variable Logarithm of five-year wealth relative				
Logarithm of firm size	0.2063 [12.68]				0.1944 [10.44]
Venture-backed dummy variable		0.0953 [1.94]			0.0992 [1.93]
Logarithm of book-to-market ratio			0.1414 [7.44]		0.1321 [7.03]
Lagged dividend price ratio				−0.2445 [−9.81]	−0.1386 [−5.03]
Constant	−1.6919 [−25.01]	−0.8923 [−39.1]	−0.7190 [−20.54]	0.0768 [0.77]	−0.9904 [−6.91]
Adjusted R^2	0.035	0.001	0.015	0.021	0.062
Number	4332	4341	3563	4341	3563

against several broad market indexes, Fama-French (1997) industry portfolios, and matched size and book-to-market portfolios to test the robustness of our results. Differences in performance among the groups and the level of underperformance are reduced once returns are value weighted.

We also show that underperformance documented by Loughran and Ritter is not unique to firms issuing equity. Eliminating IPOs and SEOs from size and book-to-market portfolios demonstrates that IPOs perform no worse than similar nonissuing firms. This argues that we should look more broadly at types of firms that underperform and not treat IPO firms as a different group.

Although small, low book-to-market IPOs perform no differently from similar small, low book-to-market nonissuing firms, the pattern of relative performance in other portfolios needs to be examined in greater detail. Some of the IPO size and book-to-market portfolios appear to exhibit either under- or overperformance. Examination of the time-series and cross-sectional properties of these patterns may be important in deter-mining the source of performance anomalies.

The underperformance of small, low book-to-market firms may have various explanations. First, unexpected shocks may have hit small growth companies in the early and mid-1980s. The correlation of returns in cal-endar time may argue in favor of this explanation. Fama and French (1995) show that the earnings of small firms declined in the early 1980s but did not recover when those of large firms did. This experience was different from previous recessions. It is possible that small growth firms were constrained either in the capital or product markets after the reces-sion. These constraints may have been unanticipated. This explanation argues that we should not view each IPO (or firm) as an event, that is, they are not all independent observations. Correcting for the cross-sectional correlation is critical.

A second explanation for the underperformance of small, low book-to-market firms is investor sentiment. The evidence from Fama-French three-factor regressions with and without the change in closed-end fund dis-count supports this alternative. If the IPO is small, "you can fool some of the people all of the time." If any type of firm is likely to be subject to fads and investor sentiment, it is these firms. Their equity is held primarily by individuals. Megginson and Weiss (1991) show that institutional holdings of equity after an IPO are substantially higher for venture-backed IPOs than they are for nonventure IPOs. The relatively higher in-stitutional holdings may occur because institutions have greater informa-tion on small, venture-backed firms through their investment in venture capital funds. Furthermore, because institutions invest such large amounts of money, holding an investment in a small firm may mean that the in-stitutional investor becomes a 5 percent shareholder, something that many institutions want to avoid for regulatory reasons. The ability to short sell small firms is extremely limited because it may be difficult to borrow their stock certificates. Fields (1996) has shown that long-run IPO performance is positively related to institutional holdings. Fields' effects may similarly extend to nonissuing, small growth companies.

Asymmetric information is also likely to be more prevalent for small firms because individuals spend considerably less time tracking returns than institutional investors do. Small nonventure firms go public with lower tier underwriters than similar venture-backed firms (Barry, Mus-carella, Peavy, and Vetsuypens 1990), and they may have fewer and lower quality analysts following the company after the offering. Michaely and Shaw (1991) provide evidence that underwriter reputation is positively related to the long-run performance of IPOs. Carter, Dark and Singh (1998) and Nanda, Yi, and Yun (1995) have shown that the quality of the underwriter is related to long-run performance of IPOs, consistent with greater asymmetric information being associated with lower returns. It might not pay for sophisticated investors to research a small firm because they cannot recoup costs of information gathering and trading. The absolute return that investors can make is small because the dollar size of the stake they can take is limited by firm size.

Finally, individuals might derive utility from buying the shares of small, low book-to-market firms because they value them like a lottery ticket. Black (1986) argues that many finance anomalies may only be explained by this type of utility-based theory. Returns on small nonventure IPOs are more highly skewed than returns on either large IPO firms or similar sized venture-backed IPO firms.

Ritter (1991) and Loughran and Ritter (1995) have discovered an area that may allow us to test the foundations of investor sentiment and rational pricing. Future tests that identify elements of investor sentiment may show that individual investors are less than perfectly rational. Alternatively, real factors may be responsible for the measured underperformance.

What are the implications of our results? First, most institutional investors will not be significantly hurt by investing in IPOs. They usually do not buy the small issues that perform the worst. Underperformance of small growth companies, however, may be important for capital allocation. If the cost of capital for small growth companies is periodically distorted, their investment behavior may be adversely affected. If any of these small firms are future industry leaders, then we should be concerned about this mispricing. Further research is clearly warranted.

15 The Future of the Venture Capital Cycle

Over the past two decades, there has been a tremendous boom in the venture capital industry. The pool of U.S. venture capital funds has grown from less than $1 billion in 1976 (Charles River Associates 1976) to over $60 billion in 1999. This growth has outstripped that of almost every class of financial product.

The supply of venture capital is also likely to continue growing. Within the past two years, numerous pension funds have invested in private equity for the first time. Many experienced investors have also decided to increase their allocations to venture capital and buyout funds. These increased allocations will take a number of years to implement.

This growth naturally begs the question of sustainability. As has been highlighted throughout this volume, short-run shifts in the supply of or demand for venture capital investments have had dramatic effects. For instance, periods with a rapid increase in capital commitments have led to less restrictive partnership agreements, large investments in portfolio firms, and higher valuations for those investments. These patterns have led many practitioners to conclude that the industry is inherently cyclical. In short, this view implies that the side effects associated with periods of rapid growth generate sufficient difficulties that periods of retrenchment are sure to follow.

Neoclassical economics teaches us to examine not just the short-run supply and demand effects. Rather, it is also important to consider the nature of long-run supply and demand conditions. In the short run, intense competition between private-equity groups may lead to a willingness to pay a premium for certain types of firms (e.g., firms specializing in tools and content for the Internet). This is unlikely to be a sustainable strategy in the long run: firms that persist in such a strategy will eventually achieve low returns and be unable to raise follow-on funds.

The types of factors that will determine the long-run, steady-state supply of venture capital in the economy are likely to be more fundamental. These most likely will include the magnitude of fundamental technological innovation in the economy, the presence of liquid and competitive markets for venture capitalists to sell their investments (whether markets for stock offerings or acquisitions), and the willingness of highly skilled managers and engineers to work in entrepreneurial environments. (The last factor in turn will be a function of tax policy, legal protections, and societal preferences.) However painful the short-run adjustments, these more fundamental factors are likely to be critical in establishing the long-run level.

When one examines these more fundamental factors, there appears to have been quite substantial changes for the better over the past several decades.[1] We will briefly discuss two of these determinants of the long-run supply of venture capital in the United States, where these changes have been particularly dramatic: the extent of technological innovations and the development of regional agglomerations.

While the increase in innovative outputs can be seen through several measures, probably the clearest indication is in the extent of patenting. Patent applications by U.S. inventors, after hovering between forty and eighty thousand annually over the first eighty-five years of this century, have surged over the past decade to over 120 thousand per year. This does not appear to reflect the impact of changes in domestic patent policy, shifts in the success rate of applications, or a variety of alternative explanations. (For a detailed exploration, see Kortum and Lerner 1998.) Rather, it appears to reflect a fundamental shift in the innovative fecundity in the domestic economy. The breadth of technology appears wider today than it ever has been before. The greater rate of intellectual innovation provides fertile ground for future venture capital investments.

---

1. It is also worth emphasizing that despite its growth, the private-equity pool today remains relatively small. For every $1.00 of venture capital in the portfolio of U.S. institutional investors, there are about $100 of publicly traded equities. The ratios are even more uneven for overseas institutions. At the same time, the size of the foreign private equity pool remains far below that of the United States. This suggests considerable possibilities for future growth. The disparity can be illustrated by comparing the ratio of the venture capital pool to the size of the economy. In 1995, this ratio was 8.7 times higher in the United States than in Asia, and 8.0 times higher in the United States than in continental Europe. (These statistics are taken from the European Venture Capital Association 1997 and Asian Venture Capital Journal 1996.) At least to the casual observer, these ratios seem modest when compared to the economic role of new firms, products, and processes in the developed economies.

A second change has been in the development of what economists term "agglomeration economies" in the regions with the greatest venture capital activity. The efficiency of the venture capital process itself has been greatly augmented by the emergence of other intermediaries familiar with the workings of the venture process. The presence of such expertise on the part of lawyers, accountants, and real estate brokers, among others, has substantially lowered the transaction costs associated with forming and financing new firms. The increasing number of professionals and managers familiar with and accustomed to the employment arrangements offered by venture-backed firms (such as heavy reliance on stock options) has also been a major shift. The market for new issues by venture-backed firms appears to have become steadily more efficient, as part III of this volume makes clear. In short, the increasing familiarity with the venture capital process has itself made the long-term prospects for venture investment more attractive than they have ever been before, in this country or abroad.

A corollary to this argument is perhaps even more important. These changes appear not to have been entirely independent of the growth of venture capital, but have been at least partially triggered by the role played by these financial intermediaries. For instance, much of the growth in patenting appears to have been spurred by the growth in the number of venture capital-backed firms (Kortum and Lerner 1998). In short, it appears as if there is a somewhat of a "virtuous circle," where the growth in the activity of U.S. venture capital industry has enhanced the conditions that drive the long-run value creation of this capital, which has in turn led to more capital formation.

As the various chapters of this volume have highlighted, much is still not yet known about the venture capital industry. The extent to which the U.S. venture model will spread overseas and the degree to which the American model will—or can—be successfully adapted during this process are particularly interesting questions. Clearly, this financial intermediary will be an enduring feature on the global economic landscape in the years to come.

16 A Note on Data Sources

Information on venture capital investments is difficult to gather from public sources. Unlike mutual funds, venture capitalists are typically exempt from the Investment Company Act of Act of 1940 and do need not reveal their investments or organizational details in public filings.

Thus, the primary sources of information in previous research on venture capital has been the companies in which the funds invest. For the subset of venture-backed firms that eventually go public, information is available in IPO prospectuses and S-1 registration statements. Investments in firms that do not go public are more difficult to uncover, since these investments are usually not publicized. Similarly, information on partnerships is difficult to identify.

The analyses in this volume seek to empirically explore the venture capital industry in considerable detail. As a consequence, it was necessary to devote some degree of time to the identification and development of new data sets. This section describes the data sources that are at the heart of our analyses.

Sources of Venture Capital Partnership Agreements

In the analysis of venture funds in chapters 3 and 4, we include only independent private partnerships primarily engaged in venture capital investments. We define venture capital investments as investments in equity or equity-linked securities of private firms with active participation by the fund managers in the management or oversight of the firms. We eliminate funds whose stated mandate is to invest more than 50 percent of their capital in other types of assets, such as the securities of firms undergoing leveraged buyouts, "special situations," or publicly traded securities. Many venture capital organizations in the sample raised LBO funds during the 1980s. We do not include such funds, even if all the other funds associated with the organization are devoted to venture capital. Venture funds that invest more than 50 percent of their capital in other venture partnerships, known as "funds of funds," are also excluded. Similarly, Small Business Investment Companies (SBICs), publicly traded venture funds, and funds with a single limited partner are eliminated. Finally, we omit organizations headquartered outside the United States because their investment opportunities or regulatory environment are substantially different from domestic venture capital funds, and their negotiated partnership terms may be expected to differ.

We use the partnership agreements collected by three organizations to construct the sample. The organizations are the Harvard Management Company, Kemper Financial Services, and Venture Economics. Each of these organizations has been involved in venture investing for at least fifteen years. Nonetheless, there are substantial differences in the funds in which each invests.

The Harvard Management Company handles the private-market investments for the Harvard University endowment. The group's files on venture investments date back to the late 1970s. Harvard's venture investment strategy was shaped by the philosophy of Walter Cabot, who ran Harvard Management between 1974 and 1990. While investing in risky asset classes, such as venture capital and oil and gas, he emphasized the importance of conducting business with established and reputable financial intermediaries (Grassmuck 1990).

Kemper Financial Services is an investment manager, also known as a gatekeeper, which has invested in venture capital on a regular basis since 1978. Institutional investors, such as pension funds, frequently seek to diversify their portfolios to include privately held assets. They may not have the resources to evaluate potential investments, or may not wish to grapple with the complications posed by these investments. For instance, venture capitalists frequently liquidate investments in firms by distributing thinly traded shares to investors. Investment managers will select and manage private investments for institutions, typically for a fee of 1 percent of the funds invested (Venture Economics 1989a). Gatekeepers will usually invest in a variety of funds, but the very oldest and youngest funds are likely to be underrepresented. Very established venture capital organizations typically have close relationships with their limited partners, who have invested in several of their funds. They are unlikely to turn to gatekeepers for funding. Meanwhile, gatekeepers may be reluctant to invest in new funds of unproven venture capitalists (Goodman 1990).

Venture Economics is a unit of Securities Data Company and tracks the venture capital industry. The organization was known as Capital Publishing when it was established in 1961 to prepare a newsletter on SBICs. Since its acquisition by Stanley Pratt in 1977, the company has maintained a file on venture partnerships. Venture Economics collects this information for its Fund Raiser Advisory Service, which provides consulting assistance to venture capital organizations that are drafting partnership agreements or seeking investors. The funds whose documents are in their files appear to represent a random sample of the industry.

All three organizations began collecting information on a regular basis in the late 1970s. The occasional earlier documents in their files do not appear to have been gathered systematically. We consequently restrict our analysis to funds that closed in the period from 1978 through 1992. We find two types of documents in these files. The first are private placement memoranda, the marketing documents that are circulated to potential investors. The second are limited partnership agreements. These are the contracts that govern the workings of the funds. The files at Harvard and Kemper generally contain both types of documents. The files at Venture Economics frequently only contain the former documents.

For the analysis of contractual terms in chapter 3, we use a random sample of 140 partnership agreements. For the analysis of compensation in chapter 4, we use all funds that meet our criteria. The search of these three files identifies a total of 543 venture capital funds that apparently meet our tests. We are reluctant to use some of the 142 funds with compensation information that are not included in the database of funds compiled by the Venture Economics' Investors Services Group. Our primary concern relates to those funds whose only documentation is the private placement memorandum in the Venture Economics collection. We are often unsure whether the fund ever closed. In some cases, the general partners may have been unable to raise the stipulated minimum amount of funds. Several files at Venture Economics contain a notation indicating that the fund never closed. In other cases, we know independently that the fundraising was unsuccessful, but there is no such notation in the Venture Economics files. Since many of the offering documents in Venture Economics files are for young venture capital organizations, there is a danger of including funds that were never raised.

Consequently, we do not include all 543 funds in the compensation analysis. Instead, we include funds that satisfy one of two conditions. Either the fund is included in the Venture Economics funds database and is coded as a partnership sponsored by an independent venture capital organization, or the fund itself is not included in the database, but the documentation indicates that it is a partnership sponsored by an independent venture capital organization, and independent corroboration of this fund's successful closing can be found. This corroboration can include its listing as a previous fund in a subsequent marketing document, the presence of a signed contract in one of the files, or a listing by Asset Alternatives. From our review, we find partnership agreements or private placement memoranda in the files of Harvard, Kemper, and Venture Economics for 401 funds that satisfied the first set of criteria. Eighteen funds met the second requirement.

We assess the representativeness of this sample by comparing these funds with a database of venture capital funds compiled by Venture Economics' Investors Services Group. This database includes venture capital funds, SBICs, and related organizations. The Investors Services Group database is used in preparation of directories, such as the Venture Economics annual *Investment Benchmark Reports*. The database is compiled from information provided by venture capitalists and institutional investors. The Venture Economics database of funds contains summary information on 1,158 funds raised between 1978 and 1992. It includes many funds whose partnership agreements or private placement memoranda were not found in the Venture Economics files.

Tables 16.1 and 16.2 examine the independent venture partnerships in the Venture Economics database that closed between 1978 and 1992. We compare the characteristics of the funds included in the sample used in chapters 3 and 4 and those not included, using t-, Wilcoxon signed-rank, and Pearson χ^2-tests. We find that larger funds by more established partnerships are significantly more likely to be included in our contract sample.[1] In addition, funds based in California (the center of the U.S. venture industry) are more likely to be included. Finally, the typical fund in the sample closed somewhat more recently than the other funds in the Venture Economics database.

Our sample of funds used in the compensation analysis in chapter 4 accounts for 35 percent of the 1,158 funds raised by independent venture capital organizations between 1978 and 1992 that are in the Venture Economics funds database.[2] Weighting observations by fund size, using

1. We examine whether the mixture of firms may have changed over time. In each of the three periods examined—1978–82, 1983–87, and 1988–92—the funds are significantly larger and the venture organizations are significantly more established than those not included in the sample.
2. Venture capital limited partnerships will have one or more closings, where the limited and general partners sign legal documents stating the terms of the partnership and initial cash payments are made. Having several closings enables venture funds to begin investing before fundraising is completed. Additional limited partners can be added to the partnership in the subsequent closings. We use the date of the first closing in the analyses in chapters 3 and 4.

Table 16.1
The characteristics of the sample of 140 venture partnership agreements. The first two columns compare the characteristics of the independent venture partnerships in the Venture Economics funds database whose first closing was between 1978 and 1992 that were and were not included in our sample. We present both the mean and the median (in brackets) of several measures. The third column presents the p-values of t-tests, Wilcoxon signed-rank tests (in brackets), and a Pearson χ^2-test (in braces) of the null hypotheses that these distributions are identical.

	Included in our sample	Not included in our sample	p-value, test of no difference
Number of observations	140	1030	
Size of fund (millions of 1997 dollars)	127.0 [94.5]	55.6 [37.2]	0.000 [0.000]
Age of venture organization at time of first closing (years)	7.34 [5.75]	3.88 [1.33]	0.000 [0.000]
Previous funds raised by venture organization	3.58 [2]	1.65 [1]	0.000 [0.000]
Fund based in California?	39.4%	28.6%	{0.010}
Date of fund's first closing	Dec. 1985 [Feb. 1986]	Apr. 1985 [Dec. 1984]	0.032 [0.027]

constant 1997 dollars, our measure of sample coverage is much better: funds in our sample account for $27.7 billion out of a total of $45.3 billion of invested capital, or 61 percent.

The first three columns of table 16.2 compare those entries in the Venture Economics funds database for which we do and do not have compensation data. We compare the distributions of the included and missing funds using t-tests, Wilcoxon signed-rank tests, and Pearson χ^2-tests. Larger and more recent funds, as well as funds raised by more established venture organizations, are significantly more likely to be included in our sample.[3] Funds specializing in high-technology and early-stage investments are disproportionately represented, perhaps reflecting their frequent sponsorship by established organizations. The fourth column of

---

3. We also characterize the investment focus of the funds. Firms typically state in their private placement memoranda whether they intend to have an industry or stage focus. Because these are imperfectly recorded by Venture Economics, we check the original fund documents. One concern may be that funds need not make investments that are consistent with these stated objectives. The partnership agreements, which unlike the private placement memoranda are legal contracts, rarely state the funds' objectives. At the same time, venture capitalists who deviate significantly from the stated goals of their partnership are likely to alienate institutional investors and the investment managers who advise them, and they may find it difficult to raise a follow-on fund (e.g., the discussion in Goodman 1990).

Table 16.2
The characteristics of the research sample of venture capital funds. The first two columns compare characteristics of funds within the Venture Economics funds database whose first closing was between January 1978 and December 1992 that were included in our sample and those that were not. Our sample includes only those funds whose partnership agreements or private placement memoranda were found in the files of Harvard, Kemper and Venture Economics. We present both the mean and median (in brackets) of several measures. The third column presents the p-values of t-tests, Wilcoxon signed-rank tests (in brackets), and Pearson χ^2-tests (in braces) of the null hypotheses that these distributions are identical. The final column presents corrected summary statistics for the entire sample.

	Funds in Venture Economics database			All funds included in our sample[a]
	Included in our sample	Not included in our sample	p-value, test of no difference	
Number of observations	401	757		419
Date of fund's first closing	March 1986	October 1984	0.000	March 1986
	[June 1986]	[March 1984]	[0.000]	[June 1986]
Size of fund (millions of 1997 dollars)	71.0	48.5	0.000	62.7
	[45.5]	[33.4]	[0.000]	[40.1]
Size of venture organization (capital raised as percent of total in past ten years)	0.42%	0.40%	0.821	0.43%
	[0.11%]	[0.00%]	[0.000]	[0.10%]
Age of venture organization (in years)	5.35	4.33	0.006	4.92[a]
	[3.50]	[1.83]	[0.002]	[3.09][a]
Fund focuses on high technology?	20.4%	7.4%	{0.000}	48.0%[a]
Fund focuses on early-stage investments?	29.2%	12.8%	{0.000}	41.8%[a]

a. The data for the entire sample of 419 differ from the subsample of 401 for two reasons. In the final column, the sample size is larger and several aspects of the Venture Economics data have been corrected with information from fund documents. First, venture organization age is sometimes erroneously entered in the Venture Economics funds database. Second, the coding of investment focus is incomplete in the Venture Economics funds database. To allow a comparison with the 757 funds not included in our sample, for which we only have the Venture Economics data, we report the age and focus of the 401 funds as coded by Venture Economics. The summary statistics about the 419 funds incorporates our corrections based on information in the private placement memoranda.

table 16.2 displays the characteristics of the funds in the final sample, including the ones not in the Venture Economics database and hence not included in the first column. The summary statistics in column four are also different from column one because the data reported in the fourth column were corrected using documents from the venture organizations.

While the sample is not entirely representative of the venture industry as a whole, these differences should have a limited impact on the empirical results. As a check of this claim, we repeat the analyses in chapter 4 using only the 221 observations where the partnership agreements or private placement memoranda were found in the files of Venture Economics. These observations are significantly more representative of the population of venture funds than the Harvard and Kemper samples. The results remain similar, though the significance falls, reflecting the smaller sample size.

Sources of Venture Capital Investments

The VentureOne Database

The analysis of corporate venture capital investments in chapter 5 employs the VentureOne database of financings of entrepreneurial firms. VentureOne, a unit of Reuters, established in 1987, collects data on firms that have obtained venture capital financing. The database includes firms that have received early-stage equity financing from venture capital organizations, corporate venture capital programs, and other organizations.

The companies are initially identified from a wide variety of sources, including trade publications, company Web pages, and telephone contacts with venture investors. VentureOne then collects information about the businesses through interviews with venture capitalists and entrepreneurs. Among the data collected are the names of the investors, the amount and valuation of the venture financings, and the industry, history, and current status of the firm. Data on the firms are updated and validated through monthly contacts with investors and firms.[4] VentureOne then markets the database to venture funds and corporate business development groups.

---

4. Information about the financing of private firms is typically not revealed in public documents and investors and entrepreneurs may consider this to be sensitive information. VentureOne seeks to overcome this reluctance by emphasizing that its database also helps firms obtain financing. In particular, firms can alert investors whether they intend to seek further private financing or intend to go public in upcoming months.

VentureOne officials suggest that two forms of selection bias may affect the completeness of their valuation data. First, in its initial years, neither the firm's data collection methodology nor its reputation in the industry were as established as today. Thus, it was less likely to obtain valuation data. Second, they are sometimes able to collect information about earlier financing rounds at the time a firm seeks refinancing. Consequently, the most recent data—which includes many firms that have not subsequently sought refinancing—may not be as complete as earlier years' data.

To help understand the impact of the missing data, we compared those rounds with and without valuation data. We found three patterns. First, VentureOne has had the least success in obtaining financing data about start-up transactions. This is not surprising. In these cases the number of investors is typically very small and concerns about secrecy are the greatest. VentureOne has also been less successful in obtaining valuation data about firms not in the high-technology industries traditionally funded by venture capitalists, but rather in the amalgam referred to as "other industries." VentureOne officials attribute this pattern to the firm's greater visibility among entrepreneurs and investors in high-technology industries. Similarly, reflecting the firm's California base, it has been more successful in obtaining information about firms based in the western United States. Finally, the observations with valuation data are disproportionately from the early to mid-1990s. Because our focus is on comparing investments by independent and corporate venture capital funds, we do not believe these patterns will bias our results.

We supplemented the VentureOne data when necessary. Some firms in the VentureOne sample were missing information, such as an assignment to one of the 103 VentureOne industry classes or information on the firm's start date. We examined a variety of reference sources to determine this information, including Corporate Technology Information Service's *Corporate Technology Directory* (1996), Dun's Marketing Services' *Million Dollar Directory* (1996), Gale Research's *Ward's Business Directory of U.S. Private and Public Companies* (1996), National Register Publishing Company's *Directory of Leading Private Companies* (1996), and a considerable number of state and industry business directories in the collections of Harvard Business School's Baker Library and the Boston Public Library. We also employed several electronic databases: the Company Intelligence and Database America compilations available through LEXIS's COMPANY/USPRIV library and the American Business Disk CD-ROM directory.

We limited the analysis reported in chapter 5 to investments in privately held firms between 1983 and 1994. While VentureOne has sought to "back-fill" its database with information on earlier venture investments, its coverage of the 1970s and early 1980s is poor. Furthermore, we were concerned that its methodology may have introduced selection biases. Although the database does not include all venture investments between 1983 and 1994, we believe that it provides a reasonable view of the activity in the industry during this period. We did not include investments made after 1994 because we wish to assess the outcomes of the investments: it may take several years until the fate of venture-backed firms is clear.

To identify independent and corporate venture capital organizations, we used an unpublished database of venture organizations assembled by Venture Economics' Investors Services Group discussed earlier in this chapter. We excluded from either classification a variety of other private equity investors, including individuals, SBICs, funds sponsored by banks and other financial institutions, and funds associated with financial subsidiaries of nonfinancial corporations (such as General Electric Capital). To determine whether a company was a nonfinancial corporation, we consulted the firm directories noted above to determine the main lines-of-business in the year of the investment. We also eliminated a variety of investments outside the scope of this analysis, such as purchases of shares of publicly traded firms and other financings.

The Venture Intelligence Database

The analyses described in chapters 7 through 9, 11, and 12 employ Venture Economics' Venture Intelligence Database. The relative performance of venture funds is an important issue for investors. Venture capitalists typically raise funds every few years; limited partners (wealthy individuals, endowments, and institutional investors) provide the bulk of the capital. An investment in a venture fund is almost always for at least a ten-year period, and funds may only be withdrawn under extreme circumstances. Thus, potential investors scrutinize the performance of venture capitalists' past funds. While venture partnerships present historical performance data in offering documents, the methodology of these calculations is frequently idiosyncratic. Furthermore, because the IPO market is so variable, potential investors usually look for a measure of relative, rather than absolute, performance.

Venture Economics addresses the need for information on performance by confidentially gathering data from venture funds and institutional investors on venture investments. The Venture Intelligence Database includes the dates of venture financings, the investors in each round, and the amount of funds disbursed. It includes firms that did and did not go public. While the database was begun in 1977, the firm subsequently encoded its earlier records on venture financing dating back to the early 1960s.

Researchers' access to this data was very restricted prior to the firm's purchase by Securities Data Company (SDC) in 1991. Venture Economics did, however, publish the names of investors in firms that went public in their *Venture Capital Journal*. Barry, et al. (1990) and Megginson and Weiss (1991) use this information (and, in the former article, cross-tabulations of these records). Much of the Venture Economics data are now publicly available as the SDC Venture Intelligence Database.

To assess the presence of potential biases in the Venture Economics database, the sample of biotechnology firms analyzed in chapters 8, 9, and 11 is examined. There is extensive data collection about biotechnology firms in other sources, which enables a detailed assessment of the Venture Intelligence Database's strengths and weaknesses. The database identifies 307 biotechnology firms that received venture capital as privately held entities between 1978 and 1989. (While the database contains earlier records, data collection was not a primary focus prior to mid-1977.) From the original sample, thirteen foreign firms are dropped that were funded by U.S. capital providers (who may face different regulatory, tax, or institutional environments), four buyouts or divisional "spin-outs" involving private capital providers, three duplicative entries of the same firm under different names (name changes are found in Commerce Clearing House's *Capital Changes Reporter* (1992), Financial Stock Service Guide's *Directory of Obsolete Securities* (1992), North Carolina Biotechnology Center's (NCBC) database of biotechnology companies (1990b), Oryx Press's *BioScan: The Worldwide Biotech Industry Reporting Service* (1992), *Predicasts F&S Index of Corporate Change* (1992), and other sources), and sixteen firms that received venture capital only after going public.

To assess the completeness of the remaining 271 firms, U.S. biotechnology firms that received venture capital as privately held firms but are not in the Venture Economics sample are identified. Documents used include U.S. Securities and Exchange Commission (SEC) filings,[5] the records of a consulting firm specializing in the biotechnology industry, Recombinant Capital (1991, 1992), the several industry directories that list privately held firms and provide information about their financing sources cited above, press releases in Mead Data Central's (1988) NEXIS ALLNEWS and LEXIS/PATENT/GENBIO files, and contacts with venture capitalists and biotechnology firms. These efforts lead to the identification of an additional thirty-seven U.S. biotechnology firms that received venture capital as privately held entities between 1978 and 1989.[6]

The significance of the thirty-seven omitted firms is assessed using three measures. First, an U.S. Patent and Trademark Office (1990) compilation of all biotechnology patent awards from January 1978 through June 1989 is used. Patenting is extremely important in biotechnology and is the focus of virtually every small biotechnology firm. Of the entire number of patents awarded to venture-backed biotechnology firms during this period, the Venture Economics sample accounts for over 98 percent. Second, the NCBC (1990a) compiles an "actions" database of events in the biotechnology industry (including regulatory approvals, product introductions, and ownership changes) from press releases and specialized trade journals. Firms in the Venture Economics sample account for over 95 percent of the entries about venture-backed firms between November 1978 (the inception of the database) and December 1989. Finally, using data from Venture Economics, Recombinant Capital, SDC's Corporate New Issues database, SEC filings, and press releases, the total amount of external financing received by venture-backed firms is determined. The Venture Economics sample accounts for over 91 percent of the financing raised by these firms between 1978 and 1989. Taken together, the results suggest that the omitted firms are less significant than the ones included.

---

5. A firm going public discloses its investors in its prospectus (the "certain transactions" and "financial statements" sections) and the accompanying S-1 registration statement (the "recent sales of nonregistered securities" section and exhibits). Detailed financial information is often available about private firms that have been acquired by public firms in the acquirers' proxy, 10-K, or 10-Q statements. Information on firms that file for an aborted IPO is available in the ultimately withdrawn registration statements. Firms likely to have made such filings are identified by the sources cited above.

6. Because firms are usually financed by multiple venture funds, the comprehensiveness of Venture Economics' information on venture-backed firms is considerably higher than their coverage of funds. When Venture Economics obtains information on the same company from several sources, its staff attempts to reconcile any inconsistencies. If they are unable to resolve conflicts, their tendency is to error on the side of inclusiveness. This is part of the reason for the inclusion of multiple records for a single venture round discussed below.

The information on these firms' financing rounds is corrected as follows:

• *Firms included in Recombinant Capital database.* The Venture Economics records are compared to those of Recombinant Capital. If they are identical, the Venture Economics records are considered as corroborated.[7] If they conflict and SEC filings are available, these are used to resolve the conflict. If they conflict and SEC filings are not available, company and venture capitalist contacts are used. If no contacts can be made, the Venture Economics data are used.

• *Firms not included in Recombinant Capital database, but with SEC filings.* The Venture Economics records are compared to the SEC filings. If they conflict, the SEC filings are used.

• *Firms not included in Recombinant Capital database without SEC filings.* Company and venture capitalist contacts are used to confirm the Venture Economics data. Frequently venture capitalists can be identified through *Pratt's Guide to Venture Capital Sources* (Venture Economics 1992a). This guide is indexed by both individual and fund, so those venture capitalists associated with terminated partnerships who are still employed in the industry can often be located. Companies are identified through industry directories (Corporate Technology 1996, MegaType 1992, NCBC 1990a, Oryx 1992). Some of the firms most difficult to obtain information about are those that failed before going public. If no contacts can be made, the Venture Economics data are used.

The Venture Economics dataset is compared to the corrected information, omitting the cases where no corroboration of the Venture Economics records could be obtained. For each firm, the ratio of the reported to the actual size and number of private financings is computed. The reporting of the amount of external financing provided is unbiased, with the ratio of total funds recorded in the Venture Economics database to the actual amount being 1.04.

The number of venture rounds, however, is overstated: the database reports 28 percent more rounds than actually occurred. The data are disaggregated to determine whether the bias in the number of rounds varies in a systemic manner: rounds are divided by the age of the firm and the

---

7. External financing rounds are not included in some cases: instances when founders contributed a small amount of funds (typically under $20,000) in exchange for common stock, or bridge loans by venture capital providers in the six months prior to the IPO, due immediately after the offering. These entries are relatively infrequent in the Venture Economics data set.

date at the time of the venture round. The spurious rounds are most frequent in older firms and in chronologically earlier records.

This pattern may arise for three reasons. First, a contract between a company and its venture financiers may call for the staged distribution of the funds in a single venture round. This may be recorded in the database as several distinct venture rounds. Second, staggered disbursements arise without design. Venture capital funds typically do not keep large cash balances, but rather draw down funds from their limited partners as needed. Limited partners will have between two weeks and several months to provide the funds. Since several venture funds normally participate in a financing round, investments may be received over the course of several months, and be recorded in the database as several rounds. Finally, Venture Economics aggregates information about venture investments from reports by pension fund managers, individual investors, and investment managers. If the date of the investment differs in these records, a single investment round may be recorded as two or more events. All these problems are likely to be more severe in later rounds, which typically have more investors. While data accuracy has increased over time, the overreporting of rounds is a significant factor in the historical Venture Economics data.

Sources of Venture-Backed IPOs and Distributions

In the analysis of IPOs and distributions in chapters 12, 13, and 14, we do not rely on a single data set to identify venture-backed offerings. Rather, the sample is compiled from a variety of sources. Although the precise sources used in each analysis differed (as mentioned in the chapters), this section summarizes the three primary information sources used to identify venture-backed offerings.

The first of these is listing in Venture Economics' *Venture Capital Journal*, which regularly publishes information on such IPOs. In the analysis in chapter 12, the collection of 433 venture-backed IPOs compiled by Barry, Muscarella, Peavy, and Vetsuypens (1990) is used. Barry et al. identify their sample using the *Venture Capital Journal*, but exclude any IPOs for which a venture capital investor could not be identified, reverse LBOs, and IPOs for which they could not find the offering prospectus.[8] For the

---

8. This information was supplemented and cross-checked in a variety of ways. For the age of the venture capital firm and the offering company at IPO, the LEXIS/NEXIS's COMPNY database was searched for incorporation and partnership filings. Ritter's (1991) IPO data set was used to cross-check incorporation dates, offering size, and underpricing. For age at IPO, the earliest incorporation date is used.

longer time period covered in chapter 14, all entries in the *Venture Capital Journal* were recorded and checked against the IPO prospectuses.

The second of these are listings of all IPOs and distributions by the funds in which two institutional investors (the US WEST Investment Trust and a major corporate pension fund) and three investment advisors (Brinson Partners, Kemper Financial Services, and RogersCasey Alternative Investments) had invested. These investors compiled, among other information, the date of the IPO, as well as the date, size, and source of each stock distribution.

Finally, many of the private placement memoranda by venture capital groups list previous investments that have gone public. While in most cases these are included in the other sources above, occasionally some additional venture-backed IPOs are identified in this manner.

Venture Capital Glossary

In the glossary we have sought to define the technical terms most frequently used in this volume. The one exception has been the terms referring to the statistical and econometric methodology that we employed, since the concepts did not lend themselves well to an explication in such a compressed framework. The interested reader is referred to Berndt (1991) and Campbell, Lo, and MacKinlay (1997).

Agency problem A conflict among managers and investors, or more generally an instance where an agent does not intrinsically desire to follow the wishes of the principal that hired him.

Agreement of limited partnership See partnership agreement.

Angel A wealthy individual who invests in entrepreneurial firms. Although angels perform many of the same functions as venture capitalists, they invest their own capital rather than that of institutional and other individual investors.

Associate A professional employee of a private equity firm who is not yet a partner.

Asymmetric information problem When, because of day-to-day involvement with the firm, an entrepreneur knows more about the company's prospects than investors, suppliers, or strategic partners.

Bogey See hurdle rate.

Book-to-market ratio The ratio of a firm's accounting (book) value of its equity to the value of the equity assigned by the market (i.e., the product of the number of shares outstanding and the share price).

Capital under management See committed capital.

Carried interest The substantial share, often around 20 percent, of profits that are allocated to the general partners of a venture capital partnership.

Closed-end fund A publicly traded mutual fund whose shares must be sold to other investors (rather than redeemed from the issuing firm, as is the case with open-end mutual funds). Many early venture funds were structured in this manner.

Closing The signing of the contract by an investor or group of investors that binds them to supply a set amount of capital to a venture capital fund. Often a fraction of that capital is provided at the time of the closing. A single venture capital fund may have multiple closings.

Coinvestment   See syndication.

Committed capital   Pledges of capital to a venture capital fund. This money is typically not received at once, but rather taken down over three to five years, starting in the year the fund is formed.

Common stock   The equity typically held by management and founders. Typically, at the time of an initial public offering, all equity is converted into common stock.

Consolidation   A private equity investment strategy that involves merging several small firms together and exploiting economies of scale or scope.

Convertible equity or debt   A security that can be converted under certain conditions into another security (often into common stock). The convertible shares often have special rights that the common stock does not have.

Conversion ratio   The number of shares for which a convertible debt or equity issue can be exchanged.

Corporate venture capital   An initiative by a corporation to invest either in young firms outside the corporation or units formerly part of the corporation. These are often organized as corporate subsidiaries, not as limited partnerships.

Disbursement   An investment by a venture capitalist into a company.

Distressed debt   A private equity investment strategy that involves purchasing discounted bonds of a financially distressed firm. Distressed debt investors frequently convert their holdings into equity and become actively involved with the management of the distressed firm.

Distribution   The transfer of shares in a (typically publicly traded) portfolio firm or cash from a venture capitalist to each limited partner and (frequently) themselves.

Draw down   See take down.

Due diligence   The review of a business plan and assessment of a management team prior to a venture capital investment.

Elasticity   The percentage change in one variable associated with a 1 percent change in another.

Employee Retirement Income Security Act (ERISA)   The 1974 legislation that codified the regulation of corporate pension plans. See prudent man rule.

Exercise price   The price at which an option or warrant can be exercised.

First closing   The initial closing of a fund.

First fund   An initial fund raised by a venture capital organization.

Follow-on fund   A fund that is subsequent to a venture capital organization's first fund.

Follow-on offering   See seasoned equity offering.

Form 10-K   An annual filing required by the U.S. Securities and Exchange Commission of each publicly traded firm, as well as certain private firms. The statement provides a wide variety of summary data about the firm.

Float   In a public market context, the percentage of the company's shares that is in the hands of outside investors, as opposed to being held by corporate insiders.

Free cash flow problem   The temptation to undertake wasteful expenditures that cash not needed for operations or investments often poses.

Fund   A pool of capital raised periodically by a venture capital organization. Usually in the form of limited partnerships, venture capital funds typically have a ten-year life, though extensions of several years are often possible.

Fund of funds   A fund that invests primarily in other venture capital funds rather than portfolio firms, often organized by an investment advisor or investment bank.

Gatekeeper   See investment advisor.

General partner   A partner in a limited partnership who is responsible for the day-to-day operations of the fund. In the case of a venture funds, the venture capitalists are either general partners or own the corporation that serves as the general partner. The general partners assume all liability for the fund's debts.

Grandstanding problem   The strategy, sometimes employed by young private-equity organizations, of rushing young firms to the public marketplace to demonstrate a successful track record, even if the companies are not ready to go public.

Herding problem   A situation when investors, particularly institutions, make investments that are more similar to one another than desirable.

Hot issue market   A market with high demand for new securities offerings, particularly for initial public offerings.

Hurdle rate   Either (1) the set rate of return that the limited partners must receive before the general partners can begin sharing in any distributions, or (2) the level that the fund's net asset value must reach before the general partners can begin sharing in any distributions.

In the money   An option or warrant that would have a positive value if it was immediately exercised.

Initial public offering (IPO)   The sale of shares to public investors of a firm that has not hitherto been traded on a public stock exchange. These are typically underwritten by an investment bank.

Insider   A director, officer, or shareholder with 10 percent or more of a company's equity.

Intangible asset   A patent, trade secret, informal know-how, brand capital, or other nonphysical asset.

Investment advisor   A financial intermediary who assists investors, particularly institutions, with investments in venture capital and other financial assets. Advisors assess potential new venture funds for their clients and monitor the progress of existing investments. In some cases, they pool their investors' capital in funds of funds.

Investment bank   A financial intermediary that, among other services, may underwrite securities offerings, facilitate mergers and acquisitions, and trade for its own account.

Lemons problem   See asymmetric information problem.

Leveraged buyout (LBO)   The acquisition of a firm or business unit, typically in a mature industry, with a considerable amount of debt.

Leveraged buyout fund   A fund, typically organized in a similar manner to a venture capital fund, specializing in leveraged buyout investments. Some of these funds also make venture capital investments.

Limited partner   An investor in a limited partnership. Limited partners can monitor the partnership's progress, but cannot become involved in its day-to-day management if they are to retain limited liability.

Limited partnership   An organizational form that entails a finitely lived contractual arrangement among limited and general partners, governed by a partnership agreement.

Lockup   A provision in the underwriting agreement between an investment bank and existing shareholders that prohibits corporate insiders and private equity investors from selling at the time of the offering.

Management fee   The fee, typically a percentage of committed capital or net asset value, that is paid by a venture capital fund to the general partners to cover salaries and expenses.

Market-to-book ratio   The inverse of the book-to-market ratio.

Mezzanine   Either (1) a venture capital financing round shortly before an initial public offering or (2) an investment that employs subordinated debt that has fewer privileges than bank debt but more than equity and often has attached warrants.

Net asset value (NAV)   The value of a fund's holdings, which may be calculated using a variety of valuation rules.

Net present value   The expected value of one or more cash flows in the future, discounted at a rate that reflects the cash flows' riskiness.

Option   The right, but not the obligation, to buy or sell a security at a set price (or range of prices) in a given period.

Out of the money   An option or warrant whose exercise price is above the current value of a share.

Partnership agreement   The contract that explicitly specifies the compensation and conditions that govern the relationship among the investors (limited partners) and the venture capitalists (general partners) during a venture capital fund's life. Occasionally used to refer to the separate agreement between the general partners on the internal operations of the fund (e.g., the division of the carried interest).

Private equity   Private equity includes organizations devoted to venture capital, leveraged buyouts, consolidations, mezzanine and distressed debt investments, and a variety of hybrids such as venture leasing and venture factoring.

Placement agent   A financial intermediary hired by venture organizations to facilitate the raising of new venture capital funds.

Post-money valuation   The product of the price paid per share in a financing round and the shares outstanding after the financing round.

Pre-money valuation   The product of the price paid per share in a financing round and the shares outstanding before the financing round.

Preferred stock   Stock that has preference over common stock with respect to any dividends or payments in association with the liquidation of the firm. Preferred stockholders may also have additional rights, such as the ability to block mergers or displace management.

Prospectus   A condensed, widely disseminated version of the registration statement that is also filed with the U.S. Securities and Exchange Commission. The prospectus provides a wide variety of summary data about the firm.

Proxy statement   A filing with the U.S. Securities and Exchange Commission that among other information, provides information on the holdings and names of corporate insiders.

Prudent man rule   Prior to 1979, a provision in the Employee Retirement Income Security Act (ERISA) that essentially prohibited pension funds from investing substantial amounts of money in venture capital or other high-risk asset classes. The Department of Labor's clarification of the rule in that year allowed pension managers to invest in high-risk assets, including venture capital.

Registration statement   A filing with the U.S. Securities and Exchange Commission (e.g., a S-1 or S-18 form) that must be reviewed by the SEC before a firm can sell shares to the public. The statement provides a wide variety of summary data about the firm, as well as copies of key legal documents.

Road show   The marketing of a venture capital fund or public offering to potential investors.

Roll-up   See consolidation.

Rule 10(b)-5   The U.S. Securities and Exchange Commission regulation that most generally prohibits fraudulent activity in the purchase or sale of any security.

Rule 16(a)   The U.S. Securities and Exchange Commission regulation the requires insiders to disclose any transactions in the firm's stock on a monthly basis.

Rule 144   The U.S. Securities and Exchange Commission regulation that prohibits sales for one year (originally two years) after the purchase of restricted stock and limits the pace of sales between the first and second (originally second and third) year after the purchase.

Seasoned equity offering   An offering by a firm that has already competed an initial public offering and whose shares are already publicly traded.

Secondary offering   An offering of shares that are not being issued by the firm, but rather are sold by existing shareholders. The firm consequently does not receive the proceeds from the sales of these shares.

Shares outstanding   The number of shares that the company has issued.

Small Business Investment Company (SBIC)   A federally guaranteed risk capital pool. These funds were first authorized by the U.S. Congress in 1958, proliferated during the 1960s, and then dwindled after many organizations encountered management and incentive problems.

Staging   The provision of capital to entrepreneurs in multiple installments, with each financing conditional on meeting particular business targets. This helps ensure that the money is not squandered on unprofitable projects.

Syndication   The joint purchase of shares by two or more venture capital organizations or the joint underwriting of an offering by two or more investment banks.

Takedown   The transfer of some or all of the committed capital from the limited partners to a venture capital fund.

Takedown schedule   The contractual language that describes how and when the venture capital fund can (or must) receive the committed capital from its limited partners.

Tangible asset   A machine, building, land, inventory, or another physical asset.

Uncertainty problem   The array of potential outcomes for a company or project. The wider the dispersion of potential outcomes, the greater the uncertainty.

Tombstone   An advertisement, typically in a major business publication, by an underwriter to publicize an offering that it has underwritten.

Unrelated business taxable income (UBTI)   The gross income from any unrelated business that a tax-exempt institution regularly carries out. If a venture partnership is generating significant income from debt-financed property, tax-exempt limited partners may face tax liabilities due to UBTI provisions.

Underpricing   The discount to the projected trading price at which the investment banker sells shares in an initial public offering. A substantial positive return in the first trading day is often interpreted by financial economists as evidence of underpricing.

Underwriting   The purchase of a securities issue from a company by an investment bank and its (typically almost immediate) resale to investors.

Unseasoned equity offering   See initial public offering.

Valuation rule   The algorithm by which a venture capital fund assigns values to the public and private firms in its portfolio.

Venture capital   Independently managed, dedicated pools of capital that focus on equity or equity-linked investments in privately held, high-growth companies. Many venture capital funds, however, occasionally make other types of private equity investments. Outside of the United States, this phrase is often used as a synonym for private equity.

Venture capitalist   A general partner or associate at a venture capital organization.

Venture factoring   A private equity investment strategy that involves purchasing the receivables of high-risk young firms. As a part of the transaction, the venture factoring fund typically also receives warrants in the young firm.

Venture leasing   A private equity investment strategy that involves leasing equipment or other assets to high-risk young firms. As a part of the transaction, the venture leasing fund typically also receives warrants in the young firm.

Vintage year   The group of funds whose first closing was in a certain year.

Warrants   An option to buy shares of stock issued directly by a company.

Window dressing problem   The behavior of money managers of adjusting their portfolios at the end of the quarter by buying firms whose shares have appreciated and selling "mistakes." This is driven by the fact that institutional investors may examine not only quarterly returns, but also end-of-period holdings.

Withdrawn offering   An equity issue where a registration statement is filed with the U.S. Securities and Exchange Commission but the firm either writes to the SEC withdrawing the proposed offering before it is effective or the offering is not completed within nine months of the filing.

References

AbuZayyad, Tarek, Thomas J. Kosnick, Josh Lerner, and Paul C. Yang. 1996. "GO Corporation." Harvard Business School case no. 9–297–021 (and teaching note no. 5–298–153).

Admati, Anat R., and Paul Pfleiderer. 1994. "Robust financial contracting and the role of venture capitalists." *Journal of Finance* 49: 371–402.

Akerlof, George A. 1970. "The market for 'lemons': Qualitative uncertainty and the market mechanism." *Quarterly Journal of Economics* 84: 488–500.

Allen, Franklin, and Gerald R. Faulhaber. 1989. "Signalling by underpricing in the IPO market." *Journal of Financial Economics* 23: 303–324.

Armstrong, Larry. 1993. "Nurturing an employee's brainchild." *Business Week* (October 23): 196.

Asian Venture Capital Journal. 1996. *Venture Capital in Asia: 1996/97 Edition.* Hong Kong: Asian Venture Capital Journal.

Asquith, Paul, and David W. Mullins, Jr. 1986. "Equity issues and offering dilution." *Journal of Financial Economics* 15: 61–89.

Asset Alternatives. 1994a. "Iowa suits test LPs' authority to abolish fund." *Private Equity Analyst* 4 (May): 1, 9.

Asset Alternatives. 1994b. "Warburg points the way toward a lower carry." *Private Equity Analyst* 4 (July): 7.

Athey, Susan, and Scott Stern. 1997. "An empirical framework for testing theories about complementarity in organizational design." Unpublished working paper. Massachusetts Institute of Technology.

Ball, Ray, S. P. Kothari, and Jay Shanken. 1995. "Problems in measuring portfolio performance: An application to contrarian investment strategies." *Journal of Financial Economics* 38: 79–107.

Balvers, Ronald J., Bill McDonald, and Robert E. Miller. 1988. "Underpricing of new issues and the choice of auditor as a signal of investment banker reputation." *Accounting Review* 63: 605–622.

Barber, Brad M., and John D. Lyon. 1997. "Detecting long-run abnormal stock returns: The empirical power and specification of test statistics." *Journal of Financial Economics* 43: 341–372.

Barber, Brad M., John D. Lyon, and Chih-Ling Tsai. 1999. "Improved methods for tests of long-run abnormal stock returns." *Journal of Finance* 54: 165–201.

Barclay, Michael J., and Clifford W. Smith, Jr. 1995. "The priority structure of corporate liabilities." *Journal of Finance* 50: 899–917.

Barry, Christopher B., Chris J. Muscarella, John W. Peavy III, and Michael R. Vetsuypens. 1990. "The role of venture capital in the creation of public companies: Evidence from the going public process." *Journal of Financial Economics* 27: 447–471.

Bartlett, Joseph W. 1988. *Venture Capital Law, Business, Strategies, and Investment Planning*. New York: Wiley.

Bartlett, Joseph W. 1994. *Venture Capital Law, Business, Strategies, and Investment Planning: 1994 Supplement*. New York: Wiley.

Bartlett, Joseph W. 1995. *Equity Finance: Venture Capital, Buyouts, Restructurings, and Reorganization*. New York: Wiley.

Baysinger, Barry D., and Henry N. Butler. 1985. "Corporate governance and the board of directors: Performance effects of changes in board composition." *Journal of Law, Economics, and Organization* 1: 101–124.

Beatty, Randolph P. 1989. "Auditor reputation and the pricing of initial public offerings." *The Accounting Review* 64: 693–709.

Beatty, Randolph P., and Jay R. Ritter. 1986. "Investment banking, reputation, and the underpricing of initial public offerings." *Journal of Financial Economics* 15: 213–232.

Beatty, Randolph P., and Edward J. Zajak. 1994. "Firm risk and alternative mechanisms for internal corporate control: Evidence from initial public offerings." *Administrative Science Quarterly* 39: 313–335.

Bergemann, Dirk, and Ulrich Hege. 1998. "Dynamic venture capital financing, learning, and moral hazard." *Journal of Banking and Finance* 22: 703–735.

Berglöf, Erik. 1994. "A control theory of venture capital finance." *Journal of Law, Economics, and Organization* 10: 247–267.

Bernard, Victor L. 1987. "Cross-sectional dependence and problems in inference in market-based accounting research." *Journal of Accounting Research* 25: 1–48.

Berndt, Ernst R. 1991. *The Practice of Econometrics: Classic and Contemporary*. New York: Addison-Wesley.

BioVenture View. 1993 and earlier. *BioPeople*. San Francisco: BioVenture View.

Black, Bernard S., and Ronald J. Gilson. 1998. "Venture capital and the structure of capital markets: Banks versus stock markets." *Journal of Financial Economics* 47: 243–277.

Black, Fischer. 1986. "Noise." *Journal of Finance* 41: 529–543.

Blanchard, Olivier, Florencio Lopez de Silanes, and Andrei Shleifer. 1994. "What do firms do with cash windfalls?" *Journal of Financial Economics* 36: 337–360.

Block, Zenas, and Oscar A. Ornati. 1987. "Compensating corporate venture managers." *Journal of Business Venturing* 2: 41–52.

Blume, Marshall E., and Robert F. Stambaugh. 1983. "Biases in computed returns: An application to the size effect." *Journal of Financial Economics* 12: 387–404.

Bradley, Michael, Gregg A. Jarrell, and E. Han Kim. 1984. "On the existence of an optimal capital structure: Theory and evidence." *Journal of Finance* 39: 857–878.

Brav, Alon, Christopher C. Géczy, and Paul A. Gompers. 1996. "The long-run underperformance of seasoned equity offerings revisited." Unpublished working paper. Harvard University and University of Chicago.

Brennan, Michael J., and Alan Kraus. 1987. "Efficient financing under asymmetric information." *Journal of Finance* 42: 1225–1243.

Campbell, John Y., Andrew W. Lo, and A. Craig MacKinlay. 1997. *The Econometrics of Financial Markets*. Princeton: Princeton University Press.

Carter, Richard, Frederick H. Dark, and Ajai K. Singh. 1998. "A comparative analysis of underwriter prestige measures." *Journal of Finance* 53: 285–311.

Carter, Richard, and Steven Manaster. 1990. "Initial public offerings and underwriter reputation." *Journal of Finance* 45: 1045–1067.

Chan, Yuk-Shee. 1983. "On the positive role of financial intermediation in allocation of venture capital in a market with imperfect information." *Journal of Finance* 38: 1543–1568.

Charles River Associates, Inc. 1976. *An Analysis of Capital Market Imperfections: Prepared for the Experimental Technology Incentives Program, National Bureau of Standards, U.S. Department of Commerce*. Cambridge: Charles River Associates, Inc.

Chevalier, Judith A., and Glenn D. Ellison. 1997. "Risk taking by mutual funds as a response to incentives." *Journal of Political Economy* 105: 1167–1200.

Clay, Lucius. 1991 and earlier. *The Venture Capital Report Guide to Venture Capital in Europe*. London: Pitman.

Commerce Clearing House. 1992 and earlier. *Capital Changes Reporter*, Chicago: Commerce Clearing House.

Cordell, Lawrence R., Gregor D. MacDonald, and Mark E. Wohar. 1993. "Corporate ownership and the thrift crisis." *Journal of Law and Economics* 36: 719–756.

Cornelli, Francesca, and Oved Yosha. 1997. "Stage financing and the role of convertible debt." Unpublished working paper. London Business School and Tel Aviv University.

Corporate Technology Information Services. 1996 and earlier. *Corporate Technology Directory*. Woburn, Massachusetts: Corporate Technology Information Services.

Crocker, Keith J., and Kenneth J. Reynolds. 1993. "The efficiency of incomplete contracts: An empirical analysis of Air Force engine procurement." *Rand Journal of Economics* 24: 126–146.

Dauchy, Craig E., and Mark T. Harmon. 1986. "Structuring venture capital limited partnerships." *Computer Lawyer* 3 (November): 1–8.

DeBondt, Werner, and Richard Thaler. 1985. "Does the stock market overreact?" *Journal of Finance* 40: 793–808.

DeBondt, Werner, and Richard Thaler. 1987. "Further evidence on investor overreaction and stock market seasonality." *Journal of Finance* 42: 557–581.

De Long, J. Bradford, Andrei Shleifer, Lawrence H. Summers, and Robert Waldmann. 1990. "Noise trader risk in financial markets." *Journal of Political Economy* 98: 703–738.

De Roover, Raymond. 1963. "The organization of trade," in M. M. Postan, E. E. Rich, and, Edward Miller. eds. *The Cambridge Economic History of Europe: Volume III—Economic Organization and Policies in the Middle Ages.* Cambridge: Cambridge University Press, chapter 2.

Denning, Paul F., and Robin A. Painter. 1994. *Stock Distributions: A Guide for Venture Capitalists.* Boston: Robertson, Stephens & Co. and Testa, Hurwitz & Thibeault.

Devenow, Andrea, and Ivo Welch. 1996. "Rational herding in financial economics." *European Economic Review* 40: 603–615.

Diamond, Douglas W. 1989. "Reputation acquisition in debt markets." *Journal of Political Economy* 97: 828–862.

Dun's Marketing Services. 1996 and earlier. *Million Dollar Directory.* Parsippany, New Jersey: Dun's Marketing Services.

Easley, David, and Maureen O'Hara. 1987. "Price, trade size, and information in securities markets." *Journal of Financial Economics* 19: 69–90.

Ely, E. S. 1987. "Dr. Silver's tarnished prescription." *Venture* 9 (July): 54–58.

European Venture Capital Association. 1997. *1997 EVCA Yearbook.* Zaventum, Belgium: European Venture Capital Association.

Fama, Eugene F. 1976. *The Foundations of Finance.* New York: Basic Books.

Fama, Eugene F. 1996. "Multifactor portfolio efficiency and multifactor asset pricing." *Journal of Financial and Quantitative Analysis* 31: 441–465.

Fama, Eugene F., and Kenneth R. French. 1992. "The cross-section of expected stock returns." *Journal of Finance* 47: 427–465.

Fama, Eugene F., and Kenneth R. French. 1993. "Common risk factors in the returns of stocks and bonds." *Journal of Financial Economics* 33: 3–55.

Fama, Eugene F., and Kenneth R. French. 1995. "Size and book-to-market factors in earnings and returns." *Journal of Finance* 50: 131–156.

Fama, Eugene F., and Kenneth R. French. 1996. "Multifactor explanations of asset pricing anomalies." *Journal of Finance* 51: 55–84.

Fama, Eugene F., and Kenneth R. French. 1997. "Industry costs of equity." *Journal of Financial Economics* 43: 153–193.

Fama, Eugene F., and Michael C. Jensen. 1983. "Separation of ownership and control." *Journal of Law and Economics* 26: 301–325.

Fast, Norman D. 1978. *The Rise and Fall of Corporate New Venture Divisions.* Ann Arbor: UMI Research Press.

Fazzari, Steven M., R. Glenn Hubbard, and Bruce C. Petersen. 1988. "Financing constraints and corporate investment." *Brookings Papers on Economic Activity: Microeconomics* 1: 141–205.

Fenn, George W., Nellie Liang, and Stephen Prowse. 1997. "The role of angel investors and venture capitalists in financing high-tech start-ups." Unpublished working paper. Milken Institute, Federal Reserve Board, and Federal Reserve Bank of Dallas.

Fields, Laura. 1996. "Is institutional investment in initial public offerings related to the long-run performance of these firms?" Unpublished working paper. Pennsylvania State University.

Financial Stock Guide Service. 1992. *Directory of Obsolete Securities.* Jersey City: Financial Information, Inc.

Freear, John, and William E. Wetzel, Jr. 1990. "Who bankrolls high-tech entrepreneurs?" *Journal of Business Venturing* 5: 77–89.

Friend, Irwin, and Larry H. P. Lang. 1988. "An empirical test of the impact of managerial self-interest on corporate capital structure." *Journal of Finance* 43: 271–281.

Gale Research. 1996 and earlier. *Ward's Business Directory of U.S. Private and Public Companies.* Detroit: Gale Research.

Gallese, Liz R. 1990. "Venture capital strays far from its roots." *New York Times Magazine* 139 (April 1): S24–S39.

Galston, Arthur. 1925. *Security Syndicate Operations: Organization, Management and Accounting.* New York: Roland Press.

Gee, Robert E. 1994. "Finding and commercializing new businesses." *Research/Technology Management* 37 (January/February): 49–56.

Gibbons, Robert S., and Kevin J. Murphy. 1992. "Optimal incentive contracts in the presence of career concerns: Theory and evidence." *Journal of Political Economy* 100: 468–505.

Gompers, Paul A. 1995. "A clinical examination of convertible debt in venture capital investments." Unpublished working paper. Harvard University.

Gompers, Paul A., and Josh Lerner. 1997a. "Money chasing deals? The impact of fund inflows on private equity valuations." *Journal of Financial Economics.* Forthcoming.

Gompers, Paul A., and Josh Lerner. 1997b. "Risk and reward in private equity investments; The challenge of performance assessment." *Journal of Private Equity* 1 (winter): 5–12.

Gompers, Paul A., and Josh Lerner. 1998. "What drives venture fundraising?" *Brookings Papers on Economic Activity: Microeconomics,* 149–192.

Good, Mary L. 1997. "Testimony before the subcommittee on oversight of government management and the District of Columbia." Governmental Affairs Committee, U.S. Senate. Washington, D.C. June 3, 1997.

Goodman, Edwin A. 1990. "Gatekeepers' 'reforms' reap negative consequences." *Venture Capital Journal* 30 (December): 25–28.

Gorman, Michael, and William A. Sahlman. 1989. "What do venture capitalists do?" *Journal of Business Venturing* 4: 231–248.

Grassmuck, Karen. 1990. "The much-praised and often-criticized 'architect' of Harvard's endowment growth steps down." *Chronicle of Higher Education* 36 (June 6): A25–A27.

Greenwald, Bruce C., Joseph E. Stiglitz, and Andrew Weiss. 1984. "Information imperfections in the capital market and macroeconomic fluctuations." *American Economic Review Papers and Proceedings* 74: 194–199.

Grinblatt, Mark, and Chuan Y. Hwang. 1989. "Signaling and the pricing of new issues." *Journal of Finance* 44: 383–420.

Grossman, Sanford, and Oliver D. Hart. 1986. "The costs and benefits of ownership: A theory of vertical and lateral integration." *Journal of Political Economy* 94: 691–719.

Halloran, Michael J., Lee F. Benton, Robert V. Gunderson, Jr., Keith L. Kearney, and Jorge del Calvo. 1995. *Venture Capital and Public Offering Negotiation.* Englewood Cliffs, New Jersey: Aspen Law and Business.

Hansen, Lars P., and Robert J. Hodrick. 1980. "Forward exchange rates as optimal predictors of future spot rates: An econometric analysis." *Journal of Political Economy* 88: 829–853.

Hardymon, G. Felda, Mark J. DeNino, and Malcolm S. Salter. 1983. "When corporate venture capital doesn't work." *Harvard Business Review* 61 (May–June): 114–120.

Harris, Lawrence, and Eitan Gurel. 1986. "Price and volume effects associated with changes on the S&P 500 list: New evidence for the existence of price pressures." *Journal of Finance* 41: 815–829.

Harris, Milton, and Artur Raviv. 1991. "The theory of capital structure." *Journal of Finance* 46: 297–356.

Hart, Oliver D. 1993. "Theories of optimal capital structure: A managerial discretion perspective." In *The Deal Decade: What Takeovers and Leveraged Buyouts Mean for Corporate Governance,* edited by Margaret M. Blair. Washington, D.C.: Brookings Institution.

Hart, Oliver D., and John Moore. 1990. "Property rights and the nature of the firm." *Journal of Political Economy* 98: 1119–1158.

Hart, Oliver D., and John Moore. 1998. "Default and renegotiation: A dynamic model of debt." *Quarterly Journal of Economics* 113: 1–41.

Hayes, Samuel L., A. Michael Spence, and David Van Praag Marks. 1983. *Competition in the Investment Banking Industry.* Cambridge: Harvard University Press.

Heinkel, Robert, and Neal M. Stoughton. 1994. "The dynamics of portfolio management contracts." *Review of Financial Studies* 7: 351–388.

Hellmann, Thomas F. 1998. "The allocation of control rights in venture capital contracts." *Rand Journal of Economics* 29: 57–76.

Hellmann, Thomas F., and Manju Puri. 1998. "The interaction between product market and financing strategy: The role of venture capital." Unpublished working paper. Stanford University.

Henderson, Rebecca. 1993. "Underinvestment and incompetence as responses to radical innovation: Evidence from the photolithographic alignment equipment industry." *Rand Journal of Economics* 24: 248–270.

Henderson, Rebecca, and Iain Cockburn. 1996. "Scale, scope and spillovers: The determinants of research productivity in drug discovery." *Rand Journal of Economics* 27: 32–59.

Hermalin, Benjamin E., and Michael S. Weisbach. 1988. "The determinants of board composition." *Rand Journal of Economics* 19: 589–606.

Holmstrom, Bengt, and Paul Milgrom. 1987. "Aggregation and linearity in the provision of intertemporal incentives." *Econometrica* 55: 303–328.

Hoshi, Takeo, Anil Kashyap, and David Scharfstein. 1991. "Corporate structure, liquidity, and investment: Evidence of Japanese industrial groups." *Quarterly Journal of Economics* 106: 33–60.

Howard and Company. 1992 and earlier. *Going Public: The IPO Reporter.* Philadelphia: Howard and Company.

Hubbard, R. Glenn, and Robert J. Weiner. 1991. "Efficient contracting and market power: Evidence from the U.S. natural gas industry." *Journal of Law and Economics* 34: 25–67.

Huemer, Jason. 1992. "Brinson Partners on a roll." *Venture Capital Journal* 32 (June): 32–36.

Hunt, Brian, and Josh Lerner. 1995. "Xerox Technology Ventures: March 1995." Harvard Business School case no. 9–295–127 (and teaching note no. 9–298–152).

Ibbotson, Roger G., and Jeffrey F. Jaffe. 1975. "'Hot' issue markets." *Journal of Finance* 30: 1027–1042.

Irwin, Douglas A., and Peter J. Klenow. 1996. "High tech R&D subsidies: Estimating the effects of Sematech." *Journal of International Economics* 40: 323–344.

Jain, Bharat A., and Omesh Kini. 1994. "The post-issue operating performance of IPO firms." *Journal of Finance* 49, 1699–1726.

James, Christopher M. 1987. "Some evidence on the uniqueness of bank loans: A comparison of bank borrowing, private placements, and public offerings." *Journal of Financial Economics* 19: 217–235.

Jeffery, Grant. 1961. *Science and Technology Stocks: A Guide for Investors*. New York: Meridian.

Jeng, Leslie A., and Philippe C. Wells. 1997. "The determinants of venture capital funding: An empirical analysis." Unpublished working paper. Harvard University.

Jensen, Michael C. 1986. "Agency cost of free cash flow, corporate finance and takeovers." *American Economic Review Papers and Proceedings* 76: 323–329.

Jensen, Michael C. 1991. "Corporate control and the politics of finance." *Journal of Applied Corporate Finance* 4 (Summer): 13–33.

Jensen, Michael C. 1993. "Presidential address: The modern industrial revolution, exit, and the failure of internal control systems." *Journal of Finance* 48: 831–880.

Jensen, Michael C., and William H. Meckling. 1976. "Theory of the firm: Managerial behavior, agency costs, and ownership structure." *Journal of Financial Economics* 3: 305–360.

Jensen, Michael C., and Kevin J. Murphy. 1990. "Performance pay and top-management incentives." *Journal of Political Economy* 98: 225–264.

Kahle, Kathleen M. 1996. "Insider trading and new security issues." Unpublished Ph.D. dissertation. Ohio State University.

Kahneman, Daniel, and Amos Tversky. 1982. "Intuitive prediction: Biases and corrective procedures." In *Judgment under Uncertainty: Heuristics and Biases*, edited by Daniel Kahneman, Paul Slovic, and Amos Tversky. New York: Cambridge University Press.

Kiefer, Nicholas M. 1988. "Economic duration data and hazard functions." *Journal of Economic Literature* 26: 646–679.

King, Ralph, Jr. 1990. "'The money corner.'" *Forbes* 145 (March 5): 38–40.

Klein, Benjamin, Robert G. Crawford, and Armen A. Alchian. 1978. "Vertical integration, appropriable rents, and the competitive contracting process." *Journal of Law and Economics* 21: 297–326.

Kortum, Samuel, and Josh Lerner. 1998. "Does venture capital spur innovation?" Unpublished working paper. Boston University and Harvard University.

Kothari, S. P., and Jerold B. Warner. 1997. "Measuring long-horizon security price performance." *Journal of Financial Economics* 43: 301–339.

Kroszner, Randall S., and Raghuram G. Rajan. 1994. "Is the Glass-Steagall Act justified? A study of the U.S. experience with universal banking before 1933." *American Economic Review* 84: 810–832.

Kunze, Robert J. 1990. *Nothing Ventured: The Perils and Payoffs of the Great American Venture Capital Game*. New York: Harper Collins.

La Porta, Rafael. 1996. "Expectations and the cross-section of stock returns." *Journal of Finance* 51: 1715–1742.

Lakonishok, Josef, Andrei Shleifer, Richard Thaler, and Robert W. Vishny. 1991. "Window dressing by pension fund managers." *American Economic Review Papers and Proceedings* 81 (May): 227–231.

Lakonishok, Josef, Andrei Shleifer, and Robert W. Vishny. 1992. "The structure and performance of the money management industry." *Brookings Papers on Economic Activity: Microeconomics* 2: 339–391.

Lakonishok, Josef, Andrei Shleifer, and Robert W. Vishny. 1994. "Contrarian investment, extrapolation, and risk." *Journal of Finance* 49: 1541–1578.

Lancaster, Tony. 1979. "Econometric methods for the duration of unemployment." *Econometrica* 47: 939–956.

Lancaster, Tony. 1985. "Generalized residuals and heterogeneous duration models: With applications to the Weibull model." *Journal of Econometrics* 28: 155–169.

Lawler, E., and J. Drexel. 1980. *The Corporate Entrepreneur*. Los Angeles: Center for Effective Organizations, Graduate School of Business Administration, University of Southern California.

Lee, Charles, Andrei Shleifer, and Richard Thaler. 1991. "Investor sentiment and the closed-end fund puzzle." *Journal of Finance* 46: 29–48.

Lehn, Kenneth, and Annette Poulsen. 1991. "Contractual resolution of bondholder-stockholder conflicts in leveraged buyouts." *Journal of Law and Economics* 34: 645–673.

Leland, Hayne E., and David H. Pyle. 1977. "Informational asymmetries, financial structure, and financial intermediation." *Journal of Finance* 33: 371–387.

Lerner, Josh. 1994. "The importance of patent scope: An empirical analysis." *Rand Journal of Economics* 25: 319–333.

Lerner, Josh. 1997. "An empirical examination of a technology race." *Rand Journal of Economics* 28: 228–247.

Lerner, Josh. 1999. "The government as venture capitalist: The long-run effects of the SBIR program." *Journal of Business* 72: 285–318.

Levin, Jack S. 1995. *Structuring Venture Capital, Private Equity, and Entrepreneurial Transactions*. Boston: Little, Brown.

Liles, Patrick R. 1977. *Sustaining the Venture Capital Firm*. Cambridge: Management Analysis Center.

Lin, T. H., and Richard L. Smith. 1995. "Insider reputation and selling decisions: The unwinding of venture capital investments during equity IPOs." Unpublished working paper. Arizona State University.

Lopez, Robert S., and Irving W. Raymond. 1955. *Medieval Trade in the Mediterranean World: Illustrative Documents Translated with Introductions and Notes.* New York: Columbia University Press.

Loughran, Tim, and Jay R. Ritter. 1995. "The new issues puzzle." *Journal of Finance* 50: 23–51.

Lutz, Henry F. 1932. "Babylonian Partnership." *Journal of Economic and Business History* 4: 552–570.

Maddala, G. S. 1983. *Limited-Dependent and Qualitative Variables in Econometrics.* New York: Cambridge University Press.

Malitz, Ileen. 1986. "On financial contracting: The determinants of bond covenants." *Financial Management* 15 (Summer): 18–25.

Manne, Henry A. 1966. *Insider Trading and the Stock Market.* New York: Free Press.

Manweller, Richard L. 1997. *Funding High-Tech Ventures.* Grants Pass, Oregon: Oasis Press.

Marquis Who's Who. 1993 and earlier. *Who's Who in Finance and Industry.* Chicago: Marquis.

Martin, John D., and J. William Petty. 1983. "An analysis of the performance of publicly traded venture capital companies." *Journal of Financial and Quantitative Analysis* 18: 401–410.

Marx, Leslie M. 1994. "Negotiation and renegotiation of venture capital contracts." Unpublished working paper. University of Rochester.

McNamee, Roger. 1991. "How to fix the IPO market." *Upside* 3 (January): 24–27.

Mead Data Central. 1988. *Reference Manual for the LEXIS/NEXIS Services.* Dayton: Mead Data Central.

Mega-Type Publishing. 1992 and earlier. *Genetic Engineering and Biotechnology-Related Firms—Worldwide Directory.* Princeton Junction, New Jersey: Mega-Type Publishing.

Megginson, William C., and Kathleen A. Weiss. 1991. "Venture capital certification in initial public offerings." *Journal of Finance* 46: 879–893.

Merton, Robert C. 1973. "An intertemporal capital asset pricing model." *Econometrica* 41: 867–887.

Merton, Robert C. 1995. "A functional perspective on financial intermediation." *Financial Management* 24 (Summer): 23–41.

Meulbroek, Lisa K. 1992a. "Comparison of forward and futures prices of an interest rate-sensitive financial asset." *Journal of Finance* 47: 381–396.

Meulbroek, Lisa K. 1992b. "An empirical analysis of illegal insider trading." *Journal of Finance* 47: 1661–1700.

Michaely, Roni, and Wayne H. Shaw. 1991. "The pricing of initial public offerings: Tests of adverse selection and signaling theories." *Review of Financial Studies* 7: 279–319.

Mikkelson, Wayne H., and M. Megan Partch. 1985. "Stock price effects and costs of secondary distributions." *Journal of Financial Economics* 14: 165–194.

Mikkelson, Wayne H., and M. Megan Partch. 1986. "Valuation effects of security offerings and the issuance process." *Journal of Financial Economics* 15: 31–60.

Mikkelson, Wayne H., and M. Megan Partch. 1988. "Withdrawn security offerings." *Journal of Financial and Quantitative Analysis* 23: 119–133.

Mikkelson, Wayne H., M. Megan Partch, and Kenneth Shah. 1997. "Ownership and operating performance of companies that go public." *Journal of Financial Economics* 44: 281–307.

Mundlak, Yair. 1961. "Empirical production functions free of management bias." *Journal of Farm Economics* 43: 45–56.

Mundlak, Yair. 1978. "On the pooling of time series and cross section data." *Econometrica* 46: 69–85.

Muscarella, Chris J., and Michael R. Vetsuypens. 1989. "Initial public offerings and information asymmetry." Unpublished working paper. Pennsylvania State University and Southern Methodist University.

Muscarella, Chris J., and Michael R. Vetsuypens. 1990. "Efficiency and organizational structure: A study of reverse LBOs." *Journal of Finance* 45: 1389–1414.

Myers, Stewart C. 1977. "Determinants of corporate borrowing." *Journal of Financial Economics* 5: 147–175.

Myers, Stewart C., and Nicholas S. Majluf. 1984. "Corporate financing and investment decisions when firms have information that investors do not have." *Journal of Financial Economics* 13: 187–221.

Nanda, Vikram, Jong-Hwan Yi, and Youngkeol Yun. 1995. "IPO long-run performance and underwriter reputation." Unpublished working paper. University of Michigan.

Nash, John F. 1950. "The bargaining problem." *Econometrica* 18: 155–162.

National Register Publishing Company. 1992 and earlier. *Corporate Finance Sourcebook*. Wilmette, Illinois: National Register Publishing Company.

National Register Publishing Company. 1996 and earlier. *Directory of Leading Private Companies, Including Corporate Affiliations*. Wilmette, Illinois: National Register Publishing Company.

North Carolina Biotechnology Center, Biotechnology Information Division (NCBC). 1990a. *Documentation for Actions Database*. Research Triangle Park: North Carolina Biotechnology Center.

North Carolina Biotechnology Center, Biotechnology Information Division (NCBC). 1990b. *Documentation for Companies Database*. Research Triangle Park: North Carolina Biotechnology Center.

Oryx Press. 1992 and earlier. *BioScan: The Worldwide Biotech Industry Reporting Service*. Phoenix: Oryx Press.

Patel, Jay, Richard Zeckhauser, and Darryll Hendricks. 1991. "The rationality struggle: Illustrations from financial markets." *American Economic Review Papers and Proceedings* 81: 232–236.

Pence, Christine C. 1982. *How Venture Capitalists Make Investment Decisions*. Ann Arbor: UMI Research Press.

Perez, Robert C. 1986. *Inside Venture Capital: Past, Present, and Future.* New York: Praeger.

Petersen, Mitchell A., and Raghuram G. Rajan. 1994. "The benefits of lending relationships: Evidence from small business data." *Journal of Finance* 49: 3–37.

Petersen, Mitchell A., and Raghuram G. Rajan. 1995. "The effect of credit market competition on lending relationships." *Quarterly Journal of Economics* 110: 407–444.

Pisano, Gary P. 1989. "Using equity participation to support exchange: Evidence from the biotechnology industry." *Journal of Law, Economics, and Organization* 5: 109–126.

Pittman, Russell. 1991. "Specific investments, contracts, and opportunism: The evolution of railroad sidetrack agreements." *Journal of Law and Economics* 34: 565–589.

Poterba, James M. 1987. "How burdensome are capital gains taxes? Evidence from the United States." *Journal of Public Economics* 33: 157–172.

Poterba, James M. 1989. "Venture capital and capital gains taxation." In *Tax Policy and the Economy*, edited by Lawrence Summers. Cambridge: MIT Press.

Predicasts, Inc. 1992 and earlier. *Predicasts F&S Index of Corporate Change.* Cleveland: Predicasts, Inc.

Rajan, Raghuram G. 1993. "A theory of fluctuations in bank credit policy." Unpublished working paper. University of Chicago.

Rajan, Raghuram G., and Luigi G. Zingales. 1995. "What do we know about capital structure? Some evidence from international data." *Journal of Finance* 50: 1421–1460.

Recombinant Capital. 1991. *Valuation Histories for Private Biotechnology Companies.* San Francisco: Recombinant Capital.

Recombinant Capital. 1992. *Valuation Histories for Public Biotechnology Companies.* San Francisco: Recombinant Capital.

Reinganum, Jennifer R. 1989. "The timing of innovation: Research, development and diffusion." In *The Handbook of Industrial Organization*, edited by Richard L. Schmalensee and Robert D. Willig. New York: North-Holland.

Riley, John G. 1979. "Information equilibrium." *Econometrica* 47: 331–359.

Rind, Kenneth W. 1981. "The role of venture capital in corporate development." *Strategic Management Journal* 2: 169–180.

Ritter, Jay R. 1984. "The 'hot' issue market of 1980." *Journal of Business* 57: 214–240.

Ritter, Jay R. 1987. "The cost of going public." *Journal of Financial Economics* 19: 269–281.

Ritter, Jay R. 1991. "The long-run performance of initial public offerings." *Journal of Finance* 42: 365–394.

Roberts, Kevin, and Martin L. Weitzman. 1981. "Funding criteria for research, development, and exploration projects." *Econometrica* 49: 1261–1288.

Rock, Kevin. 1986. "Why new issues are underpriced." *Journal of Financial Economics* 15: 187–212.

Ross, Stephen. 1977. "The determination of financial structure: The incentive signalling approach." *Bell Journal of Economics* 8: 23–40.

Sah, Raaj K., and Joseph E. Stiglitz. 1986. "The architecture of economic systems: Hierarchies and polyarchies." *American Economic Review* 76: 716–727.

Sahlman, William A. 1990. "The structure and governance of venture capital organizations." *Journal of Financial Economics* 27: 473–521.

Sahlman, William A., and Howard Stevenson. 1986. "Capital market myopia." *Journal of Business Venturing* 1: 7–30.

Schultz, Paul. 1993. "Unit initial public offerings: A form of staged financing." *Journal of Financial Economics* 34: 199–229.

Securities Data Company (SDC). 1992. *Corporate New Issues Database: A Tutorial.* Newark: Securities Data Company.

Seyhun, H. Nejat. 1986. "Insiders' profits, costs of trading, and market efficiency." *Journal of Financial Economics* 16: 189–212.

Seyhun, H. Nejat. 1988. "The information content of aggregate insider trading." *Journal of Business* 61: 1–24.

Shiller, Robert J. 1990. "Speculative prices and popular models." *Journal of Economic Perspectives* 4: 55–65.

Shiller, Robert J., and John Pound. 1989. "Survey evidence of diffusions of interest and information among investors." *Journal of Economic Behavior and Organization* 12: 47–66.

Shleifer, Andrei. 1986. "Do demand curves for stocks slope down?" *Journal of Finance* 41: 579–590.

Shleifer, Andrei, and Robert W. Vishny. 1986. "Large shareholders and corporate control." *Journal of Political Economy* 94: 461–488.

Shleifer, Andrei, and Robert W. Vishny. 1992. "Liquidation value and debt capacity: A market equilibrium approach." *Journal of Finance* 47: 1343–1366.

Shleifer, Andrei, and Robert W. Vishny. 1997a. "The limits of arbitrage." *Journal of Finance* 52: 35–55.

Shleifer, Andrei, and Robert W. Vishny. 1997b. "A survey of corporate governance." *Journal of Finance* 52: 737–783.

Siegel, Robin, Eric Siegel, and Ian C. MacMillan. 1988. "Corporate venture capitalists: Autonomy, obstacles, and performance." *Journal of Business Venturing* 3: 233–247.

Sirri, Erik R., and Peter Tufano. 1998. "Competition in the mutual fund industry." *Journal of Finance* 53: 1589–1622.

Sloan, Allen. 1997. "Feeding frenzy over Internet firms' IPOs likely to leave investors with heartburn." *Washington Post* (May 27): E3.

Smith, Clifford W., Jr., and Jerold B. Warner. 1979. "On financial contracting: An analysis of bond covenants." *Journal of Financial Economics* 7: 117–161.

Standard and Poor's Corporation. 1993 and earlier. *Standard and Poor's Register of Corporations, Directors and Executives.* New York: Standard and Poor's.

Stein, Jeremy. 1988. "Takeover threats and managerial myopia." *Journal of Political Economy* 96: 61–80.

Stein, Jeremy. 1989. "Efficient capital markets, inefficient firms: A model of myopic corporate behavior." *Quarterly Journal of Economics* 104: 655–669.

Stern, Richard L., and Tatiana Pouschine. 1992. "Junk equity." *Forbes* 149 (March 2): 40–42.

Stiglitz, Joseph E., and Andrew Weiss. 1981. "Credit rationing in markets with incomplete information." *American Economic Review* 71: 393–409.

Sykes, Hollister B. 1990. "Corporate venture capital: Strategies for success." *Journal of Business Venturing* 5: 37–47.

Teoh, Siew, Ivo Welch, and T. J. Wong. 1998. "Earnings management and the long-run market performance of initial public offerings." *Journal of Finance* 53: 1935–1974.

Titman, Sheridan, and Roberto Wessels. 1988. "The determinants of capital structure choice." *Journal of Finance* 43: 1–19.

Turner, Nick. 1997. "Xerox inventions now raised instead of adopted by others." *Investors' Business Daily* (January 28): A6.

Tyebjee, Tyzoon T., and Albert V. Bruno. 1984. "A model of venture capitalist investment activity." *Management Science* 30: 1051–1066.

U.S. Department of Commerce, Patent and Trademark Office [USPTO]. 1990. *Technology Profile Report: Genetic Engineering, 1/1963–6/1989*. Washington: USPTO.

U.S. Department of Commerce, Patent and Trademark Office, Office of Patent Depository Library Programs [USPTO/OPDLP]. 1989. *ASSIST Disk Notes*. Washington: USPTO/OPDLP.

U.S. Department of Commerce, Patent and Trademark Office, Office of Patent Depository Library Programs [USPTO/OPDLP]. 1990. *CASSIS/BIB User's Guide*. Washington: USPTO/OPDLP.

Venture Economics. 1986. "Corporate venture capital study." Unpublished manuscript.

Venture Economics. 1987. "Stock distributions—Fact, opinion and comment." *Venture Capital Journal* 27 (August): 8–14.

Venture Economics. 1988a. *Exiting Venture Capital Investments*. Needham: Venture Economics.

Venture Economics. 1988b. *Trends in Venture Capital*. Needham: Venture Economics.

Venture Economics. 1989a. "Investment managers—A force in the venture capital industry." *Venture Capital Journal* 29 (September): 10–17.

Venture Economics. 1989b. *Terms and Conditions of Venture Capital Partnerships*. Needham: Venture Economics.

Venture Economics. 1992a and earlier years. *Pratt's Guide to Venture Capital Sources*. Needham: Venture Economics.

Venture Economics. 1992b. *Terms and Conditions of Venture Capital Partnerships*. Needham: Venture Economics.

Venture Economics. 1998 and earlier. *Investment Benchmark Reports—Venture Capital*. Newark: Venture Economics.

VentureOne. 1998. *VentureOne 1997 Annual Report*. San Francisco: VentureOne.

Wallace, John, and Jim Erickson. 1992. *Hard Drive: Bill Gates and the Making of the Microsoft Empire*. New York: Wiley.

Wallsten, Scott J. 1996. "The small business innovation research program: Encouraging technological innovation and commercialization in small firms?" Unpublished working paper Stanford University.

Weisbach, Michael S. 1988. "Outside directors and CEO turnover." *Journal of Financial Economics* 20: 431–460.

Weitzman, Martin L., Whitney K. Newey, and Michael Rabin. 1981. "Sequential R&D strategy for synfuels." *Bell Journal of Economics* 12: 574–590.

Welch, Ivo. 1989. "Seasoned offerings, imitation costs, and the underpricing of initial public offerings." *Journal of Finance* 44: 421–449.

Welch, Ivo. 1992. "Sequential sales, learning, and cascades." *Journal of Finance* 47: 695–732.

Williamson, Oliver E. 1979. "Transaction-cost economics: The governance of contractual relations." *Journal of Law and Economics* 22: 233–261.

Williamson, Oliver E. 1983. "Organization form, residual claimants, and corporate control." *Journal of Law and Economics* 26: 351–366.

Williamson, Oliver E. 1985. *The Economic Institutions of Capitalism: Firms, Markets, Relational Contracting*. New York: Free Press.

Williamson, Oliver E. 1988. "Corporate finance and corporate governance." *Journal of Finance* 43: 567–591.

Wilson, Robert. 1968. "The theory of syndicates." *Econometrica* 36: 119–132.

Name Index

Subject Index

abnormal returns (ARs), 275–276
adverse selection, 188
agency costs
  contract restrictions related to, 44
  effect on provision of capital, 129–130
  in entrepreneurial firms, 142–144
  expectations of, 132
  factors in decline of, 33–34
  free cash-flow, 145
  of intangible assets, 132
  in R&D-intensive firms, 149
  related to funds selected, 35n6
  related to tangible assets, 139
  and relationship to high book-to-market
    ratio, 132–133, 144
  theoretical predictions, 139–140
  venture capitalists' minimizing of, 164
  venture firms mitigate, 130–132, 183
angel, 151
ARs. *See* abnormal returns (ARs)
assets
  intangible assets of firms, 3, 128, 132
  liquidation value, 143–144
  relation of tangible assets to probability of
    venture financing, 163–164
  specificity of, 143–144
  tangible assets of firm, 128, 132, 139, 143
associate, 4n3

biotechnology equity index
  construction of, 216
  in timing of financings by biotechnology
    firms, 219–223
  in timing of IPOs, 216–217
  in timing of private financings, 216, 218
biotechnology firms
  distribution of board members by round of

    investment, 174–175
  equity stakes in venture-backed, 197–198
boards of directors
  changes related to change in CEO, 176–
    180
  classifications of board members, 174–175,
    178
  determinants of composition of, 172–175
book-to-market
  in analysis of firm performance, 296
  as determinant of stock returns, 283–284,
    296
book value, 284

call options, 38, 142–143
capital
  access to, 127–130
  factors in fundraising raising, 240
  sources of venture capital, 5
  staged infusions as control device, 139, 142
Capital Asset Pricing Model (CAPM), 308
carried interest, 20, 99, 102
CARs. *See* cumulative abnormal returns
  (CARs)
certification, 207–208
chief executive officer (CEO)
  correlation of replacement with board
    membership changes, 176–178
  reasons for replacement of, 176
closed-end funds, 6, 290, 292–293
  discount, 313–314
coinvestment. *See* syndications
common stock, 110n6
compensation
  assumption in calculation of variable and
    base, 91–94
  base, 70–74